COMING HOME

————— Notes for the Journey —————

Stephen G Wright

Coming Home wonderfully captures all that is good in contemporary spirituality. Unencumbered by institutional baggage, Wright weaves a hugely uplifting vision of our encounter with the Beloved, the divine presence that enriches what it is to be truly alive. In this book, Wright's rich experiences, not only from his own search but also drawn from those people he nursed through the final stages of their lives, become the signposts along a journey that so many in our day are recognising. This is no dry tome, but a highly readable work that flows with an immediacy that is compelling. Wright draws on a rich array of sources to place his own story in a context that is infused with the wisdom of many ages. He is a true guide for those ready to work towards finding their way Home.

Dr. Les Lancaster, author of 'The Essence of Kabbalah' and 'Consciousness: the Marriage of Science and Mysticism'.

Coming Home is a shining jewel that will serve every spiritual seeker, filled with rich wisdom from across the worlds traditions, offered with heartfelt authenticity of someone who has really walked the talk. It is well referenced, full of inspirational suggestions and stories and offers practical ideas for 'coming home'. Grounded in the author's experience of the joys and struggles that come with the search, the challenge of engaging with a tradition, it invites the reader into the life affirming vision that the way Home is accessible to everyone with the right support. Stephen Wright is an articulate and practical guide to usher you deeper into the beauty of your own soul.

Miranda Macpherson, author of 'Boundless Love' and 'The Way of Grace'.

Wright de-genders the language used for God in a characteristically lucid, personal and helpful way. Coming Home is a lovely meditation - so rooted in everyday experience, so honest. And it is simultaneously straightforward, without contortions or long diversions into the complexities of feminist or other theologies, while also being profound in touching the heart of the matter; the heart of his Beloved. I'm sure that it will help to open up and make even more meaningful the way for many fellow travellers, because there is recognition and affirmation that traditional masculine God language and its baggage can be difficult.

Lesley Orr, feminist historian and member of the Iona community.

Coming Home is the revelation of one man's challenging journey through life, offered with love and uncommon compassion. Wright writes as friend to friend; he does not masquerade as someone with a halo or special insights from on high, but as a no-nonsense traveler who has discovered what works, and doesn't work, for him. He laughs at his failures and never takes his achievements too seriously — and his achievements are considerable. The result is a captivating volume that can assist anyone searching for deeper meaning, healing, and fulfillment. There is a special quality to this book, and I cannot imagine how anyone's life would fail to be enriched by this luminous, enchanting offering."

Larry Dossey, MD author of 'One Mind'.

For Jeannie

British Library Cataloguing in Publication Data: catalogue record for this book is available from the British Library.
ISBN 978-0-9560303-7-5

Design layout and typesetting by:-
Barry Marshall, be...creative
Home Farm Office, Eamont Bridge, Penrith, Cumbria CA10 2BX
www.becreativecumbria.co.uk

Acknowledgements

For their great help with editing and suggestions I am deeply grateful to Jean Gray, Jeannie Sayre-Adams and Kristopher Drummond. Ian Webster I thank for all the patient backroom work that enabled me to be lost in the computer without interruption. Barry Marshall's work through all the stages of production is deeply appreciated.

A number of examples of individual experiences are included in this book, taken from the accounts of some who have been with me seeking spiritual direction. In all cases the names have been fictionalised.

Contents

Stuck to the rock,
afraid of the unknown open sea,
the shell-domed limpet clings
to home from Home.
Deaf to the call of the ocean,
"Come to me".
Deaf beneath the time-hard shield.
Blind: facing stone and stone.
Blind: encased and lightless.
In the womb, isolation,
in the tomb, salvation.
"Oh break me, break me again.
Let wind and wave do their will.
Let the Master find the servant,
let the servant leave home for Home."
The choice of god for God.
Choice! In the image of God are we made?
Choice – the bitter call to sweet redemption,
the reunification of source with Source,
the call forever rilling patiently through
the long night waiting to be heard.
We pour out of buildings onto
blistering black tarmacked sunblasted city streets
in high summer,
bikeroared, roaddrilled, deafening, heatflattening
summer in London or anywhere.
Out into the heat,
the unashamed unforgiving heat.
We choose to enter the furnace,
we choose the heat.
The searing heat (compassion cooling the suffering soul),
a brick melting heat; roasting identity.
Heat concealed, in the loving heart.
Unleashed, the limpet calls: "For freedom",
burning shell from shell.
Hearts on fire,
hearts on fire.
Bring more oil,
bring more oil.

Introduction to the second edition

The thought that we are separate from God is just that – a thought. Separation is an illusion.

Coming Home brings us to that truth.

How we 'get there' requires us to address some serious questions about what we think 'life' is all about, whether life as we know it is the only life, who or what is God (if there is one), why we bother to ask at all, indeed who is the 'I' that is doing the asking? Assuming we get some answers, then how do we live our lives with these truths? These and other such questions lie at the core of our spiritual search. The essence of this book is to offer guidance in that quest.

The modern spiritual supermarket offers choices for our search as never before. That can be both liberating and confusing. Sometimes we find what we are looking for in an established tradition, sometimes a "here's one I prepared for you earlier" approach simply doesn't work and we need to find our own way. Along with the old forms, new forms of worship and awakening are emerging which integrate different beliefs and practices into new personal and collective patterns. Boundaries between religious beliefs while being shored up in some quarters are shifting and merging in others. Interfaith, multifaith, interspiritual, New Age and Old Age approaches offer a potential and range of spiritual exploration as never before. This search for meaning and purpose in life, the longing for something 'more', the hope of the transcendent and the yearning to help and heal a world that is broken in so many ways – this is the very stuff of spiritual inquiry.

Spirituality isn't just a theory, it's a practice. It summons us to discover our uniqueness and through that our essential unity. We are called to see who we really are and through that recognise the common ground of our humanity in the vast cosmic drama of the Divine.

I have added lots of new material in this edition to develop some of these ideas in greater depth, especially in relation to different spiritual practices, and fleshed them

"The thought that we are separate from God is just that – a thought."

out with more real life examples. I trust these will strengthen the use of this text as a handbook for spiritual awakening, for *Coming Home*, grounding and integrating theory and practice in everyday experience.

I've also included more recent evidence from research in different scientific fields that support the emergence of a healthy spirituality.

We are all invited Home, to be at Home in ourselves while we live and breathe, awake to the sacred now. Not everyone takes up the invitation, but these pages set out what I hope is useful and maybe even wise guidance for those who do. If following this invitation is a kind of journey into an unfamiliar landscape, then it's a good idea to have a trusted guide, map, compass and a means of communication along with us.

Thus I advocate drawing on the strength of four key supportive elements on the Way – our Soul Friends (such as a spiritual director, minister or therapist), our Soul Foods (ways in which we nurture ourselves such as through scripture, the arts or nature), our Soul Communities (groups of fellow seekers with whom way share our travels, for example at a place of worship, meditation group or retreat) and lastly our Soul Works (the spiritual practices which support depth and discernment such as prayer, contemplation, labyrinth walking, fasting and many more). A deep exploration of these four themes forms the backbone of *Coming Home*.

I made a conscious commitment to de-gender God in this edition, the reasons for which are explained in the opening chapter. Mainly this is because, like so many seekers, I do not experience the Divine as exclusively male. I'm mindful also that we may limit God by our labels and produce unhealthy consequences in the long term for both men and women.

Thus, while I've sometimes used the word God in the text, it is with the understanding that it is not the anthropomorphic God of which I write. I have used gender free grammar and names interchangeably – Sacred Unity, Source of All, the One, the Absolute, the Self and mostly the name that is most dear to me personally, the Beloved. The latter is favoured in many scriptures and mystical writings not least because it conveys a sense of intimate and loving relationship with the Divine and not just the unknowable nature of the One. Please feel free to transpose any other name that is your personal preference. The only exceptions where God is a 'He' are where I have quoted directly from other sources.

I've built my approach using three core ideas common to many spiritual traditions – God, Soul and Ego - the latter being an all round name for the little or false self, the 'me' of identity and personality , the *ahamkara,* with all its conscious and unconscious elements. I've used these concepts to provide a foundation for exploration of the main themes, but I do so with caution. Each does not exist in separate silos but as a flowing and dynamic expression of what it is to be human in the All-that-is. I've also drawn extensively on the roots of my own tradition and the guidance of my 'guru', which I hope adds depth while at the same time embracing truths from many different traditions and philosophies. I do not advocate any one belief system, proselytising is absolutely not a function of this book. I have referred to my own tradition simply to offer examples of truth and what has worked for me.

At the time of writing, I've never known such a period when there has been so much political and religious turmoil worldwide. Old certainties and structures fall away. Individuals and political organisations increasingly default to shadowy fear-based retrenchment. War, famine, disease and ignorance stalk the land. It's an old and familiar pattern. This time it's different. Our climate seems to be spiralling toward disaster. The Holocene age, where people have flourished for over 10,000 years, has drawn to its close. We enter now the Anthropocene epoch; human activity is profoundly and probably irreversibly changing our earthly home. If ever there was a time for a deep and widespread shift of individual and collective consciousness, this is it. It is not all doom and gloom. Across the globe there is far more good than all that is wrong. Millions of people are working to stay open-hearted and work for the collective good. In these pages we will explore at least one contribution we can all make: personal awakening and transformation through which we may discover and strengthen our own particular path of service. Coming Home reconnects us - to ourselves, each other and the All-that-is. It is not a summons to self indulgence, but a pathway to spiritual renewal for the good of all.

SGW. Mungrisdale.
January 2017

"The thought that we are separate from God is just that – a thought."

Part 1

"Home, is where one starts from."[1]

A letter

Dear Unknown Friend,

There is a word on this keyboard, the one I am using to write this letter, to the right of my hand. It says "home" and if I press it the cursor is taken instantly back to the place where it began. If only the spiritual life were that simple! Nonetheless, dear Unknown Friend, this book comes to those perhaps like yourself who look for that key. The return Home is rarely so rapid. In everyone lurks an often unspecified longing, an empty space that aches to be filled, a 'there must be more than this' feeling in the depths of our being. It's there waiting to have the ignition button pressed and for the long, slow, joyful-painful burn to get under way.

There comes a time when beneath the protecting or imprisoning shell we may get a sense that it's time to break loose, to set out and face the ocean of possibility in calm or storm. For some it happens at times of shock or trauma such as fierce illness, bereavement, loss of work or a relationship. For others it can be a gradual awakening or fuelled by mind-altering substances or an unexpected deep plunge into mystical union. For me, as my life took a sudden jolt in a direction the-I-who-I-thought-I-was did not want to go, it felt like a neck-wrenching, handbrake turn in an old car or a sudden scary skid on ice. The loss of control was exhilarating and terrifying, the kind of loss that is complete and entire. You end up, if you are lucky, with the deep relief that you can breathe again as you are brought to halt facing the wrong way. All your life has flashed before you and death may be more than facing you. Life after this is never quite the same again.

Some 30 years ago, that hurtle through a particular spiritual crisis known as burnout cracked the familiar shell of who I thought I was. I suspect each of us has a particular catalyst - moments in time that change us, make us take stock, pull us around

"We are all here to reclaim that Home; it is our birthright."

to another way of being. Moments when truth and illusion, after vying for authority down a lifetime, break the old truce and one finally gains the upper hand. And the truth is what sets us free. That freedom does not always feel welcome. The chains may be gone, the door of the cell burst wide open, but better the devil you know...a creature long caged may be surprisingly unwilling to run free into the unknown; the cage may be cramped, but it's a safe cage. It keeps things out, as well as in.

The shift can happen in seconds, it can be in the long slow curve of a lifetime or it may never happen at all. Some never turn while others have never quite moved off in the first place – away from Home. I have encountered many people down the years who seemed to have always felt at home in the Beloved, the Friend, the One, the Absolute, Ultimate Reality, God/dess. They appeared to have no memory of ever having fallen from that Source and felt no need to search. But for most of us the fall away from Home into the great forgetting happens early on. The quest to find our way back can begin at any point in our lives, not necessarily with the spiritual kick to our consciousness that a sudden crisis can bring.

This book is about that journey Home, that urge to seek something which we know is there but which has sometimes lain long forgotten at the back of the mind, on the tip of the tongue not quite able to be expressed, some irrepressible urge barely touched upon. Sometimes it drives us on powerfully and unaccountably, we know not where, yet impelled towards some ineffable 'something other', the numinous, the *mysterium tremendum.* It is the search that seems to be a primary quality deeply ingrained in what it is to be human, driven onwards by a sense of something lost, although we may not be quite sure what – some sense of original perfection, harmony, home, an inner Eden where we were at One.

We are all here to reclaim that Home; it is our birthright.

Much of our secular, 'this-is-all-there-is', materialist society regards such searching along a continuum from toleration to irrelevant to fun to slightly odd to dangerous. Some of the religious can equally signal the search as irrelevant – they already have the answers so why not just do as they do? Authentic faith, worship, spirituality, mysticism have been cleansed from our culture in so many ways that it is left mutilated rather than free. Spirituality gets reduced to an afterthought in the busyness of everyday life. Those who pursue such things are often viewed as out-dated or deluded. Already, dear Unknown Friend, by picking up this book you have marked yourself out as slightly weird, a little odd, drawn to something that many others would dismiss (at least publicly). So if this marks you out as a bit deviant from the mainstream, welcome to the club! You are not alone; there are millions more members - despite the cultural pressures vast numbers of people, the great majority, still participate in some form of religious activity or spiritual quest. To want to see beyond the self may be regarded as irrational by some people, but for others to *not* want to see is the madness.

Thus the spiritual seeker often feels somewhat alien to prevailing mores, at least at the beginning, until the work of maturation and integration enables us to live in the world with equanimity, compassion, service and understanding. Spiritually mature persons may be judged quite crazy by the rest of society, because their values often stand in contrast to what the rest of the world says is true. Film star Bette Davies [2] remarked that "Old age ain't no place for cissies." – the same might be said of the place of spiritual enquiry. It's not a place for the faint-hearted.

I recall feeling at Home as a child, a sense of being safe and at one with the world that was only in part cultivated by the safe working class background into which I was born. In 1949, England was still emerging from the aftermath of World War II, but for kids like me it was a time of unprecedented opportunity rooted in a diminution of fear. Millions of us from poor backgrounds were being given opportunities by the great reforming Labour government of the post-war era on a scale hitherto unimagined. For the first time, huge numbers of parents like mine no longer had the same relentless financial anxieties associated with homelessness, ill health, lack of education, unemployment and other dark spectres that lurked in the lives of the poor – for the state was building houses, providing health care, education and social benefits at unprecedented levels.

Kids like me were to grow up in a world transformed because fear of finding the money to meet the basic securities of life no longer depended on savings if you had them, or charity if you could find it. State-governed redistribution of income and an extension of the principle of the Good Samaritan infused many levels of health and social support that dramatically changed the landscape of possibility for a whole nation.

"We are all here to reclaim that Home; it is our birthright."

At the same time, freedom from fear accompanied the breaking down of the old order that was to see decades of social transformation under way. The certainties of my parents – of knowing your place, of being defined by what the established order of class or religion or government furnished you with – began their dissolution. For more people than ever before the influences of change in the decades to follow, still running their course to the present day, moved millions of people from being defined objectively, by what society told us we were, to subjectively, by using our own benchmarks of self-definition. This 'subjective turn' [3] unleashed forces of change (which in their own way fed back to the 'turn' to stimulate even more change) that were to affect above all the religious/spiritual backdrop into which I and millions of others emerged. The search for the 'I am' in this post-modern world was to be found less and less in the givens of a particular religion or social class into which you might be born, but by the fruits of a personal interior search often outside those constraints.

Here is but one example of that 'turn'. I walked through central Dublin recently, a huge billboard advertising banking services caught my eye. One of Ireland's major banks had seen fit to show two gay men, 'pioneers' of Ireland, on full public display. How this country had changed, I thought, from my first visit here 40 years ago. A major cultural shift has been underway that has seen, among other things, the collapse of the authority of the once all-powerful Roman Catholic Church. Ireland, in the teeth of fierce opposition from the church, became the first country in the world to vote by a majority in a plebiscite to legalise same-sex marriage. Ireland has become a state where it's OK to be gay, a pattern that has emerged in many countries across the globe, at least in the 'developed' world.

What happened in Ireland in 2016 did not arise suddenly, but it's an example of the slow building of the wave of change of the subjective turn, where the demand for personal liberty trumps the power of rigid authority. This movement was under way in my childhood, although of course I was blissfully unaware of it. The narrow, mostly comfortable, limitations of family life in our council house kept me oblivious of much that was moving beyond.

Anyway, I had my escape routes. My mum always said I was a daydreamer, for I recall hours as a child spent just staring at the sky or the trees in the garden or ly-ing in the grass. I could not explain then, but I was not daydreaming and my mind was not wandering off into some fantasyland; I was simply feeling utterly present in those moments. I did not have the words to express that I was feeling completely at Home, at One with everything, in Love - the presence of something that was both within and without me. Years later, a dear Soul Friend, said such moments are when we are "touched by God". Under this Touch, in this Presence, the world continued around me and I felt both part of it and witness to it. I thought everybody felt like this, experienced the world like this, but if they did they never said so.

We are all here to remember that we are bearers of that Presence; this too is our birthright.

At the time, on the few occasions I attempted to explain what was going on inside me, I was dismissed or judged strange, until I began to think that it must be me that was wrong, that the way others saw the world must be the right way simply because they said so and they were grown ups and there were more of them than me. When I grew up and shared these intimations the response in most quarters was the same except by then, armed with psychology or physiology, the responses were more barbed – that they were something to do with my poor parental relationships or the search for a loving father I did not really have at home or a flush of endorphins in the brain. So I learned to shut up about them and even forget about them.

Thus the seeds of separation were sown, the road to Home-lessness set down. Only later in life as I met many seekers along the Way did I discover that countless others also felt what I felt as a child. That for all kinds of reasons the 'I' that I was to become (or who I thought I was) and the world had conspired to push or pull me away from Home - for a while.

In the Jewish mystical tradition it is said that we know the Divine in the womb and then start to forget after we are born or perhaps are pushed into forgetting by life's painful experiences or the demands of simply growing up and learning to fit in. The essence of this book is about exploring how we remember.

That is *re-member* – join again to that from which we have been parted. How as

"We are all here to reclaim that Home; it is our birthright."

we shift into adulthood, our own personal story determines how we respond to that forgetting and to the world, with love or fear, with hope or despair, with a consciousness of Yes or No. Often our social and educational systems reinforce the forgetting, knocking us ever more into the No place instead of the Know place. In the former we drown out the original wisdom embedded in us, in the latter we are revived into it.

A point of disillusionment sooner or later turns up in our lives, the point when we start to seek new answers. The old ways of being, seeing and doing no longer suffice. The seeds of the soul are stirred, pushing up to a new life, so that we may start to expand beyond the limitations in which our egoic personalities have imprisoned us. That is not to condemn or do battle with such a personhood, rather to recognise that its role of mastery is finished and it is time to both break free of it and then accommodate it in a new way.

This book is rooted, dear Unknown Friend, not only in my personal experience of the collapse of who I thought I was and the tentative awakening to who I might be (with the passage through times of stillness and turbulence on the journey between the two), but also the many others with whom I have shared and worked down the years. Each passed in their own unique way along the same trajectory. It was in part their promptings, dear Unknown Friend, which suggested that this book if written might help others. In the mountains where I live the wise person does not set off without map and compass. Beautiful as they are, they can be dangerous. The spiritual life can indeed feel like a climb across mountainous terrain, but we can go there with at least some mapping provided by those who have walked the Way before us.

Thus I offer you here, dear Unknown Friend, a map with rivers of rich experience, a range of hills of diverse approaches to spiritual awakening and deep valleys of wisdom from the perennial philosophy. I'm not so sure that I will be saying anything new. Truth is truth, yet each generation must express this truth in its own way for its own time and circumstances. For some of us the quest for Home is a deepening in life of something we have never lost, for others it is seeking something new when our earliest sense of home no longer fulfils; to others it is a return to what was known, but seen again and known differently.

These pages are also for those like myself who are or have been in exile; who might feel no allegiance to or cut off from a particular tradition, yet are seeking heartfully nonetheless. Perhaps you are on the threshold of spiritual enquiry or a religion, or maybe you feel disconnected from the latter completely. It can certainly be hard to be associated with religion these days as it gets such a bad press and is blamed for all the ills of the world. True, religious organisations have often become corrupted and fed that perception. Religions can seek to serve not the Divine, but the will to power. The latter can mask itself as religion, but corrupts the soul's longing to its own ego ends. Much of 'Old Age' religion reeks of this while much of the 'New Age' movement is about building up the power of the ego, the 'false self', rather than demolishing it. We will explore these issues in more depth later as well as, dear Unknown Friend, looking at the pros and cons of being part of a religion or otherwise in the search.

Meanwhile, perhaps you have done a lot of spiritual work, but are wondering, "What next?" Or maybe you have become disheartened. It could also be that you are looking for something new or to deepen and strengthen what is already yours. Whatever your longing, dear Unknown Friend, my hope is that these notes made along my own Way may inspire and nourish you along yours. Simone Weil [4] writes of those who are "unable to cross the threshold" of faith, the "immense and unfortunate multitude of unbelievers" who are by accident or design on the margins of or disconnected from religions, yet questing sincerely nonetheless. I hope this book may help you, dear Unknown Friend, to get clearer about the Way for you, about what barriers to overcome, what thresholds if any to step over. Some, as we shall see, view the spiritual seeker as someone trying to find comforters to dull the pain of being in the world or escape from it. But to be 'spiritual' does not mean that we engage in a mysterious non-natural way of being, divorced from everyday experience. It is to possess qualities of life, love, compassion, acceptance and non-attachment that engage us *more* in life, but more sensitively, lovingly and with awareness. Soul and spirit are not false, unreal, separate realms but true in their own way and deeply embedded in the human experience and the whole cosmic order.

But who or what is this Home of which I write, dear Unknown Friend? It has many names, locations and genders. Is it a place or a way of being, a person or a state of consciousness? Is it somewhere else or here, now? Is it in time or in eternity? Theologians have dissected it, philosophers pronounced upon it, mystics immersed

"We are all here to reclaim that Home; it is our birthright."

themselves in it and some scientists and sceptics dismissed it. It is the One, the Absolute, the Beloved, the Friend, The Presence, God/dess, Source of All, Sacred Unity, Holy Wisdom, Eternity, Heaven from which we came and to which we shall return. And when we are ready for that return it happens in the twinkling of an eye, the distance no more than the same seat in which we sit, closer than our own breath. For some even the word or notion of 'God' is itself an obstruction. We will look in detail about how to respond to our difficulty around the 'G' word for that is itself grist to the mill of spiritual practice. There's many a rut like this on the road Home.

However, if God is love as many claim, when we know love we know God and love is boundless. The infinite faces of the Beloved cannot be reduced to the face we see and think is the one and only. The Beloved, with invincible attraction, draws us Home (fulfilling the promise at our incarnation) and appears to us in whatever guise we are ready to embrace. For some this is found in images of a male God in the clouds or in Isis pouring forth the power of the moon or the wonder of the cosmos or the harmony of the Dao or the quiet moment at home with family or a spirit guide found in a hedgerow or in an icon of the Christ or Krishna or the Buddha or… or…or…The infinite possibility of God cannot be pinned down to one person's version, nor can we, despite our best and sometimes even violent efforts, get everyone else to see our Beloved in exactly the same way that we do.

It seems that the longing to come home to the Beloved is deep in all human beings; no matter how it is blocked out or distorted, it is still there. If there is another maxim in this quest it is the words of E. M. Forster [5], "Only connect". Connection with the Beloved, with our deepest self, with All-that-is, with others - this is our hearts' desire. Connection is a kind of homecoming. Indeed we might well be called not so much human beings as human belongings. When we cannot belong we are more likely to get sick, as the many studies on loneliness have shown and which I will explore with you later. Relationality and the quality of our relationships is the key to our sense of belonging, of connectedness, of feeling at Home in the world and that which is more than the world…and to keeping us healthy. Connection through the way we feel is what binds us together.

Relationships founded in common interests, say of work or politics or sport or religion or the way we look or the things we own or value, have their limits. If we depend on agreement in them for connection, at some point we may disconnect when our views start to diverge. Relationships rooted in shared ideas of this nature must be transient. However, if we seek to connect through our shared stories we find the common ground, for in each of them no matter how different the detail, contains our experience of love, fear, disappointment, joy and so forth. A different kind of bond forms, a connection, when we see how each other has felt in the ups and downs of our lives, for we both know what fear and joy and love and sorrow feel like. We don't have to explain, we know, and these feelings are universal and intransient. Here is our common bond, the root of connection to each other. It is in part a homecoming when we live and relate in the world from that common bond.

Home is also mirrored in some ways in the ordinary home we try to make for our everyday lives, a place of safety, security, individual expression and relating. It is reflected in the childhood household into which we are born and which, if we are so blessed, was a place of love and security, but from which all of us must depart if we are to emerge as fully human. Then, perhaps long after the departure and having established our individual identity, there are moments of ripeness, perhaps just one, perhaps many in one lifetime. These are the moments when we are ready to turn, to become more aware, to shift the way we are in the world and try to get a little closer to something that we had forgotten or pushed to one side, something for which we had nonetheless been quietly waiting.

This adaptation from a website prayer[6] offers us some of the reference points for the landscape we will be exploring:-

> Home is the cradle of life.
> Home gives the gift of self.
> Home is where we find one another.
> Home is the space of our intimacy.
> Home is the harbour of our security.
> Home is the shelter of our growth.
> Home is the sanctuary of our love.
> Home is the treasury of our memories.
> Home is the temple of God's presence.

"We are all here to reclaim that Home; it is our birthright."

Home is the warm hearth of our love.
Home is the heart of all our longings.
Home is the hand of forgiveness.
Home is the source of all healing.

In this book I offer more detailed explanation of what it is to seek and find Home, while being mindful that the journey there (and it feels like a journey for a while) is not without its cul-de-sacs, lost directions and even intersections of danger. It's also a journey of breathtaking views, inspiring encounters and stunning experiences. In the pages that follow there are examples from real life, stories from wise teachers and suggestions for bringing greater depth, integrity and authenticity along the Way as we draw ever nearer to Home.

Each of us experiences Home in our own unique way. I offer no prescription of what religion to follow (or not), no image of the Absolute that is right or wrong. With over seven billion of us on the planet we cannot all stand in precisely the same place as each other and see the Divine from exactly the same angle. The image will be unique to each of us. I do not say, "This is the Way and this is the only Way". In the modern spiritual supermarket we are spoilt for choice, but I may make some recommendations on the quality of the goods on offer, how to discern what is worth buying and what to leave on the shelves.

To aid this discernment, a spiritual gift we will explore in some depth, I offer four significant approaches in the search. They are more, dear Unknown Friend, than spiritual exercises to solve life's problems or make us feel good. Their substance is in the way they encourage us to make a conscious participation in the search, to get our 'stuff' out of the way so that we connect deeply with our souls and let the Divine speak to us. Out of a habit formed in childhood and initially unquestioned, I almost wrote the G word there! You may have noticed, dear Unknown Friend that I have studiously sought, except when quoting others, to avoid words about 'God' that assume a gender. What is your response to that? Perhaps you are comfortable with it, perhaps curious, indifferent or hostile? Stay with me, we shall use that response to inform us in these pages. Your reaction may already be a way in which the Beloved is speaking to you.

When we start to 'listen', how we 'hear' the Divine 'speaking' to us is unlimited in its possibilities. From a hunch or intuition, to 'hearing' a still, small voice within, from the advice of a Soul Friend to the inspiration of a beautiful day, from the dirt in the street to an inspiring piece of music, from a profound piece of scripture to a silly programme on TV. We are surrounded and infused by the Divine consciousness knowing itself. It floods relentlessly into our awareness at every level if we are open to it. The Beloved will speak to us, reach out to us, in whatever way we have the willingness and capacity to receive. The four soul paths outlined in this book help us to access that awareness and offer resources by which we discern the true from the false, the mystical from the psychotic.

We will explore, dear Unknown Friend, how we try to deny the consequences of a life without meaning and driven by deep seated fears in the unconscious, perhaps using one or more 'addictions' to drown the pain of such a life in drink, drugs, sex, work, compulsive communicating or whatever other form of addictive behaviour we can find. We have an enormous menu of options available to us to avoid the hunger in a life of essential separation, to fill up the hole in ourselves from which we have emptied the Divine. Whether it has to be 'God' or not to fill this hole will be part of our exploration when some might argue that politics or social action or material gain might suffice.

Whichever course we take, all *things* must pass. Our journey along the way will discern if there is a *no-thing* that does not, that is in time and space yet not captured by them. In a life lived however fully engaged in the world, there is the undercurrent acknowledged or not that it will all pass away, we must pass away. No matter how we dress it up in confidence that "this is all there is" or "I am happy to live my life, I don't need a God or an afterlife" – somewhere beneath lurks an unconscious unyielding despair and fear of mortality that feeds on a denial of the numinous. Either that or we transfer our hopes of being 'saved' on to the false gods of material fulfilment, demagogues, social movements that promise heaven on earth and any number of other psychological security blankets. The Absolute does not pass – he/she/it is not a 'thing'. In the Beloved lies the immortality of the essence of who we are, shorn of our notions of a separate, egoic, transient self. Here we find a different awareness of 'life' that we may come to know while in this 'ordinary life' and beyond, a true life that is out of time and in eternity where 'endings' and 'beginnings' have no meaning.

"We are all here to reclaim that Home; it is our birthright."

Until then, if we do not seek flight from the world or resignation (masked as accep-tance, but maybe really a resignation that is saying "yes" to hopelessness), then the other way is to seek power in the world. If there is no 'God' then we may make our-selves 'Gods', and therein lies so much of the misery that has crashed upon human-ity down the ages. The pursuit of our own will to power perverts the divine image in religion, politics, commerce and many spheres of human endeavour. In the hands of those who are ignorant and have not done the deep inner work, any system, not least a religious one and however well meant, will find its original intent corrupted.

This Beloved, dear Unknown Friend, is not some panacea, some trick of the mind to fill a hole in our consciousness, to wall out the despair of the world, of mortality, which might otherwise encroach upon us. It is not the 'God' of so much atheist com-mentary, some of which we will explore, or interpreted from many scriptures, invari-ably male, often angry, damning and destroying upon a whim. Nor is this Beloved a fabrication of the unconscious, a honey-pot of fantasy and projection to sweeten the bitterness of birth and death and the bits in between. For birth and death are of the body, held in the Divine, a life lived in space and time which dissolving in its own time frees the soul completely towards Home. As to what this 'soul' is, that is a matter we will explore more deeply in the next chapters.

Many times in this book we will refer to the Beloved and perhaps we will edge a little closer to knowing the One who, simply by picking up this book, may be call-ing you Home. That which radiates from this Source, that invisible, unconquerable magnetic pull, grace, the Holy Spirit, the divine energy - is already working its way in you. And what is this 'God', dear Unknown Friend? Here I offer some personal reflections from someone mystically inclined and rooted in long years of enquiry and experience.

The One that is the focus of this book and in which our being and belonging have their Home, is sometimes like the hidden guest at a party, the Friend of all, who no one remembers inviting yet everyone is too polite to suggest otherwise. This is the Divine that is simultaneously personal and transpersonal, immanent and transcen-dent, knowable and unknowable. Nietzsche [7] argued that "He who has a 'why' to live can bear almost any 'how'". In being and belonging we find the answer to the 'why' on which we can base our values and reasons for living. In coming Home we seek that answer, and perhaps find that it is also about seeing what life expects from us rather than what we expect from life. We also learn along the way that it is not so much a matter of *being* a Christian, Jew, Moslem, Hindu, Sikh, Daoist or whatever religious or philosophical tribal identity we give ourselves, but forever *becoming* one of these. In the unbounded becoming on the way Home, we are never a 'this' or a 'that', but always expanding into the infinity that is the Divine, of being a work in progress, an exquisite unfolding work of art.

Some people begin the search for this One, this Oneness, early on and spend a whole lifetime seeking. It is the ground of absolute truth, union with All-that-is, a consciousness unbounded by space and time wherein we touch the eternal, get a sense at last that 'I am not alone' and that there is 'more than this'. When we touch this numinous realm, even if only for a moment, life can never be the same again. We may get a hint or superficial sense of it in the mass movement of a rock concert, a football crowd, a demo' or a religious gathering. The feeling that we are all 'us' hints at our unity, our immortality. This mass 'now' of like-minded people creates a faux transcendence, a religious experience that gives us a glimpse of something 'other', but is unlikely to be transformative, to shift us out of the essentially mech-anistic participation in the world as it is. At the same time we may see even this surface experience as an invitation to go deeper, a carrot dangling on the end of a stick to tempt us to look for 'more'.

Others avoid such a search until pressed by some circumstance or other to enquire. Some just stay asleep to it and the promptings that come along from time to time. Maybe, in what was no more than a flash of insight or moment of mysticism, we sense that Presence through the mist of time, tantalisingly out of reach. Others just get drunk on the Beloved from the first encounter and remain intoxicated. Which-ever way is followed, it seems that few, if any, in the end (and it may come at the very end of life) can resist "being gripped by the field of gravitation of heaven"[8].

As the irresistible gravitational pull to wards the Beloved gains hold we may find all our definitions being challenged not least the gender of the One – He? She? It? No matter how much we strive to apply our definitions we may discover paradox and perplexity, a being-ness beyond gender, in all genders yet contained by none. In the first edition of this book I found myself clinging to a 'Him' after many years of

"We are all here to reclaim that Home; it is our birthright."

cultural influence and theology. After lots of debate, dissonance, gender analysis, doubt and discussion I decided I'd avoided taking the tougher option of writing of God without gender. Once I applied myself to the task, it turned out to be not that difficult after all.

As it is, I rest in awe of the nameless one who can bear any name while acknowledging the distortions (affecting both women and men socially, culturally, psychologically, spiritually) to which an exclusively patriarchal deity can lead us. Indeed many have argued that the split from the primordial mother Goddess and the worship of the exclusively male God has deeply damaged human consciousness and the way we have treated the world and each other down the ages [9,10]. In my day-to-day life I frequently slip across boundaries to names of different gender, but I am mostly left with the simplicity of the Beloved. This word, found in some scriptures and favoured by mystics, is one on which I settle most. I use it in prayer, conversation and contemplation as it reflects a loving intimacy I feel and is less likely to alienate others.

However, dear Unknown Friend, no matter what words I use in this text, please call the Divine what you will, what works for you in your own particular relationship to the Source-of-All, I don't mind and I'm sure the Beloved doesn't. You may find one word suffices for a lifetime. You may find words come and go as you transform. I long ago let go of the separate, anthropomorphic 'Him' perched on a cloud, bearded, grey and English, firing spiteful thunderbolts at anyone as 'His' fancy takes 'Him'.

The Dao, our Buddha nature and other considerations of eastern faiths are much less inclined to see the Absolute as male. The 'people of the book' – Islam, Judaism and Christianity, are rather more locked into masculine language for the deity. Mystics and contemplatives seem more likely to escape this limitation, while for others God remains resolutely 'father'. The Old and New Testaments consistently refer to God as 'He' in English translations, while the original Hebrew and Aramaic words (*Elohim* in Hebrew and *Allaha* in Aramaic) are not gender driven and refer to a Sacred One who is beyond definition and has no opposite, a Sacred Unity, a Holy One who holds diversity in one.

Furthermore, the Beloved is not fixed in heaven, or standing outside of hell. Heaven is not above nor hell below, in a geographical or astronomical sense, but in a metaphorical, a conscious sense where the lower is a concept of density, darkness and (apparent) absence of the Beloved and the higher is the lighter, open, overt Presence. But these are only perceptions. They are constructs, labels, made by frantic minds, including mine, along the Way demanding fixity. Such minds struggle to deal with experiences and concepts that are ineffable, numinous, nebulous, paradoxical, indefinable or mystical – the truth of the Divine who is no-thing yet not nothing. As a child I knew this truth, it's just that I was told I was wrong

The Old-Man-In-The-Sky-God I came to know was introduced to me at church and school. He (sic) was remote, intimidating and seemed forever to be angry with the Jews or being nice to them according to his whim. He was not interested in the pain and suffering that, even as a child, I was witnessing in the world. He was constantly finding fault with us, meting out punishment and telling us how wrong we were. He sent his child into the world with the expressed intent of getting him killed, and set up Judas as the fall guy. He was there backing wars, the monarchy, the police, schoolteachers and every other part of the establishment I encountered, but seemed to not give a damn about the victims of war, or famine, or the unemployed or the homeless. He was a ruler hitting your hand or a cane across your bottom in class. He was a lonely room at home where you were sent because he didn't like what you had done. He owned lots of buildings that were empty most of the time. He expected you to give him money or whatever else you had although he owned everything anyway. He liked some people, especially ladies who wore hats and went to church on Sunday. He did not like young men with spots, those who had long hair and those who thought about what was underneath girls' sweaters. He disapproved of sex and come to that of anything that seemed fun, exciting, colourful or joyful. He liked white people best and white men were his favourites, especially if they were kings or policemen or headmasters. He liked men and women who married and lived together forever and had 2.3 children in semi-detached houses and had nice cars. He did not like single girls who got pregnant, anyone who enjoyed sex either solo or with someone else and especially a same sex someone else. He ignored anyone who was not English and people with old bangers or who lived in terraced houses with outside toilets. He was forever handing out judgements while wagging his finger and was waiting to give me hell (literally) when I died unless I pulled my socks up (also literally).

"We are all here to reclaim that Home; it is our birthright."

When this 'God' died to me I came to know another. 'He' ceased to be a forbidding cartoon character; the God word simply became a metaphor, a symbol for some-thing infinitely more subtle and profound, remote and yet closer to me than my own breath. This God ceased to be a God of domination, of hierarchical power forever directing, controlling and intervening. This 'new' God, the Beloved, is one of rela-tionship, interconnectedness and co-creation. This is not a God thundering down power from on high, but a God of service, like Jesus at the last supper washing the feet of his followers; a God in all things yet contained by none, a God of mutuality, sharing, with us and in us. So, dear Unknown Friend, please fasten your seat belt before you read on, for a different perspective on God is about to be offered if you're still stuck with a separate Old-Man-In-The-Sky. Mystics and contemplatives do not see God as separate, male, remote or angry. In fact we do not see God as a 'thing' at all. Some of the qualities and experiences of God can be described, but this God-self is beyond definition. Still we try.

This Beloved, my Friend (as the poet Rumi often calls him) I know is with me now as I write these words, is the sitting, is the writing, is simply known and being known, the whole universe, every universe, is a mirror to the Beloved knowing the Beloved. I fumble and flounder in this relationship along the Way in a being who smiles ("But how can you smile if you don't have a mouth?") at my efforts and still loves me (would do no other). The Beloved is all and none, the single and the general, every-where and nowhere; has no face yet everywhere I turn I see the face. The Beloved is light containing all light; brilliant, impenetrable, and would blind me were my in-sight not veiled to protect me. My Beloved is also dark, darkness itself, unknowable, hidden. Yet this darkness is luminous and here the Beloved is revealed as well. In all things yet contained by none, the Beloved contains all in a magnificent *panen-theism*, everything in the Divine and the Divine in everything, Sacred Unity. This Beloved, this God, is transcendent and beyond me, yet immanent and personal.

This Beloved to whom I am so close and in whom I find the deepest reality does not exist. Yes, does not exist; created things have their own existence governed by the laws of time and space. But the Beloved, in whom time and space are contained, does not exist in the same sense that we do, beings that are born, live and die. We know existence. The Beloved is no finite creature; timeless, this One is in eternity, is eternity. Eternity is not forever. Forever is a condition of the physical reality of time and space. Eternity is neither; it is the *aeternum* (Lat.), that which is without origin or movement, ungoverned by the laws of physics, no beginning and no end. It is sometimes in these numinous glimpses of eternity (encountered in loving relationships, moments of wonder, deep spiritual practice or mystical union) that we 'see' the Beloved, 'see' heaven. When all our concepts of the Divine slip away, we 'see' the Beloved simply *is*. To come Home to this truth after physical death is heaven. To know this truth while embodied is to bring heaven to earth.

In our efforts to define God, theology eventually wraps itself in layer upon layer of obtuseness and obfuscation. God is no thing. We may use phrases like 'God is love' or 'God is eternal' or 'God is good', but these are ultimately mere efforts and only describe qualities of the Divine, not the nature or depth of the reality. All definitions are ours, arising from the limited frame of egoic consciousness that wants names and facts and certainty. If the soul laughs it must do so at these efforts; like a parent watching a child struggle with a complex puzzle, a parent who knows the incredible simplicity of the answer for which no words are needed.

This Beloved that is no-thing, remote and shrouded in myth and mystery, is yet accessible, reachable and closer than if sitting right next to you on a bench, as close as sitting *in* you. This Beloved loves unconditionally, boundlessly, infinitely, abundantly all creation, none specially, all uniquely. This love pours out for all who wish to drink, and for those who don't. My Beloved knows all, yet still I pray; dances with me in countless forms and relationships, questions and certainties. Nothing is required in return, not least worship, adoration or acknowledgment, yet still I offer them. Believers and unbelievers are loved in equal measure. Carved over the door of Carl Jung's home in Switzerland are the words *'Vocatus atque non vocatus deus aderit'* – 'Bidden or not bidden the God is present'. Whether we want God to be present or not makes no difference, the Divine is not under our control and there is no time or place that God is not.

This Presence, this bidden or unbidden God, is not indifferent. The Beloved is the one in whose heart all is well, all that is right and wrong, saint and evildoer, good and bad, loving and fearful; all is gathered and made whole. Everyone and everything is invited and welcomed Home.

"We are all here to reclaim that Home; it is our birthright."

I wonder, dear Unknown Friend, if like me you were taught to fear God, or at least the God a lot of people thought God to be? I don't recall feeling this fear even though I was told that I should do because "the Bible says so". In the Hebrew texts we find the word *yirah*. It is translated as 'fear' but the meaning is subtler and better expressed as awe, the kind of shudder we get when we are both exhilarated and overwhelmed by something too big to take in. Often I heard then as I do now of God's 'holiness'. I used that word in those days, but knew not what it meant. Now I know it and cannot express it adequately in words, for who can put into words that which is utterly whole, at-one and ungoverned by the boundaries of time and space? The reality of such Being-ness is so utterly awesome that I am both deeply enamoured and shaken before it, not least the overpowering love that is its nature. Words fail, but feelings do not and thus is this holiness known by the way it makes us feel – inspired, blissed out, shaken and stirred, terrified and transported. This is *yirah*.

This radiant love is no mere sentimentality. It's power is so great it can reduce us to tears when we open to it, leave us trembling and on fire with it. It cannot be overcome, radiating sun-like on and through all. It does not differentiate. It is the *shekinah,* an overpowering divine love that pours out so abundantly that to a simple ego consciousness it seems wasteful. Touched by awareness of this some are sent into rapture that they long to embrace, some into panic from which they would flee. To the former it is bliss, to the latter a burning pain. I've been touched by the presence of so many who, when faced with the possibility that they are loved completely as they are, feel the need to shut the door and get the hell away from it.

Please let me tell you of a childhood experience of this, dear Unknown Friend. I was in the back garden at home on a sunny July day with high clouds in a bright blue sky. The wind was brisk and unusually cold, my mum came out with a blanket for me, an old yellow blanket from my bed and wrapped me in it. I lay on the grass transfixed by the beauty of the world around me including the bits I might otherwise have ruled out as ugly – the broken fence, the dilapidated shed, the sooty, red bricks of the houses crowded around me, the smell coming up from the mill down the street. It all seemed so *perfect*. Perhaps it was my mum's loving gesture or just the sense of being so warm and the sun on my face, yet I felt the sun was more than just above me. It seemed to be radiating equally all around my body, that I was surrounded by the sun and that this same shining was also coming from inside my body outwards. There was nowhere this radiance was not. I was so overwhelmed I was moved to tears. It was a feeling beyond joy and it was tinged with an edge of fear to it, that the I-whoever-I-was would disappear or that I would lose it and never feel like this again. *Yirah* and *shekinah* in one. Ah, but of course all this could just be childhood delusion – or not; a subject we will be exploring later.

Meanwhile, in the esoteric traditions, alongside holiness and love, there is a third primary quality to the Divine, justice. Justice as order, the foundational quality of All-that-is; there is a pattern and unity, a vast similitude, to all planes of reality that is unbreakably sure. No matter what forces might seek to fracture this order, its tenacity and absolute certainty cannot be gainsaid. To act justly is to act according to this divine order. No matter what 'laws and conventions' we may create, in time this justice will break them if they run counter to this divine order, which is thus restored.

These planes of consciousness are perfectly placed, but there is sometimes a tendency in some teachings to deny the world of matter as a delusion, which must be escaped. Coincidentally the word matter is closely related to the root word *mater* (Lat. 'mother'; related also to words like matrix, mare, metre) and expresses something of the feminine nature of the earth, the mother. It is in turn closely related to the *maya* of Hinduism and Buddhism, the female *shakti* or consort of the Divine (like Mother Mary in Christianity) out of whose free-play the world of form emerges, the divider and measurer of the One that is no-thing which thus becomes things. To escape from or deny the world of matter no doubt is a driver in the denial of the feminine, the consequences of which I explore later. The spiritual life is not about escaping and devaluing the world of matter and denying its reality, an *acosmism*, rather it is to come to full awareness of it, to appreciate and value it as one would look upon a work of art. This conventional realm comes to be appreciated and loved, simply because it is conventional. Thus it is redeemed, rendered part of the whole rather than separated out to feed a sense of duality.

Perhaps, dear Unknown Friend, the God I knew and the Beloved I know rings some bells for you. Perhaps there are similarities between my childhood experience and the God who sometimes dies when we grow up. Perhaps you are confused because you are certain God is male and you thought you'd got 'Him' defined. In the end, they

"We are all here to reclaim that Home; it is our birthright."

are all words, perceptions, struggling to make sense of something that is no thing. The Divine is incomprehensible to human thought except by metaphor and allusion, which is why only the poets, artists and musicians seem to get close. But perhaps in mythology and the arts lies the secret, for we cannot define or know the Beloved fully; the clue is in the name. A name that speaks of love suggests we can know the Divine through what we 'feel' with the eye of the heart, in relationship.

Thus, facts seek to tell us what we *know* about the Beloved. Myth and art tell us what it *feels like* to know. Like millions down the ages I have been a seeker. I do not assume or reason than this Presence is there, I know this truth at some deeper level than intellectual discourse. This 'knowing' and its nature will be explored in this book.

Meanwhile, this 'knowing' reveals that there is nowhere the Beloved is not and nor is this Prescence indifferent. We can hear in the silent universe, this vast theophany, where each star and each molecule, each cell and beast, each grain and mountain when asked, "Who is God?" responds, "I Am". The Beloved is seen with the eye of my heart, where each moment breathed is full of that Presence which says only one thing, "I love you". The nature of the Beloved is the eternal I Love You, the I Love You from which all creation pours and into which it returns. All the creation sings I Love You, for that is the Beloved's song.

This beloved Sacred Unity I know is big enough to embrace the thought of non-existence and thus is not offended by atheists or those who make no acknowledgement. The Beloved is beyond ego concepts like offence, does not demand those things that our egos crave – money, power, worship and so forth. So abundant is the love of the Beloved that it pours seemingly wastefully into where it is not recognised or requested. Yet love from the Infinite is not wasted, for waste is to suggest limitation, ultimate shortage. There is no shortage in the Beloved, not least of love and not least of patience. This love flows where it will, our judgements of it are irrelevant and its fulfilment a mystery.

One of my favourite paintings is 'The light of the world' by William Holman Hunt. It hangs in Manchester city art gallery. It depicts the risen Christ figure knocking at a weed-overgrown door, which, having no handle, can only be opened from the inside.

This door (to the heart) has clearly never been opened before and indicates that it is up to us whether we choose to let the Divine enter. Thus it is with the Beloved who is no spiritual bully, does not force the Self upon us in a violent sense, unless the relentless outpouring of love, which ultimately overcomes all, shall be deemed a violence. Even when the resistance is great, the soul, which longs for Home seems to have ways of bypassing such obstructions from our egoic 'false' self, and inviting the Beloved in. The unconscious is just that part of our consciousness, the mind, that our egos cannot yet see. It is part of our being in the world and the soul seems to have the knack of forming an allegiance with it to subvert ego power, perhaps by leading us into situations where the Divine burglar can find the hidden entry point. The Beloved and the soul in a holy conspiracy find a way!

However, this is not to say conversely that the Beloved is some separate, spiritually passive entity waiting for us all to wake up by our own efforts. This love is grace, the Divine saving and strengthening influence radiating constantly into our lives. The Beloved is pouring out love to draw us Home. The soul is not without attunement to this, for it is locked onto the Beloved, its own nature, it knows where Home is and rests in it whilst simultaneously experiencing incarnation. Perhaps the soul does not so much go Home as get free of anything that inhibits the fullness of knowing Home and draws with it all that it has been whilst being a 'person'. The ego, the personhood, the false or little self, the mind product, that collection of identities and drives whose names are legion that we call the-I-who-I-think-I-am and which we may believe for a while has an existence of its own (Ah, the seductions of power and fear!) can bend all its efforts to hold back the inevitable, but give way it must.

The Beloved is the one who loves us so greatly, that we were let go into separation so that we could leave Home. And the Beloved is the one in eternal waiting for each prodigal son and daughter to return to Union, wealthy with all that we have been, impoverished of all we thought we were. Saints and holy men and women as well as the broken and the disreputable have known the Beloved manifesting in this ordinary reality. The Beloved is the One ever present but never fully seen, the invisible guide hidden in the fog of the life that is not life, until Life that is beyond life bursts through and we weep at the wonder of our immortality. And in all of this the soul is safe, for the we-who-we-think-we-are does not own it. What does not belong to us but is of the Beloved cannot be sold or destroyed. Your soul, dear Unknown Friend,

"We are all here to reclaim that Home; it is our birthright."

is indeed of the One. Just as the Beloved is infinite and indestructible so the soul is a hologram of that infinity and indestructibility imbued with boundless possibility.

Dear Unknown Friend, perhaps my words have provoked in you the question of who or what the Divine is for you, perhaps a conventional view or something other, an inclination to the mystic like myself or a distant deity? No two of us see the Beloved in exactly the same way. There is a Sufi story of a group of people blindfolded and taken to meet an elephant for the first time. The one who touches the trunk thinks the elephant is like a snake, the one who takes the tail thinks it is like a rope. One touches a leg and declares it to be like a tree. Likewise, no one of us can see or know all that is the Beloved, although perhaps the mystics come closest in their experience of union. However, after a while, we may lose the desire to describe the whole of the Beloved anyway, rather simply experience the relationship.

Even as I write this it's quite possible that another universe has burst into being, and another and another. The Beloved is like that. The poet [1] wails, "Where is there an end to it?" Perhaps there isn't, and thus we must lose the fear of the boundless unknown and immerse ourselves in the joy of endless exploration. "Nobody gets into heaven", Ram Dass once told me. Look at that phrase again dear Unknown Friend and let its teasing truth roll around for a while. While we are busy being a somebody, loaded with our thoughts, identities and self-definitions then we remain in separation. It really is easier for a camel to get through the eye of a needle [Matt:19.24] than for a rich person to get into heaven if we are wealthy and overblown with ego identity. To become no-body (ah, to surrender so fully!) we find that Nobody does indeed get Home! And surrender to the Divine is either full or not; it cannot be conditional for that then is not surrender. The endless journey Home can seem like that as we work, cheerfully and wearily along the Way, not so much getting 'there' as continuous discovery, surrender, expansion of consciousness, falling into forgetting and then remembering again. Always Coming Home.

When we are ready for Home we have let go of the desire to be a 'me', have surrendered our will so completely that 'somebody' is annihilated in the Beloved. (Look again at those words – surrender, annihilation. Scared? Good. We'll explore that later on too. Notice also how 'scared' and 'sacred' are near twins!) All that we thought we were is surrendered (according to some traditions perhaps over many lifetimes) and the soul then completes its ineluctable destiny. Home, being re-united, immortal, invisible, self and selfless. So, we can take heart, for we are not annihilated into nothing, we return to oneness in God, into total Love. If we know what its like to love a person, imagine what it's like to be merged with a love so complete that all doubt, separation and fear are lost in eternity.

The Soul Work for this voyage is not about going 'up' to heaven but 'down' into ourselves, where strangely enough we find heaven lies. It is the *kenosis*, the emptying of the self in order to find the Self. In surrendering our identity to the Beloved we do not lose our freedom to be ourselves, we find it. It is the *fana' fi-l'llah* of the Sufi's, the annihilation of everything into the beauty of the Divine, beyond limited concepts of existence. Refined, liberated and surrendered of identity, we re-find our true identity in the One from whom we came; the tiniest door of time is now open to us.

"Nobody gets into heaven" is not a council of despair but of joy! Thus the great paradox, in losing ourselves, we find our Self, at Home. All names, all states, all experiences lead here, eternity where 'here' and 'where' have no meaning and the glorious paradox of oneness and individuality are held in perfection.

Enough for now. Perhaps some challenges, some questions have arisen. I hope so! Then let us be about the Work and all shall be made clear in the pages that follow.

May this book be a guide and comforter, dear Unknown Friend, as you follow the Way Home.

Seek the One, the Beloved; seek Home, dear Unknown Friend. There's nothing else!

Yours, in anticipation,
A Friend

"We are all here to reclaim that Home; it is our birthright."

Sometimes the light was so close,
so very close,
that flesh seemed thin.
Sometimes high,
like the noontime over a summer lake.
Sometimes dim,
like a waning moon behind a vapour trail.
Words slip out and crack,
like paving stones
under the tracks of Krishna's tanks;
each thought broken
in the pointless shards exploring
the Truth:
that there is nothing to say.
And oh the perfection,
whole in its partial wrong,
whole in its partial right.
Made clear in the crucible of our despair.
Burnished in the furnace of our hopes
and dreams, our dreams great and small.
All dreams.
It was and is and shall be all a dream.
Be reasonable Buddha,
the night is long
and the lamps we strap unto ourselves
grow dim.
Is there no one with a light to help?
We cannot break the chain,
the rust has set its links.
"Surely it's time for tea?"
If there is no God, is there no help?
"No milk or sugar, please."
He missed the point,
I'm sure He missed the point.
Suffering arises not

from attachment to possessions,
relationships or events
or even the gifts on the Christmas tree,
but detachment from You.
We feed the million hungry ghosts.
The compulsion of the blackbird
stuffing the beaks of chicks
in the nest by the cherry tree.
She dies eroded by labour in the summer heat.
The soul starved of You
waits for the next season,
or the next.
And sometimes when feeling lucky
or maybe on a day when the police stop you for speeding
or maybe when you miss your train or
during a treat when the chocolate tastes especially good,
sometimes, just sometimes,
we wake up.

Part 2

"Adam and Eve were driven from the Garden of Eden because of the kind of knowledge they reached for – a knowledge that distrusted and excluded God. Their drive to know arose not from love but from curiosity and control, from their desire to possess powers belonging to God alone. They failed to honour the fact that God knew them first, knew them in their limits as well as their potential. In their refusal to know as they were known, they reached for a kind of knowledge that always leads to death"[11]

Leaving Home: a wander in strange lands

<u>The subjective turn</u>
The council estate of immaculate gardens and red brick houses that shone in the rain gave way to Cemetery Road. Here, as a small child, I felt I could breathe. Here the built area had not invaded. A small farm and open fields had somehow eluded the planners, developers and factory builders, leaving a green island bounded by the encircling grey slate roofs and forests of mill chimneys. Here were skylarks. I would watch them rise, singing, and sometimes even into my late teens I would lie for hours beneath them in wonder; hymns with wings on blue sky summer days. In this space it always seemed lighter, open, more free. There were views and the sound of wind in the trees and the mystery of long grass. Black and white cattle watched you watching them. On a summer's day the sky was endless. In grey, wild winter it pressed down on the terraces and gunmetal streets far off. It was a place where somehow I could feel my own breath, as if some restraining corset had been removed and, unleashed, something inner seemed to soar and roll. Here I was happy; perhaps I was happy elsewhere, but here I knew I was.

I cannot offer a particularly heavy deprivation narrative. My family was poor, my mother a hard working coper and my father remote in job, booze and betting shop. It was not expressively loving, but it was good and warm enough. I was safe and well fed (on a diet so high in animal fat and sugar it might in other times constitute child abuse!) and the first of that generation born into the reforming times after the

"We are utterly safe, loved, worthy and right as we are in our very essence."

Second World War that was to open up, for working class kids like me, horizons of which our parents had never dared dream.

It was a time of transformation, for the culture and community that at once held and nurtured me also restricted and repressed me. For thousands of my generation and background, better fed, educated and housed than any before, the walls were about to give way; the sheltering walls, the imprisoning walls. Church was one of them; most people belonged to one church or another. British society at every level was wrapped up in it; it was almost obligatory. I arrived into a world where religion, as never before, was about to become an option, a personal choice, and not something you had to do because that was what you were supposed to do.

This was the time that was to give birth to a movement, the post-modern, the desire to break free from old places and old bonds and old customs, some forever, but not necessarily for better, as John Lennon was to sing. Out of this milieu grew the revolutionary movements of the 1960s, the summer of love, the shaken and stirred cultural norms where old certainties of church and state, of social conventions from cradle to grave were never to be the same again. This was the era in which the 'subjective turn' [3] was born, a time when an enormous cultural shift, long in the germinating, accelerated; an era when who we were in the world was to be changed. Here a fermentation was under way that transformed self-definition - no longer by whatever rules the law or the church or society or the community or the elite or whatever objective other cared to define us. These hitherto accepted ways were inverted; definition was to come now from a different direction, by our own selves, the subjective, the I, me, mine of self-identification on a scale unparalleled.

Thus the organised religions became increasingly sidelined, just one view among many. My generation and those that have followed it have grown up in this world of apparent self-definition. It is a world of "believing without belonging" [10], the apparent freedom to pursue our own spirit without boundaries or rules. It was a reaction in the post-modern world to the totalitarianism of the modern that had been perceived as rational, systematic, logical and progressive. This modern worldview arguably reached its apogee in the cataclysm of the Second World War where totalitarian systems clashed and crashed in appalling destruction. The post-modern world set itself to liberate us from this "cold and cerebral" way of seeing humanity "by injecting a sense of choice and even playfulness" [13].

Out of this grew the unwillingness to define moral absolutes, holistic thinking, the ecology and many personal liberation movements, a wariness of logical thinking and 'progress'. But was this a real escape or a way of avoiding difficult questions? Was it a new way of action or a retreat into self-indulgence? Was it freedom from totalitarian religion or unwillingness to take on the tough spiritual work of being in long-term communion with and commitment to fellow travellers? Has religion really been abandoned, or have we created a whole new religion, the New Age?

While the New Age may not fit traditional patterns of religious governance and organisation it seems to have its own rules, moral codes, puritanical attitudes and approved behaviours that are nonetheless a religion by any other name. There may not be an Archbishop of Glastonbury or a Grand Mufti of Sedona, but there is a plethora of New Age teachers, writers and pundits whose courses and written and spoken words are followed with religious, awed fervour. Yet they sometimes seem without firm foundations, untested and lacking the spiritual truth that has taken millennia to emerge. We may lay claim to individual freedom, but many of us seem consciously or unconsciously willing to surrender that freedom to the latest fad, to style rather than substance, to the superficial rather than the deep, to the new rather than the tried and tested. In the flight from meta-narratives, all embracing worldviews, spirituality and religion are split into endlessly competing camps of seemingly equally valid viewpoints.

We may celebrate the choice and diversity, but perhaps the price is great spiritual confusion, lack of firm ground and sloppy, even harmful, ethical systems. The open vista of freedom may in fact be a spiritual waste land (see Part 3) where we can pillage a bit from one faith, a bit from another, a bit from this or that currently trendy guru and construct something that keeps our personal, subjective inclinations happy. However, this may bring with it an atomised spiritual world, where 'doing your own thing' overrides collective action, negates individual and collective responsibility, abandons rites of passage which hold families and communities together and reduces self definition to 'I shop, therefore I am'. Individualism is a blessing in that it helps to keep us safe from oppressive groups, a curse when it keeps us from connecting and working communally.

"We are utterly safe, loved, worthy and right as we are in our very essence."

At the altar

But I return to a small boy, in grey flannel short trousers held up with braces. His shirt has a badly fitting collar. His feet have short ankle socks and brown crepe soled sandals; Brylcreem flattens his hair and a little quiff has been added at the front. Time for church, with mum and dad; I have no other memories of church with them but this one. It's Sunday and for some reason the memory is of Pentecost, although I was only maybe six or seven and cannot say the occasion fits with that word, for it was only decades later that I came to know what Pentecost is. It is also linked to Passover, and being passed over was about to take on new meaning for me. Wesley Methodist Church was full, as it always was in those days (sleepy then in its certainty, unaware of the mass evacuation to come with the next generation). The service progressed and I have no particular recollection of its content, except perhaps the same tedium I experienced in every childhood church service, expressed in kicking legs and 'ants in your pants' wriggling with threateningly whispered "keep still" or "behave" from mum and dad.

The time for communion arrives and we shuffle forward to the altar rail. There's a man in a black suit and some sort of something going on but I can't make head or tail of it. The queue shrinks and I am kneeling down, mum to the left, dad to the right. They kneel with hands cupped and raised. I do the same. I watch it all, head bowed, through screwed up eyelids, searching from side to side. The man in black drops a little cube of white bread in my dad's hands, says something about it being a bit of Jesus' body and I am confused - by what little I know about Jesus and the idea of someone giving you a bit of a human body, which it patently wasn't, more likely a bit of Warburton's 'white-sliced' bread. The man in black passes over me and offers the same to my mum. I am ignored. I feel profoundly confused, emotions run riot but I am not sure what they are - only later when fully grown do I make sense of them: lost, shamed, ignored, angry, sad, cut off...I do not think in my short years that I had ever been hit with such emotional turmoil. I wondered what I had done wrong, what was wrong with me - and it had to be my fault of course. The man in black returns, this time with a shiny silver cup, which he holds to my dad's lips. He takes a sip, words about Jesus and this time blood. The image of Jesus' blood in that cup knocks me into deeper confusion. I can't see into it, but there's a hint of red on the edge of dad's lips. I am passed over again. The same words, mum drinks too.

What set in then was panic that there must be something very bad about me, that I am being cut off because I am not good enough and my mind races to think of something I must have done to deserve this punishment. And it felt like punishment, like the time I was sent to bed without biscuits because I had been naughty. The reason this time escapes me, my mum telling me off for being bad always seemed confusing to me. Inside there is a kind of splitting feeling, like some part of me that feels at home in myself and the world, and some other part fierce and strong that has a power of its own. A power rooted and growing in something as yet quite inexplicable, never hitherto quite so deeply experienced, yet willing to break away, to go its own way for that way would lie power and safety and separateness, away, yes away on the deep and hurling wave that is fear, mighty enough to tear that childhood sense of OKness in the world and into a final sense that would be the seedbed of my experience of the world in my early adult life – that I was a thing of separateness. Pulled away from something in which I felt inherently at one, worthy, loved, in that moment was deep realisation of the cruelty of the world; the birth of suffering and disconnection. Some part of me had broken loose from the child I had been. It was that moment in the Garden of Eden repeated in every life down the millennia, the moment when we become aware of our sense of self, of our own essential isolation cut off from that idyllic place where the world seemed one and, despite the niggling events of childhood, from which I had until now not finally made the break. Feeding on the soil of fear, the polar opposite of the love that had hitherto bound me into a sense of oneness in the world, the 'I' who I thought I was for many a long year had taken root to grow into the man.

Exile

I did not know it at the time but this early experience, manifested in countless different guises but the same in its essence, is common to all human beings, for we all desire to be and to belong, but must also separate. The Enneagram (see also Part 8) is a useful aid to spiritual enquiry, which draws on the impact of early experiences like this; how they can influence the whole development of our personality and our response to life. All those deep-seated fears in the egoic self arise when we are split off from our connection to our Source usually by some childhood experience. We forget the primal truth that we are utterly safe, loved, worthy and right as we are in our very essence. To compensate for the pain of this loss the egoic 'false' self demands to be fed with experiences of being powerful, in control, right, loved and worthy and so on.

"We are utterly safe, loved, worthy and right as we are in our very essence."

Cut adrift from its truth in the Beloved and undermined by its belief that it will die, the ego searches outside itself, with almost pitiful heroism, for immortality, relevance, affirmation and compensation - beliefs, occupations, power and other persons. Thus the we-who-we-think-we-are constructs things – roles, relationships, status, 'success', organisations and religions - to fill the void. The flight from the centre where we have been so wounded is the opposite direction to our real needs. The route required is inward bound to return to this 'Eden', this truth; it is the Way Home.

To feel that we do not belong, are 'wrong', unloved, unsafe, cast out, cut off, exiled, excommunicated – all these and more become our deepest fears. In fact the word fear (*d'hel*) in Aramaic (the common language of the people and which Jesus spoke [14]) has to do not with fear of death or pain or punishment, but with fear of being excluded, driven away and banished from home and family. In pre-modern cultures this was one of the greatest terrors, for there was no chance to hop on a train and go to another city. People largely lived and died locally in small family, tribal units. To be cast out from this meant the pain of living alone, a kind of death. In modern culture exclusion is still used as a means of control; some religious organisations (such as the Amish or Jehovah's Witnesses) and cults and sects of all sorts will 'shun' people by ignoring them, cutting them off from normal social discourse or family and community connection if they have in some way transgressed the group's rules.

Each of us has our own unique breaking point, sometimes sudden and shattering, sometimes slow to emerge, but the point is the same. A belief in a sense of on-your-own-ness, out of which the individual is fashioned, may be one of these. The sense of brokenness from an incomprehensible yet very real source can be so complete that our response to the world is to root ourselves ever more deeply in the fear from which it grows and go on the attack; pouring out our distress, quite unconsciously, on the rest of the world in our abuse of the creation, others, ourselves. The root of the violent response to the world lies here. Here also is the slow drip of the human condition, each drop falling into a bottomless chasm that never fills unless there is more – money, sex, booze; the relentless pleasure principle filling the void.

Nowadays, in my work as a spiritual director, I am struck by the common descriptions people give to this place of disconnection. Paula's words are typical, 'When I'm in this place in myself I feel completely alone, angry, frightened and powerless.

It's dark and cold. I feel very, very small and vulnerable. God has disappeared, or maybe I've sent Him away." This is exile. This is hell.

Paula mirrored the kind of feelings I met decades before. My communion story is my earliest memory of the cruelty of separation, of being excluded from something because there was something 'wrong' with me; that first sense that, if I am here at all, I am here on my own. Other things went on in parenting and early life to reinforce that sense of worthlessness – plenty of inner work there when the time was ripe! No matter what I might live or love, that undercurrent of loss and separation would be ever present and the fear of it drove countless joinings and separatings down the years all in search, consciously or unconsciously, of that oneness, that One.

Was this just an illusion? Is there really no One, just a longing in a broken psyche for something lost, a substitute parent, a dream of love? Was all this 'God stuff' just transference, the hope that something would save me from death or at least after death? Was the subsequent search an inevitable by-product of psychological maturation when we grow more deeply into our individuality? Was this merely a victimhood response, the realisation that I was no more than a random mass of atoms somehow and mysteriously formed in the world and cast out to find its way until at the end it dissipates and merges into the earth as if it had never been (except in the memory of those left behind)? "Is that all there is?" Peggy Lee [15] sang, and if "Yes" is the answer, the only despairing response is to "break out the booze and just keep dancing".

Or is that separation itself an illusion? We may discover that Home is here and now, not in some other time and place. We may sense occasionally a Presence nudging and calling us Home not to a place but into a state of awareness, an awakening to a truth and life radically different from what we once thought truth and life to be. This summons home is sometimes barely perceptible like a tiny voice that we just about hear through the others in a crowded room. Sometimes it is fierce and almost deafening as if demanding we respond. This call may come regularly in our lives down the years under countless guises – a certain inner prompting here, a seemingly casual yet out-of-the-box encounter there; it seems to not want to give up on us. It is neither bullying nor threatening, just a patient loving invitation, a wait for us to come Home. Then it may be that if we choose to listen and respond the sense of a

"We are utterly safe, loved, worthy and right as we are in our very essence."

journey gets under way. Like some spiritual space probe, we launch courageously into the unknown and reach our apogee whence the inevitable trajectory to base takes hold. Then we return, knowing more deeply the place from which we came and enlightened with all that we have gathered along the way.

The spiritual tourist
Almost fifty years later I am sitting in the abbey on Iona feeling that a circle, or at least an arm of a spiral, has been completed. I hung onto Christianity in my childhood and went through the motions of membership of the Methodist church, but my heart was never in it. Maybe I thought that if I said I believed and I belonged, with the latter arguably being the more important undercurrent, then I would eventually 'get it' and feel safe and sound in my faith, in my family, my community, in the world - as everyone else seemed to be. (Later I learned that so many I met along the way were no more at Home than I; they had just learned to mask it better.) It's an odd, passive way to look at religion really, a bit like believing that if you sit around in a garage long enough you'll turn into a car. Coming Home requires active engagement with the work rather than waiting around in the hope we'll get zapped into enlightenment. In fact, I rather doubt the oft-repeated stories of instant enlightenment. It's more a question of patient and persistent work and not so much seeking answers as asking the right questions.

As for myself, the teenage push and pull to break away accelerated me out of small-town England; at 18, leaving behind church and community, I set off. And after all it was the 60s and there was sex and drugs and rock and roll to discover. Yet in each encounter down the decades that followed, that empty place was yearning to be filled. Marriage, for a while, brought love and glorious children. Lovers, careers, material success, cars and clothes, all the usual hedonistic foods I consumed in abundance. Then when they did not satisfy and when the burnout crunch came, an overt spiritual search got under way with accelerating pace. The long-buried hunger was now ravenous for satisfaction and I ate and drank long and deep in the quest to be full-filled.

I passed through atheism and politics as solutions, soaked up the faith of the Hindus, Daoists and Buddhists. Wondered at Islam. Journeyed with shamans. Sat with Jews and Quakers, Zoroastrians, Alpha-coursers - every faith I can think of was picked up, chewed over, put down. I sat, too, at the feet of spiritual teachers of world repute.

I devoured every spiritual book I came across and supped every drop of the New Age brew in all its flavours. I stayed with some favourites, mixing and matching for a while. I tried drugs, dreams and deprivation in search of answers. I met people of great love and great evil and walked into situations of great bliss and danger. I was blessed to have people along the way, especially one wise woman, to whom this book is dedicated, who stuck by me from the moment of the first painful awakening to ease me, sometimes push me, along the path when it looked like I may veer off course into self-limitation or spiritual self-gratification and materialism.

I met a man of big love, Ram Dass, who came the closest I ever got to what I thought it was to have a guru. He was clear this was not his role or identity. Teacher or maybe just Soul Friend were the closest we got to labels. Only later did I find my guru and, as is sometimes the way of these things, he turned out to be right under my nose all the time. I met a woman, Mother Meera, who teased for a while along the way with the remote unreachableness of her powerful presence (or was that my projection?). I met a loving partner who kept me grounded on the earth. I encountered a woman who took me to the edge of reality. I had my personhood unpicked by a deft psychotherapist, my original intent uncovered by a compassionate astrologer, my awakenings questioned by a kindly, elderly 'abba' in the Anglican Church. In action, inaction and interaction with so many I learned the pleasures and pitfalls of the spiritual search. I learned especially of the seductions of being a spiritual tourist, shifting from one experience to the next and never really going deep. That would change.

The spiritual supermarket
When I was a kid that spiritual search was a one-stop shop with only one product on sale – you could buy anything you wanted as long as it was Christian. Different flavours it was true, but much the same in essence. Religion in my community in those days was like the local corner shop. Mr Thirkell's grocery on the corner of Ainsworth Road near my home in Radcliffe was but a short walk for the essentials of life, with limited stock for limited people. The demise of his shop mirrored the demise of religion, for by the 1960s he and his little business was swept away before the unbeatable onslaught of the supermarkets. The supermarket of the spirit, which grew at the same time, largely undercut the religious monopoly by offering choices my parents' generation never had.

"We are utterly safe, loved, worthy and right as we are in our very essence."

Now we can pick our religion like we can pick our pizza – a little bit of this and little bit of that according to personal taste. In the vast freedom to choose in the secular west, it is easier than it has ever been to seek out a faith, or none, that suits us. The trouble is (aye there's the rub) sometimes the freedom to choose is the freedom of the superficial. Spirituality becomes a dipping-in to the bits we like, a dipping-out of the bits we don't like when the going gets tough. Nobody ever said the spiritual search was easy, certainly not the great teachers on whose teachings the world's faiths are founded. Those who say it is easy peasy are probably the ones to avoid. You can wander at leisure in the spiritual supermarket trying all the tastes on offer, but depth of spirit requires digging, discipline, dedication, direction – none of which are popular in a quick fix, celebrity obsessed, narcissistic culture.

Looking back, I can see that inclination in myself to stay superficial. Heights and deep water always scared me – perhaps metaphors for what frightened me about spiritual exploration. I learned as a child to be afraid of stepping outside the norms, of being too adventurous or breaking the rules. Often in childhood the light in us is shrouded by an accumulation of dark fears from our parenting and social expectations. My dad would threaten to "beat the living daylights" out of me when I was a kid if I misbehaved. It was more threat than action, but let's look at that phrase. All of us experience things in life that beat, by fear and its various guises, the light out of us. The search for Home as we wander from one option to another is the search for the light, a restoration and a rediscovery that we are the light. Our earthly home, if we are lucky, may be a place in childhood or adulthood where we feel safe, free from the challenges of the world, a place of respite where we can express ourselves, know intimacy, love, creativity. Such a home is the safe womb in which we rest, and from which we venture out into the world to do and to be.

Safe and saved are closely related words. The earthly home of ordinary reality can be our sanctuary in the everyday world, and it's not surprising that we invest huge amounts of time, money and energy into seeking and maintaining a home. Freedom from want of a home is one of the foundation stones of human rights. But the earthly home must pass away, or at least our attachment to it for its nature is essentially transient. At any moment it can be taken from us. It may happen in the process of maturation as we leave home to establish our own place and relationships. It may happen through sudden financial crisis, ill health or disaster, either natural or human-made, that tears it away from us, perhaps forever. Our ordinary home is inherently temporary, no matter what securities we put in place to tell ourselves otherwise.

Consciously or unconsciously this drives our search for ever more material security, longevity, perfect health and relationships. We can pour a lifetime's energy into meeting these goals only to find when we get there that the goalposts are as far away as ever, that we can never have 'enough', that safety, home and security are not absolutes no matter how hard we try. We find that immortality and denial of death are fantasies – at least according to our initial understanding of what 'life' is. The home we make in ordinary reality is never permanent, never quite satisfies. At some level we know this however much we try to drown it out; we expend so much of our lives trying to make it otherwise, all to no avail. Death and change are inevitable; indeed the Tibetan Buddhist Sogyal Rinpoche [16] wrote that these are the only certainties.

I think he is wrong. There is another certainty. When we seek and find another kind of Home, even while we continue to participate in the world as usual, we discover something very special. And note it is to dis-cover, to remove the cover from something that by implication is already there. Indeed, it's worth noting at this point that so many of the words we use on the Way are repetition words – we dis-cover, reveal [re-veal, take the veil off], remember [re-member, join again] and recognise [re-cognise, know again]. The Hebrew expression Lekh Lekha, often translated as an encouragement to leave and travel (as Yahweh told Abraham to do), also suggests an inward travelling to discover our interior landscape. We do not so much travel towards home as re-turn to it. Thus, everything we need to know is already inside us!

This is the Home all the great spiritual teachers offer us, what we seek is already within. It is to discover the "peace that surpasses all understanding" [Php. 4:7], a transformed consciousness, a new life. From this awareness, this re-newed way of seeing, we witness and participate in the world from a radically different perspective. This eternal, immortal Home is found when we realise that the life lived between womb and tomb is but one dimension of life. This new life can feel like we have been rescued or saved from a kind of drowning in something, while not really knowing at the time that we were drowning. We dis-cover a vast new horizon

"We are utterly safe, loved, worthy and right as we are in our very essence."

of possibility opening up before us. If the Beloved is infinite and immortal the soul, being of the Beloved, is infinite and immortal too.

Saved

This immortality and infinity does not place the Divine out of time, but deeply engaged in it; does not make the Beloved an aloof observer, but a loving participant. The bond of love between soul and Beloved (the two who are One), between Bride and Groom as some mystics describe it [17], is unbreakable and boundless. This love is not only reflected in the love we have for persons or things, but also a love that is the very source of the All-that-is. When we fall into this love or are guided towards it or find ourselves broken into it, we come to know our true Home that is not transient. The approaches outlined in this book, if they have any goal at all, seek to edge us towards these truths.

It is here, at Home, that we are 'saved' as some traditions may term it, where we are 'enlightened' – a-light with awareness of reality, its nature and our place in it; the deep love that holds this vast work of art together. If all the dimensions of reality are a work of art, then there is artistry and intention in it. The universe and the realms seen and unseen are not indifferent but arising out of something that is no-thing, the very ground of being itself, Love. To be 'saved' is to come to know that God the Beloved loves us - no qualifications, no conditions, no limits, absolutely none. To know also that nothing, no thing, can separate us from that love, not even death, for 'death' as we understand it is mere death of the body. Our physical manifestation is just an infused binding of atoms and molecules, the medium through which we, our deepest selves, experience the reality of space and time.

It is in this plane of reality that the fear of death is ever present – at some level our egoic personality knows its transience. This fear of death welling up from the deep unconscious drives vast amounts of human behaviour. The Freudian emphasis on sexuality as the primary energy behind so much of human behaviour is perhaps seen as less potent when balanced with the psychoanalytic understanding of the impact of our deep-seated fear of mortality. Along with other fears such as being unlovable, unworthy, unsafe or powerless (and their unholy neighbours such as shame, anger or despair) it feeds the beasts of a feverish search for certainty, power and immortality. Death, or at least an egoic, false self perception of it, lies at the root of our existential angst, the darkest fear lurking in the unconscious of every person. In affluent and safe societies, death is less immediately apparent for most people. Those living in less cosseted societies or in a hand-to-mouth existence live with a more direct fear of death. And yet even for the affluent the fear of death nevertheless saturates our lives in other ways. We are driven to avoid our fear of it through countless distractions and neurotic fixations or pursue the delusion of immortality in wealth, status or success. Loss, failure, shame or unworthiness can all feel like a sort of death when we are stuck in this plane of consciousness.

Affluent societies create cultures of death-denial by investing heroic energy in 'success' in what is seen as 'life' while side-lining death, or at least the possibility of a personal experience of it. We sanitise death by residing it safely in hospital or hospice. We rarely see real death in the home, but remote on the TV news or in the artifice of the TV crime thriller. Meat for food, if we eat it at all, is often presented in such a way as to distance us from the reality of the killing it involves. We engage in relentless activities and addictions, constructions and creations, occupations and investigations…anything to drown out the deep-seated fear of our mortality, anything to keep it firmly pressed back down into the unconscious. Anything, that is, until those moments of trauma and loss or almost accidental deep reflection or when death forces its way into our everyday lives – then and only then might we face that terror that has lurked under the surface, biding its time.

Yet the paradox of having to face death can be the route to get free of its grip. The Buddha described the greatest of all animals in the jungle as the elephant, and the greatest of all meditations as being that upon death and dying. When Jesus said, "Let the dead bury the dead" [Luke 9:60] he was not being unkind, but forcing us to look at what death really is. If our consciousness is stuck in the limited perceptions of what the ego or false self considers it is to be alive, then we are not really alive at all, merely existing in one dimension of reality, one plane of consciousness.

Many traditions include teachings, reflections and meditations upon death not as morbid preoccupation, but as a means of unlocking its tight embrace. Going into our deepest fear is also the way to be 'saved' from it, to learn in this place what it truly is to be 'alive', to dis-cover the true nature of our immortality in the eternal Home in love. Doing this work while embodied and alive can be like taking off some tight and restricting clothing that

"We are utterly safe, loved, worthy and right as we are in our very essence."

we have worn for so long, but not seen how it has limited us because we got used to it the way it was, indeed that's the way we thought it was supposed to be. Facing up to and integrating our fear of death is a primary way for us to be saved (by love) from the illusions of the false self and set free into our true Self.

In short the movement towards the Beloved requires us to shed our preconceptions of self and know that which is beyond the self. That shedding requires at least some degree of suffering in the process of annihilation/humiliation. We 'die into life' (see page 344) and break free of the slavery of death. Through that we may experience 'enlightenment' – touching eternity where love prevails, free of the fear when time-bound and knowing pure awareness. Yet this awareness is not neutral, it is not indifferent, for it takes us to a profound *loving* awareness of this reality, the only authentic response to it. In turn this may lead us to act compassionately to help others get free of the living death that they may not even know constricts them. This service does not mean we impose our own, ego-driven solutions (such as an inflated desire to 'save' everyone), but to seek the ways of compassionate transformation that all the great teachers have offered us. It is in our relationship with the Beloved that we come to really 'see' ourselves and our agendas and through which we are transformed.

To be saved in this sense brings a different possibility of the 'second coming' in the Christian tradition. Christ is not some being who has gone away to return at some future point, re-embodied and ready to judge the living and the dead. Someone once said to me that they were convinced that Jesus would return in this way and I know this is a belief common to many. I wouldn't rule it out, but a different interpretation (rooted in an alternative approach to scriptures which we will explore later (page 234) led me to say, "Actually, to me he's never been away." The cosmic Christ consciousness ungoverned by time and place is available to each of us now. Always has been, always will be. In each awakening, each moment of realisation of truth or glimpse of eternity, each flood of recognition of the love that 'saves', this is a kind of second coming, a bursting through into this reality at a personal level that scatters the power of the false self and awakens us to the wonder of the All-that-is. This comes to us not as a kind of cosmic prize for agreeing to certain doctrines or striving to 'do good'. This birthright is here, now, if we come to it with an open heart and a "condition of complete simplicity" [1].

Re-examining our motivation for the desire to change and to be 'good' is part of this process of becoming 'saved'. The motivation of healthy longing for the Beloved is not the same as unconscious fears of avoiding divine wrath and punishment or covering up for past misdeeds. Anyway, it is questionable just how much we can do to change ourselves. No matter how many books we read or courses we follow or practices we try, in the end these may only serve to put us in a place of doing the work and showing up – the fullness of transformation is in the grace of the Beloved, the infusion of that love which powers change once we've cleared away our stuff and stand forth in waiting, for as long as it takes, for that power to do its work. We don't need to change for the Beloved to love us, but it may be that once we dis-cover how much we are loved by the Beloved, we want to change ourselves. The change comes from the in-breaking awareness of that love and in that sense is not under conscious control. Once we 'get' that love, the change happens. Such a beautiful paradox – the desire to change stops us changing, but has to be there for the change to happen; yet when we stop *trying* to change, then it begins!

The light of enlightenment is not the same as the light of sun or moon. It is a light that permits clarity of vision and insight, the light of awareness, expanded consciousness, an open fearless heart. It is not a light that chooses to hide itself in a private room just to keep one individual happy. Its very nature demands that it radiate way beyond its source. Enlightenment spreads to others, will not be contained, while the holder of that light is also blessed. The emphasis of this trip changes from our initial search for something for ourselves into sharing something; less about trying to get joy than wanting to give it.

And we may literally feel and look 'lighter' when we are thus saved – less careworn and anxious about the world as we come to live with greater equanimity and more in the moment in loving awareness. Thus to understand 'saved' we can let go of all those religious definitions that hook us into the idolatry of a method or a person. Love loves to love. When we open to that we know what it is to be saved…nothing less than a life transforming, authentic encounter with the reality of the unconditional love of the Beloved. After that, life is never the same again. Fear loses its grip on our souls and we are set free; it is the truth that sets us free. No longer do we have to be afraid that we are not loved or worthy or safe or right or any other inner criticism we have embraced down the years. These old messages are now seen for what they are - lies, taken and woven by our egos, to survive, to control. The love that loves to love has driven them back and we are saved from them.

"We are utterly safe, loved, worthy and right as we are in our very essence."

Frightened men and women who are not yet 'saved' create megastructures of thoughts and organisations that coalesce into the iron girders of fearful religion or politics or social systems of control – designed to keep the perceived forces of chaos (to them) at bay and only those 'in the know' shall be allowed to be part of the in-group and (in the case of religion) 'saved'. Of course that's one of the oldest tricks in the psychological book. If we see the 'enemy' as unclean, 'other' and outside ourselves, the cause of our and the world's misfortune (*ressentiment*) we avoid seeing the shadow inside ourselves.

During a recent radio interview with a priest about sexuality, I felt a strong impulse to reach for the 'off' button and had a hunch that many other listeners may well have felt the same. He drove home his views using words like 'sin', 'salvation', 'the enemy', un-aware it seemed that when people rant about religion like this we do not hear the Be-loved, we hear them. That's the paradox of such fiercely expressed dogma – it does not draw attention to truth but to the person who is speaking. It does not save, it alienates. The perceived 'enemy' was in fact in the speaker himself. That's what happens when people have engaged in some form of religious or spiritual work, but have not done the inner work on themselves to resolve the shadows in their unconscious.

The genuinely religious life does not simply avoid the shadow and comfort our egos. It does not tell us we are 'saved' because we behave according to certain rules or believe certain things. That way lies a constant effort to be on our best behaviour in the hope of staying 'saved' or of some reward (heaven) later or fear of punishment (hell) if we don't. Approaching the spiritual search in this way is about trying to make the ego good, but this has its limits. True, following religious rules may provide a kind of solace and sometimes cause some people to reign in the worst aspects of their otherwise harmful behaviour, but it is a strained, fragile and superficial goodness. Fear and desire are dubious bases for a healthy spirituality. The surface behaviour may appear 'good' but beneath it is all manner of unresolved stuff that means it is not really authentic. And inauthenticity is mightily draining, it takes a lot of energy to keep up an act, it usually leads to burnout and there is the risk that the underlying shadow will leak out in other ways, perhaps as illness or outbursts of fear, anger and even violence towards others. Furthermore, by this approach, the soul has still not been set free and the ego wrestled into service while a fundamentally unhealthy dynamic between ourselves and the sacred has been set up, reducing the Beloved through transference to a projection, an authoritarian parent who rewards or punishes.

The authentic religious life aids our transformation. It is true alchemy, turning that which is leaden into gold. We come to see all the fractious parts of ourselves and heal, forgive and integrate them. The ego becomes whole and strong through this process not as a separate, driven entity, but as a servant, a loved and loving wholesome identity through which we can act in the world. We are guided towards wholeness in ourselves and in the Divine, into communion in the Beloved, not into dualism of God and self as separate or the creation of an image of God who rewards and punishes. I am reminded of a Rasta man on a beach in Jamaica. As a storm gathered he exclaimed, "Jah's comin'." I said, "No, Jah's never been away." To suggest that God is in the storm, but not everything else, is to split the God who is One. To be 'saved' is not about reward or escape from punishment from a deity who is separate from us, but to know love. Spiritual practices that nurture contemplation of these truths and draw us into a direct encounter with the Divine set us free from the delusions of separation and the ego driven agenda into living fully and lovingly in the world, in the Beloved.

The dissonance, contradiction and inauthenticity in religions that grows out of dualism do not just affect individual persons. When acted out collectively the unresolved darkness they bear, masked as light and strengthened by sacred words, can unleash just as much violence and oppression on the world as any political movement. Religion stuck in this unhealthy, corrupt paradigm offers only rules to live by rather than personal transformation. Those who can, turn away from it and seek instead material, sexual or whatever fulfilment. Those who cannot, may find themselves ground down by the iron boot of nasty, oppressive, theocratic regimes.

'Being in the moment' has become something of a cliché and can be distorted into a false 'saved'. Just living 'in the moment' or in the 'power of now' can become a form of self-regarding nihilism, of living without care for others, or the future or the past or the planet. For the 'in the now' is just a perception, a facet of the eternal 'now' that is contained like all time, in the Divine. Living in the moment of the love we find in eternity, yet grounded in our experience of space and time, the duality passes into non-duality where "all time is irredeemably present" [1]. In this 'now' there is no escape from the ties of time and space. Instead we come to live fully in them with love and compassion, for we have come to rest in that love. An authentic expanding consciousness means

"We are utterly safe, loved, worthy and right as we are in our very essence."

we embrace all of life and are spurred to act according to our qualities in, for example, liberation movements, eco-consciousness or healing work.

Until we are liberated from dualism, our egoic self is locked into a kind of death cult. Under the surface it is always terrified of its own termination (which as some level it knows will happen some day). The work along the Way saves us from this enchainment. Worrying about death is just another form of attachment. It's a mighty fierce attachment, but an attachment nonetheless. There is no death of the soul. In a sense while we are afraid of death we are already dead as we noted in the Jesus story above. The spiritual life teaches us to let go of our fear of death, indeed in a sense to live as if we are already dead, dead to the ego and its entire agenda. Having thus died, saved from the grip of this fear, we die into life ever more free of the grip of our thoughts and desires. The soul does not live in time and space, it lives in eternity from which its only response to our trapped-ness in the world of time and space is compassion. Thus we are paradoxically born into life anew, each moment. We become, as Underhill [18] writes "fully human capable of living the real life of eternity in the midst of the world of time".

I did not grow up in an overtly loving family; love was rarely demonstrated and never spoken of. While I knew that my parents loved me I very rarely experienced it. The same can apply to our (mis)understanding of the love of the Beloved. We may know that 'God loves us' as an intellectual concept, but unless we have experienced it we can never know the truth of that deeply, nor be transformed by its power. Indeed the fear that the love may not be there, or may not be given to us for whatever reason (e.g. "I'm not good enough" or "I don't want to lose control") may be the very thing that keeps people away from surrendering to that love - better keep the defences in place than risk the pain of something that might not be there or even reject us. Knowledge of the love of the Beloved is not enough, just like knowing that we are loved in our families is not enough, it is the *experience* of it that is life transforming.

This love does not just show us as we are, as some psychological therapies and tests would do, but also shows us how we might be and how to get there. This penetration of divine love is what transforms us far more and far more deeply that any analysis, therapy, knowledge or spiritual practice can. We can only be fully available to others when we are fully open to the love of Beloved. Once we are transformed by this love we enter into the fullness of our humanity. This comes first. We run ourselves into a cul-de-sac of we think we can 'sort ourselves out' under our own steam and then open to the love of the Beloved as an afterthought.

The egoic personality thinks and acts imperially, its *modus operandi* is at root the acquisition and exercise of power and control. It sees the world only through the reflection in its own narcissistic mirror. The seeker on the Way comes to see this trap and in seeing it has the choice to respond differently to the world, to respond by thinking and acting soulfully rooted in an awareness of eternity. Thus the soul-ful person brings to the suffering of the world not a retreat into self-preservation, or a distorted understanding of 'now', but redemptive action, justice and mercy blossoming in countless forms. We become, as Bourgeault [19] describes it, "an energy-charged field of holy presence". We come to rest in the deep place of trust that Mother Julian [17] found when she wrote certain that, "All shall be well and all manner of thing shall be well".

Lastly, even the terms 'saved' or 'enlightened' look like completed states or end points. There is a need for caution here. There is no 'there', rather a subtle and more nuanced condition of eternal becoming; less a linear progression and more a spiral journey in and out of time. Otherwise the risk is that our little egos will just get hooked on the idea of yet another goal to be achieved. Paradoxically, we are saved or enlightened when we are no longer attached to either, no longer desiring of a state of completion or an endpoint! We shift from an ego orientation hooked on a fixed state to be achieved to the possibility of always becoming, always Coming Home – liberated to reflect the ma-jestic, boundless possibility of the soul in the Beloved.

Spiritual emergence and emergency

The prophet wailed at the transitory emptiness of life. "Vanity of vanities! All is vanity" [Ecc.1:2]. Vanity in Hebrew is *hevel* - meaning vapour, wind and things transient and im-permanent. The passing nature of ordinary reality has led many in all spiritual traditions into the quest for the possibility of a non-ordinary reality (arguably the 'real' reality), the landscape of the soul, the Absolute, God. The writer of Ecclesiastes seems to have been a mystic like a Buddha or a Mother Julian. Having looked through the window of perception of one reality, he or she saw another.

Such shifts in boundaries, such spiritual emergence from our established way of seeing

"We are utterly safe, loved, worthy and right as we are in our very essence."

the world can produce either gradually or suddenly a profound transformation in the way we live our lives. Spiritual emergence is when we start to wake up from the sleep of ego identity and perceive who we really are. Lancaster [20] writes of "untying" the knots of our personality and "entering into an undifferentiated state of consciousness" as a transitional phase before reforming in a transformed state. We unfreeze, move then re-freeze into a new condition (and may do so many times). Clearly this transition phase is high risk without proper preparation and support, the forms of which we will explore in these pages.

Spiritual emergence happens with this support at a pace and pattern that our egoic personhood can handle. Spiritual emergency happens when we are not ready for it, perhaps because of hallucinogens or trauma or trying to 'go it alone', rendering us inchoate and incoherent. Instead of breakthrough we plunge into breakdown. We can become more fully human, or we can crash into mental instability, but going back again does not seem to be an option. Or rather, there is an option and that is to attempt to go back again and invest great energy in doing so, but this is not viable, the seeds have been sown. It's a bit like the old song: "How you gonna keep 'em, down on the farm, after they've seen Paree." A glimpse of greater possibility stays with us and worms its way into our consciousness no matter how hard we try to deny it.

Thus for some these moments of numinous intensity, these sudden visions or insights, these times of being 'touched by an angel' can be affirming and life transforming. For others they can be chaotic and destructive. It's as if some persons, especially those who have not yet done the preparatory work or have perhaps sought shortcuts or not ac-cessed wise counsel, have the equivalent of a massive computer download without the 'hard wiring', the psychological and bodily infrastructure to handle it. What could have been a spiritual emergence instead becomes a spiritual emergency. Instead of bursting renewed through the doors of perception into the arms of unconditional love, we crash headlong into fear, disruption and psychosis.

It's possible to enter numinous and mystical states and then return functional to or-dinary reality or disintegrate. They can be part of our gradual transformation into new stages of spiritual maturity or just experiences that make no difference to the way we are. It's quite possible to be someone who has non-dual consciousness yet still exhibit immature or antisocial behaviour. Thus states and stages are not the same thing as will be explored further in part 5. Someone who has done much work on themselves, deepened their spiritual roots, whose mental state is coherent and is willing to surrender into nurturing guidance will have a very different response, say, to a month's silent retreat or *vipassana* insight meditation, than someone who has avoided inner work or whose mental health is fragile. Our stage of maturity, the strength of our ego structure and the 'holding' by our Soul Friends and Soul Communities will significantly determine whether the spiritual insights along the Way lead us into dysfunction or healthy integration.

There's an inclination among some seekers to avoid the psychological/emotional work and think that we can leap straight to the spiritual. In my work as a Soul Friend I often encounter this phenomenon among some people with mental health problems. In part, because of the social stigma associated with mental illness, some prefer to think of themselves as having a spiritual crisis rather than a mental health one. They may come to think that some spiritual practice alone will save them rather than accepting medication or therapies. Others can see spiritual practices as a kind of spiritual materialism, adding more trophies to their belts. Then there's the simple thinking that getting into Soul Work looks easier than all that painful grubbing around in the unconscious. If we are not careful, our neuroses can just get their hooks into the spiritual work – someone who hasn't dealt with their fear of powerlessness can see the spiritual life as a means of finding control, another who feels worthless may look to becoming an accomplished meditator so that others will offer admiration, yet another may try to avoid inner pain by filling life with endless spiritual experiences. However, getting our interior household in order is a prerequisite to the spiritual work. Being a competent householder readies us for the deep transformative work of Coming Home.

As well as the fear of social stigma, many of us have internalised feelings that we are shameful, unworthy or 'bad' if we have a mental illness. This reinforces the inclination to shift our attention from the psychological to the spiritual. Another tactic is to try spiritual solutions for psychological problems, believing that more prayer, meditation, shamanic journeying, mind altering experiences and so on might help, when they tend to have the opposite effect. As we will explore later, there is no bypassing the emotional work if we are to develop an authentic spirituality. Seeking to lead just a 'spiritual life' will not keep us 'high' and save us from suffering.

"We are utterly safe, loved, worthy and right as we are in our very essence."

While the pain of the mystical/spiritual crisis or emergency can be confused with psychosis, emergence, if nurtured rightly, is transformative rather than destructive. As a result we become more present, more whole, more loving, more forgiving, more functional in the world and not less. Our compassion extends beyond the self; we become more accepting, inclusive and embracing of others and ourselves, more discerning rather than judgemental. We are also likely to be more trusting and able to work collaboratively with others, fostering a sense of humility and the possibility that we are not always right or have to be in control or at the centre of things. In becoming these 'mores', a spiritual emergence ultimately enhances rather than diminishes our humanity.

Authentic spiritual awakening can thus be a source of profound, alchemical change for the better in the way we live our lives and see our place in the world. Whether it is judged as madness or mysticism depends a great deal on the manner of the emergence, the observable effects and the cultural backdrop. If we are among people who are spiritually savvy, we can be nurtured onwards, if we are not we can all too easily be considered mentally ill. Mystics and spiritual seekers learn quickly who it is safe to talk to so that they do not get branded insane and locked up in psychiatric clinics!

There have been many points along my own Way when I could have fallen into selfish and destructive patterns. Drugs that alter our state of consciousness (I've taken a few) can leave us wanting more, wishing to repeat the 'high' experiences and circumvent the tough inner work. There can be deep inner drives, to succeed, to get 'there', to get through the pain – these are the grist to the mill of patient inner attention rather then chasing shortcuts. Often I have wondered, "Am I getting it right?" or " Am I missing something?" Such thoughts come rolling in from time to time. Where they come from, well, that's where we have our work cut out for us. Meanwhile I have found a Buddhist saying helpful. "When in doubt about where you are meant to be, look down at your feet"!

With full awareness, the process of surrender requires us to enter into the perfection of each moment and live it fully, being and doing whatever is true for us at that precise time. The soul has its own wisdom; left to itself until we are awake it is careful to take care of the personality/ego structure it carries. It will not expose it to things about itself or take it into new territory until it is ready. If however that wilful ego of ours gets a grip and tries to bend the soul to its way, tries to be God in effect, then we risk all manner of difficulties. We do the work and trust that each shift will unfold in its own good time. Trust is something we will explore a little later. Our egos with all their attachments trust little except themselves.

Attachment even unto 'past lives'
When Jesus said that unlike the creatures of the earth and the air, he had nowhere to lay his head [Mt.8:20], he was doing more than bewailing his inability to get on the property ladder. He was offering us a vision that when we become fully and perfectly human (one understanding of the concept of the 'Son of Man') we let go of our attachment to a permanent physical place which we own. Instead the place where we rest is deep within our own consciousness, in the love that knows us as we are known, the birthplace of our essence, the soul's origin. Here is our internal, eternal Home, a place of utter safety, connection and oneness that allows us to be fully in the world yet not bound to it.

From this centre we can engage with the world and its rich opportunities and challenges of every sort. Here we recognise the paradox of the fundamental impermanence of worldly phenomena, participating while being free of them at the same time. The Buddhist and Hindu traditions speak of this as non-attachment. In early Christianity we find the expression 'dispassion'. In coming Home to love and being non-attached it does not mean that we disconnect from the world and love less. The latter would be detachment, a condition of indifference. I have met not a few spiritual teachers who believe they are non-attached but who really manifest detachment. Anyone who has plunged into the depths of the spirit, perhaps by profound contemplation or a mystical insight however brief, will report that the All-that-is is anything but indifferent. If the quality of the very ground of being, of the soul itself, is loving awareness then we cannot divorce ourselves from the hope of attaining that ourselves.

Thus it is that while some seekers claim to look for non-attachment, really it is detachment they unconsciously seek. And why should this be? It is in order to avoid the pain of involvement, commitment and responsibility. Detachment is a desire of the ego, the false self, for control, to escape fear and avoid pain. Non-attachment

"We are utterly safe, loved, worthy and right as we are in our very essence."

is still love, perhaps more strongly committed and in some ways more painful than ever, but it is love without clinging. In being in Love, at Home in our deepest selves, in the Divine, we are able to love more not less.

Non-attachment, therefore, is not about ignoring our responsibilities and disengaging from the world. On the contrary we can approach worldly participation more compassionately and more meaningfully when we see the suffering that attachment can produce. Coming Home is not about dropping out from the suffering around us and inside us, but about embracing it, engaging without becoming trapped or overwhelmed by it or striving to push it away. When the struggle in us to keep suffering at bay evaporates we are able to hold the light and dark of the world with equanimity and compassion. Letting go does not mean ignoring our place in the world, rather it is to fulfil it, but from a completely different place within ourselves. In this place we know that fundamentally there is an OK'ness to the All-that-is. Deep beneath, within and around the reality in which we live and move and have our being [Acts 17:21] there is a Love vast and incomprehensible and yet it can be felt deeply and personally. It holds and enfolds everything into itself.

It is taught in Buddhism that 'suffering is' and that the cause of this suffering is attachment. There is an additional perspective. It may be that the cause of attachment itself is rooted in the fear that we are separate, cut adrift from our Source, detached from God. Perhaps when we reconnect to that source, shifting our centre of gravity from self to the Beloved, then the need to get attached to things or to persons falls away. Fear diminishes when we rest in the perfect love of the Beloved. The cause of suffering is not only in the endless desires of the ego driven by fear to find power and control in the world, but also in the struggle to become non-attached under our own steam, by the efforts of the mind. Thus while our work along the Way is to cultivate non-attachment, perhaps an addition or even an alternative approach is to overcome our detachment from the Beloved. Personally I find myself quite attached to the Beloved, but it's quite a different form of attachment that is not clingy. I think it's called love. In this love I learned that I am never alone. Thus strengthened when the Work got tough I found I always had the presence and strength of an ally upon which to draw.

Now, of course it could be that the notion of such an 'ally' is just an illusion or a transference or a projection to make me feel good in an often bitter and meaningless world where no matter how I lead my life, death is going to come at some point. The experience of the Beloved is not something that can be tested empirically and subjected to a randomised controlled trial so it's hard to show how 'real' this Presence is.

I've had some interesting discussions about this among various faith groups both atheistic and theistic. Perhaps it's a consequence of being mystically inclined, which of course some dismiss as delusional. Yet I can't help feeling that being part of a tradition that embraces both the personal and immanent as well transpersonal and transcendent Other might have something going for it. In a rather heated debate with one teacher I was told that God was just another attachment, a mind phenomenon that I really needed to let go of if I wished to become enlightened. Well, if that's so, I'm clearly a spiritual chicken unable to do what's tough. On the other hand maybe some delusions are worth hanging onto for the comfort they bring! The truth is this Being is so much more than a comforter and often a great challenger, and there's a certain 'knowing' that I am not alone that simply won't budge no matter what spiritual routes I've taken down the years.

Meanwhile, here is an example of what can happen when our attachments in our Soul Work go awry. Jeannie and I once booked into a hotel in a certain new-agey place in the UK. As the owner opened the door we were ticked off for standing on the sacred crystal star (difficult not to, it being placed in the pavement in front of the door, and it was dark). A little nonplussed, we nevertheless entered as the owner introduced herself ("I am Isis") and then Osiris, her husband. I commented how curious to have such ancient names of Egyptian Gods, only to be reassured that they were not just named thus, but actually were Isis and Osiris reborn. I bit my tongue to avoid asking what on earth two mighty beings, creators of the universe, were doing running a B&B. So I let that pass, as I did the comment that 'he' was also King Arthur returned. Now these folks were perfectly serious and probably harmless. Or at least I thought so until next morning when Osiris/King Arthur passed through the breakfast room on his way to the 'rebirthing pool' with a young woman. We ate our sausages, vegetarian of course, to the accompaniment of the moans and screams next door.

"We are utterly safe, loved, worthy and right as we are in our very essence."

When our egos get a grip on spiritual insights they can run riot with them. The truth, as we explored above, is that we are *all* part of All-that-is. Thus in the vast pool of consciousness the beings, the stories, that were Osiris and Isis and King Arthur are there just as much as we are. Sometimes, in an effort to make sense of such visions we personalise them, make them ours, or go crazy with the enormity of the download when our ego structure just can't handle it. Often it's simply that, lacking discernment in ourselves or from others, such phenomena get hooked into our unconscious needs (such the desire to be special, worthy, powerful or immortal) and become 'true' to us. Thus attachment is not just to things or to persons, but also to thoughts.

Let's develop this notion of past lives a little further, for I have lost count of the number of people I have sat with who have acquired a strong attachment to them. We can be offered past life regression, for example with a hypnotherapist. Many accounts have been written of recovered memories from such experiences. Some faiths are rooted in the notion of having many incarnations, working through 'karma', and moving up and down various scales of evolution of consciousness from the earthly to the angelic, from the imprisoned to the free, and back again according to how authentic and compassionate we have been. Reincarnation has been a common theme throughout the ages, and even in the early Christian story we see the intriguing allusion to John the Baptist being Elijah re-born [Matt.11:14].

The idea of 'Past-lives' is an interesting theory. For some it is a truth, for others poppycock. Einstein [21] wrote how he could not conceive of a God who rewards and punishes, nor could he conceive of physical survival after death or of many lives and so forth. He regarded such notions as "for the fears or absurd egoism of feeble souls." Enough for him was an "inkling of the marvellous structure of reality" and "the reason that manifests itself in nature". I have certainly done past life work myself and been intrigued by the possibilities, but there are some pitfalls here if we get too attached to them. I've noticed for example that there is a tendency to have our past lives include people who were famous, powerful or distinguished in some way – hence the B&B owners above. I have encountered many others who are stuck in the idea that they have to 'work out' some unresolved issues – suffering, grievance, forgiveness and so forth - from a past life.

A lot of my working life has been spent nursing people with mental health problems who believed that they were Jesus, or Mary or Krishna, or for that matter Isis, Osiris or King Arthur. The only difference I can see between the Isis and Osiris of an English B&B and the Isis and Osiris of the local psychiatric unit is that the former were A] careful who they talked to so as not to get admitted to hospital and B] were able to function and pay their bills. Hanging out as Isis with a like-minded group who believe in the possibility of past lives and reincarnation will elicit a very different response compared with telling people you are Isis in a suburban supermarket.

Another experience comes to mind of a holiday on Iona. It was Youth Week in the Community programme and after the evening service in the abbey church; the congregation was invited to come to the refectory for a cuppa. I duly joined in and witnessed forty or so awkward adolescents struggling with relationships and acne. Mindful of similar agonies in my teenage years, I found myself playfully and inwardly muttering "Thank you God for not making me a Buddhist or a Hindu, I really don't want to have to come back and go through this again".

The serious point behind this discussion is twofold. Firstly that it's not so much what we believe but why we believe it; what the nature of the attachment is, if any. Does belief in past lives provide a milieu for all manner of projections from our unconscious in this life i.e. feelings of powerlessness or insignificance or wound-edness or the desperate need to avoid mortality that we prefer not to acknowledge? Likewise could being an unbeliever suggest a fear of having to live a life over again? Thus all manner of motives can be loaded onto our understanding of past lives as either true or a form of escapism. Secondly, we can see how our attachments and neuroses can be loaded onto such experiences. Past life work may inform our lives, but getting hooked on it can distort our full participation in this life. Lastly, there is simply the possibility as suggested above that our individual humanity, or more accurately our consciousness, is far more magnificent than we believe it to be; that our egos can only interpret things personally, unable to embrace the soul's vision that All-that-is, every past life, in a vastly expanded view of consciousness is part of each of us. For some such a possibility is too great a vision to hold.

Past lives may be a blessing, if true, to inform how we live truthfully and with loving

"We are utterly safe, loved, worthy and right as we are in our very essence."

awareness in the present. They become a curse if they reinforce our attachment to our place in it or get distorted by ego inflation or keep us from seeing where we need to transform.

The hungry ghosts
Getting free of all our attachments is a principle aspect of the work along the Way. There are plenty of them. The ego exists in a condition of constant incompleteness that is why its demands are legion and relentless. This conglomeration of our personality traits, our identities, roles and histories that we have created and have had created for us exists in one plane of reality, driven by fear of non-existence. At some level, conscious or unconscious, it knows it is finite; fear of death is its fundamental driver. Thus vast amounts of human activity are designed to create immunity to this fear and immortality through countless inventions and distractions. We deny it or develop roles and systems that give us a sense of control, success, relevance, purpose and meaning in a neurotic defence against death. We invest enormous energy in these defences – our occupations, our interests, politics, belief systems – and build equally enormous structures around them such as religious or political organisations or nation states. We even go to war to defend them. We make 'idols' of these and our identities, they colonise what we come to believe 'life' is. Until we break free of this limited conception of what 'life' is we are trapped.

Sometimes the energy needed to shore up these defences can indeed drive us crazy. There lies a paradox; sometimes madness is a perfectly sane response in the face of the incoherence of ordinary life. It may be just another way of escaping the suffering (denial, drink, drugs, shopping, sex, status chasing are but a few of the others). The alternative is to raise our awareness and to plunge deeply into participation in the life force of which we are a part. Escaping the grip of these powerful agents is often mighty difficult.

The insatiable appetite of the false self's hungry ghosts is mirrored in the "principalities and powers" [E.g. Eph. 6:12, Col. 1:16] – people in positions of authority and organisations be it religions, nations, political organisations, workplaces or educational institutions). These too can take on a life of their own driven by the collective consciousness of the participants. Indeed, because they can outlive us, they can seem super-powerful, offering us in return for allegiance the chance to participate in immortality and overcome the deep seated fear of death. We can sub-sume our personal desires and moral decisions into the needs of the wider organi-sations in return for the superficial rewards of belonging and investment in a future. Like the internal hungry ghosts, these external powers draw upon our deepest fears and they too prove ultimately fragile in their powers and promises. For, in time, all institutions fail, collapse or corrupt their original (however benevolent) intent. The good priest is cast out for defying orthodoxy, the free-thinking teacher fired for failing to stick with the curriculum, the loyal mill worker made unemployed and pen-sion-less by the collapsed business. All persons invested with great authority, they too must die – demagogues who promise the earth must someday go to the earth, military leaders fail in battle, religious zealots take their followers down with them.

When we place our trust in the powers and principalities to 'save' us or rely on well-fed hungry ghosts to keep us from the fear or mortality, meaninglessness and pur-poselessness, then we have made idols of them. These false gods (as opposed to the relationship we find in the Beloved) may seem momentarily to be our saviours, but they are always essentially untrustworthy and will invariably betray us.

The soul, unlike the egoic personality, is in a condition of completeness, an absence of fear (of death, first among other things). The soul being grounded in Sacred Uni-ty, the Beloved, is therefore fearless and perfect of itself. Hungry ghosts or powers and principalities do not seduce it. It is calibrated towards Home while infusing the personhood, the ego and the body. In some schools of thought it has chosen to be so, to serve its divine source through its experience of the dense reality we know as ordinary life. In almost all traditions the language of getting free of the ego power is quite fierce – notice how often words like surrender, annihilation, letting go, power-lessness and so forth arise in the spiritual discourse. Wilber [23] writes that the ego has to be made into "toast". I'm not so sure about that. Killing something, even a recalcitrant ego, is somewhat suspect. Perhaps it is more accurate to say that its power has to be made toast: its roles and identities then integrated and subsumed into service.

So many of the signals in our culture, a death denying culture, scream at us that life should be about anything but surrender of personal power. On the contrary, we should be demanding individual expression, power and control at all times – what's the

"We are utterly safe, loved, worthy and right as we are in our very essence."

point of life otherwise? It's little wonder that seekers can feel afraid of commitment to the Way when faced with such fierce language and requirements for letting go. Eventually, of course, death will prevail if we have not transformed while alive. This egoic personhood, the ego, the little or false self must be wrestled, not to say loved, into submission one way or another. Those who intentionally seek Home look to this to be while we are still embodied.

Personally, after many years of spiritual practice I can say that it gets easier – falling into forgetting and into the hands of my ego needs and desires only happens about 20 times a minute now! Sweeping away the ego's power is long-term patient work. A power shift takes place over time. The false self is gradually brought in service to the soul, the Beloved, instead of itself. The false idols in the hungry ghosts, principalities and powers lose their allure. The master must become the servant. Authentic spiritual practice is not about 'empowering oneself' and acting it out in the world. That's an ego trip, rooted in the desire to find meaning and avoid death by becoming powerful, wealthy or successful. It's a trip we can take to develop an identity in order to surrender it (or get stuck in it). Ultimately, as we pass through the self-empowering stage we may discover our essential powerlessness.

Much of this seems counterintuitive to conventional wisdom. Of course we should want empowerment, of course we should have control, of course the I-who-I-think-I-am must be affirmed and enhanced. Although all these surrender words are scary, that is because we may find it difficult to see the freedom that flows from this letting go. Evelyn Underhill [24] explains that it's not so much the work of addition, rather subtraction, and cites Richard of St. Victor who notes that, "The essence of self purification is self-simplification." This "complete abandonment in God" that she describes, this willingness to "sacrifice everything" or come to the "condition of complete simplicity" that Eliot [1] portrays is but a fierce passage beyond which a great blessing is received. The blessing is one of finding life rooted in the soul-Beloved dynamic, a true life and immortality in eternity outside of the transient life of the fear-of-death driven ego. False idols, whose only ultimate realm is death, tumble. True life is found in the Divine in whose life and love there is no fear.

A truth in all traditions is that the everyday understanding of life i.e. that which starts at physical conception and ends at physical death, is false (see 'dying into life' page 344). This grand neurotic illusion is a powerful addiction with a relentless appetite; it must be fed constantly so that we do not have to face that deepest of fears. In Buddhism, the countless 'hungry ghosts' of the ego are insatiable. The *nafs* in Sufism equate to those egoic drives that are selfish, materialistic, foolish, always demanding. In early Christian texts we find them equated with 'deadly sins', passions or demons. We find the principles of non-attachment emerging, for example, in the writings of the 6th century mystic John Climacus [22] who describes the need for 'dispassion', to not be trapped by passions (i.e. attachments) to money, power, status, success, security, sexual gratification and so forth that distract us from the Beloved. Jesus' teachings are full of cautions about the dangers of attachment, such as the impossibility of loving the Divine and money [Matt 6:24]. Time and again we see him warning of attachment to things or to persons or to our inner desires, urging us instead to love the Beloved and each other more than such things.

In the words of the great English mystic Walter Hilton [25] when the Beloved says to him "I am God. Then may you see that I do all your good deeds, and all your good thoughts, and all your good loves in you, and ye do right nought. Nevertheless all these good deeds be called yours, not because you work with them principally, but because I give them to you for the love that I have to you…cease then ye of the beholding of yourself, and set yourself at nought, and look on me and see that I am God." We learn in this surrender of our essential ego powerlessness without the Beloved, that we do not so much hold onto the Divine as realise that it is the Divine who holds us in union. We don't have to do all the work any more, the Beloved works through us: liberation.

We are asked, therefore, to abandon our agendas and perceptions of self in order to be filled with the power of the Beloved and act in the world in service thereof. By thus setting "ourselves at nought" as Hilton wrote we come to the deeply humbling recognition that the we-who-we-think-we-are is essentially empty, *hevel*. As the ego power is dissolved we come to do what we do not for ourselves but for the Beloved. Whatever is given to us in this life, no matter how we judge it, is from the Beloved and it is therefore a gift of love. It can be very hard to see that sometimes, especially when there is suffering. Yet, beyond our ego judgements and experiences, love is what's going on.

"We are utterly safe, loved, worthy and right as we are in our very essence."

When we begin to get what *life* really is, beyond our ego structure, then we can enter a kind of resurrection where we are no longer governed by fear. As we tune in to the essential immortality of our deepest self, the fear of death begins to lose its grip. Even the ego can begin to soften into this truth, learn to relinquish its need for control and slip into service. The polarising battle between false self and true Self becomes a truce. Integration and cooperation become possible.

As the power of the false self gets subverted, our way of seeing shifts more and more. Most religions have 'rules' to live by. Designed to curb our personal lust for power and keep 'God' in charge. The 'Ten Commandments' are a well-known example [Ex 20:1-17] that have become a deeply embedded cultural influence worldwide. At one level following these rules is a good way of stopping people doing bad things. The trouble is it requires a lot of discipline, social conventions and legal structures to get great numbers of people to stick with these rules. Feeling 'forced' to do and be good brings with it all kinds of fears, repressions and neuroses as well as the exhaustion that comes from *trying* to be nice all the time.

However, when our soul is released from the power of the ego and we are awakened, we simply do not desire – to kill, to have power over others, to steal, to dishonour or feel co-erced into loving the Divine. In other words the 'Ten Commandments' cease to be *orders* that we are to follow in order to please an authoritarian deity, get our reward in heaven and be socially acceptable. Instead they become a *promise* to us, a reward, a fruit of the spirit that emanates from doing the Work and reconnecting with the Beloved. We are liberated from attachments, desires, 'sins' - we simply no longer wish to do these things. We no longer have to invest energy in striving to be good; goodness simply flows from us effortlessly. A fearsome command has transformed into a beautiful promise.

After all that's been said about our false self, we might seem a bit harsh on the poor thing. We can be gentle on our ego identities. They too have their part to play in the unfolding of our consciousness, our life's purpose. In order to surrender, we have to have something to surrender! In order to have grist to the mill to purify our way to the Beloved, we have to have something to work on. Getting into a battle with it or trying to destroy it just sets us up for more conflict and stuckness, such hostile energy just distracts us. We can have compassion for the ego too. It still has a place of service, but as it looses control (fighting all the way) to the authority of the soul it can be fully integrated and suffused with the soul; set in its rightful place as it learns where real power lies. Hubris is the forgetfulness of the true nature of power and its source and the belief that 'I' have power. It prevails until the ego meets its all-consuming nemesis – the heart's desire for home reunited with the embrace of its Beloved.

An internal compass

It seems the spiritual search is universal; everyone seeks meaning, purpose, direction and connection in life. We all at some point, perhaps continually, seek answers to all those great existential questions like "Who am I? Why am I here? Where am I going? How do I get there? Is there a God?", and indeed, "Who is it who asks these questions?" We all pursue love, joy, relationships, work and activities that nurture and feel 'right' to us, which bring a sense of being and belonging. This pursuit may or may not be God-centred. Spirituality is an expression of the will to live in what might at times seem like a meaningless and purposeless world. Through this embrace of depth we may find the courage to live fully, to connect to the All-that-is in the face of death and so discover the true nature of life, death and immortality. Spirituality is to long to make a difference, to love and be loved and to live on in those we love. Spirituality lies at the very roots of what it is to be human. Religion can be seen as the ritual, liturgy, doctrines and practices that we may collectively enter in our spiritual life to codify and unify it with others, and which may provide answers to those existential questions. Thus, on these premises, everyone is spiritual but not everyone is religious.

While spirituality for most people embraces some form of deity or transcendent realm, this is not universal. What seems to matter is that we believe in something and that we feel we belong to something and each other, not least because a great deal of research suggests there are direct health benefits when we do [26]. On balance, those committed to some form of spiritual practice and/or religious connection are more likely to live longer, healthier and happier lives than those who do not. There is no evidence that one belief system is superior in these benefits than any other and there may be downsides – for example some ill people can get worse because they think they have failed in their spiritual work or their faith, or that God has deserted or is punishing them [27].

However, if we follow the research about belief to its logical conclusion, does it mean that any belief is OK? Belief in a religion or politics or a psychological theory

"We are utterly safe, loved, worthy and right as we are in our very essence."

may sound innocuous, but if that belief is in Satanism, Nazism, White supremacy or eugenics or, for that matter, the tooth fairy, the earth as flat or that the world is doomed on a particular date, does it mean that any belief is OK? Such beliefs may bring some people the comforts of meaning and belonging, but are they healthy, are they true, are they moral?

Something that is meaningful to us might turn out to be harmful to ourselves and others such as participating in 'black magic' or surrendering into an exploitative cult. A cult *per se* is not necessarily harmful, unless it fetishises its beliefs or leaders as absolutes of moral authority and seeks to control the participants, perhaps by excluding them from engaging with families or ordinary society or meting out punishments that are dangerous and physically, spiritually or psychologically harmful.

Likewise, I recall working with an addict once who did not fit the stereotype of the wasted human being. He was a highly successful professional and looked every bit the shiny, healthy, energised person. He told me about the pleasure of driving home from work at the end of the day and how he was looking forward (with a smile) to his evening trip. In the long term the destructive effects of addiction are well known, but at that time he saw it only as giving him meaning and purpose in life, indeed he spoke of it as one might speak of a lover. Discernment (part 5) is an essential quality that must be cultivated if we are to 'see' what is truly healthy no matter how meaningful and purposeful a belief might seem to be.

Another important consideration arises about beliefs. What what seems to matter is not what we believe but why we believe it. Fear-based belief systems emanating from the shadow of the unconscious will drive beliefs and actions that seek only pleasure, 'power over' (page 261), certainty and exclusion in order to shore up a (fragile) sense of identity and immortality. Love-based belief systems seek 'power under', are comfortable with paradox and the unknown and search for connection and inclusiveness. Fear-based ways of seeing the world are rooted in deep-seated unconscious terrors of mortality, powerlessness, worthlessness and other such chthonic forces in the psyche. Love-based ways of seeing the world emanate from a deep-seated knowing of both personal and cosmic OKness, rooted in a sense of being loved and lovable, that transforms the shadows of the psyche. The authentic spiritual life is about such a transformation, drawing each of us out of fear into a love for and from the Beloved, the All-that-is.

If belonging to a belief system has health and wellbeing benefits, it is therefore questionable if this applies to all of them equally. I might get a feel-good factor from belonging, for example, to a political or religious movement where everyone seems to agree with me and idolises the leader, but such movements are always impermanent – movements and leaders fail and die as does our sense of belonging, immortality and hope when they do. If we invest our needs for certainty or power or worth in the impermanent and if such investments do not aide the transformation in our 'way of seeing' (see below), they are ultimately unhealthy for others and ourselves.

Curiously the healthiest and happiest people in one study were not those getting support from their religious community, but those who felt they were giving most [28]. (Now, who was it said that, "It is more blessed to give than to receive"? [Acts 20:30]) What seems to be going on is that the spiritual-religious paradigm offers people a sense of centre, meaning and connection to others and to the Divine in an often lonely, meaningless and chaotic world [29] without which we seem more prone to all manner of physical, mental and social ill effects. Indeed recent studies on loneliness suggest it is as lethal as smoking and obesity [30,31,32]. Little wonder, then, that groups of people coming together in religious or spiritual pursuit may find health benefits. If nothing else they find a sense of companionship, which appears to aid good health.

If loneliness is deadly, why should this be? It is possible that lonely people may indulge in the comforts of excessive drinking or junk food or they may be more likely to suffer from mental health problems. However, it is also possible that something much deeper is going on. If we look at the evidence from the field of psychoneuroimmunology (PNI) how we feel affects our physical wellbeing [33] – feeling good tends to equal a healthy immune system, better cardiovascular condition and so forth. There was a reason why our ancestors sent people into exile or some modern social and religious groups 'shun' people – exile can be a good way not only of protecting the group, but also a less obvious way of killing off dissenters or the opposition.

"We are utterly safe, loved, worthy and right as we are in our very essence."

Loneliness is not the same as solitude – loneliness suggests a state of being on one's own yet longing for company and relationship. Loneliness is a feeling. Solitude is a condition of being without company yet without desire for it. Loneliness is usually involuntary and invariably painful, solitude voluntary and often longed for. The solitary does not wish for company, indeed prefers the peace and opportunity for introspection without the demands that the presence of others can bring. We are not so much human beings as human belongings. Those engaged in the Work may find a different quality of belonging that is not contingent upon the company of people or acceptance by social or religious groups. Loneliness disappears when through our Soul Works we come to be at one in non-duality, in the All-that-is. Perhaps the solitary finds company enough in him/herself and in the Beloved (but with due discernment that it is not a faux solitude masking the desire to avoid the discomfort and challenge of being with other people).

I have explored the connection between spirituality and health in detail elsewhere [34], suffice to say here that, taking a broad sweep across the research, we can suggest that people with the following in their lives are more likely to be happy and healthy: -

Faith - not necessarily in a 'God', but simply having faith in something (politics, sport, nature etc.) that gives meaning to life.

Fellowship – family, friends, community i.e. the power of relationships.

Fulfilling work – that brings creativity, meaning, purpose and rewards to life.

Free Giving – such as voluntary work and contributions we make to others without requiring a reward other than the 'good' feelings intrinsic to giving.

Something is going on therefore that affects the human condition, not least our health, which is associated with the spiritual aspects of life. When we engage with these four 'F's healthily, then health itself seems to ensue. When we do not, then other problems arise. For example, we can be part of a Soul Community or have an occupation that can be oppressive and abusive yet we may not recognise this unless we have the opportunity to stand back and look afresh.

One theologian, John Macquarrie, saw spirituality very simply as a "way of seeing" [35] not with our eyes but with our awareness. How, drawn from the reference points of our experiences and our beliefs, we "see" who we are in the world and how we relate to others, how we know our place in the cosmic order and find meaning, purpose and connection in our lives. Religion can be seen as the conduit through which we channel and express our "way of seeing". This "seeing" can also change as we encounter beliefs and experiences that challenge our status quo - sudden insights, trauma or the presence and stories of great spiritual beings like the Prophet, the Buddha or Jesus. We can thus change our way of seeing joyfully, but can also be left feeling challenged and confused. Bourgeault [19] illustrates how Jesus uses parables to "break the ego operating system". We may notice a Jesus here who seems less interested in religion than in transforming human consciousness.

Transformational experiences or intimations of Ultimate Reality can easily be dismissed as madness or delusion [36,37,39,39,40] and when linked to 'God' can be judged simply as the need for an 'opium' to dull the pain of an unjust world and an instrument to keep people under control (Marx), a sign of neurosis and transference arising from the need for a father figure (Freud) or consolation in the face of the sorrow of the world (Feuerbach). Others link the desire for a deity with our own desire to be one (Sartre) and find our own meaning in the world. Carl Sagan [40] argued that 'God' is used to fill the bits we can't explain by science: the "God of the gaps" who will disappear once science has filled the gaps. While Thomas Hobbes [41], in his magisterial 17th century 'Leviathan' wrote, "Fear of things invisible is the natural seed of that which everyone in himself calleth religion".

Recent studies suggest our brains are 'wired' for God [42] or that we may be genetically programmed to connect with the Divine [43] – the outcome of an evolutionary process that advantaged a religious tendency because it helped people survive and find meaning in a distressing world. Physiologists place the mystic, ineffable experience as an effect of an outpouring of serotonin or endorphins, or a product of electrical discharges in temporal lobe epilepsy, while others have shown that it can be induced by various hallucinogens [44]. Some [45] veer towards the oriental understanding and activation of 'kundalini' energy, a force that lies dormant within us, coiled in the region of the spinal column and, when awakened, "connects us to the energy of creation and profoundly elevates consciousness". I suspect that some

"We are utterly safe, loved, worthy and right as we are in our very essence."

drug treatments and recreational drugs mimic the kundalini experience; hence so many people have intimations of breakthroughs in perception and awakening with them.

As an aside, I've noticed that many people I work with who say they are atheists have not so much moved towards atheism as away from the woundedness associated with faith. Likewise I often encounter people who say they have stopped being Christian/Buddhist/Jewish etc…(take your pick) and instead become Christian/Buddhist/Jewish etc…(take you pick) not because of a deep commitment to that faith or a calling into it, but as a running away from the horrors they see in the other and the personal hurt they might have experienced. The deep spiritual work here is not so much embracing their new tradition as resolving those shadows that have led to the need to flee in the first place. Whatever spiritual path we follow, whatever practices we chose, a root question along the Way is always "Why am I doing this", then using this question and the answers we flush out to discern our motivations – obvious and hidden. The Way of truth requires us to be clear about the ground of our intention so that we may transform the shadows in the unconscious into the light of the conscious.

I have also been bemused by how many persons I have met of atheist persuasion who, when you scratch beneath the surface of these sometimes fiercely held beliefs, secretly hope that the Divine is real. And further, that flight from the mystical, from the transcendent, from the possibility of something 'beyond' is just another form of denial of something fearful (fear that it is there, fear that it is not there!). If so much of human behaviour is an attempt to deny the deep unconscious fear of death as described in much psychoanalytic theory, then maybe atheism is a way of denying the fear of the possibility that there really is a Beloved. To face this and be open to the 'real reality' of a profoundly intimate 'something other' is itself full of fears – the challenge to long-cherished beliefs, terror at the thought of intimacy or what such an experience might do to our ego structure. Perhaps a deep fear in humanity is not just that of our certain termination, or at least death as the ego understands it, but a fear of a love so powerful and all embracing that the false self, the ego, fears suffocation and annihilation in it. Perhaps it is not so much death we fear as overwhelming love. Yet it is through the latter that we might discover the very thing the ego longs for – true immortality.

Someone whose spirituality has evolved and healed beyond the need for a rigid religious structure often has a lot in common with the atheist, for they too have turned away from the false 'God' portrayed in so many religions, what Cornwell [46] calls the "trash and tinsel that passes for him". In that sense I find myself to be an atheist too, for it may be clear from these pages that the notion of a singular, definable (male) god is anathema to me. Curiously enough, the early debates about God in the Old Testament were not about the reality of the Divine, but about whether God was one or many, kind or angry; that God is real, a Presence, was a given. Only much later do we see the notion of atheism as a philosophical position arising. However, I can't help feeling that some of the more strident atheist commentary comes from some unhealthy stuff rooted in the unconscious, about past wounds or fears of authority figures. Whatever we believe, what is arguably more important is why we believe it. Cornwell again succinctly notes, "Many people who have turned away from religion – even with a sense of hatred, rejecting all its idiosyncratic externals – to embrace scepticism, agnosticism, even militant atheism, are perhaps as much in the desert, in the 'dark night of the soul' as any contemplative." What they might be fleeing is "not God at all, but the false or the inadequate representations" of God.

By rejecting, even hating "the trash and tinsel" we may paradoxically find ourselves being drawn to what God, the Beloved, really is, free of the religious distortions that get in the way. Furthermore, "If God gets to be defined as 'Being itself'", as Maslow [47] points out, or as "'the integrating principle of the universe' or as the 'whole of everything' or as 'the meaningfulness of the cosmos' or in some other non-personal way, then what will atheists be fighting against?" Maslow proposes that once we let go of an anthropomorphic God then there is much common ground for agreement among believers and unbelievers on the 'integrating principles' or 'the principle of harmony'.

However, to return to the reasons why most people 'believe', is an interest in spirituality, religion, a Sacred Unity, a God therefore just some kind of neurosis, mental illness or deficiency that with the right treatment we can cure or with the right education grow out of? Is it just good health insurance evolved by some Darwinian process to assist our survival? Is God therefore merely a delusion, a product explainable by one or more of these catalysts?

"We are utterly safe, loved, worthy and right as we are in our very essence."

Like millions of others, I experience God in my life, I know God at a different level of knowing (what the ancients called *gnosis*), which transcends scientific analysis or easy description in words (although Poets like Rumi, Eliot or Whitman get close). When asked if he believed in God, Jung [48] famously said, "I do not believe, I know".

This 'knowing' is elucidated further in Evelyn Underhill's [49] classic text on mysticism in which she describes five distinct stages, moving from the purgation of old ways of seeing to union with the Divine. Many people report such mystical union, and it is probably far more common than is generally believed, as indicated by the work of the Alister Hardy Trust [50]. Recent research [51] is increasingly supporting what many spiritual traditions have always claimed – that consciousness is more than the product of the brain and that the Absolute is not a delusion but a reality. I have explored mysticism in more detail in the companion volume to this book *Contemplation* [52]. Underhill [18] defines it simply as "the art of union with reality. The mystic is one who has attained that union in greater or less degree; or who aims at and believes in such attainment." Mysticism does not send us off into chaotic states of near-madness, mystery or detachment from ordinary reality, but draws us into a deeper, authentic relationship of integration, communion and union with the Beloved and a deeper engagement with the world. It is from this union that belief and action spring.

The real reality is not what we 'think' it is. What many see as a 'not real' non-ordinary reality is to the mystic the real reality. The mystic, having come home, longs to rest there and maybe help others find this Way too. Spiritual practice helps us break free of the bonds of the intellect and the judging ego that has assimilated the unreal as real. We are purged of a limited frame of awareness, which sees only one plane of reality as possible and which keeps judging and analysing the things that we otherwise never truly know, the world of facts and 'common sense'. This purging, this spring-cleaning, releases us to discover the deepest reality, our true 'I-Amness' (see page 391). We stop spending our time "rearranging unimportant fragments of the universe" [18]. Having thus let go of attachment to one limited perception of reality, wisdom and loving awareness accrue. This shift permits not a rejection of ordinary reality, rather a willingness to embrace it, but from a completely different viewpoint.

The response to 'ordinary reality' is one of compassion and a willingness to partic-ipate in it, not from an egoic stance of control or defence, but perhaps by finding some small way of serving that enables others to wake up – to get free even while in prison, to see the illusion of the jail for what it is. We don't wake up just to escape reality, but to seek full union with all reality/ies as well. Ordinary reality is trapped in time, it is forever becoming and it is full of multiplicity. The mystic journey of awak-ening takes us into a different plane of consciousness in which the former reality is held; a new awareness of eternity, being and unity. Uniting with that reality, or per-haps more accurately reuniting, might be seen as an intention along the Way. Such a reunion is life transforming, but it can also shock us into serious problems of spiritual emergency if we are not ready for it, as we have noted above.

Few people I have met have had the sudden, blinding, life-changing awakening to Truth that Saul/Paul experienced on the road to Damascus [Acts 9:1-31]. For most of us it's the steady plod up the mountain with many an apparent slip along the way. Sometimes there is indeed the urgent shake that comes in many different guises. It may be the earth shattering experience traumatic in its own way of falling in love, where the love is so intense and our egos are so thinned by it that we come close to seeing the Beloved in the lover, the soul feels it has found its mate.

Falling into love with someone in this way can be the ego shattering experience that projects us into a new way of seeing. It may happen also with the overwhelming love we may feel for the newborn child. Shaken and stirred this way has its coun-terpoint in trauma – loss of a loved one, illness or burnout. A patient with cancer I met recently told me that she had learned to love (the terror of) her cancer because, "Without it I would have stayed asleep. My cancer was my spiritual awakening." The horror of cancer paradoxically contained a gift.

A spiritual awakening thus shakes the tectonic plates of our consciousness; our usu-al way of seeing is perturbed. As a consequence, the often dramatic emergence of this new way of seeing shifts our perspective; life that was once seen as normal, full of the usual ups and downs, may now seem strange and alien before us, a new waste land that no longer seems our home [53,54]. We have become "strangers in a strange land", as Robert Heinlein [55] expressed it in his science fiction story. The shift in ourselves has made us look out on the familiar landscape and see it as

"We are utterly safe, loved, worthy and right as we are in our very essence."

unfamiliar. We may feel like an alien as our whole way of being in and perception of the world is shifting. Others may begin to see us in the same vein as our values and priorities shift, we're not quite in the mainstream any more. This, and perhaps the perplexity of others at the change in us, can be a frightening place to be.

Yet more paradox is found when we may find ourselves feeling some sense of lightness of being amidst the perturbation, as awareness dawns of the possibility of a new Home being present while living in the old one at the same time. If where we used to be is no longer home, then where is Home now? Whether we are shaken rapidly out of our way of seeing things or whether the shift emerges through gradual attention in spiritual work, we may hear some echo within that keeps calling us onwards. Through the shadow of the fear of unknowing we may be excited by the joy of possible discovery, ready to plunge headlong towards the light.

Healing old wounds
I mentioned earlier a visit to Iona, that glorious isle where it is said the veil between realities is thinnest. This leads us into another aspect of where the spiritual search might take us – sometimes not to a different spiritual tradition, but to a familiar one. Back, in some senses, to where we started but with a new way of seeing, as Eliot reminds us [1]. On Iona an ancient Christian site has in the last century been revived and renewed, providing one of several homes to a religious community that is open, inclusive and Christian and which is spreading its message way beyond the boundaries of the island, its Glasgow base and its widely dispersed membership. On my first visit, over 35 years ago, I hovered around the edges of the services in the abbey church, moving into its noiseless sacred space only when no one else was there. Late at night or early morning I would pass through its ever-open door to sit in silent contemplation.

However, by chance if chance it be, within the space of a few months I encountered people and situations that were to drag me out of my anti-Christian trench. What follows is not a suggestion that we all have to return to or discover Christianity; I offer these words merely as an example of what can happen along the way. Each of us will have our own experience. It may be as in my case a call to return to something long abandoned, or we may voyage into a new faith, or none at all and we will explore the implications of all these paths later on.

My hostility to Christianity, as I explored other faiths down the years, had grown not lessened. That early childhood lesson in exclusion was compounded in adulthood by the endless messages emerging from pretty much every branch of the church that there were some who were 'in' and some who were 'out'. Doctrines and dogmas were all that seemed to matter and the public face of the faith appeared venal and contemptible marred by bickering, division and hatred of anything and everyone of one sort or another – women, gays, other religions, other Christians, anyone who didn't slot into a particular sect's beliefs. My opening of the gifts of other faiths had caused me to leave the Christian parcel largely ignored.

In nursing school I watched a film about Pavlov's dogs – those famous experiments which showed a dog salivating when food was presented accompanied by a signal such as a bell. After a while the dogs salivated when only the bell sounded. A signal of something can produce a response even if the thing associated with the signal is not present. That woundedness I experienced in Christianity, feeling abused and excluded even from childhood, led me to a default position through much of my adult life when the word Christian came up. A sort of Pavlovian hostile response had been set up at the mere mention of the word Christian or the sight of things associated with Chrisitanity such as the cross or a priest's robes.

It took me a while to realise this hostility wounded only myself, that in closing my heart even to one person, let alone a whole tradition, I was also at some level closing my heart to myself and to the Beloved. Closing our hearts, even if we think it's only to one person, is always generalisable; at some level, subtly and invasively, it touches every relationship. The lessons of all the great teachers, not least Jesus in his specific call to love our enemies, contains a great truth that when we fail to love it is ourselves we wound as much if not more than the other.

Participation in church life in later years has taught me much about love, not least that just because someone disagrees with me or is even hostile towards me, it doesn't mean I cannot love them and see beyond surface impressions of personality and recognise (re-cognise) that beyond egoic ideas and identities, there is a soul there just like myself, indeed the same as my Self. This love can only be authentic,

"We are utterly safe, loved, worthy and right as we are in our very essence."

otherwise we become just another person of faith indulging in chronic niceness because we are supposed to love our brother and sister. The Work on the Way Home
helps us to realise our true nature, our essential unity in the One, through which we
discover and reveal the unconditional love that lies at the heart of each of us. That
love can extend even to those who seem to be against us.

At the Interfaith Seminary (a ground-breaking course, led at the time by the char-
ismatic Miranda Holden, training ministers and spiritual counsellors across faith
boundaries) that I attended some years ago in London, we were coming to the
end of the Christianity module. Our facilitator for the last day, Revd. Ray Gaston,
entered a room full of mostly arms-folded students, myself included. He opened up
the flipchart, wrote the word 'Christian' on it then asked us to call out our responses. I thought at first this man must be a fool. He was in a room full of people who
were mostly escapees from Christianity. Wounded by it, the majority of us were on
the hunt for some other roots instead and were unlikely to have anything good to
say about Christianity. For the next hour he, a man of the cloth, just stood there
and took it; an outpouring of venom, suffering, anger and grief splattered onto the
flipchart. The small group of half a dozen or so on the same course, who were committed Christians, heard all this and were moved to tears.

As the tide abated, he stood there very quietly and said something quite remarkable, three times. "I'm sorry, that is not Christ, that is not Christianity and you should
not have been treated like that." Sorry – three times. There wasn't a dry eye in the
room when he'd finished. Many of us saw and were able to let go of something that
had affected us adversely in so many ways.

Now Ray was not responsible for all that had happened to the group down the
years, in fact he wasn't even born when (some) Christians were inflicting their distorted faith on us. So why did the apology have such a healing effect? Firstly his
sincerity and humility were profoundly moving, secondly he stood there as a representative of a tradition. He was in communion with the Christian church, warts and
all, past and present – that connection, that identification not restricted by time and
space is part of what being in community, in communion, is all about. Ray could
not personally take the blame for the past, but as an agent of that tradition whose
mantle he had voluntarily donned, he now took part in its collective consciousness

and could speak on its behalf.

His non-defensive, humble response allowed many of us in that roomful of students to re-examine our hostility to the Christian faith. Something began to turn in me then, a growing realisation that, despite all my spiritual work down the years and the heart openings and the deepening of my compassionate potential, I certainly wasn't willing to extend that to Christians and Christianity. Furthermore there came realisation that my anger wasn't hurting anyone else, only myself; my closed heart perpetuated the suffering.

Then a dear friend, who had found herself while at the Seminary returning to her Christian roots, poked and prodded me with difficult questions. Once on a long and glorious drive along the west coast of Scotland she just turned to me and said, "Have you ever thought of turning to Christ?" I was speechless and felt like a brick had just dropped into my guts, something I was neither willing nor able to then explore. Yet it was one of those moments when something that is said can touch us at a deep level, beyond words. It is the kind of experience we can have as if an inner red flag has been raised and demands "Attention!", and we know the matter is going to come back to haunt us no matter how much we try to avoid it.

Then someone with whom I'd been friendly for years, a retired Canon from the Anglican church, became quite ill and we would spend long evenings together ex-ploring our favourite poem, Eliot's 'Four Quartets'. As a result we talked of matters of faith into the late hours lubricated by not a little fine port. This 'abba', through loving and simple spiritual fathership, began to open doors in me, those old barriers of anger at feeling attacked and excluded that had long been locked. I also began to realise that this gentle man, Christopher Pilkington, was not the only one in my life. Two others, Revds. Stanley Baxter and David Wood were there also gently, sometimes fiercely nudging my perceptions of Christianity, Christians and Christ. I became aware of how I'd put these things in my own self-defined boxes and how incredibly confining these boxes were.

For some reason, I hadn't quite spotted that these three men were there. Perhaps it was because they were never 'in your face' about their faith; perhaps it was because they were deeply righteous men filled with a passion for justice, fairness and inclu-

"We are utterly safe, loved, worthy and right as we are in our very essence."

sivity. Maybe it was because they did not define themselves, or me, by rigid identity labels. Or perhaps it was my denial, not wanting to admit that some Christians could be nice! Whatever, they became my 'three wise men' who fed my soul in their own ways down the years without me realising much of the time that such was the gift of their friendship. Despite their doubts about the church, they each had the same resilience to remain in it and work for transformation rather than abandon it and to see that faith was not dependent on the way it gets to be organised. I admired their tenacity, their love of God and their capacity to transcend theology and doctrines.

It may have been just coincidence, but these experiences were converging before I took a holiday on Iona that year, determined to enjoy the time of spirit in the abbey, but remain on the periphery of the community and its services. It was Sunday morning, communion was about to happen and for some reason I cannot explain to this day, I decided to go along. (Is this what is called a Divine possession – when you do something that seems out of character and beyond conscious control?) I sat at the back, on my own, aware that I had arrived armed to the teeth (with my guardedness, resentment and cynicism) waiting for what would surely come, some dogmatic statement about sin or damnation or hell or some other unloving and excluding words.

No doubt I would, as I had before when attending a church service that I could not avoid (the compulsory birth, marriage and death rites of passage), remain aloof to the whole hypocritical show. I was wrong-footed. No such words came; instead I heard only words that were loving, questioning, tentative, humble and inclusive. I remember being overcome by a profound sense of sadness and struggled to see where this might be coming from. I was hearing words from the warden, Kathy Galloway, in her sermon that were entirely welcoming and compassionate and something just didn't fit.

At that moment I had the strong feeling that my parents, long dead, were sitting either side of me. I could smell the tobacco haze that always hovered around my dad; the scent of the 'Imperial Leather' soap my mother loved. Communion was under way and I was prepared to sit it out, when the abbey seemed suddenly silent and still even though people were moving and speaking. In this silence I heard a voice. It was a voice I had heard many times before, on the inside rather than in the ears, not so much words alone as wordsandfeelings combined. It just said "You are welcome at my table, everyone is welcome at my table, come eat and drink with me." I was struggling to hold back the tears and maybe to hold onto my sanity, but I had known this voice before, come to trust it. Three times I heard it. Then the moment passed, and I took communion. I knew it was time.

Inner voices? Intuitions? Synchronicities? Spiritual journeys? Religions? Soul searches? Home? What is all this nonsense about? I have been and am like millions of others, a seeker, a desirer of truth, a lover longing for the Beloved and a traveller heading Home. Such experiences are not uncommon and probably every reader has had similar along the Way. I offer my story here as an example, but it is just mine, and it could be any faith or none; each of us brings our own unique pattern to events like these. They illustrate the general principle of how numinous happenings can lead us deeper into truth along the Way, but they can also be seductive and side track us into blind alleys.

In such experiences may lie madness or mysticism, deep irrationality or pure truth. How can we discern what is truth? Can those inner voices and other promptings be trusted? Do we dismiss them all, as explored above in much atheistic and scientific debate, as mere phenomena of no value or neurosis or psychosis? After all, it is risky territory - some seekers go to the edge and fall over into ego-inflation or craziness or disease or death. Some get lost and give up - falling back into familiar ways that numb the hunger. Some fall under the spell of cults and false prophets, dehumanising faiths or empty soullessness.

The way Home is fraught with pleasures and pitfalls. How can we walk the path with some degree of safety and equanimity? How can we sift out truth from untruth, the wise from the foolish, the false from the genuine? Often the boundaries are blurred, our faculties too limited. Was my Iona experience at communion and the memory of my parents just another deluded moment, an old memory surfacing and nothing more, or an act of grace?

Finding our way Home is not a solitary affair that can be pursued without guidance; the risks of delusion and distortion are immense if we attempt to do so. The process is not helped by doubts we may have about the world's religions and their inclina-

"We are utterly safe, loved, worthy and right as we are in our very essence."

tion to ossify and separate rather than nurture and set people free to come Home. There can be doubts and prejudices too about the whole notion of 'God' as I've explored above. Beyond these difficulties, perhaps we need to be wary of casting away in these individualist times the very real treasures to be found in the traditions that have emerged over thousands of years. Rich stores of teachings and practices are held therein, with many common approaches that have been tried and tested down the years. They have primarily evolved, however distorted over time, to hold us in the safe arms of love and nurture our awakening while we deal with the inevitable risks and accompanying shadows.

On our way Home we need map and compass, companions and guides until we get to know the route well ourselves. It is to these that we turn next.

And shadows fall here,
sometimes like a dark swallow
skimming over an inverse lake.
Sometimes like the black fog of a burning oilfield,
bitter, acrid, enveloping this
our small infrequent world
in the terror of the uncreation.
The darkness unbound, beckons. Come! Come!
And some take off like flame-bound moths,
and others plunge,
reckless,
into that black night.
None escape.
The shadow waits at the edge of the flame,
the unknown shifting margin
where light and dark, vying for authority,
surrender in truce to You,
You!
Who holds both light and dark in Your
perfect,
undimmed
thought.

Part 3

"The history of the world, with the material destruction of cities and nations and people, expresses the division that tyrannises the souls of all men"[56]

The Waste Land

<u>Swimming the spiritual river – sometimes less is more</u>
In a Glasgow hotel you can go to the 'Soul Therapies' room. Here a sign says you are welcome to "a peaceful haven within the heart of the city…switch off, kick back and enjoy the wide range of treatments and therapies on offer." And you can kick back into reiki, facial massage or a mineral salt scrub, then have a 'fake bake' in the tanning machine and get a bikini wax or a manicure. In a popular newspaper, there's a section called 'spirit' where there is advice on home décor and lifestyles. There's a company called 'Spiritual High' selling drugs to the post-rave culture. A magazine column advertises 'soul mates' – where specifications of personality traits and preferences invite the perfect partner.

Just about every city has its alternative therapies free paper selling the wares of the healing armies. One example I came across in San Francisco had 150 pages and a thousand ads' and a menu of everything from hypnotherapy sessions to provide help with your 'inner child processes' to 'spiritual breakthroughs' via 'intuitive coaching' to find your 'soul mate' or your 'true spiritual self' (at $750 an hour). From London to Lisbon, from Berlin to Brisbane, from Moscow to Minneapolis, everywhere it seems offers the same fixes for the soul.

It's little wonder that assorted sceptics can have a field day of mockery about matters spiritual when our culture has so successfully dumbed down one of the most profound insights that humanity has ever come up with – the possibility of soul. A meaning-lite, money making feeding frenzy has been engendered in the popular use of soul – usually referring to little more than the tickling of the ego's pleasure centres; the bathing of the personhood in sickly-sweet comforts. The various organisational cultures we use to run the world - be it capitalist democracies or theocracies or dictatorships – all in their own

"The soul has its own designs and will not be refuted."

ways seem to distort, corrupt and empty our language and indeed our everyday consciousness of the depth and significance of the very essence of what it is to be human.

In the free market system that now dominates the world, spirituality has been privatised, reducing it in many quarters to a product ideally packaged and ready for marketing to the consumer society. We human beings come to be seen as little more than our egos, our personalities – 'who I am' becomes the plaything of multiple attachments to countless roles, identities and functions. 'I am' is what I do, what I earn, how I look - and all of these things can be bought and be tempted into buying things. Privatised spirituality does not socially engage; it is about the self and all the comforts that the self demands. It avoids deep transformation or being a source of compassion in the world in service of others.

Religions too can fall into this trap, reducing their work to commodity and control, which from time to time causes schism and fracture to break these bonds (e.g. the breaking away of George Fox and the Quakers from the Anglican church, the Prophet's founding of Islam in the face of the corrupt faith he saw around him, Guru Nanak's forging of Sikhism in the presence of entrenched Islam and Hinduism in India). Neo-Pharisees tend easily it seems to gain the upper hand in all spiritual traditions from time to time, reducing the authentic religious experience to rules to be followed or a commodity to be bought at a price (of rules, indulgences, trinkets) and thus controlled. Being part of the right group, conduct or rituals in such circumstances takes priority over an authentic and life changing relationship with the Beloved. Such an approach to spirit and religion rips the heart and soul out of them.

Growing in the same fertile ground of commodification are new therapies arising by the day, with old ones resold, restyled, repackaged – all planted and raised for the market hall of the personhood. In its endlessly shifting garb and restless hunger, the ego demands ever more food to keep it feeling good, more therapies to shore up its ever crumbling boundaries, more sweet, fluffy, feel-good junkets just to keep going. This ego pleasure seeking can capture the spiritual life as well.

Spiritual materialism sets in all too easily, even when our consciousness expands, our egos can get a grip on it. It's as if, frightened at the prospect of the loss of power and control, the ego takes a look at the spiritual experiences on offer and says, "Right, OK, this looks interesting, let me take charge of it". It ensures it keeps in charge by becoming a relentless inner critic or inflationary demon. It keeps us longing for and distracted by one superficial experience after another. It maintains a pretence of wanting a relationship with the Beloved, but really only wanting to want one.

Wanting something and being content to stay with the wanting, is quite different to making that leap of commitment to act upon it, to carry it through with all the fierceness that such a spiritual exploration can demand. At some level, many people want to stay just with the general desirability of connecting to spirit and having lots of experiences, but really don't wish to go any further, because unconsciously either they know the risks and don't want to lose ego power or they know also at some other level that it would be tough work - what Ram Dass [57] calls the "crisp trip".

A kind of spiritual acquisitiveness thus festers away, fed by these experiences and their trinkets - a blessing from a worshipped 'guru' here, a crystal there, a shamanic course here, a weekend's fasting retreat there and so on *ad infinitum*. The ego has thus made a 'hungry ghost' even of the spiritual life, capturing it and filling it with insatiable desire for more spiritual experiences and powers. These attachments can become very strong and, to paraphrase Eliot [1] once more, we can end up having the experience but missing the meaning. Superficial attractions, however strong their pull, just stop us from going deep. The seeker has to get past the enchantment of spiritual experiences at some point, otherwise they become havens for our various neuroses or narcissistic entertainment or sources of addiction to keep us from transforming. Unless the experience is transformative rather than acquisitive, it cannot be used to guide us into our path of service.

If there is a truism about coming Home to the Beloved it is that 'sometimes less is more'. Going deeper into few rather than dipping into many; letting go of attachment to multiple extrinsic baubles and distractions of whatever sort is part of the Work along the Way. We can experiment with many options, but sooner or later we need to do a bit of sieving to discover what is essential and let go the rest. This helps us recognise what really matters, what is intrinsic to us, our way of being, to the expansion of our consciousness and the opening of our hearts. When we get caught up in trying to 'do it all' then we need to examine the underlying motivation. That often flushes out where there is work to be done, perhaps on our unconscious

"The soul has its own designs and will not be refuted."

fears that somehow unless we experience everything we won't 'get there', or maybe frantic activity is a way of not being still and quiet and thereby avoiding the pain that we fear lies beneath.

I can certainly see some of those patterns in myself in the early days. I swam the length and breadth of the new age river to try everything I could, fearing that I might 'miss something'. Fear often brings into the cold light of day those parts of consciousness where we have not yet learned to trust and love the Beloved, and ourselves, completely.

There is much talk in discussions about spirituality of 'following our soul path', 'finding a vision' and so forth. The universe is indeed a co-creative process; we play our part and are played upon, lead and are led. Yet there is another possibility - that we do not so much plough our furrow (which can seem like mighty hard work at times) as discover and follow a furrow that has been ploughed for us. By whom? Perhaps in that time when there was no time, in eternity when our soul mapped out this earthly adventure, or perhaps by the Beloved who opened a pathway for us to follow, experiencing it in our soul's own unique way yet certain of returning Home. The notion that what we need and where we are to go is somehow mapped out for us, in the contract as it were, may help us to ease off the accelerator a little, maybe we can trust that things are moving as they should. Trust, that's a big one. I will return to that later.

Some of us live and die captured by the limited, fearful egoic world. The ego is our instrument for being in the world, for living a life set within certain parameters, but despite outward appearances it is a fragile thing. Some wake up spontaneously from the ego's grip and know 'it doesn't have to be like this'. Some gradually awaken, prompted by an inner restlessness that seeks answers. Some are touched by the influence of mind-expanding drugs, a traumatic life event, a stunning vision of the numinous 'other' or a breakthrough in deep spiritual practice. Some like myself crash and burn when they can no longer take it. Sometimes the soul just punches through or maybe the ego personhood power implodes to allow it to escape. Whichever, life can never be the same again for those thus transformed. Into this unknown landscape the soul now emerges, and sees clearly the waste land of the country it once inhabited. For some people this can produce a spiritual crisis as we explored in the previous chapter. The old way of seeing the world is exposed as an illusion, but what is real now with this new vision? Where do we go for affirmation, discernment and deepening?

Our culture, now deeply rooted in the possibility that human beings can be happy and healthy with ever more scientific advances, material comforts and designer bodies and babies, becomes a sweetshop of transient comforters where the language of soul and spirit and the depth and potential it offers, is lost in the superficial, the seductive and the short term. Not much help can be found here. That people cannot ultimately be satisfied with ephemera, that the insatiable desires of the personhood are exhausting and that there is a longing for 'something more' is demonstrated in the filled waiting rooms of millions of therapists, healers and counsellors.

As some of the congregational religions, seemingly ever more stuck in dogma and decline [3,58], fail to respond to this deep human urge, they relinquish the territory of the soul to others who can bring heart and meaning to the search. But to find the true and the deep, we may pass through many distractions and false paths along the way. The genuine friend of the soul is rare in a market place filled with snake oil salesmen and women. As an example, it is perhaps no irony that one of Europe's most recently wanted war criminals, Radovan Karadzic, was able at the turn of the millennium to reinvent himself as a spiritual healer and teacher and hide safely among the unquestioning crowds. A few mysterious words, an enigmatic presence, some well-chosen clothes and beads and the right style of hair fit the seductive image of the wise man/guru. How easy it is to exploit the vulnerable seeker. There are thousands like him, but how to find the authentic ones? Sometimes to find the charming prince or princess, you have to kiss an awful lot of frogs.

Despite myriad distractions and pitfalls, we can have confidence. At some level, as I have suggested, the soul has its own designs and will not be refuted. It is a wonder how the work goes on even while we seem lost in ordinary life. Conscious attention co-creates the transformation, but whether or not we choose or forget to participate or go wandering off, the soul has its own longing and will continue to work to transform us whether we work with it or not.

"The soul has its own designs and will not be refuted."

The Work seems to have a momentum of its own, taking us into our deepest truth. We can carry on as if the I-who-I-think-I-am is at the centre, but the truth is 'I am not the centre, *the* 'I Am' is the centre', something that we will explore further in the next chapter. The soul does not need anyone or anything; it is OK in itself, in its pure I-Amness. Everything we need to know is already inside us. There is nothing wrong or lacking in the soul. From the ego's perspective nothing is certain, everything is scary. From the soul's perspective everything is certain, everything is safe.

Trust

Our egoic natures, the little or false selves, trust little but themselves. The basis of their existence is fear and fear stalks the waste land from end to end. No nook or cranny escapes its influence. Learning to trust, something that cannot be seen or measured only felt, is the Work along the Way. Spiritually mature people have learned to trust deeply in the reality of the Beloved in which we learn we are utterly loved, safe and worthy as we are.

This is trust. On the far southwest corner of Iona the cliffs drop into the Atlantic. It is a place of nesting seabirds in the spring, where peregrines stoop on inattentive rock doves and you can watch a 'bonxie' (great skua) dissecting an oystercatcher with surgical-like precision. I once saw a bonxie take an oystercatcher out at sea, swooping up from behind to strike it down then drop on it, holding the hapless bird under water. The oystercatcher struggled for three or four minutes, flapping its black and white wings on the surface as the predator rode its back and pushed its gasping red beak under water again and again and again. Exhausted, it eventually gave way to death and the bonxie plucked and picked it clean there and then. Later a raft of feathers and stripped bones drifted onto the rocks. The nesting birds watched all this from their cliff top safety. I wondered if they wondered who might be next, or if they sat relieved knowing a full-bellied hunter meant life for them for at least another day.

I doubt if birds think like we do, but on those same cliffs that autumn when most had abandoned the ledges whitened with layers of excreta, a solitary chick remained. The young fulmar, product of a late breeding and still with a haze of down over its immature plumage, sat hunched against the rock face as a bitter October wind hurled itself against the granite. I drew close, perhaps no more than a dozen feet away, but it barely flinched at my presence while the parent birds pitched and rolled around me, screaming at me or maybe the chick or both. Was it a scream of warning to me (fulmars can projectile vomit a vile fluid when threatened) or to the young one still impassive and motionless as the heaving Atlantic thudded a hundred feet below?

It stood up, the parents soared back and forth, calling, calling – was it an entreaty, a pleading to get air-bound before it was too late? The chick responded only to stand, looking up and down then stretch and flap its wings, then sit again, then rise. I was close enough to look into its eyes and it into mine. Again it stood, flapping weakly against the wind, the parents' calls seemed more urgent, rapid and intense. I'll swear that young bird was working things out, looking down at the sea, at its parents, at me. It may have been just my projection of feelings and thoughts onto something that may or may not possess either. Had it flown before? It seemed not. Was it the lateness of its hatching in the season that had delayed its flight or the fear of the wild sea below, the deathly drop, the rip and tear of the wind rushing up the cliff face?

I edged closer another foot and the chick continued its dance of hesitation, bobbing up and down on the spot, wings stretched then retracted repeatedly. Then a pause; that look in the eye right at me and some sense of a moment of recognition of myself and the sea-roll and the cliffs and the updraft as danger, all danger. At that point if ever I have seen a bird think, it was then. If ever I have heard a bird speak, it was then. In a tiny moment out went the wings, and with its eyes closed and I'm sure I heard it shout, "Oh, **** it!" And it launched itself outwards, dropped into the air only momentarily, before its wings took it; an unloosed kite, whipped aloft and way across and over the clifftops as if a master of flight. Something in that bird at that point, weighing up all the options of destruction, made a choice and on outstretched wings and placing its trust in something it could not see, just went.

Deep trust is like that. It requires no reasoning, no working out. We simply come to know at some profound level that the Beloved is real and no matter what ego judgements might creep in, we are absolutely taken care of. A golden thread binds us to our Source, unbreakable and guaranteed to reel us in, back Home. The sense of being attached by some sure thread reminds me of another story that illustrates trust.

"The soul has its own designs and will not be refuted."

I've never liked heights. At least heights on the edge, like a building or cliff. Up in 'planes is fine. But with edges, my legs go wobbly even when just watching someone else on a cliff edge in a film. It feels like a deep, primordial, ungovernable response. On a climb up the quarry face at Camas (Isle of Mull) I did wonder how the hell I got here? Why did I say yes to the group leader when he suggested a climb? One of those things we find ourselves doing that goes against the grain and yet we feel a kind of possession, some other will taking over and governing, overriding our normal responses.

On the way up I came to see how much in life I had edited down my options. How often I had allowed definitions of myself "I can't do", "I don't like" to govern who I am and who I might be. I came to see that scaling a rock wall or abseiling off it does not remove fear of heights. Perhaps such fears are after all a blessing, keeping risks to life and limb at bay. No, it is the judgement of the fear that counts, the defining of myself by a fear and then seeing myself as somehow 'bad' or 'wrong' because of it. I learned something on that rock wall - about surrender to my skilful guide and his words of encouragement. Just like my nursing days, when patients could do no more and indicated, "Over to you, nurse" and in the surrender how important it was to say "You can" rather than "You can't". Just handing ourselves over and hearing those 'can' words encourages, transforms and drowns out fear. Just like the Beloved really.

I learned or was re-minded that I can still do it and it's OK to be afraid at the same time. I saw something in the many readings and teachings along the Way that to be afraid is equated with 'wrong', a sign of lack of spiritual strength or maturity. Nothing of the sort. Fear is just a feeling like any other; it is part of being human. What counts is whether we react to it, giving way in unawareness, or responding from a place of awareness. In the first case the fear has the power, in the second the Self is in its own power. Therefore we can ask where in our own lives do we feel fear, give way to it? Do we add to the burden by carrying with it some sense of badness that we are afraid? What are the definitions of ourselves (I'm too big/too small/not clever enough/not fast enough/too old/too young/too small/too anything) that govern and limit our lives? Just because we think it, doesn't make it true. Thoughts and feelings aren't facts.

I learned something on that climb and that clifftop moment with that young fulmar. I learned in the former to trust another human being and hand myself over to his guidance, just as I expected others to do with me when I worked as a nurse, just as the Beloved expects of me. Nothing less than absolute trust. I learned too that it's OK to be scared and how trust can overcome it, far more deeply than that old cliché about feeling the fear and doing it anyway. This trust, this fearlessness, does not come from abandonment to my own resources, rather from the faith that I am not alone, that even if I fall, I will be held up. Faith is something we will look at again in Part 7.

Soul

The language of the soul has been proletarianised; the spiritual cat is now out of the religious bag. The religions no longer have a monopoly on the discourse about the soul. This can be at once liberating, but also has brought the attendant risks of pandering to the needs of the ego, in the mistaken belief that keeping the latter happy is what life is all about. This loss of soul, this emptiness at the heart of our culture, is in part driving the search consciously or unconsciously for alternatives to satisfy the deep hunger which at some level every human being feels; that "God shaped hole" [59] that Sartre posited. The loss of attention to the soul is perhaps the single biggest omission of the modern world, especially the secular and materially driven Western culture. It catalyses the unhappiness of many, despite material prosperity and freedoms undreamt of by our ancestors. Religions are often unable to respond to the need and the freedom of choice, stuck in beliefs that a 'sticking-plaster' God is what people want to make everything all right.

In facilitating retreats and workshops both in the UK and abroad, I have been struck by how much the language of the sacred has been lost and, in countries influenced by Christianity, so much of the sacred story too. Mention a story from the Bible that might have been part of my childhood schooling or throw out a word like 'sacred' or 'eucharist' and you can be met with a sea of blank looks. The same applies if I bring in stories and words from other traditions. For huge numbers of people the language and stories of the sacred are meaningless. I suspect that a culture is in deep trouble when it no longer has such a memory. That is not to bemoan the loss of Christianity particularly, rather it is something deeper, the loss of a sense of the sacred that has gone with it. It's not as if it has been replaced by another sacred,

"The soul has its own designs and will not be refuted."

instead the gap has been filled by the superficial language and stories of the egoic personality. Reality TV has replaced the Real.

The response of some religions has been to batten down the hatches or try to. In seeking to hold to orthodox or strict interpretation of scripture or symbol, the reverse of the desired effect is achieved. People turn away. As Campbell notes [60], "The problem of the theologian is to keep his symbol translucent, so that it may not block out the very light it is supposed to convey." Unfortunately, absolutism, certainty and rigid interpretation can block the symbols, stories and liturgies. Campbell goes on to note the serious consequence of the inclination to 'fix', for example, the stories in holy books (of all faiths). What should be poetic and mythical, which leads to transformation, becomes doctrinaire and stultifying. "Whenever the poetry of myth is interpreted as biography, history or science, it is killed. The living images become only remote facts of a distant time or sky. Furthermore, it is never difficult to demonstrate that as science and history, mythology is absurd. When a civilisation begins to reinterpret its mythology in this way, the life goes out of it, temples become museums, and the link between the two perspectives is dissolved. Such a blight has certainly descended on the Bible and on a great part of the Christian cult."

Most people in the post-modern world do not respond to a tradition when "the life goes out of it" and seek answers elsewhere. The inner longing is subtle and seeks the experience of the Divine rather than rigid rules. Some long for the Beloved in varying degrees of inner spiritual pain or crisis while others just feel that prompting for 'something more' and want answers through a willingness to enquire and understand. In prosperous libertarian countries we have more freedoms than ever before to explore that inner need, yet poll after poll suggests that the congregational religions fail to meet it for many people, that the New Age market lacks depth and that no amount of designer clothes, homes, orgasms, babies, bodies or relationships can satisfy the longing for happiness [61,62]. Instead we see the emptiness, anomie, disaffection and disconnection that arises when we attach ourselves to material gains or cultural distractions. The environment, politics, relationships – every aspect of the human experience and the world we inhabit is diminished when attention to soul is left out.

In his poem, The Waste Land, Eliot [63] captures the disjointed conversations, the disconnected relationships, the sterility of language and the dark and dull existence of a soulless society. Without soul, families, relationships, cultures, nations fracture and fragment. Purposelessness, nihilism and ennui ensue, the pain of which is drowned by the addictions to drink or drugs or sex or TV or shopping – the pain-killers for the broken heart, anaesthetics for the personhood lost in the meaning-less, countless options for the countless holes in our consciousness that can never otherwise be filled.

As the soul has dropped off the map, psychobiological models have come to dominate, framing human beings as little more than the products of mental and bodily processes. We are nothing that cannot be analysed, measured, weighed and investigated in this form of scientific reductionism. Soul, if it is considered at all, is consigned to the realms of the religious or the therapy room and studiously kept there. Although there are signs of change, such as recognition by the business community that profits are linked to the wellbeing of the workers and their degree of spiritual support [64,65,66] or the greater willingness of the political worlds to work with the religious, these are as yet drops in the ocean. A culture that has no sense of soul is a culture that is not whole, and a culture that is not whole is not holy. With no sense of the sacred, of the possibility that we are far more than what can be known by the ordinary senses, then the one reality, the one self is all that in relentless despair we are left with. We may fall into nihilism, or to loving and living only for the moment, or to doing the best we can for our children and ourselves and hope for the best. Or maybe the world and its resources come to have no meaning or purpose but to make us feel good, and the pursuit of the feel-good is destroying our world, both internally and externally.

Baring [10] warns us, "What happens to us if we exist without relationship to anything beyond our own consciousness? We are left bereft of the relationship with the cosmos. Psychic energy that has nowhere to go implodes on itself, undermining the social order." We see this emptiness, this collapse of meaning at every level; it is found in Sartre's 'Nausea' [67] or Eliot's 'The Waste Land' [63]. It is the completion of the fearful prediction in Yeats' [68] 'Second Coming'. When there is no consensus of supreme values "all the institutions and social structures of society are weakened; morality becomes a matter of everyone's convenience" and with nothing beyond ourselves we become "inflated because we behave with god-like omnipotence; diminished because we are

"The soul has its own designs and will not be refuted."

imprisoned in an image of reality…which limits and constricts our growth." [10]. Our planet and other people become something we can use and abuse at our will. As Baring points out, because we are all connected at the quantum level, when some change then millions more may change. In a holistic universe where everything is connected, what affects one affects all. Another perspective is that the world is not just a Gaia or a theophany or a hologram, but a self-generating work of art, and if the latter, who could not stand back and wonder at the awesome pattern where every part of the picture is perfectly in place? How does seeing something as a work of art change our relationship to it?

All this requires us to shift our consciousness and our view of the cosmos from random atoms colliding in a random universe to the awesomeness and possibility of one that is purposeful and co-creative. We are part of it and it is part of us. Just as we are conscious, so is the cosmos in ways that we can barely comprehend with the five senses. The reality we can see is not limitless dead matter upon which we act, over which we have or seek control; it is a living thing, conscious of itself. How differently we might relate to a living thing than to a dead thing.

The question of what 'God' is, therefore, is not the question; the question is who asks the question? Our limited five senses are really good for getting us around the realm of time and space at the level of ordinary reality, but to enquire into the deeper levels of reality we need to cultivate spiritual senses – insight, discernment, compassion, envisioning, receptivity – the senses of the heart. To assume that we can 'think' our way to Sacred Unity with normal brain function alone, or touch the One with tactile receptors or hear with the ears and see with the eyes or taste upon the lips – all these senses are involved in our perception but only skim the surface of possibility. To know deeply we must go deep, drawing on planes of consciousness that these sensors are ill-equipped to know, depth of consciousness that can only be plumbed in our Soul Works such as prayer, contemplation or meditation. Using the works of the spirit, the toolkit of the mystics, the mystic way unites with *all* reality.

Our relationship towards the Beloved can thus take two main approaches. The first is the rational and objective, where we try to 'work it all out' drawing on what our five senses tell us to be true. (They're not wrong; they just can't get the full picture). It involves lots of judgements, measurements and interpretations (limited if you want to get to the One, very useful if you want to build an aeroplane). The second is the mystical, the relational. We don't so much seek to believe as to know. In the first we develop a subject-object relationship, an "I-it" to borrow from Buber's [70] philosophy. In the second we interpenetrate and connect in an "I-Thou" that betokens union. Mystics are not special people, they have just found the relational way to the Beloved, to the All-that-is, a way that seems to be much less hooked on definition, power or control; willing to engage with ordinary reality from a perspective of greater equanimity, humility and service. In the end it's all 'real', it's just that with our ordinary five senses we only penetrate part of this reality.

Meanwhile, the egocentric view of humanity as the sole owner of consciousness and at the centre of the universe and ourselves is shifting, gradually. Modern science, such as the work in quantum physics or the Heartmath studies, is not only nudging us away from ourselves as the centre, but also from the brain as the centre, the driver of consciousness. The heart, traditionally the seat of the soul, is emerging as a new realm of enquiry and understanding of consciousness [69]. For example studies on the electromagnetic field of the heart show how it is over 70% bigger than that of the brain. We do not end at our skin; the heart rates of people in close proximity are transmitted to each other. Heart health and coherence or harmony can be profoundly affected by whether we visualise and feel loving feelings and experiences or fearful ones. These studies, together with those on loneliness and disconnection cited earlier, are indicating the intricate and complex subtlety of human consciousness – it's far more than the firing off of electrochemical processes in the brain.

A couple of years ago I was asked to speak at a conference for several hundred doctors and nurses on brain death during Brain Awareness Week in the UK. It was my lot to follow a well-known scientist who had done much work in the UK and internationally on brain death and coma. His session was deeply appealing to much of the audience. He was so certain. We can feel very assured by certainty in others. The nub of his case was this: the function of the brain can be measured, 'vegetative' (a horrid word for all it conjures up about brain-injured people) states can be assessed and given certain criteria, by which we can be assured the person is really 'dead' and then life support machines be switched off.

The seductive simplicity of this argument left me feeling strangely nauseated.

"The soul has its own designs and will not be refuted."

Needless to say, my subsequent session where I expressed serious doubts about this approach went down like a lead balloon in some quarters. Any suggestion of uncertainty about the nature of human consciousness, of humility in the face of human illness, of reverence for the possibility that we might be more than the sum total of our cerebral atoms and their functions was uncomfortable to many. More recent work, such as on 'locked-in syndrome', has sabotaged those previous certainties about brain death. The simple approach of brain dead = consciousness death is very seductive. After all, it so much easier if you are caught up in the difficult business of caring and really tough decisions at the end of life to feel, to need to feel, that our actions are rooted in reason and logic. Introduce the concept of soul or the possibility of the real Self that is not the same as the personal self or the possibility that the brain is not the only repository of consciousness or even that consciousness is not so much in the body as the body is in consciousness - and the steady ship of certainty is holed below the waterline.

Without soul, then...?
Thus far I have used the word 'soul' without question, but what does the word 'soul' mean? It seems like it is one of those things that it is impossible to define; yet everyone knows what it is. The soul is of the Divine who is indefinable, but to Schweitzer [71] it was, "the sense of something higher", something that stirs in us "thoughts hopes and aspirations...reaching out to the world of goodness, truth and beauty and the desire to breathe in the world of light and never to lose it". The soul is the deep inner energy of all life, indeed of all matter, the ground of being that connects us to all beings and to the Beloved in whom the All-that-is is sustained. The soul is the seat of reverence for life and love and the road to it is through the heart, for it is our feelings that reflect back to us the joy of life, but also those places where we are summoned to heal. The heart is almost universally seen across faiths as the gateway to the soul, to the Beloved, to Sacred Unity and Ultimate Reality.

The notion that we might have souls, that we are not so much human beings having a spiritual journey as spiritual beings having a human journey [72] goes against the grain of much of modernity. One example springs to mind when I was involved recently in an enquiry where abuse of patients with Alzheimer's had been a prominent feature. While making the right noises about caring, some terrible things had been done to these patients and a cardinal feature of the underlying problem was that a significant number of the staff – fairly conventional nurses and doctors – were not facing up to the underlying, unconscious hopelessness they felt about their patients or the deep fears their patients' condition touched in them about their own mortality. Although much work was going on with 'reality orientation', the only reality accepted was ordinary reality. The patients were seen as ultimately lost causes in their own form of (declining) vegetative state. This shadow in the unconscious was occluded by "chronic niceness" [73], but ultimately leaked out. Behind the mask of caring lay some deeply uncaring feelings and actions, which, being unacknowledged, led to these vulnerable old people being abused.

Health problems that diminish personal identity, like Alzheimer's, challenge our very notion of what it is to be human. Imagine a situation where first we forget our names, then whatever job we had, then how to dress, then how to eat, then who our family is and so on – eventually a point is reached either gradually through such diseases or suddenly as with severe brain damage where all identity is lost to us. Who we are or were resides only in the memory of those who know us. "Who am I?" becomes the key unanswered spiritual question, unanswerable by the ego self because it has been dissolved. This illustrates two other key points.

Firstly that the ego tends to get a bad press, yet it is essential in the formation of identity and mind function; without an identity there is nothing to surrender to the Beloved. It is also the ego that develops an imagination, an ability to see and reflect upon itself. The ego is the individualiser, the identity creator, and it is a vital part of our way of being in the world and in our coming Home. Thus it too plays its part in the dance with the soul that leads to awakening. Both have purpose in each other, but what has to change is the relationship between the two. The ego's mastery is destined to be turned into service of the soul.

Secondly, what is left if the personality has passed away? We still tend to treat the person's body with honour in recognition that it was once a person and as a mark of respect to his or her loved ones. We pay great attention to dead bodies, go to great lengths to 'lay them to rest' and have fought wars over the relics of saints or soldiers. But, and it's a big but, if the person has 'gone' then really all we are dealing with is a bag of flesh and bone, so why not simply get rid of it – it's not a person any more after all? To some extent switching off ventilators or calls for euthanasia are rooted in

"The soul has its own designs and will not be refuted."

this thinking. And yet most of us feel intuitively that there is 'something there' even though there is no response any more. It may be our projections onto such persons, our memories or our inability to deal with our own mortality that keep us wanting to keep them on. But it may be that we are sensing, regardless of our religious beliefs, that there is indeed something there, some presence, some witness - the soul - that is more than the mere identity that has gone.

Another example of what happens when we reduce people to their identities occurred when I got involved in a debate in the professional press about the nature of mental illness. On current evidence at least one in three of us is likely to experience mental illness (at least as currently defined, see the previous chapter on spiritual emergence) of some sort during our lifetimes. I help a charity, the Sacred Space Foundation, that was set up to support people in spiritual crisis, including that particular spiritual crisis known as burnout [54]. A spiritual crisis throws our lives up in the air, all sense of certainty and security can be lost. Things that were once ordinary in our lives – work, relationships, a sense of purpose - become meaningless, confusing and frightening. Often this gets diagnosed, unsurprisingly perhaps, as a mental illness, especially depression. After all, most of us live in a culture where sanity is reduced to how well we can adapt to living life the way things are. QED those who cannot or will not, and who see things differently, can expect to be made to feel that *they* are the ones with the problem. Many mental health professionals who had bought into this paradigm of sanity responded with hostility to this debate, seeing no place for a spiritual perspective. Letters from patients and some other mental health practitioners were quite different.

One, a doctor now working as a General Practitioner, described the devastating effect that a psychiatric diagnosis has had on her life and the stigma it has left behind, even though her problems have long since been resolved (after being made worse by psychiatric treatment). Another, also an ex-patient but also a mental health nurse wrote of how "any public criticism of psychiatry often meets with an aggressive response". Another suggested, "There are still thousands of nurses not driven by wanting to really be with people". Two psychiatrists also felt critical of their own discipline, but curiously felt unwilling to speak out publicly because of pressure to conform to the status quo. One said he felt "like an alien at some of the case conferences when I feel my blood start to boil at some of the totally mechanistic ways people view our patients". Another wrote, "we only think about the brain and refuse to acknowledge the possibility that there might be something else that makes us human".

However, other calls for change are getting louder and not just from the health care sector but from the wider scientific community. The current dominant paradigm, which sees 'mind', 'consciousness' and 'personhood' purely as products of the brain, is being broken as suggested earlier. The reduction of human beings to biological processes where 'who we are' is relegated to the outcome of a bunch of neurones and neurochemicals is being challenged more now than it has been in many decades. The idea that when we break down, we can be rectified if we can be tweaked with the right chemical or psychotherapeutic spanners is increasingly being seen for the simplistic modernist notion that it is. Although I have focussed on mental health care here, because of my recent experiences, no part of our culture has escaped the consequences of soulless models. So, let us return to ask what is this 'soul' thing with which so many in the modern world seem to have a problem?

All spiritual traditions down the years have sought to define what soul is and it comes in many guises and explanations. To the Greeks it was *psyche* (a term we use today to refer to the conscious and unconscious mind – hence *psyche*ology, *psychi*atry) and *pneuma* the life giving spirit. In Hebrew *nefesh* and *ruach* describe the individual soul and the divine spirit respectively. In early Greek and Hebrew thought little attention was given to individual survival after death, the Greek *Hades* and Hebrew *Sheol* were realms where the dead continued only as shadows and memories. The *nefesh/psyche* went to *Sheol/Hades* and the body returned to the earth at death. The *ruach/pneuma*, being of the Divine, returned to its source. Subtle differences also arose about the origin of the soul. Some beliefs inclined towards the soul as an inviolate aspect of the Divine that incarnates and returns after death, while the Hebrew *nefesh* is not so much a pre-existent entity but rather an emerging and growing one through the experience of being embodied.

A few centuries before Christ notions of individual immortality began to arise, including the possibility of the soul as part of the Divine and the ground of individual existence. Known as the Real, True or Highest Self, the 'I Amness', 'that of God' in everyone, the Essence – it suggests a quality of consciousness, presence and being

"The soul has its own designs and will not be refuted."

that is in or holds but is not of the ordinary or 'false' or 'little' self as the Hindu tradition describes it. This true Self is, paradoxically, Truth itself - indefinable, non-dual and a condition of pure and infinite uncreated awareness. It is unmanifest, rather than a 'thing'. But that is not to say that it is nothing, rather it is no thing, a subtle difference, which we will explore in later chapters.

The ego or false self is likened in some traditions to a caterpillar that knows only that it's a caterpillar. Only when it breaks down and is transformed into a butterfly is its true nature revealed. Other views see it rather like an onion, the layers of which we have to peel away until we get to its core. I tend to the view that if that's the case it's quite some onion with infinite layers! The ego has so many identities, stories and distractions that we can spend a lifetime, maybe many lifetimes, peeling away at it. Maybe one option as we will explore later is to find ways to renounce it, transform it, let it be and be open to the possibility of seeing the world through the eyes of the soul instead. It's not that the ego is not real or that the true Self is the only real, it's just that they are two very different planes of reality. Our Soul Care does not seek to destroy one and embrace only the other, but to draw all into one, into non-duality. The awakened person is liberated from the trap of duality and sees the whole in full awareness.

We need to be wary of seeing the ego or false self as something that we need to attack and destroy, a common theme in some quarters. Developing such a war-like consciousness is questionable. Rather, we may learn to accept and integrate it into the fullness of our being, something which has served us but which now needs to play a very different role in our lives. The personhood, ego or false self, that strange conglomeration of 'who-I-think-I-am' through which we initially find our place in the world, is a very useful thing to have for getting around, relating, separating, connecting but it is essentially a false self not *the* Self. When we live and move and have our being in the pure awareness of the latter, then that is freedom.

Thus the false self whilst having its own real-ness, is not all that we are, indeed it is not what we are at all. Our true Self is the soul. Influenced by the Sufi tradition Almaas [74] sees the soul as "the true nature of everything. It is my nature, but it is also your nature. It is the nature of birds, cats, trees, rocks, everything. It is not the rocks, not the cat, not your body, not you, not me. It is the inner nature of these. It is what allows them to exist. That is the nature of Essence, the nature of everything, it is what is sometimes called God." In the soul, in our essence which is both personal and transpersonal, found in all things yet contained by none, we not only find our individuality we also find unity with All-that-is.

Descartes famously pronounced, "I think therefore I am" (*Cogito ergo sum*). But thinking is the realm of the mind out of which, influenced by culture, experience, heredity and other factors grows that conglomeration of self-will known as the ego. The latter is very useful in its own way for acting out our roles and functions in the world, but it has its limitations. The soul, the essence of All-that-is, is beyond language and thinking. It simply is. It is the uncluttered 'I Am'. The ego believes in itself. The soul knows it is of the Beloved. The ego wants to live forever. The soul being of Sacred Unity knows its immortality. The ego is a created thing that wants to be in charge, to be 'God'. The soul knows it is in the heart of the Beloved and wants only to love its Beloved. The ego desires to be, the soul is the 'I Am'. The ego self-hood, the person is the medium of being in the world, but it is not the true, absolute Self, no more than the part played by the actor on the stage is real.

On this basis, Descartes might better have postulated, "I Am, therefore I think." Thinking emanates from the ego, but this has no existence without soul.

The little or false self, the ego, is the instrument by which we participate in the world, but we can spend a lot of time believing that the instrument is all that we are. However, without soul, without the knowing of our Essence we are caught up in the waste land where the barren interior landscape is bedevilled by a gnawing and ultimate despair, no matter how it is dressed up in worldly fun or liberation to 'be who we want to be' (which usually means an inflated pursuit of the ego's agenda). The interior waste land is reflected in the exterior – the degradation of our cultures, indeed of the planet, and the murder and mayhem in the world are a mirror image of the interior degradation. People who are ensouled tend to find it easier to form loving relationships with themselves, with others, with the world and that which is beyond and within all these. The landscape of the ego, of personal selfishness, is ultimately a horizon of fear, for the ego knows at some level that its power is temporary. Thus rooted in fear, it holds these unconscious and sometimes not so unconscious fears at bay by an endless hunt for self-gratification - more, more, more of everything. In Buddhism these are the "hungry ghosts" that haunt our consciousness,

"The soul has its own designs and will not be refuted."

with bloated bodies but pinhole mouths; they can never suck in enough to satiate their needs. In contrast, when we act in the world from an ensouled place, from the Home of complete love, which rests within, our response to the world is transformed. We no longer have to suck in everything to meet our desires - there is less exploitation, more compassion, less fear, more love.

The downgrading and destruction of our planet is one of the less attractive results of modernity, and its denial of the sacred, the essential soul unity of and reverence for all things. A "significant part of human life is erased"[75] when external reality is treated as the plaything of our egoic personhoods, removing the support of the human soul. The mediaeval Arthurian legend tells of certain holy wells or sanctuaries for the refreshment of the traveller, guarded by maidens who, on request, would proffer the water in golden bowls. But king Amagons abused this hospitality, raping one of the maidens and stealing her bowl. The result was that everything was instantly changed. The whole land went to waste, nothing would grow, human bonds broke down and vast suffering ensued. Arthur and his knights undertook to remedy this by prayer to heal the land and to rediscover the vanished holy site to restore its wholeness. Their task was useless, for at its roots the destruction was spiritual. Only by the discovery of the Holy Grail, the renewal of Essence, the re-consecration of the relationship between humanity and the cosmic order, could the waste land be transformed back to its former nourishing harmony.

The "waste land comes when the spiritual is abandoned in favour of the material. Inner nature is rejected and eternal truths are forgotten"[75]. The re-discovery of these eternal truths is a central task for the spiritual search. We cannot recreate what has been lost. We live in new times, new circumstances and hankering after the past is to pander in its own way to the agenda of the false self. If a tradition is lost, so may be the conditions that sustained it. The renewal of soul in the waste land of our culture is arising paradoxically from the very newness that helped to set it aside. The essence will be the same, but its form and manifestation will be different and unique to its time. We see it now in the shifting sands of the reordering of the religions, the movements in our understanding of the nature of consciousness, the ecology movement, the rise of 'integrated' or holistic health care, the burgeoning interest in personal development, new forms of monasticism, going on pilgrimage and taking retreats. These and other indicators suggest that the waste land may also be the fertile ground for a renewal and reintegration of essence, of soul, into health and wellbeing. The alternatives are there, becoming more known and drawing greater allegiance [76,77].

Meanwhile there are more than a few timely reminders on a daily basis that the recovery of the soul for the world might seem to have a long way to go. Perhaps it is an ego pipedream that it might be otherwise, for at some other level the world is unfolding perfectly and the ordinary experience of the world is just a mirror image of the superficial experience of our egos. At some deeper level this vast work of art in which we participate and co-create may be happening exactly as it should. Thoughts of loss of a spiritual golden age and the possibility of creating a heavenly future are just that – thoughts, an ego perception of one level of reality trapped by limited perceptions of time and space. Perhaps many dimensions of reality are end-lessly unfolding in each moment and we might see this truth that brings, what? The peace that surpasses understanding when we witness this mighty artwork through the eye of the mystic, they eye we all hold if we but open to it. Yet, in this reality, however we experience it, we can only try and do our bit. A theme we will return to later.

I was in London at the time of the July bombings in 2005. Looking at what moments before had been a reasonably ordered city going about its peaceful business, my friend said, "It makes you want to give up on humanity doesn't it?" Any act of may-hem since that time - and there have been many - will produce similar comment. In view of the carnage, the waste land made starkly real before our eyes, this might seem a reasonable response. But I watched most ordinary Londoners in the reports of this wonderful diverse city recognise that an attack on one is an attack on all. In fact looking at the victims – with so many faiths and races represented - an attack on London has now become an attack on the world. I watched the response of nurses, police, ambulance and fire officers and others who worked their hearts out to help and heal. I watched people of faith and none echo the words of Julian of Norwich that whatever confronts us now, a belief in God, humanity or some greater realm of being – of Love – through this "all shall be well and all manner of thing shall be well." In love and the expressions of love there is not despair but hope, for the fearful waste land ultimately cannot stand against a re-creation that emerges from the being of the soul.

Thus it is not so much about creating as re-creating (forever) conditions that propitiate our egos' judgmental and fearful perceptions of duality (good and bad, past and present, right and wrong, birth and death), but conditions that nurture constant spiritual emer-gence. As Campbell [60] again reminds us, "We need to render the modern world 'spiri-

"The soul has its own designs and will not be refuted."

tually significant'…making it possible for people to come to full maturity through the conditions of contemporary life."…."a transmutation of the whole social order is necessary, so that through every detail and act of secular life the vitalising image of the universal god-man who is actually immanent and effective in all of us may be somehow made known to consciousness." We cannot wait for the world to change. Instead we can dis-cover the "immanent and effective" in ourselves so that every one of us becomes our own hero in our own way rather than reliant upon another. Heroic because we see and feel the despair in the world and ourselves and, from a deep place of faith in the soul, in the Beloved, refuse to give way to them.

The tension between these apparent two worlds, the one of bliss and the one of suffering, the one of the spirit and the one of the material, the one of life and the one of death is an unnecessary one arising from the grip of the ego. As we mature in our spirituality, shifting from seeing with the eye of the ego to the eye of the soul, we come to perceive this more clearly. There is no 'this world' and 'the other world' (although it can certainly feel like that a lot of the time) for a truly spiritual, holistic way of seeing is able to embrace the paradox of opposites, the challenge of diversity. Indeed, in some ways the binary soul-ego or true-self - false-self is a distorted dualistic dichotomy. Beneath and beyond our efforts to explore and explain, essentially it is all One.

The inclination to be binary in our approach to the Work ("Now I'm being spiritual because I'm praying, now I'm not because I'm shopping) can cause us not to see the grace where we are right now. Underhill [24] writes that, "What matters supremely to our soul's growth is how we lay hold on life; whether we let it just go on without giving it significance, or whether we so respond to the mesh of circumstance, that through and in it we find God. Our job, our environment, however narrow, is always adequate to this, because there is no place or circumstance where God is not. It is consoling to remember that circumstances can do nothing to us, to our deepest selves, because they can neither help nor hinder, save in so far as we do or do not direct our will through them to God. We are not required to adjust ourselves to circumstances by some awful wrench; but to let circumstances be, let them happen, be quiet in them and do our best without fuss; and then God will come to us in them, however hostile to our own notion of spiritual life, peace and happiness they may be."

The tendency to separate the ordinary from the spiritual is something we have to address along the Way and we will explore further in later chapters. The Gospel story of Mary and Martha [Lk 10:38-42] is a classic teaching on this subject. Martha was busy grumbling about the housework she had to do while Mary seemed to have the better deal, just being with Jesus and anointing him with expensive oil - spiritual intimacy with Christ. Had she (Martha) got out of such dualistic thinking and seen that her work of hospitality was an equally contemplative gift and paid full attention to it in the moment, she might have felt more at peace in herself. Her problem seemed to be that she was being dualistic, not able to adjust her awareness to see that the Beloved was just as much in the household duties as being still with Jesus. It's all One if we can but see it. The Work is there to help us see.

It does not have to be a case of Home or the world but Home in the world, seeing all of it as one, of All-that-is, unfolding exquisitely and elegantly in Divine consciousness in which the waste land too plays its part. The world is a spiritual waste land; but it is also a land that blooms and sings with beauty and possibility. Pundits often bemoan the neo-barbarism of post-modernity that is seemingly bereft of a moral compass, of a religious ethic, of a code of the soul. But it has always been thus and we need to see things in proportion. The waste land exists as it always has contemporaneously with the exquisite beauty of the face of the Divine. Our choices may determine which prevails at any one moment.

The waste land lies all about us, but what lies about stems from within. 'As above, so below' is an important spiritual principle; 'above' or 'below' not in a physical sense but in the sense of more or less evolved spirit and consciousness. The more expansive and loving, the more creation tends to mirror it, and vice versa. When we turn to our hearts, to love and the very roots of the soul, the waste land is transformed, not in some linear lurch from a lost paradise into hell and back again, but in the endless attentiveness to soul. The waste land is eternally becoming and fading in each conscious moment, with each breath. Acknowledging, nourishing, choosing soul is the searching for and finding of the Holy Grail and thereby perhaps the world shall be changed because our way of seeing is changed: alchemy - the lead of perception becomes the gold of awareness. The waste land is what we encounter when we are exiled from Home, when the soul, trapped in the ego's relentless pursuits, longs to be free. When freedom comes, we can embrace the waste land as part of All-that-is, just like ourselves.

"The soul has its own designs and will not be refuted."

"What is God?" is not the question.
The question is who asks the question?
Who?
Between the I and the not-I,
twin bridged by time and space
(necessary for movement)
lies the canyon of the unknown,
the bottomless.
Do not go here stranger alone,
do not go here accompanied.
Come prepared,
come naked in your unpreparedness.
For here be the faultlines of your psyche,
the waiting earthquake of the soul.
Here, words and thoughts are broken
in the caverns of despair.
Dreams split like apples dropped
from towers onto concrete pavements.
Hopes drown in oceans of tears.
Do not go here, stranger.
Do not go here while you're a stranger.
We all stand on the bridges.
Some retreat to try again.
Some fall, some rise.
Near or far all pass, all enter
and stepping through the iron gates
of the exit, look back
(do not look back – pillars of salt, pillars of salt!
Abraham wailing in the desert).
Rabbit-eyed with fear
we see the long road buried
in the rubble of imagination,
bordered in fires
stalked by other guards looting the rich pickings.
Don't wait, go on, go on!

Beyond the gate and up the rose-climbed wide wall
where the bell rings in an empty sky,
a high hill, sunless and moonless.
And there in the distance,
no further than under your nose,
a glimpse,
of something half remembered,
of something half forgotten.
Set in the genes
or tattooed on the underside of the skull.
Embedded at birth, first birth,
the eternal, internal compass home.
The immortal hand outstretched
to bring the bride stripped bare
waits to take you to the seat
by the lily pond, by the lake of dreams,
the waters of compassion, whose droplets
are Your substance.
Love.
When all has been said and done,
only Love.

Part 4

"Fate has flung me into the wastes of
Memphis.
Go and tell fate: turn me round and hurl
me again
Until I behold the wilderness of Judah
And reach the fair heights of the far north
And wrapped in majesty of Elohi's name
I'll don the splendour of his holi-
ness, and whirl."[78]

Escaping Memphis: leaving the waste land and heading home

My childhood in the 50s was poor by modern standards, but all my basic needs were met. I had food in my belly, shoes on my feet and clothes on my back. The state paid for my schooling and health care and provided a modest home. My dad had a poorly paid job, but it was steady money and with a little 'overtime' he earned enough for a seaside holiday once a year perhaps a week in a caravan and maybe a bike for me at Christmas. My mum kept the house (and me) as clean as a new pin. Today I meditate with a mantra, a skill I learned easily because my mum began each day with them – "Have you washed behind your ears?" "Did you do the back of your neck?" "Have you put clean underwear on?" These rolled off her tongue daily before I left for school and her antiphon to my usual "Why?" was always the same, "Because what will people think if you have an accident?" It took me a long time to grasp the logic of my mother's thinking. If I'd had an accident (and I did once and ended up at the hospital and the first thing my mum did was to tick me off for being so stupid and the second was to check the back of my ears!) then surely the state of my cleanliness was the last thing she needed to worry about. But no. My childhood society was governed by one overriding thing – the fear of being 'shown up' – shamed.

"The exterior waste land is a reflection of the interior waste land."

Letting go

Nowadays, with all that went on in my family it would be called dysfunctional. Emotionally impoverished, we nevertheless had a kind of safety and we were certainly clean. And there is not a moment of it that I do not cherish though much of it in retrospect was scary, painful and suffocating. Yet, if not that then not this and there is no part of my life now that is not full of blessings. I have in my time worked with many profoundly wounded people, and one thing I have noticed about their healing is the liberation that comes from a deep acceptance and, yes, love of their past even when aspects of it would be judged brutal. That level of forgiveness, where we go beyond perceptions of right or wrong or 'letting people off' for hurts done to us, sets us free to discover our true essence, to come Home. Healing our relationships with our primary authority figures, with the past, is invariably a prerequisite for healing our relationship with arguably the ultimate authority figure – the Absolute, the Beloved, the Source of All. Those who undertake the spiritual work while attempting to bypass the emotional work will find this renders incomplete their relationship with the Beloved. Coming Home involves healing and integration of all that we are, we cannot miss out the bits we don't like or that we think are too tough to deal with. Woundedness, a closed heart, an inability to forgive and let go – all these and more whether conscious or unconscious are the grist to the mill of our work along the way that cannot be avoided.

Forgiveness is a letting go of our desire, our hope, that the past was anything other than it was [79]. In the 'nowness' we know that the past and future do not exist. Clinging to hope that the past could be other than it was is clinging to something that is not real, no matter how powerful a memory it might be; it is not real. Our capacity as human beings to worry about past or future is amazing, putting so much energy into something that does not exist. The past is gone; the future is not yet.

There are essentially two ways of being in the world. The first is that of victim. Life happens, full of suffering and maybe some joy; it happens *to* us, and there's not much we can do about it except try to take control of it or escape from it or accept with stoicism the overused cliché that 'whatever doesn't kill you makes you stronger'. Perhaps with that comes a degree of resilience, an ability to cope with whatever life seemingly throws at us. The second is to see life as something in which we participate, co-create. Life events are not so much done *to* us, as summoned up *by* us. That is not to say that the Way is one of spiritual sado-masochism, demanding suffering in order to transform, rather it is a call to embrace suffering and joy and see what they have to offer us, where we find our attachments that keep us stuck – to things, to ways of being. In this view we can transform our 'way of seeing' [35], to live with more equanimity in the world. It is the 'ah, so' quality of Zen Buddhism – "I am happy" – "Ah, so"; 'I am sad" – "Ah, so". Our life story as willing participant shifts our view, it enables us to see events as opportunities for transformation, as wake up calls to discover our deepest truth, opportunities to embrace the extremes of life and all that lies between as rich treasure, to be carried with us when we go Home. Cavafy [80] captures this in his poem *Ithaka*:-

> Keep Ithaka always in your mind.
> Arriving there is what you are destined for.
> But do not hurry the journey at all.
> Better if it lasts for years,
> So you are old by the time you reach the island.
> Wealthy with all you have gained on the way."

There is much evidence [36,81,82,83,84] to suggest that those who can embrace the suffering in their lives and not just cling to happiness can find the enrichment of transformation, healing, expanded awareness and compassion. I have lost count of the number of people I have worked with who have found grace and illumination when they have been able to 'forgive' in the deepest sense of the word, i.e. found expansion of compassion and awareness of themselves and others when they have been able to look at some challenge in their lives and see what it has gifted them.

I recall one man, for example, who said "Don't get me wrong, I wouldn't wish cancer on anybody, but if I didn't have it, then I wouldn't have changed the way I am, wouldn't have grown so much closer to my son." Another, a woman abused as a child, said that "I'm almost glad it happened all those years ago, does that sound perverse, because I am now so much free-er because of it, so much more understanding of how others hurt and how to help them." A man facing prison said, "I've lost everything, but that's meant I've found myself". These people and many others like them were not in a place of saying, "Yes, please, bring it on, let's have more pain", rather what they were able to do was to find the shining diamond in the deep pit, the glimmer of light in the darkness that enabled them to forgive, to let go, to not be governed by it, to find redemption and freedom with it.

"The exterior waste land is a reflection of the interior waste land."

'Beloved' and 'suffering' don't seem to be words that sit well together at first glance. How to explain suffering if the Beloved is real? "How can there be a 'God' when there is so much horror in the world?" is a common refrain. People have tied themselves in theological knots for millennia attempting to answer this question. The following vignette illustrates some options, please pick your own – personally I think it's probably best to abandon too much thinking about it, but perhaps we can discern that evil and suffering too have their purpose when viewed from other planes of consciousness.

My friend had a bad foot injury, which immobilised her for months. She got caught up in feelings of foolishness and victimhood ("Why me?") from the self inflicted wound and catastrophising about what might go wrong next. Down the ages, people have sought to find reasons why bad things happen:-

- First it might just be random events things in a random universe – shit happens, it's not personal and it has no meaning.

- Second, it could be Karma – the law of cause and effect (often reduced simplistically and erroneously to suffering in this life because we were bad in a previous one).

- Third, it could be sabotage rooted in the unconscious, putting us in a place where we have to stop or seek help; a wake-up call to something going on deep within that requires attention.

- Fourth, and closely related, it is part of the soul's plan, its 'contract' with the Beloved, to go deeper into the life experience or to experience more of the nature of non-attachment, divorcing from the willpower of the ego.

- Fifth, it could be an 'Act of God' to stop us in our tracks, to wake us up or to punish us.

- Sixth, it could be the malevolent use of psychic power by other persons who wish suffering upon us.

- Seventh, it could be the work of demonic power(s); the 'enemy's' enjoyment at our suffering or trying to ensure our capture by chthonic forces.

Some of these options make us just powerless victims or seduce us into the nihilism of the meaningless life of a meaningless world. Others require acceptance of certain theories of past lives, of opposing forces of light and dark, of a separate judging God, of a powerful unconscious over which we have little if any control – all of which we explore in more detail in these pages. Regardless of the cause, experience suggests that all suffering contains the possibility of grace, a nugget of deeper awareness and healing waiting to be seen and integrated. Somewhere within, although maybe obscured from view at first, is the potential and gift of a deeper transformation, a setting free of the true Self from the all-embracing power of the ego. In all suffering - if we can work through it with insight, hope and faith - we invariably find another step towards liberation is available to us.

We may or may not be able to choose our suffering, but we can perhaps choose our response to it. To stand over and against it, live fully, not get attached, go deep and realise as the mystics do that what we see is only on the surface. Beneath it there is a profound resonance of 'all shall be well' (all of which, of course, could be ego pipedreams to reassure us!). Meanwhile, maybe it's best just live well, love your neighbour as yourself, act justly, love mercy and walk humbly with the Divine…and let the rest take care of itself.

And what suffers? Certainly we do so when entirely ego identified, but when we move to our 'I-Amness' we 'see' things differently. There is a very different response (as opposed to reaction) when we say, "I am suffering" to when we say, "I am experiencing suffering". Whether there is a Deity wrapped up in all this or not is another matter. Once, after a cancer diagnosis, I went on retreat and hung out with my fear in a church by the sea, a place of solitude I have grown to love down the years. I got into a fierce internal argument [85] with this 'God' and spewed out a lot of anger and decided 'He' didn't exist as I stomped out of the church. The gorgeous scene as I stepped outside took my breath away. I had an intense feeling of simply being alive and sighed to myself, "God or not, it's still a beautiful day".

It seems counterintuitive to want to stay with suffering. We naturally fear the pain (of whatever sort) so want rid of it by any means; otherwise we might be overwhelmed by it and disintegrate. A Jesus story is helpful here. When summoned to the tomb of his dead friend Lazarus, Jesus wept [John 11:35]. Notice he did not try to avoid the pain and sorrow, he allowed himself to feel. He did not fear disintegration. His life,

"The exterior waste land is a reflection of the interior waste land."

like most of our lives, teaches us that actually we can hold suffering and stay with it. We don't have to be afraid of it, we can move through it then do whatever we have to do. Some along the Way want to avoid suffering, yet we may learn that we can be with it and not be overwhelmed; even use it to transform and influence our work. The Soul Care approaches mentioned in this book are there to help us in the event that we do not have the strength as Jesus did to stay with deep and painful feelings.

Although there may be gifts in the paradox of suffering I do not suggest that we sadomasochistically invite it in. Rather, the Work enables us to 'see' and find different options for how we deal with it. Suffering is one way to get free and therefore a grace, but, and it's a big but, we need to remember that the gift is *in* the suffering; the cause (such as cancer, bereavement or some other pain) is not itself the gift. Those of us involved in therapeutic or caring work need to be really careful with this. Telling someone in agony from a stroke that it's a gift when they do not have that plane of spiritual awareness is brutal. To him or her it's not a grace, it's just suffering and they want out of it.

For example, faced with a life threatening heart problem I felt the fear very deeply and wanted to escape, but I also sat with all that I was experiencing to see what there was in it to learn, what it might be teaching me, how might I live my life more fully, what needed to change? I thus was able to embrace the suffering with many different options. To someone who cannot see or has not been given these options, well, suffering is just hell and we cry out to be free of it. Some religious people can embrace illness with humility because their faith in the loving Presence is strong, others may become more ill with their suffering because they feel that God is punishing them or has abandoned them. A person who is fasting can endure because it is a spiritual practice, a person who is starving sees things very differently.

Forgiveness is the 'seeing' of the whole of ourselves that brings with it reconciliation, integration, wholeness. The pattern is quite simple – the agent is grace, the method is forgiveness, the outcome is atonement – at-one-ment. We'll return to this theme shortly.

The law and the Work
The inner work we have to undertake along the Way may seem frightening. Sometimes

we may avoid this by focussing on the intellectual side - becoming theologically sound and really knowledgeable about matters spiritual and religious. Yet without the deep emotional and psychological work there is an inability to fully connect with others and ourselves. Even worse, without the grounding in the personal work that has produced the requisite humility and healing, we may apply these spiritual learnings in damaging and pathological ways.

Storr [86] offers a fierce critique of false teachers and gurus and illuminates how they can so easily corrupt spiritual knowledge. Once the ego gets a grip on these teachings it can do much harm to the person and to others. Thomas Merton [56] writes, "the most dangerous man in the world" can be the spiritual seeker "who is guided by nobody. He trusts his own visions. He obeys the attractions of an interior voice but will not listen to other men. He identifies the will of God with anything that makes him feel, within his own heart a big, warm, sweet interior glow. The sweeter and warmer the feeling is, the more he is convinced of his own infallibility. And if the sheer force of his own self-confidence communicates itself to other people and gives them the impression that he is really a saint, such a man can wreck a whole city, or a religious order or even a nation: and the world is covered by the scars that have been left in its flesh by visionaries like these".

Healing, holiness and wholeness are closely related words. Holy work, Soul Work, is not just undertaken by immersion in holy books or religious rules in the hope that if we do so diligently, enough of them will rub off on us to cleanse us, produce enlightenment and bring us Home. I have met so many seekers who believe that a pharisaic approach like this to the spiritual search will make everything OK. The Pharisees were an ancient Jewish sect who saw themselves as guardians of religious laws, strict observance of which was the only route to God. They tended to affect a 'holier than thou' attitude, challenged Jesus and ultimately sought his death. Jesus said the law was love - of God (*Allaha* in Aramaic), neighbour and self, from which right behaviour and enlightenment would proceed. Following the rules was less important than the content of a person's heart, for it was and is through the heart that we do good and find our way Home. Jesus' earliest followers were not known as Christians, that term was to come a generation later, but Followers of the Way [Acts 22:4 and 24:14] - of love and compassionate action that was revolutionary for its time and place.

We can find common threads of this Way in almost every faith tradition. Often,

"The exterior waste land is a reflection of the interior waste land."

whenever it arises within a religion that has become ossified and rule bound. the orthodox establishment will do all in its power to eradicate it. Primarily the tension arises between those who believe that faith is one of a personal, mystical relationship with the Absolute and those who see the only right way as following certain rules and doctrines. Once a religion gets hidebound by rules, we can guarantee that somewhere along the line a movement of the Way will arise to shift it or break away. As we explored in the first chapter, this pharisaic approach is rooted in fear (of death).

I got into the rules myself at one stage. If I could only follow them properly, eat the right food, do the right rituals, then I'd get to God and goodness. We can see the unconscious fears that lurk behind such an approach. Of course, doing good does not necessarily mean that we are being good. If our heart is not truly in it, then what emerges is inauthentic and sometimes transparently so. We fool ourselves if we believe we are fooling others; most people can see through the phoniness of our 'chronic niceness' [73]. Our capacity to be and become fully human for ourselves and others is thereby diminished when stuck in such falsehood. All the great spiritual teachers have iconoclasm in common. As the age in which each lived produced straightjacketed faith, they challenged (often at great price) such rigidity. They established certain rules for their followers, but these were inherently paradoxical – rules designed to break rules, rules that at some point must be left behind on the journey and transcended.

This is not to say that there are no 'laws' or 'rules' at work along the Way. Spiritual searching without controls or discipline - without subjection voluntarily to rules designed to hold us while we seek, rather than suppress us - this is not freedom. It is spiritual anarchy, self-indulgence, irresponsibility and arrogance. It can be very difficult to know when rules are there to help or abuse, especially when we are vulnerable in our spiritual immaturity or in crisis. We cannot always rely on our own discernment. That is why the practices advocated in this book, such as the need for Soul Friends or Soul Communities, are essential.

Not all rules are bad. A walk through any city would be chaotic and dangerous without the traffic lights and signs and the Highway Code to keep us safe and guide us on our way. Thus it is with surrender, where we agree to follow certain rules on a spiritual search, such as following those of a community retreat or the teachings of a true master. But in emptying our wills we do not have to empty our heads. We still need to get help in discerning what is right and true, of knowing when a rule is there to help subvert our will into the Beloved or to have power over us so that we can be abused.

We have all kinds of modern psychological terms to understand why people slavishly follow the rules – co-dependency, projection or transference. Somewhere along the line we learned, for example, that we are not good, whole, loved or safe and all wrapped up in deep seated fear of annihilation. The way to overcome this for some is to put the effort into doing good, doing the right thing and bottling up the underlying pain. Bound by these interior ties, reinforced by the suffocations of family and society, it is hard for the prisoner to break free. A kind of religious Brokeback Mountain [87] emerges where conformity to collective norms locks us in an iron cage of repression. In this waste land of the spirit the suffering for those who long to transform can seem endless. The exterior waste land of toxic disconnected relationships with everything - the land, society, other people - is a reflection of the interior waste land where we feel disconnected from our loving source, essence or soul within.

Yet the waste land is not without hope, for in its mud there are seeds of freedom. While it is full of suffering, it is also the place of spiritual awakening, of friendship and loyalty, of joy and creativity, of environmental and social activism. That is its paradox. It may be muddy, but it is a fertile mud. In the darkness the light of awareness is waiting to be re-membered, re-born and schooled into being. What we seek to make us free lies, literally, right under our noses, within the very existence we already have. In the Shvetashvatara Upanishad [88] its location is charmingly specific: "The Self, small as the thumb, dwelling in the heart". The Self is within, waiting to be stirred into life, and it is the soil of the waste land that carries the potential for that awakening.

<u>Cracks in the ceiling: crisis as opportunity</u>
All the great spiritual teachers frequently exhorted their followers with words like, "Awake", "Behold" and "See". What were they asking them to see? The seeing was not so much a change of physical vision, but an interior seeing as we explored in John Macquarrie's work in Part 2. It is a shift of consciousness, a *metanoia*, a trans-

"The exterior waste land is a reflection of the interior waste land."

formation of understanding, an en-lightening to awaken to the nature of reality and to enter a new reality, the very source of peace itself and a new vision of life. Life that is not transitory but eternal. This new life is not elsewhere; the invitation is to awaken to what is already present in the here and now.

What makes the existing vision crack? Why should the scales fall from the eyes so that we at last see clearly and can be re-born into a new way of being? Why should we be set free of the waste land, yet full of compassion for it and willingness to stay in it not least so that others might be stirred to life too? As I suggested in Part 1, for some it is a plunge into the real pain of spiritual crisis while for others it is the steady drip into our consciousness of a new way of seeing, sometimes with sudden lurches in changed awareness where the prospect of Home on the horizon is a tantalising glimpse. A spiritual crisis is a tough place to be. Much of our approach to it in a secular world is to either class it as a mental health problem or ignore it or suggest a holiday. Indeed, many would argue that spiritual work without the crisis is just as tough, but spread more thinly over time!

I recently searched the web and found over a million references to spiritual crisis/ emergence. Numerous organisations and individuals are offering more imaginative approaches than a diagnosis of psychosis. Many of the websites of religious organisations seem more willing to acknowledge its existence – a territory which arguably has always been their own but sometimes lost to dogma and rigidity [3]. When the religions pull back from responding to spiritual crisis and emergence, either by ignoring them or inhibiting that direct experience of the Divine in favour of the rules, new priests colonise the vacant lot such as the still burgeoning army of gurus, therapists and healers of the New Age movement.

However, the religions have a rich tradition of know-how in relation to spiritual support. While psychiatrists like Grof [36] and his colleagues, and organisations such as the Interfaith Seminary in London have very much pioneered the modern response, others have rooted their approach in age old traditions such as theologian Margaret Guenther's [89] concept of 'spiritual midwifery' as the right role of the therapist/ healer/counsellor in relation to the person in crisis or seeking spiritual maturity. To midwife is a different way of working than in conventional roles of medicine and therapy, for the midwife does not see the person as wrong or diseased, rather he or she is there to help a perfectly natural process to occur. The person is not sick, but pregnant with the possibility of transformation. The soul is not sick; it is simply looking to emerge fully into being.

Anyone who has experienced spiritual crisis will know that it is arguably one of the most painful of human experiences. It is a heightened sense of being trapped in the arid landscape of the waste land, yet in becoming more aware of it the pain is exacerbated because no way can be seen out of it. As the amount of energy required to keep things stable increases, we become more and more depleted, exhausted and heartsick with the effort. The greater the exhaustion the closer we get to a state of almost complete mental, physical, social and spiritual collapse. The deepest truth about our Self is seeking to be born out of the tight constraints of our old way of seeing and like all births it can be a painful process. We may project the cause of the pain onto many things – a failing relationship, a difficult job, a fierce illness, a financial worry – but the real cause lies deep in the soul, the essence of our Self seeking freedom and truth. This is not to negate the very real suffering emanating from, say, a failing relationship or sickness, but to suggest that these may be the symptoms of an underlying emergence rather than the cause.

Often the process is an unconscious one as we call to ourselves challenge after challenge that brings us closer to the edge, even though consciously we may think we do not want these things to be happening. I am reminded of a wealthy man 'caught' shoplifting, a closeted gay man publicly outed by risky relationships, a woman in an adulterous relationship exposed by an 'accidental' leak of emails. Thus while we may feel like a victim of circumstance, that may just be a very egoic view. In these circumstances it is as if the heart is saying, "I can't stand this way of being any longer and I'm going to break you to get free."

Although breakings like this may seem terrifying and tragic, it may be that they are only happening because at some level we are ready and able to handle them. What arises for us in life from this deep source is rarely more than we can handle if we are willing to work with it. We have the Work we have because it is a gift of love from the Divine, not a test or punishment. What may be happening is a deep summoning up, from our unconscious, of situations that will provoke us into another way of seeing. Others might see this as grace, the Holy Spirit at work, worming its way into our lives

"The exterior waste land is a reflection of the interior waste land."

so that we may hear the call Home. Often at some point the awareness of our inherent helplessness sinks in. In that place of dread we come to know that we cannot do this alone; that we need help, the help of grace, the Holy Spirit, the divine energy, call it what we will for the soul to complete its journey Home.

The suffering at such times is deep and at every level – physical, psychological, social, spiritual – when old ways of being in the world no longer work and disintegrate. We are like a frightened voyager, pushing out to sea in a storm. The safe harbour has been left (painfully) behind and is lost to sight beyond the horizon, but the new haven is not yet visible. Caught in the middle, there is only the terror of the unknown. Our normal ways of functioning in this state almost grind to a halt; disease (dis-ease) in many forms can occur in each of them the more we resist. A few can become so distressed as the pressure mounts that severe physical or mental illness or even suicide can result. We can fall prey to the views of others who may exploit and abuse us in this vulnerable questing state (and not a few inauthentic gurus and religious leaders have capitalised on this down the years – and still do). The suffering is accentuated because the cause is not clear to us and our usual resources for dealing with it do not seem to work. The vision of how we might be without suffering eludes us, so we can stay stuck in the way we are, while exhausting ourselves trying to deal with the status quo.

Nothing less than a complete transformation in our way of being in the world is called for and, whether we perceive it consciously or whether it is bubbling along in the unconscious, this too can be terrifying. The levels of fear, panic, pain and distress in our lives are often unprecedented. This is spiritual crisis, and whether it becomes emergence or emergency, as we explored earlier, depends on our response and the circumstances in which it is happening.

Some respond by becoming a victim of circumstance - bad things happen and there is little or nothing we can do except give up, fight back or try to maintain the status quo. Struggling to keep going in the face of what seems like an attack can be immensely energy intensive, leading to the collapse known as burnout. Some things can be ruled out as unhelpful. 'Job's comforters' (people telling us constantly that it will be all right, or making endless suggestions for change) just make us feel worse. Irina Tweedie [90], in her classic account of spiritual awakening (punctuated by periods of crisis) in the presence of a Sufi master, draws on a verse from the Sanskrit epic the Ramayana and writes: "There are two ways Thou canst love me; either I should be so perfect that Thou hast to love me, or I will surrender before Thee, and Thou who lovest thy creation, Thou willst love me for myself".

At some point in the midst of spiritual awakening surrender is the only viable option. There is a certain inevitability about it, a sort of primordial interior programming to which we must all at some time (perhaps after many lifetimes, according to some traditions) respond and begin the journey Home. There is also a certain inevitability about the time it takes each of us to pass through and deepen that process. I have a hunch that some-how the soul has a pre-planned timetable of its own which can be neither held back nor accelerated. That we can either go with the flow or fall into forgetting and hold back, in which case the process embodies different levels of spiritual pain. The more we resist, the tougher it feels; the more we surrender into the process the less bumpy the ride. But to surrender is also a great challenge. The ego fights tooth and nail using every strategy in its deception toolbox to retain its power and the status quo. In those 'liberal' cultures, where individualism and the personal spiritual search are in the ascendant, concepts and actions like surrender do not come easy.

Furthermore, some faiths disavow the possibility of interior exploration – keeping the shadow of the unconscious and the tricks of the ego firmly under wraps is preferred, because they are 'evil'. Better to adopt the approach of the Pharisees instead – ignore the internal process and just behave ourselves. Yet, constraints like these cannot hold back the power of the soul within, punching to break through what has held it in place for so long. The ego has served its purpose. It has been in charge long enough, arguably keeping us safe as we have individualised and forged our path in ordinary reality. But now it is time for it to give way, to move from being master to servant, and it rarely does so without a fight and a lot of pain and much risk. The apocalypse (from the Greek *apokalupsis* - meaning to reveal, to uncover) is not about a literal end-time destruction as is sometimes suggested. That is just an egotistic interpretation of time and space and the dualistic battle between good and evil. Rather, the apocalypse happens in every moment of surrender as the ego gives way before the Beloved, every collapse of the consciousness of ego identity into the numinous consciousness of the soul.

Some might be put off from the spiritual search because they do not like the sound

"The exterior waste land is a reflection of the interior waste land."

of this tough work and especially the idea of surrender. However, the search is not about following our bliss, tempting as this is, but more a consciousness of 'Not my will, but Thine'. Yet, paradoxically, in making that surrender we find the bliss. Bliss is not happiness; that is an ego mirror image of something far deeper. Bliss is an experience of the soul, of union with the Divine, of the lover reuniting with the Beloved. In surrender we become saturated in God, in the bliss that is beyond mere happiness. Ruysbroek [91], mediaeval mystic, writes that in the Beloved we are "lost, drowned and liquefied into an unknown darkness". Depending on our point of view, that thought is either joyous or terrifying, perhaps both.

Furthermore, surrender is not a *stasis*, a fixed condition, but a process, forever un-folding and transforming. There is no endpoint, at least not until the soul completes its journey Home into that timeless place where 'then' and 'now' have no rele-vance. Meanwhile there is a need for ongoing and expanding insight, for all kinds of things emerge that can call us back into forgetfulness. Surrender includes a quality of watchfulness for such distractions, a prayerful humility without striving that keeps us relaxed but ready and alert to the signs of those temptations that tug us away from the spiritual life.

In the meantime, if spiritual crisis is experienced, the immediate task is to get out of the situation, perhaps if possible away from the home and the workplace and retreat from the battle - as happens with the people who come into our retreat facilities at the Sacred Space Foundation in Cumbria. Inevitably I am drawing here on the many years of experience at the Foundation and the development of 'what works'. And what works is a formula tried and tested down the ages and found in many spiritual traditions.

Thus, spiritual crisis is not a time to try to make solutions happen – this is a time to come to stillness, to wait and see, to get out of the situation and find the space to allow the solutions that are waiting within to emerge. There are lots of possibil-ities, but getting at least temporarily out of the present environment and creating the space (the sacred space – where there is time for the soul to be heard) for the next steps is a priority. Resting, re-energising and recuperating – looking after our physical wellbeing by eating, exercising and sleeping better are part of the process, coupled with time to reflect on what is going on with us. This problem cannot be solved alone, so disconnection in retreat is not the answer, reconnection is what is called for, so the support of a wise counsellor and Soul Friend who can guide us through the process is essential.

Birthing within us what needs to come forth is arguably unsafe alone (look at the near death turmoil that even great spiritual masters like the Buddha or Jesus or the Prophet went through) – we need a 'spiritual midwife' as suggested earlier, one or more, to accompany us through this phase. As we re-collect what has gone on, we can start a process of re-visioning our lives. Notice again how almost all the verbs in this process are words of repetition – the journey is not so much to new lands, but a remembering of somewhere we already are. Using all kinds of insight and awareness building processes, such as guided meditation, the Enneagram [92] (a form of personality inventory which assists spiritual insight, see chapter 8) and spiritual direction, we can begin to return to that place in ourselves where we feel at Home – recovering a sense of meaning, purpose and connection in life – the very stuff of spirituality.

Thus we learn to live our lives with what has heart and meaning for us with a deeper connection to our spiritual needs. Equally, we may find that the revisioning process enables us to stay in our ordinary lives with greater equanimity, because something in ourselves has changed, some shift of consciousness or awareness that helps us to be with old roles and relationships in new and less hurtful ways. The crisis of spiritual emergency does not mean that everything has to be demolished, rather, and perhaps more likely, we are able to stand more firmly and compassionately in ordinary life because we now see it so differently.

On the other hand this can also be a time of painful letting go. Whether this happens in the intense time of spiritual crisis if we experience it, or through the steady work of attending to our spiritual needs and awakening (gradual emergence rather than critical emergency) we may have to face up to changing some aspects of our lives that no longer nurture our souls. How we let go of or change roles or relationships depends upon our awareness. We can terminate them in anger and bitterness. We can become resigned (a kind of passive disconnection) to them and their underlying inauthenticity. We can work with them to transform them into a new alignment. Or we can let them go as lovingly and consciously as we can.

"The exterior waste land is a reflection of the interior waste land."

The process of refinement helps us to let go as lovingly as possible of old habits, values, roles and relationships that are no longer nurturing and keep us feeling like we are sacrificing ourselves. This is high-risk territory, as we will explore in part 5 when we look further at discernment, which, without careful support, can be a painful process for others as relationships or jobs or other interests are seen to be no longer part of our way Home. If we are not careful and our egos get a grip on this, we can find ourselves riding roughshod over others in our driven, spiritual search. There is a delicate balance here to know what is right to let go and what we must keep.

The awakening of the spirit within and the journey Home can be and is a profoundly joyous and blissful experience, but as I have suggested it is also a high-wire path as the Work refines us ever more, harmonising our will with the Will. Like all journeys it needs careful planning perhaps taking into account that it will last years and cannot be hurried. Recognising this, the religious traditions down the years have evolved tried and tested means of helping this birthing process. For this reason alone we need to be wary of rejecting religions, for they have often had millennia of experience to find out what works and what does not.

Soul Care: The four pillars of wisdom
Religions have often failed seekers in so many ways, tending to be containers of orthodoxy rather than nurturing us like a womb, developing and setting us free. Religions can help us as Soul Communities with the business of seeking meaning in the early stages of self-discovery of our place in the cosmos. There's an inclination in some faiths to remain stuck in this phase rather than encouraging the seeker to escape early notions of self; to die to the self and live instead in the Self (see page 344). However, it's important to be cautious about dismissing religious traditions because of this stuckness or shadow sides. Later I will explore the value or otherwise of engaging with a religious tradition in our searching. For the moment we can draw attention to the rich experience that the long histories of religions can bring to our search. Four key Soul Care themes can be identified that need to be in place, which have been commonly used in spiritual 'midwifery' down the ages:

1. Soul Friends – in the Celtic Christian tradition this is the *anam cara*. This is not an

easy journey alone and what is needed is the support of one or more wise spiritual directors, counsellors or mentors to whom we can turn for guidance. These teachers, mentors or guides are people who have walked the path before us and know how to support us in times of need. I have met a few in my life, who know how to challenge and guide lovingly. Such guides exhibit a kind of fierce love, holding us with deep compassion and understanding, yet not letting us get away with our illusions and delusions. Through shared spiritual practice and loving, but challenging, dialogue we are encouraged toward spiritual maturity. In individualist cultures one of the spiritual challenges is overcoming the resistance to surrendering to the authority of the Soul Friend [93,94] (or perhaps more accurately to the authority of the Beloved whom the Soul Friend serves) but without him or her we risk many dangers, not least psychosis, ego inflation or a messianic complex if our interior impressions go unchecked and unchallenged. The New Age tendency to say OK to everything, to allow us to avoid surrender into the Divine and make Gods of ourselves instead is not the approach of the true Soul Friend, who may lovingly direct us quite firmly when he or she sees we are going astray or becoming aggrandised by our experiences. Our Soul Friend knows we are going astray for he or she has long since acquired map and compass of the soul's landscape. This wisdom (because they have also done the personal and emotional work themselves, freeing them from the risk of corrupting the work with ego agendas for power) is rooted in the humility of the true servant.

2. Soul Communities – groups of people with whom we feel at home and who lovingly nourish our ongoing spiritual awakening. It might be a fellow group of meditators, sangha, mosque, temple or church group - there are numerous possibilities. It might be a permanent community, such as belonging to a religious organisation a temporary community, such as a course or retreat where we share with and relate to others for a while. The Soul Community adds to the checks and balances that can keep us safe in the sometimes disorientating, not to say almost crazy time when one way of seeing is replaced by another. Such a paradigm shift can be full of joy but can also be cataclysmic. We can contrast the spiritual awakening that occurs in a spiritual community such as a monastery, convent or modern day, well-run retreat centre, to that which takes place in unbridled freedom – such as unsupported weekend courses without follow-up or in centres of New Age teaching where the attention to creating even temporary 'holding' communities is limited or non-exis-

"The exterior waste land is a reflection of the interior waste land."

tent. The holding quality of the healthy Soul Community enables us to pass through the transformation and the maturation work with greater likelihood of coherence, safety, integration and wholeness, rather than either repressing or leaving us to wander the streets or return home frightened or ego-inflated, disorientated, perplexed and alone.

3. Soul Foods – the inspiration of scripture, poetry, music, art, nature and so on that refresh, renew and revitalise us. And, literally, good food that nourishes our body e.g. many organisations offering spiritual support stress the need for a healthy diet and lifestyle free of toxins. It's a truism that as we become more spiritually refined, we become less tolerant towards unhealthy things be it foods, drugs, situations or people. Things that 'feed' us in every sense of the word can be included here, such as being in environments of peace and beauty, with people who are loving and nurturing, listening to words and music that have heart and meaning for us, having access to complementary therapies and healing approaches such as the laying on of hands and the deep relaxation that comes from bodywork such as massage.

4. Soul Works - developing spiritual practices which keep us on track and take care of us and foster deepening insight – meditation, prayer, yoga, retreat time, sacred dance, tai chi, exploring our Enneagram, labyrinth walking – there is an enormous range of possibilities. Soul Works are the practices alone or in groups with our Soul Communities, that help to keep us centred and at home in ourselves while also moving us ever deeper into awareness of Truth and our true Self on the journey Home.

These four elements together support our work of spiritual exploration along the Way. They provide us with the structure for the next four parts of this book and we will explore each of them in detail to see what we can expect.

Without them, insights can leave us buffeted by the interior storm, sometimes even bringing great personal danger to others and ourselves. People have been known *in extremis* to commit suicide or desert their loved ones or carry out terrible acts upon others. For example, a flurry of newspaper reports in the UK recently discussed several individuals who had committed murders because "God told me to". The line between madness and mysticism is a fine one. If we receive revelations in the midst of our spiritual awakening it can be hugely difficult to sort the wheat from the chaff unless our Soul Care principles are in place.

When we are young (spiritually) we may not like it, but there can be a lot of sense in someone who checks that you have changed your underwear and washed behind your ears! Even without the extremes of spiritual crisis, these four Soul Care principles are essential to a healthy and maturing spirituality; they help to prepare the ground so that the seeds of the soul can flourish, the Will of the Divine work fully in us. Our community, our practices, our directors and our sources of nourishment are there to encourage and guide us when we feel lost or discouraged, when we encounter challenging or arid times. They are there to share in the joy and celebration too. If you have not already done so, it might be worth taking stock right now and answering the questions:

In my spiritual quest who is my wise and trusted Soul Friend to guide me safely on the Way?
Where is my Soul Community that nurtures my spirit and both challenges and encourages me?
What are the spiritual practices, my Soul Works, to which I am committed?
What Soul Foods do I have in my life that nurture, challenge, encourage and inspire my search?

We need to take care of ourselves during the alchemical process of our awakening and the transformation of who we think we are into who we truly are. With Soul Care in place the intense spiritual pain of spiritual crisis diminishes, or the struggle of the steady plod up the mountain can be less wearisome, but does it ever go away? If the soul is of the infinite, then there are infinite possibilities for its expansion, its awakening. To the cry "Where is there an end to it?" Eliot's [1] response was unequivocal, "There is no end, but addition."

Often, underpinned by fear, we seek to set goals for spiritual work, seeking that end point when we will be 'there'. We are not what we achieve. Our goals will not make us happy, only our being. All the hurts, challenges and obstructions are just the stuff emerging from our unconscious that gets in the way of our move into being and provide the grist to the mill for enlightenment. There are no goals, more a sense of trans-

"The exterior waste land is a reflection of the interior waste land."

formed attention and a refinement of our attunement to the world, through and for Love. There is no 'there'.

A Sufi wisdom story [74] suggests that in spiritual awakening we may seek to set goals of avoiding suffering or seeking the blissful experience, but both are ego distortions. *Isa ibn Maryam* (Jesus, son of Mary) saw some people sitting miserably on a wall by the roadside. "What's the matter?" He asked. "We have ended up like this because we have been afraid of hell," they replied. Isa blessed them and went on his way and came across another group, also wailing and in pain. "What's the matter?" He asked. "We desired paradise and it has made us like this," they answered. He blessed them as well, continued his walk and came across a third group. They looked indeed like people who had suffered much and yet their faces seemed to shine with joy. "How is it that you are like this?" He asked again. "The Spirit of Truth," they answered, "and this has made us let go of lesser goals of seeking bliss and avoiding pain." Isa blessed them too, for they were the ones who thus attained heaven and came to be in the Presence of God.

When the seeker finds the "Spirit of Truth" there is a passing beyond pain. It is not that pain does not exist, rather that our consciousness around it and towards it has been transformed. It is not detachment, but non-attachment, an age-old truth found in all the great faiths, that to be free of desire, even desire for bliss or escape from suffering is freedom in Truth: "Without desire, we can plumb its depths; with desire, we can only see its externals."[95]

There are certain eternal elements to this state of consciousness, this level of healing, and in my experience it is always the same – the process is one of forgiveness, the agent is grace and the outcome atonement. Through the way of forgiveness we come to accept and integrate all the parts of our being – our history, our personhood. This process is not sustained by the will of the ego, in fact the ego has no place in it at all except to get out of the way, to have its power broken. It is fed and watered by grace in surrender to the Absolute however we experience this, the power that is of an indefinable, immeasurable source – it is spirit, energy, consciousness, call it what we will. It has many names in all belief systems, but it is the same agent of transformation that moves once our own will gets or is pushed out of the way. That movement is towards union, wholeness (holiness), healing – the atonement – the at-one-ment, from which place of consciousness we may see Truth and the perfection of the path we have taken towards it. Towards Home.

"The exterior waste land is a reflection of the interior waste land."

It is easy to know one.
It is easy to know two.
But to understand that one and one are two,
we have to learn the and.
Connection into disconnection,
the breaking of the empty vessel,
the holes in the net,
the vacant room,
the blank page,
the incalculable value of the space contained.
In our hollowness is our fulfilling.
In our emptiness is our purpose.
Hold my hand and I yours,
let these roses cover the flesh
and the fleshless,
for what you see is not who I am,
what you see is not who I am.
As we reach out for the Beloved
we fall through the door
barring one reality from the next.
A door when pressed dissolving
in the resolution of my hand.
From the tea shop of memory
to the wine bar of action,
berobed in splendour,
beyond cloth or stitch.
Satiated in optimism
and the ground of our action,
where doing and being slip into
unity
along the trajectory of
dissolution, illumination, integration,
into the peace
of service.

Part 5

"World crises multiply and everybody deplores the shortage, or even the total lack, of 'wise' men and women, unselfish leaders, trustworthy counsellors etc. It is hardly rational to expect such high qualities from people who have never done any inner work and who would not even understand what is meant by the words." [96]

Soul Friends: "God heals; I make the tea"

<u>Of Gods and gurus and those alongside</u>
He'd been in retreat for a week and we'd worked together for many hours each day. His cancer diagnosis had thrown his whole life into uncertainty, and his response was to return to a search he had abandoned as a teenager. It wasn't that in his youth he had ignored questions about the meaning of life, it was just that the answers he got from his church at that time did not fit with life as he was living it. Anyway it was the 60s and there were the Beatles and the Stones to enjoy, free love to pursue, drugs to play with. Thus it came to pass that in his middle fifties facing death he was looking for hope, looking for God at last.

It was a humbling experience being in this man's presence as he groped his way toward something that he knew must be there. To watch him pass beyond thought and word and simply be, drowning himself in the Self. We didn't talk in much detail about what he saw or heard or felt, just exchanged knowing looks, understanding looks. No more was necessary in those shared moments of knowing; the kind of knowing that indeed requires no words or explanation. Through the oceans of tears he wept for himself, for his family and for the world he began to see clearly that which he sought, not far off but right under his nose. The tears of pain turned into tears of joy; water turned into wine.

The spiritual search is full of paradox. In going deep into ourselves we also are turned out of ourselves into the ecstasy – *ex-stasis*, out of the static or usual perception of self – into new possibilities. Under the guidance of a spiritual director that process can be passed through safely and, in a culture where feelings are sometimes held in suspicion, the space is created for those feelings to be expressed. In

"This is what happens when soul talks to soul."

ex-pressing, literally pressing or pushing out, we have the opportunity to see some-thing from a different perspective, to find a new way of seeing, especially if there is someone around with the wisdom to help us do so and translate this into action.

When he left he said, "I don't know how you can do this day in and day out. How do you cope with all these people crying all over your floor all the time, all that anger and bitterness that comes out." I suppose I could have come out with all those off-pat counsellor clichés – about having good supervision, or taking care of myself, or knowing my limits and all that kind of stuff. But the only thing that popped out of my mouth was, "It's easy, I'm not in charge".

One of the ways the soul is nourished is in the relationship between the person and their spiritual guide. The spiritual director (often used synonymously nowadays with the term spiritual counsellor or accompanier) is found in all belief systems. We see this bond between teacher and student in the 18-year apprenticeship of the novice druid to his/her master, in the relationship with the *murshid* (one who guides aright) in Sufism, the Socratic *iatros tes psuches* (soul healer), the *staretz* of the Russian Orthodox church, the 12 years of training of the ascetic with the Hindu *guru* or *baba*, the roles of sheiks, rabbis and priests – in many forms the essential elements of the Soul Friend, the Celtic *anam cara*, are found. These various names for the Soul Friend are used here in the sense of the wise spiritual guide, usually someone who is more spiritually mature than ourselves and with whom there is a clear direc-tor-directee relationship. I differentiate this from the use of *anam cara*, companion or accompanier in the general sense of friends met along the Way with whom we mutually share our experience in order to learn. We can find many *anam cara* in this sense, not least in our Soul Communities (Part 6), where loving and supportive dialogue helps us along the Way.

The concept of the guru needs a little explanation here. While there is a quality of spiritual direction in the relationship with the guru, strictly speaking the guru is rather more. Caplan's [93] extensive survey challenges much of the New Age and maybe not so New Age notion that 'we can do it on our own'. Everyone needs trusted teachers and guides along the Way. I have been blessed with many and some have been with me from the very beginning. Ram Dass has been a consistent teacher down the long years since I went through what might be called an 'awakening', but so too has Jeannie my closest soul companion. Teachers can come to us in many forms – persons, books, art and nature. The world is infused with them if we pay attention. Teacher and guru are often used interchangeably, though there are some subtle and yet significant differences. The teacher points the Way. The guru *is* the Way. Thus the guru is a Soul Friend, but a Soul Friend is not necessarily a guru.

The guru is a much-debased concept in our culture (we have business gurus, medical gurus, political gurus and so forth – to imply extensive expertise and wisdom in something), but a real guru is infinitely wiser. Arguably we all need one, that is, a manifestation of the Divine free of ego. Some believe that such persons walk the earth from time to time, although false gurus seem to abound [86] who can exploit us by drawing upon our insecurities and our projections upon them. After all, "The attractions of being a trickster guru are many" – lots of opportunities present themselves for power, money, sex and avoiding the ego self [97].

Ram Dass has his guru, Maharaji (Neem Karoli Baba) whom he experienced as the embodiment of the Beloved. I almost wrote 'had' his guru, for Maharaji left his body in 1973, but to Ram Dass he is still very much alive, the relationship and guidance has continued beyond Maharaji's physical death. I once said to Ram Dass, "I envy you, you've had a guru whom you have met in this life and with whom you still feel connected. I've never really had a guru, despite thinking I might have found him or her from time to time, but no, they fell short". To my surprise, he exclaimed, "Of course you have!" "Who?" was my puzzled response. "It's Jesus," he said.

The guru does not have to be physically embodied, and the truth of Ram Dass' words hit me like a thunderbolt. How could I have missed something so blindingly obvious? How could I have allowed all the fog of my religious doubts and denials get in the way of the relationship with the being that is/was Jesus and whom I had known since childhood? Who despite all my wanderings down the years was deeply embedded in my culture and my psyche. Who in the deep plunge into mysticism was invariably there staring back at me offering loving guidance every step of the way. I recognise that such a story could be the stuff of delusion, but please bear with me, I will explain more of this shortly.

My youthful struggle with faith in the Methodist Church required me at the time to

"This is what happens when soul talks to soul."

believe (literally) things that were not believable, from the creation story in Genesis to virgin births. Although much of modern biblical scholarship has defused the rigidity of thought in Christianity and religion generally (but not everywhere), what struck me decades later was the need to move beyond faith as believing *about* to believing *in*; not to allow those 'believing about' [98] blockages to get in the way of the relationship.

The Christian cross is rich with symbolism, particularly the cross that has come to be associated with Iona, the cross with a circle. The horizontal beam can be seen as symbolic of the transcendent, transpersonal, unmanifest, unknowable Divinity; indefinable, beyond words, reaching out boundlessly inside and outside of space and time. The vertical beam is the direct line of communication from above to below, the immanent Beloved, personal, knowable; the one in and with whom we can have a relationship, closer to us than our own breath, knowing us better then we know ourselves. The circle binds and holds both in harmony; and at the centre is the point of intersection where all duality is lost and all possibility is contained. The possibility of both transcendence and immanence is the foundation of the relationship with the authentic guru. The relationship we have with the Soul Friend with whom we meet in person from time to time is quite different, as we shall see.

Meanwhile, I suspect we all have a guru whether recognised or not, but it is not for me to prescribe one to others, and I even hesitate to offer my story; proselytising is absolutely not a role of this book or indeed part of my role in life at all. I offer this account simply as an example of what the guru is and as encouragement to explore whether such a being, embodied or not, is relevant and available to us. Maybe when we come down to it the guru is the same thing or being throughout the ages just wearing a different mask.

In this age of individual expression and aversion to authority, the authentic spiritual path invariably requires conscious engagement with the wiser being. This relationship calls for discipleship, discipline and discernment to enable us to sniff out the false guru or Soul Friend. The unresolved in their psyches can emerge in destructive ways. Such was Jim Jones who led more than 900 of his followers to mass suicide in Guyana in 1978. The spiritual search down the millennia is littered with the bodies of false teachers and their followers, in all faiths and none. Authentic Soul Friends are free of the power of the ego's agenda and live and move to help others find their way Home, not to secure power, money or god-like status for themselves.

Perhaps ultimately we may discover the inner guru on our way to individuation as Jung [99] suggests. This seems not to require the extinction of the guru–student relationship, rather that maturation of the latter so that the two become one. It is in the relationship that this is forged as we move from attraction to the worldly "spirit of the times", as Jung phrased it, to reunion with the "spirit of the depths". Yet this guru, this "spirit", does not demand that we become like him or her, rather that we become like our true selves (and then paradoxically by becoming our true selves we become like the guru). I cannot become Christ-like, if that is my desire as a model for the perfect being, by trying to be him. He was a one-off, as we all are. Rather our task along the Way is to discover and fully manifest our true selves, then paradox-ically we become Christ-like by being the unique being that we were born to be. The guru/teacher helps us to see that, for as Jung describes it in the Red Book, "The knowledge in the heart is in no book and is not found in the mouth of any teacher, but grows out of you like green seed from the dark earth."

The authentic Soul Friend for most of us is a wise person who lives and speaks truth, who educates us, but in the true sense of education (from the Latin, *e duco*, to lead out). He or she does not place words in our hearts and minds, rather by being a truth seeker helps us to recognise, re-cognise, that truth which resonates and already ex-ists within. My relationship with my guru and the many teachers in my life, such as Ram Dass and Jeannie, have been like that; always loving, even if sometimes very fiercely so, to draw out from myself that which was already there rather than enforce some image of their truth or themselves upon me. Such Soul Friends do not de-mand we surrender our authority to them, rather they coach us into surrender into the authority of the Beloved they serve and through that to our own inner authority – which turns out to be the same thing!

The *anam cara* model as Soul Friend is not one of hierarchy in the sense of one per-son having control over another, but in the true sense of the word from the Greek *hierarchos* – 'holy order'. Hierarchy tends to have negative connotations because our early experience of it may be associated with the abuse of power in the hands of ego driven persons. The authority of the Soul Friend is sapiential, i.e. rooted in their

"This is what happens when soul talks to soul."

sacred wisdom, rather than authority based on position. The former is 'power under' as servant, the latter is 'power over' as master. The Soul Friend is one who comes alongside the seeker in solidarity with their searching, but in terms of wisdom and experience is 'more' than the seeker. Both are taking a journey, both are vulnerable, but the Soul Friend draws upon their longer and richer experience, their glimpses of the route on which both are engaged. With this Soul Friend we find ourselves mirrored back so that we can learn. In this mirror, as John Philip Newell [100] writes, "If we look with God's eyes, nothing on earth is ugly".

Before this Soul Friend we find the one to whom one's inner self can safely be opened hiding nothing. With the Soul Friend we feel safe because we are not judged, yet we are loved. But this is not a fluffy feel-good-all-the-time love, for it is sometimes also terrible and raw. It forces us to confront our demons, to do the work on our shadow, to live authentically and face up to things in ourselves and in our lives that are false to fact. Sometimes we cling to our demon, as Jung [99] again reminds us, because without realising it we have made a god of it. We may not like our particular form of suffering or whatever shadow it is we possess, but it is ours and we sometimes grasp it for fear of having nothing, no real God, to replace it. To abandon it would be to abandon our god and risk the fall into the abyss of isolation, abandonment and despair; an abyss that, paradoxically, invites us through it to discover the real Beloved who has been reaching out to us all along. The job of the Soul Friend is to hold us through this time as we let go of our false gods.

The Soul Friend comes alongside us in what might otherwise be an overwhelmingly frightening task - to name our powerful inner demons that distort the fullness of our lives. Fear, anger, shame, self-hatred, worthlessness – these and other powerful feelings and the things we do to avoid them such as feeding the 'hungry ghosts', as we explored in Part 2, lurk in our shadows. Exposing them to the light of awareness, naming them, is an important step in getting free of them. This work needs loving support, wisdom and accompaniment. Relationships, work, hopes, expectations, values, self-perceptions, ways of thinking and doing - all these and more are thrown into question, seared by the fire of love that "intolerable shirt of flame" [1] until we are burnished of anything that is false to truth.

Self actualising and expanding our awareness can be traumatic as we wake up. A kind of shock wave of spiritual emergence can follow when we see the limitations of the life we were living with all its delusions and the enormity of the new vision unfolding before us. Awakening can bring us face to face with the horrors in ourselves and the world that we have denied. We can cross the bridge into a new reality of love and freedom from fear. The crossing, however, is assisted and less scary and disorientating when the Soul Friend and our Soul Community are there to hold and accompany us so that we do not fall into despair or try and retreat.

Sometimes this means the role of the Soul Friend is to direct, to tell us, the 'directee', what to do! Horror of horrors in this individualist, autonomous culture where we are all leaders and in control now! Spiritual direction by the Soul Friend differs because the intention is different in this 'holy order'. The Soul Friend's sapiential authority is driven by compassion. Free of the need for ego power, their authority fructifies in service through knowing deeply their role and themselves in the exercise of 'power under'.

I recall being taken aback in my first meeting with Ram Dass when he quite clearly instructed me to do three things. He was very firm in this. What matters of course is not being instructed but the consciousness with which it is done. In this case, even though I resisted, it was clearly done to jerk me into awareness that I was in danger and needed to take care of myself. There was no sense from him that he wanted me to do something for him, rather he wanted me to do something *for myself*. That's the big difference. By the use of his authority, Ram Dass was teaching me about my own - a quality I have met in many Soul Friends along the way. "One has to be a light to oneself; the light is the law"…"You cannot be a light to yourself if you are in the dark shadows of authority, of dogma, of conclusion," wrote Krishnamurti [101]. Remember too that all authentic teachers tell us *we* are that light and wish to liberate us with that truth. They do not require us to serve only their light.

Midwifing the soul
Some spiritual directors work almost full time as such, accompanying and counselling many seekers along the Way. For others it is a part of a wider role, such as that of the parish priest. Personally, I prefer the term director, even though the concept of 'direction' is often unwelcome in our Western individualised culture. I look at it this way - if you get lost on the way home and you stop and ask for help, do you ex-

"This is what happens when soul talks to soul."

pect to be counselled or directed? At the same time direction is not just a one way process from 'higher' to 'lower', there is mutual exchange at work in which both can deepen their capacity to relate, to know each other and themselves as human beings, to know the Divine more. I have never, in all the countless sessions of spiritual direction I have offered, left the session not feeling somehow closer to and known more deeply the other, myself and the Beloved.

A friend and fellow interfaith minister, Sam Wernham, writes [102] how she came to the work with many questions about it. "Really it was a question about myself – am I good enough? Or do I know enough? Or who am I?" What she came to understand was that "the ground of being able to spiritually counsel another is deeply rooted in God, in knowing that who I am fundamentally is made by God and beloved of God. When I know this is true for me, I can hold this is deepest truth for another and within this truth we are one." She goes on to write, "I experience spiritual counselling as a journey, a relationship between two equal souls who are learning together that they really are deeply connected to and loved by their One Source. When I sit with another person in this way I experience a kind of deep stillness, a loving presence that seems to flow through me from the Source. As God looks through my eyes, feels through my heart, listens through my ears and speaks through my voice, that person before me is the most precious thing. Whatever is concerning them matters and holds the seeds of freedom. Being deeply attentive to whatever is unfolding in someone allows healing to happen."

My friend's summary encapsulates the essential qualities that we can expect of the spiritual director - that sense of not being 'in charge', of waiting upon God's guidance, of offering hospitality, mutuality and friendship, holding the safe sacred space that allows grace, the Holy Spirit, the Divine energy to be manifest. To be so present with someone, the spiritual director must have done much healing and emotional work upon him or herself. Otherwise the helper who is not healed risks bringing all manner of constricting, even dangerous, personal shadows into the relationship. One of the hallmarks to look for in the Soul Friend is that they have done this work, that they are themselves emotionally well-rounded human beings and have been brought to a place of humble service free of ego agendas such as the need for power, relevance or admiration.

The depth of humility that arises from this work allows us to come to know that we can be in control of very little, for as TS Eliot [1] put it, "humility is endless" and is of profound service to others. As my friend concludes "Does it really matter whether I feel God or not? Does it really matter what I know? I simply hold the space. God heals. I make the tea." The relationship with the spiritual director is essentially a Divine infused one with the intention of allowing the inbreaking of the grace/spirit of the Beloved into the relationship. It is the seeking of the *parousia*, the bursting of the 'kingdom', heaven, Ultimate Reality, *nirvana* (lit. 'blowing out') into consciousness, into ordinary reality, the transformation of the way of seeing and being. Sacred unity bursts in because we have invited it, (even though sometimes we think we did not do the inviting!)

This sense of effortless effort is reinforced in Guenther's [89] remarkable study of spiritual direction. Likening it to midwifery (which is essentially a natural process of aiding the birthing of something, which already exists, into the world.) she writes, "When in doubt, I always assume that God is at work, that is, the person is pregnant." She writes further of the relationship between counsellor and counselled as fundamentally hierarchical, "not because the director is somehow "better" or "holier" than the directee, but because, in this covenanted relationship, the director has agreed to put himself aside so that his total attention can be focussed on the person sitting in the other chair" yet it is "a hierarchy which is a gentle and perhaps transitory one."

If there is a hierarchy at all it is a hierarchy, a *hierarchos*, of wisdom as I have suggested; of expanded consciousness. However, in the transmission of that wisdom we cannot expect the spiritual director to share everything with us at once. We mature spiritually at different paces [103] moving along a trajectory from what some see firstly as a 'conformist' stage. This is characterised by orientation towards results, black and white thinking and dependence on a group or person or thing to sort it all out for us and give us the right answers. Later we may move to a 'conscientious' phase where we are more willing to see exceptions to rules and able to embrace individual traits and roles; there is more commitment to and dependence on ourselves. Thirdly there is the 'interindividual' phase. Here there is greater toleration of self, others, paradox, mystery and the embracing of spiritual development as a way of life rather than a fixed goal.

"This is what happens when soul talks to soul."

We need to be wary of applying psychological models to spiritual processes, but these concepts do help us to understand that our degree of maturity will affect the kind of Soul Care approaches that will work for us and those that will not, which kinds of books we are ready to read and which will go over our heads, which kind of spiritual practices will 'work' and those that will simply confuse or alienate. The spiritual director is able to help us discern what it is best for us. Jesus was not being cruel when he spoke of not throwing pearls before swine [Matt. 7:6]; he was stating a spiritual truth about not giving things away to people when they are not ready to receive them and honour their value. Our spiritual director encourages development in us that enables a free flowing transmission of wisdom, sometimes teasing or pressing us, lovingly, along the Way to draw us into deeper maturity. S/he makes sure that we are not so confused that we cannot mature, but challenged enough so that we are encouraged to press on. It is a fine balancing act, hence the need for the effective and wise Soul Friend.

Spiritual direction thus takes an unusual approach, some would argue unique, towards inner enquiry. By offering a loving, safe haven in which to find meaning, inner peace and wisdom it provides the space, the sacred space, for truth to be revealed and integrated. Some spiritual directors are affiliated to particular religions, others non-denominational, but the best stay open to all comers and feel no need to fix the 'directee' into their tradition. To do so, the Soul Friend incorporates deep listening, acceptance and spiritual practices (such as meditation, guided visualisations and prayer) within the framework of each person's beliefs. Thus spiritual direction can help people of any faith or none, to access the clarity needed to resolve inner conflicts and lead a joyous, meaningful life.

This accompaniment can take many forms, sometimes in fixed appointments sitting in a room together, sometimes walking alongside, sometimes in groups, sometimes in what might at first hand seem brief and casual conversation yet, if we can spot it, some pearl of great price has been dropped into our consciousness that we may not appreciate until much later. I have a particular room at home, the Sanctuary, specifically set aside to meet people. It is free of interruptions and there is attention to beauty, warmth, smell and lighting conducive to insight and reflection. It is a safe sacred space held with the intention of encouraging freedom to speak and be heard. Sometimes we just sit together in conversation to see what comes up (spiritual direction is not about just turning up when there is a 'problem', but part of an ongoing, perhaps lifelong, encounter to explore the spiritual depths). At other times we may walk side by side in the hills or sit in the garden. Sometimes there will be rituals, prayers, visualisations and guided meditations, at other times long silences while we wait to see what the spirit is saying to us. All this and more is part of a rich flow of senses and perception that permits a safe environment and relationship to foster awakening.

Spiritual direction is not intended as a medium for instruction about the rules of faith or only one interpretation of the holy books. It is a companionship of mutual exploration and respect in the search for truth. Some hostility and misunderstanding has emerged around spiritual direction as it can sometimes be reduced to enforcing and reiterating dogma and doctrines rather than personal awakening. I recall one man, an Anglican priest, who came into retreat suffering from burnout. The Christian retreat centre to which his archdeacon had sent him decided the problem was demonic possession. A young woman had made a serious mistake in the workplace and faced the sack, but was told by her imam that it was God's way of punishing her for refusing an arranged marriage. In both of these examples spiritual direction had taken the form of one person or group imposing their version of truth on another. This kind of approach is not spiritual direction or soul friendship, it's judgmentalism rooted in fear and ignorance. It is what happens when directors bring their unresolved ego work into the relationship and are unable to get themselves out of the way to be fully present for the directee.

For most people, spiritual direction is specifically concerned with the Beloved, a Source, an Absolute. God is central to the relationship however envisaged. There is an explicit understanding of the truth of this Presence and a willingness to thus engage towards transformation – which includes knowing that we are loved deeply as we are, turning away from the blasphemy in the ego that insists otherwise, and coming to rest in the impact of loving ourselves as the Beloved loves us. The spiritual director mirrors the Beloved back to us, for he/she does not see us as 'wrong', but whole/holy and searching to express that wholeness.

Spiritual direction with a Soul Friend is also revolutionary. The intention of spiritual enquiry and the work with the Soul Friend is not to produce a state of spiritual

"This is what happens when soul talks to soul."

passivity and acceptance of the status quo in our lives. Sometimes counselling and psychotherapy may risk settling for rearranging psychological material, enabling people to resolve their conflicts and problems with the world and learn to live in it as it is. They may seek that which is 'wrong' or 'broken' about the person. The application of psychiatric methods along with societal expectations can lead to efforts to shut down or reverse spiritual emergence (especially if it manifests as a crisis) and restore someone to 'normal'. This can be far more damaging than the crisis itself, for there is no going back. The old life as lived cannot be restored except at the expense of great inner pain and repression.

Spiritual direction offers the reverse of rearrangement or repression. It seeks to hold and guide the person through this process of awakening and rebirthing into new life. It does not encourage passivity and acceptance of the way things are either for the individual or the wider world. "Spiritual direction is concerned with healing and reconciliation, not with adaptation to current values, but with the transformation of consciousness"[94]. In so doing, spiritual direction is not an instrument of the status quo (as some argue that religion and spirituality are) rather it is an instrument of change. For the transformation of consciousness brings a transformation in our way of being and action in the world. The fate of the soul and the fate of the world are intimately bound together.

Soul Friends and psychology
A key feature of the work of the director is to help us find truth through testing and discernment, for the path to spiritual awakening is littered with illusions and delusions. Stafford Whiteaker [104] writes, "A spiritual director or guide is someone who helps you in your spiritual journey by being a good listener and soul companion, and by making suggestions for meditating, reading, study or prayer. Such directors and guides are often religious men or women, clergy or lay people who have had the special training and experience in helping people with spiritual matters. The important thing is that the person helps us with discernment and is someone with whom we can feel very comfortable and to whom we are able to entrust our confidences." Finding that person with whom we feel comfortable is not always easy, although perhaps the cliché that 'when the student is ready, the teacher turns up' may have a ring of truth about it. Meanwhile many religious organisations, websites, counselling journals and retreat guides are among the sources of information. The

search for the right director is itself a rich opportunity for spiritual learning.

The spiritual director can hold a safe and loving space where we can explore our spirituality and all that has meaning and purpose for us in life. Nowadays, spiritual direction has the benefits of the discoveries of psychology to draw upon and often a Soul Friend will explore our psychology as much as our spirituality. They are good at helping us see through and get past the various places in ourselves where we get stuck. Getting ego inflated, failing to see the unconscious at work, getting caught up in projections or transference, occasions of feeling disconnected from Source, the tendency to turn interest in the Self into self-interest – these and other quagmires are familiar territory to the wisdom of the Soul Friend.

In the daily work of spiritual direction, it is noticeable how many people have psychological blockages that create spiritual blockages. Mike was an experienced meditator who came along because of difficulties in his marriage. His wife was following her Roman Catholic tradition and they had been getting into serious arguments about the existence or otherwise of 'God'. We spent some time, playfully, applying the word 'exist' to God (an idea explored in the first part of this book). This got us into an interesting debate in which he became more and more angry about the 'God' word. When we explored this it was clear that his whole image of 'God' was negative.

He claimed to be an atheist, which was odd because he had very definite views about what 'God' was like. Words like 'bad tempered', 'murderous', 'unjust', 'domineering', 'inconsistent' and so forth fell from his lips. As our exploration unfolded it emerged that he had been brought up in a very hellfire protestant sect and was taught that unless he believed certain things and lived a certain way he was going to hell. He was neither able to believe nor live those things so abandoned his church in adulthood. It also emerged when we talked about his parenting, that his father in particular had been remote, domineering, punishing and shaming with him. Much the same qualities he applied to 'God' in fact.

Mike gives us an example of a common phenomenon, our tendency to project onto the Beloved the early experiences of authority figures in our lives, such as parents or organisations. It is very common to find the main obstruction to a relationship with

"This is what happens when soul talks to soul."

the Divine is a distorted concept of God, exacerbated in the modern world from two broadsides, the domination of the secular agenda and the dreadful face of God conjured up by acts done in the name of God. It is almost impossible to turn on the TV or radio or pick up a newspaper without someone or some group somewhere unleashing murder and mayhem and claiming to be doing so in the name of God.

Mike spent a lot of time revisiting his relationship with his parents and learning about forgiveness, but he also spent a lot of time, in visualisation, prayer and meditation revisiting his beliefs about the Divine, getting past the images he was stuck with, and discovering a source of boundless love that opened his heart and brought him to tears. The image of 'God the monster', as he called it, turned out to be a false God. Psychology and spirituality here spiralled around each other, taking him to new levels of understanding. Thus his journey to the Beloved began by finding out that "whatever we think God is, God is not"[105]. At some level, the Divine Being is beyond definition, neither this nor that - *neti neti*, in Hindu thought.

Participants in a workshop I was recently facilitating got into saying what they thought God is. God is "good", "knows the future", "His (sic) kingdom is not of this world". There is a strong tendency in us to reify God, because the alternative of the mystical and contemplative Way with its disinclination to towards definitions and concepts can be difficult to grasp (until we experience it). All these words carry the weight of ideas with which many of us are so familiar, rooted in theologies, stories from childhood and our own deductions. The trouble is they risk locking the Divine into our egoic, judgemental way of seeing things. God is not 'good' for God is beyond concepts like good or bad, not caught up in the future because God is not trapped by time, not possessed of a (masculine) kingdom in some other place for in God there is no 'other'.

In the Old Testament, Moses [Ex. 3:4] presses Yaweh to identify himself (sic) so that he can give the people a clear image. He wants a label, a name, a fixed Idea he can give to his recalcitrant and wayward people – something he can go back down the mountain and say to them who or what God is. After all, they've created a golden calf to worship, something they can see and feel and onto which they can project their beliefs. I suspect Moses may have been somewhat frustrated by God's elliptical answer, "I am who I am", a subject I have explored at length in *Contemplation* [54] (see also page 391). He may well have preferred something a little more definitive to help control his restive followers. The Beloved's mysterious 'I-Amness' may leave us frustrated by its lack of definition while also releasing us into a boundless exploration of the infinite.

Spiritual direction allows a drawing upon the person's resources (spiritual) that counselling and psychotherapy often steer clear of, and usually involves practices – such as joining in prayer and so on that tends to be outwith the counselling role. Spiritual direction is not about maintaining a professional distance, but a fluid merging of boundaries, a mutual participation in a unitary process whose outcome is always certain in the long or short term. It is indeed a high-risk strategy in conventional terms of counselling, but with the learning and application of the skill of both getting out of the way and opening to the Beloved, it may be that the birthing of something miraculous and wonderful can be witnessed.

Yet spiritual direction, in being different from counselling and psychotherapy, also has an ally in them as we have seen, for the fields are compatible and "frequently share raw material' [89]. Aronson [106] emphasises this mutual territory and the limitations when he writes: "Meditation is beneficial and it may not solve one's psychological issues. Psychology is helpful, and it does not necessarily address spiritual concerns. For a balanced psychological and spiritual life, we in the West can benefit from both meditation and psychological assistance. One approach does not preclude the other. At their best they can mutually inform and enrich each other. In the end there are also some differences between the traditional and modern visions and these can be respectfully acknowledged."

I've noticed that many people deepen their spiritual search after a period of counselling or psychotherapy. It is almost as if these approaches first help by clearing the ground of old problems, wounds and disappointments that then frees the soul to take flight on its search for Home. Jones [107] echoes the value of this preliminary cleansing when he writes "The therapist, the counsellor, the psychiatrist can help us on our way. They can rescue us from a particular block, get us back on our feet, can teach us to accept ourselves so that we can be on the move. But they cannot answer for us (nor would the best of them want to) those burning questions concerning the purpose and meaning for which we long. The spiritual guide cannot answer them

"This is what happens when soul talks to soul."

either, but there is within the world of spiritual direction a conscious commitment to faith in God."

This was my own experience as well, working with a fine psychotherapist, Judi Ledward, at the time of my early crisis. She gently and sometimes not so gently led me to face up to some things about myself, dig up some of the nastier skeletons in my unconscious cupboard and begin a process of healing. It is still a source of curiosity that I ever turned up on her doorstep. To this day I have no memory of finding my way to her or by what means I overcame my inherent resistance to inner exploration – I was fine thank you very much! Sometimes angels in our lives are real people who turn up when we need them and some force, some spirit outside of our conscious control, seems to impel us towards them (or them towards us). My friend Larry Dossey, when I told him of this exclaimed, "You were possessed!" Years later, my re-entry into church on Iona had the same quality to it. Whether the possession is one of divine intent or an egoic impulse, well, that is the very stuff of discernment with the Soul Friend.

Spiritual direction may thus build on the work of psychological enquiry, but takes on a different direction not least by drawing on elements sometimes considered outwith the remit of the counsellor or therapist – grace, prayer, the invocation of the Other, sacraments, the laying on of hands and so on. The Beloved is very much at the centre of the spiritual direction relationship, where the seeker is becoming more sensitised to and developing a relationship with the Beloved. All this is taking place within the human connection between director and seeker, itself a powerful agent of change. This relationship may of itself be beneficial to some who find themselves starved of others with whom they can have the level and depth of communication and conversation they are looking for.

Soul Friends and friends
Seeking insight can also happen to some degree in our relationships with friends. Is the Soul Friend that same kind of friend? The relationship with the spiritual director-Soul Friend tends to be more transitory, for being a soul companion suggests a journey, where the companionship is shared while the journey lasts, but not beyond it. The spiritual direction friendship is different from social friendship, for "My director is my friend but I am not his. He knows an awful lot about me and I know very

little about him...It's not an ordinary friendship. My spiritual director is friendly, open and human and shares stories. She's not someone I see at other times: so there is a specialness about it. It's a spiritual friendship in a liminal space...you put yourself in a liminal space so that things can happen which might not happen in a more fixed place or more fixed relationship. There is space for the Holy Spirit; a space which is there when we meet and doesn't exist anywhere else. It's a friendship dedicated to God; that's what makes it spiritual and something different" [108].

And yet it seems possible that as the relationship evolves, ordinary friendship can emerge. However, where this happens, it introduces all sorts of personal dynamics that may limit or make more difficult the flow of the seeker towards that which they seek. Sometimes our time with a spiritual director may last a few sessions or be spread over a lifetime, and a unique form of mutually nourishing Soul Friendship may emerge. It is rooted in humility, hospitality, humour, respect, connection and service to God. It is these qualities that will determine how mutually beneficial towards the Beloved the relationship can be rather than the boundaries we try to apply to the relationship.

There can also be a 'confessional' quality to our relationship with the Soul Friend. I use it here not in the sense of being heard in some partitioned chamber and bringing a list of our wrongdoings to the Beloved via an intermediary. I refer instead to the opportunity for *metanoia* (see page 333), for seeing those aspects of ourselves where we have fallen into forgetting and become lost or disconnected on the Way Home. Here the intention is not to punish ourselves or beg forgiveness, but to see more clearly, and learn, so that we may reconcile our relationship in the Beloved.

It can also be a tough relationship. For spiritual direction is not about telling us that whatever we are experiencing is OK. I have several people in my life from whom I have intentionally sought spiritual direction. There is Jeannie Sayre-Adams, with whom I have shared this spiritual search now for some 30 years. In our work together at the Sacred Space Foundation, in our co-authoring and teaching, and in our day-to-day relationship we have become mutually supportive of each other's souls. Sometimes it challenges and stretches us in every sense, but always deepens the love. In the crucible of that human relationship, a drawing closer to the Beloved has been the profound result for both of us. That dance of love and Soul Friendship

"This is what happens when soul talks to soul."

is a high-wire act, but where it works, and my hunch is that it is rare, two persons can become a significant mutual foil, dance partners in an unfolding consciousness of, and relationship to, the Beloved. In such a relationship, there is no end to the possibilities of that unfolding.

Many others have been with me along the Way, most significantly Ram Dass whom I have already mentioned. At home, a small group of wise friends and sometimes-fierce advisers have been with me as Soul Friends down the years. There have been many others where the relationship was brief, perhaps no more than a chance meeting where some mutual spiritual exploration and illumination took place. It is important not to negate or overlook the possibility of spiritual direction arising in the innumerable encounters in which Soul Friendship is offered. At the same time, the consistent and continuous relationship with our spiritual director/Soul Friend is the main aspect I encourage here; there is no substitute for it.

Certainly this is the common pattern that has emerged in different faith traditions around the world. The central idea is that subjecting oneself to the wisdom of the spiritual director is itself an aspect of spiritual work and in this surrender emerges the role of the spiritual director. As the barriers dissolve, the directed one finds their way Home through the direct transmission of wisdom, of the perennial philosophy in all its guises, from one person to another. Further, it may not be just transmission, but also a kind of catalyst role through which the seeker is so shaken and stirred that they discover and birth their own truth that lies within.

Transference is a risk in the work of the spiritual director or teacher – the inclination of those who are not yet fully aware to project onto the authority figure the need for a loving and all powerful 'parent' who will save us. We can fall in love with them, but also hate them because of the neuroses they stir up and the fear of someone controlling us. We may have deep fears of loss of power to others. Yet the reality is that given the right circumstances we will throw ourselves at the feet of others who can seem to make the world OK for us and parent us – demagogic politicians, faux preachers and false gurus down the ages have known full well how to play this game, even engaging whole populations in their essentially destructive paths. We can be seduced by their veneer of omnipotence and their ability to make us feel that we are at one with them - safe, saved, part of the union. This is what happens when unresolved shadows in ourselves encounter the same in the teacher who has not done the emotional work on themselves.

My early encounter with Ram Dass led me to hero worship him, to idealise and place him on a pedestal as someone who'd got it all sorted and could do the same for me. This form of transference is unhealthy for Soul Friend and seeker alike and something to which the Soul Friend must be alert so that neither they nor seeker fall into its traps. The Soul Friend is our effective guide precisely because they are fully aware and human. When I noticed Ram Dass having everyday chatty conversations with others, sitting in his sports car or listening to 60s soul music, I learned about the importance of his ordinariness. In the human ordinariness of the Soul Friend is their specialness. The teachers need to use the loo (!) like the rest of us, they have ordinary bodies too, as indeed did the founders of all the great faiths, and we need to be wary of getting stuck in our projections onto them, making them models of some idealised being beyond normal physical needs and functions. This neither liberates the Soul Friend nor us and it inhibits the full flowering of the spiritual direction relationship. We come to the Soul Friend because of the loving wisdom they can offer and which they can reveal in ourselves, not to make idols of them. (If any Soul Friend suggests that we should do the latter with him/her then this is probably a relationship best terminated.)

To become thus attached to the Soul Friend or to give way to the abuse of power is a kind of spiritual infidelity in which we betray the Divine, and ourselves. Some teachers say, "I am God". In a way there is truth in this, but the would-be guide who has not done the inner work distorts this. The ego gets a grip on it and thus shifts it into a power trip, where it leads the person to mistake being *of* the Divine, with being *the* Divine. For a person to say "I am God" is like a mirror saying, "I am you". The inner work approach is distrusted in some faiths, which believe that accessing the Divine can only be mediated by a priestly caste. The Soul Friend is not such a gatekeeper. He or she may happen to belong to a holy order of one sort or another, but their actions are very clearly those of companion and guide not mediator. I suggest that no one stands between us and the Divine but ourselves and if there is a mediator, it is an aspect of the Beloved alone.

Do not expect an easy friendship. The Soul Friend works with us to turn up the heat

"This is what happens when soul talks to soul."

on the fire of the soul longing for its source. I have probably only met Ram Dass in person a dozen times on a one-to-one basis, plus Skype and phone calls and a few emails (reinforced with the benefits of books and recordings) and the enormous blessing of a week long retreat with him at his home. Yet in each of those encounters he would take no prisoners of my delusions! His has been a deeply loving presence, but that love has sometimes been fierce and burning, pushing me into taking stock of what was true and authentic and what were my ego driven distortions. We can expect the love of the spiritual director to be fierce love. Like any good friend he or she will speak truth to us, even if it is tough to hear, but always do so lovingly.

In my first meeting with him I was taken aback that he was so directive, being quite clear about the risky place I was in and he gave quite specific instructions. He taught me something then about spiritual direction; that it is not always about soft and fluffy encouragement, but sometimes about being direct and challengingly so. A spiritual director who does not challenge, test, push, question is not a spiritual director. Sometimes we can expect to be told we are doing fine, sometimes he or she can deliver a spiritual kick in the pants (lovingly)! Subjecting ourselves to the discernment and discipline process of spiritual direction does not fit comfortably in the individualist material culture where we expect to achieve only self-gratification and congratulation. While, as I suggested above, the spiritual director is one with whom we should feel comfortable, it is important to recognise that discomfiture is part of the process too and that often we have to stick with the process of the relationship precisely because it is tough to do so, that is part of the discipline of spiritual work.

What happens when the relationship with the Soul Friend gets challenging – is it thus because it is necessary for us to learn and therefore we must stick with it? Or is it an abuse of power from an unhealthy or false director? The modern spiritual supermarket can sometimes make it too easy to indulge in spiritual director-hopping simply because we don't like the difficult stuff, yet it may be that hanging in there is exactly what we need to do when it gets challenging. A spiritual pick and mix opportunity can lead us to just pillage the bits we like and avoid the rest. Discernment is needed to help us decide whether it is better to use the challenges as the spiritual work precisely because it stretches us or whether it is time to move on.

The wheat from the chaff

To help us in our 'way of seeing' and especially seeing differently, many individuals and organisations are available offering retreat facilities either for quiet time alone or in groups and with or without access to a director. Likewise a spiritual director can be seen on a regular basis without going away on retreat. Once one has been found it is wise to check out clearly what background he/she has, what style of working, costs and other arrangements that are to be met (taking account of the caveats I have listed below). Not all spiritual options or those who teach them are without risk. Sorting out the deep from the shallow, the flaky from the serious and the safe from the potentially dangerous – such issues also draw us into the spiritual practice of discernment. As yet there is no nationally recognised training or registration system for spiritual directors in the UK. There are strong arguments against this within the field through fears of 'professionalising' what is essentially a human skill and calling.

How to discern the true from the false? Check out the person and the setting and be wary of those who:

■ Do not walk their talk – preaching love or claiming to live at a higher level of righteousness then branding as wrong or evil those who disagree with them.

■ Ask you to abandon all critical thought and follow them blindly – authentic directors ask you to follow the truth not them. They are self aware enough to know their limitations, when to say 'no', when to refer you to others for help.

■ Suggest that they have special gifts such as the capacity to heal others, transcend the laws of physics, have unique insights into the failings of others or infallible wisdom.

■ Spend a lot of time telling you what *they* think and very little time listening to what *you* think. The authentic Soul Friend is a good listener, is able to restrain themselves so that there is space for the relationship to flourish, recognises the mutual learning in the relationship, helps with discernment so you can decide what it true.

■ Say that their knowledge is secret and can only be given to an elect few who

"This is what happens when soul talks to soul."

have been initiated to their standards. (Can you imagine Jesus or Mohammed or the Buddha saying that their wisdom was secret? They may have been cautious about to whom they revealed their wisdom according to their readiness for it, but they did not regard it as belonging only to them and to be denied to others).

■ Demand all your money, possessions, body – the real guide gives away freely to humanity not to acquire wealth or power over you, though he or she may set tough spiritual tasks to gain the knowledge and it is fair to ask for reasonable payment for the time and effort.

■ Instruct you to get rid of all your relationships and activities not connected to the 'faith'. This especially includes cultish behaviour where you are told to cut yourself off from others who question the path you are taking and its effects on you. No matter what faith they belong to themselves, the spiritual director has a quality of openness and inclusiveness to those from different beliefs or who disagree and never asks you to disconnect from the world.

■ Run an organisation that is really a big business rather than a service; unreason-ably high fees for teaching/time or being asked to sign up to escalating pay-ments for 'advanced' teachings are other warning signs. Matters such as fees or donations and the timing of sessions are always made clear.

■ Tell you your lack of enlightenment is entirely your entire fault because you're not giving enough money, obedience, sex etc.

■ Use bodyguards or minders to keep followers remote or indeed have troops of followers at all. This means especially followers whose purpose is to affirm his or her importance and protect them from facing up to their ordinariness, denials and fallibility.

■ Gather around them only those who agree with them and denounce others who disagree as traitors, false or too dim-witted for their wisdom.

■ Have no tradition or field of expertise to draw upon – the good director is a repository of wisdom who helps you unravel that wisdom in yourself and they have the strength of a spiritual tradition and spiritual practices such as prayer and discipline to draw on.

- Have no ongoing direction/challenge themselves. The Soul Friend is a model of integrity and is accountable to others not least their own Soul Friends.

- Are part of an organisation with pressure groups to make you conform rather than encouraging faith and trust.

- Tell you their way is the only way – the director's work is to help you find the truth in you not impose his/hers on you.

- Demand that you remain in their sphere of influence rather than take what you need from them and move on.

- Leave you feeling controlled, intimidated, abused or exploited rather than loved, liberated, nurtured and encouraged.

- Focus the attention on their teaching and themselves as opposed to the teachings and presence of the Divine. The Soul Friend always places the Beloved at the centre of the relationship and is always open to being surprised by the direction the Will might take.

- Suggest that they be worshipped rather than the Divine.

- Lack a sense of humour – avoid any who are always grim and have no ability to laugh at their own ridiculousness or a good joke.

On the last point, over the years I've come to appreciate the importance of humour as a healthy quality of the Soul Friend. Laughter has a kind of energy that can shift the fiercest pain. There is a necessary trickster, clown and scallywag quality in the teacher that can radically alter our way of seeing ourselves and the truth. I've laughed until I've cried with many a Soul Friend and many a 'client'. Humour and humility are closely related. Beware the Soul Friend who can't belly laugh at the world and him/herself. Laughter shows we are human, that we have the humility to see our own foolishness and still love ourselves. The Soul Friend thereby teaches by

"This is what happens when soul talks to soul."

example what it is to be fully human.

In my early days of awakening one of my teachers gave me an exercise: 'Imagine Jesus laughing.' You could put the name of any of the great spiritual leaders in there instead of Jesus. We often assume them to be austere beings. Actually, taking Jesus as an example, there are many of his sayings that contain jokes, for example the camel and the eye of the needle parable [Matt.19:24]) would have had his audience in tucks because, knowing the precise setting, they would have seen the incongruity and ridiculousness in the story. Once, at a meeting with the Dalai Lama after a grand entrance with his entourage, the whole audience rose to its feet to honour him. He sat down on the chair provided for him, but it was way too big for him. He dangled his legs over the edge, rocked back and forth and giggled like a child at himself. Everyone else erupted into laughter. His wisdom was not diminished by his childlike ordinariness; on the contrary it was enhanced by it.

Sometimes, even if we are astute enough to discern our way through the points I have listed above, choosing a Soul Friend can still be a hard decision to make alone. Thus other aspects of Soul Care as outlined in Parts 6, 7 and 8 provide us with checks and balances if we are unsure of our relationship with a spiritual director. Of course this includes discerning what the guidance of the Beloved might be.

Meanwhile, it is worth remembering that just because someone has acquired deep wisdom in one thing, it does not necessarily mean they are wise in all things. Wise spiritual teachers know their limits. The Dalai Lama comes to mind again; at one meeting I attended in Manchester he was asked a convoluted question by a young man about the struggle he was experiencing in his marriage. The audience was hushed, expecting a profound, holy response from a man who dedicates a large part of his life to spiritual practice. He thought for a while then said, "Ask an expert! See a marriage guidance counsellor!" I warm to teachers like that who have the humility to know their limits.

If we have a problem with our family, then maybe a family therapist is the best person to seek out. If we are worried about our job, then maybe a union adviser can help. The Soul Friend may have wisdom in many areas of life including family, work and other matters and it's true that many of life's challenges overlap. My problem with ill health or a relationship may be taking me into new terrain of meaning and purpose, the spiritual realm, with which my doctor or counsellor cannot help. However, the primary role of the Soul Friend is to help us find our way to truth in Sacred Unity, our relationship with ultimate reality, the Beloved.

Although we may seek out a Soul Friend, there is no guarantee that we will be taken on. Those skilled in this service tend to be in high demand; they have to say 'no' and feed the ones they can who come close and trust that others will feed the rest. We can expect some sort of 'selection' to take place. Clearly there are many different levels of awareness in our consciousness and not everyone is fully receptive to the deeper work and indeed may become disorientated by it or corrupt it if their interior household has not been set in order first. Some people, for example, may feel they have a spiritual crisis when the crisis is really psychological as we have explored in Part 2, and would be better off accessing other forms of help.

Jesus cautioned about 'throwing pearls before swine' [Matt.7:6] and seemed to reserve some of his teachings for a select group rather than all and sundry. This was not done as a mark of superiority or arrogance, but as compassion for others who were not ready for some aspects of his message. The Soul Friend works at different levels with different folks, trusting that each contributes to growing competence and potential in others and that the ripples spread outwards to others from there.

The Buddha is famous for his exhortation to his followers, "Be a lamp unto yourself." But he did not intend this as a license to go off and do our own thing in the spiritual search without restraint or guidance. He was encouraging his followers to be acutely aware of false prophets, gurus and teachers. A nurse friend of mine recently attended the much-publicised Alpha course seeking to renew her Christian faith, but she left when it was made clear to her that homosexuality was a sin. Her son happened to be gay and she could not square the condemnation by the course facilitator, with the loving, responsible, wonderful human being that is her son. It's a common approach for leaders to quote a holy book, chapter and verse, to justify a particular stance and to keep people toeing the line in (their) faith. This often comes with a failure to explore the conscious and unconscious drivers behind such beliefs.

"This is what happens when soul talks to soul."

"What sayest thou?"

It's always struck me as odd that some religious people have had such a hang up about sex; it's a subject guaranteed to start a feverish poring over the holy books to find a clause to support an absolute position. It strikes me as odd, not because of the view, but because of the way the book is elevated as a perfect document to be interpreted literally. In monotheistic faiths, this seems to be a kind of blasphemy, raising the book to the same level of perfection as the Divine. Most people of faith see their holy books as spiritual material for reflection, interpretation and challenge in the search for truth. Likewise, those in ministry in healthy faiths are not held up to be beyond challenge. The absolutist position is horrified by both these aspects, and tends to view with dismay the interpretative approach and/or the challenging of authority that bringing our own lamp to the search suggests.

George Fox [109], a passionate force behind the establishment of the Quakers (the Religious Society of Friends) in the 17ᵗʰ century was motivated in part by the ossified state of the beliefs and practices of the established church. He was regularly challenged and imprisoned by people who would quote scripture at him in an attempt to dismiss his ideas. When these people would say, "The Bible says this", his response would be, "But what sayest thou?" Like the Buddha, he saw it as wrong to follow any person or belief system blindly, rather we must bring the light of our own reason, our lamp, to shine upon them – to expose the truths and the deceptions. The words of Jesus have often been used to justify the repression of 'sinners' in all manner of quite horrendous ways, yet there was no greater iconoclast than Jesus when confronted with the fundamentalism of his time.

The Sufi, mystical heart of Islam has an interesting tale to tell about the healthy approach to Soul Friends in particular, and religion in general. When faced with the certainty of an authority, the tale of the donkey and the Mullah is brought to mind. Mullah in Islam is a title of respect meaning teacher or scholar of religious matters. Mullah Nasrudin crops up in many Sufi stories, a figure associated with an unconventional approach to testing and teaching others about their uncritical attachments to persons or beliefs. Nasrudin borrowed a neighbour's donkey one day and the neighbour called at his home some time later to ask for it back. Nasrudin denied that he had the donkey, only at that moment for the sound of braying to emerge from the back of the house. The neighbour heard it and demanded its return. Nasrudin, faking a shocked expression, asked indignantly "Would you take the word of a donkey over the word of a Mullah?"

A healthy spirituality is cautious about taking on board the advice of authority figures uncritically. Yet it can take courage to listen to the advice of our own heart and trust our own knowledge and experience. In all faiths it is taught that we must not accept things blindly, but use reason and enquiry. St. Paul, for example, advised followers to "Test everything" [Thess.1.5:21], echoing the Buddha's call to be our own lamp. The moral of the Sufi tale is simple, be very wary of trusting authority figures and believe the donkey not the Mullah! Beware of making Gods of people. All are of the Beloved, and in some the veil of the ego has become so thin that they seem to shine with divine light. But they are *of* the Divine not *the* Divine. The One, the whole, the Sacred Unity within and around each of us is to be honoured and worshipped, not the aspect that bears it, no matter how wonderful our Soul Friend or any other person we happen to meet might be.

The Soul Friend and discernment
Many, a great many, times in my life I've had 'experiences' that have not leant themselves easily to rational explanation – synchronicities (or coincidences?), visions (or daydreams?) and so on. Once I met up with someone while on retreat and attending Mother Meera's darshan. A week later as I went to a meeting in London I passed her on the street. A week later I saw her in Glastonbury. Random chance? A prompting that I should take the trouble to connect with (or avoid) this person? Was I being stalked? Was I unconsciously stalking her? Likewise I have had countless experiences of inner promptings, conversations with the Beloved, guidance, visionary and mystical encounters and insights, including once hearing a voice so clear that it played no small part in leading me to live where I live and serve as I do now.

Each of us will have inner and outer 'experiences' like this in our own way and of infinite variety. What do they mean? Do we keep them to ourselves or share them? Are they true voices, urgings and images of the spirit, divine intervention, our souls or whatever we believe - sent to nourish us into deeper Truth on the way Home? Are they divinely inspired synchronicities designed to wake us up and summon our attention to where the Will wants us to go? Or are they things of deception, magical thinking where we conjure up connections and truths where there are none,

"This is what happens when soul talks to soul."

emanations from wounds in the shadows of the unconscious or maybe the work of malign forces to distract us from and distort the Truth of the Way? Are they delusions, an ego thing to make us feel important, the desire for the 'high' of an experience, something to tell others about so we feel special and above the common run of humanity, signs of psychosis, the authentic voice and guidance of the Beloved? Please take your pick from all of these and more. All such experiences are the grist to the mill of discernment. Discernment and judgement are often used interchangeably and I don't wish to get into heavy hermeneutics here, but they are not the same thing, at least when it comes to spiritual inquiry.

Judgement is about subjective choices between good or bad, pleasant or unpleasant, likeable or unlikeable, right or wrong - full of value-laden views. Discernment is the work of in-sight to see whether an experience, a situation or a relationship is true or false. I could have pursued contact with that person in Glastonbury - thinking we are supposed to get to know each other or simply dismiss it as random chance, could have thought it spooky or felt wonder at the universe that such coincidences are possible. Judgement would have me see this with an "Oh wow! How weird this is?" or "How wonderful that I'm having an experience!" and so forth. Likewise, how about those inner promptings - is that a true voice of the Divine or a sign of schizophrenia, or perhaps a sudden rush of endorphins, or a sign of stress or maybe an overindulgence in caffeine or MDMA? Discernment holds this, sees all the little seductive traps and demands to know if it is true - by checking facts, by seeing all the possible motives and deceptions.

Judgement tells us something is pleasant and nice or repellent and repugnant. We are inclined to push away the latter and cling to and replicate the former. Judgement is an ego skill, designed to keep fear at bay and boundaries in place, even if it means cutting people off from us. Judgement splits, creates a consciousness of duality, takes us out of a sense of oneness and connection to All-that-is. Judgement desiccates, denies us the blessing of seeing the whole picture and the interconnectedness of all things.

At a recent performance of Akhnaten, an opera by Philip Glass, I stood outside the theatre at the interval. A couple had decided to leave, reeling off their dissatisfactions with this or that backdrop, movement or colour. Their judgements of the superficial, albeit matters of personal taste, blocked them from getting deeper into the music and experiencing the profound spiritual depths of this work of art. Out on the streets of London a dishevelled homeless man was begging from a shop doorway. Well-heeled folks pushed past him with varying expressions of indifference, disgust or hostility. I stopped, patted his dog, gave him the coins from my pocket and in a few minutes heard his story of sorrow rooted in a profound injustice done to him. He could have been just spinning me a line to get some money, but I didn't think so and the encounter was heartfelt; human-being-to-human-being across the gulf of disconnection that judgement would otherwise have put between us. I couldn't rescue him, but I could give him food for his belly, and for his dog…and my time and attention. I could use his story to bless my own good fortune and strengthen my resolve to play my small part supporting economic justice in my country.

The judging mind is the antithesis of the contemplative mind. With judgement we are inclined not only to decide whether someone is right or wrong, but also to close our hearts to him or her. That hurts us as much as the other person. When Jesus warned us against judging others [Matt.7:17] I don't think for a moment that he was just offering a moral lesson about the rights and wrongs of judging other people. Rather, he may have been indicating that once we get into judgement of our experiences, the diverse and other parts of ourselves, we can get caught up in grasping the 'good' while pushing away the 'bad'; this attraction-repulsion dissects, separates, creates duality and is distracting and energy draining. Judgement causes suffering to ourselves as well as others.

Discernment sees the whole picture and does not place value judgements upon it, but seeks to see the Truth that is in it; the Truth that it is. It is a quality of non-duality, of the contemplative mind that embraces and 'sees' All-that-is and its essential, sacred unity. In all this lies, mantra-like, the question "Is this true?" – a question at the root of discernment and which we can bring to every life experience. Discernment is an art of the spiritual life (which is really all of life) and like all art it is enhanced by constant practice. It's a continuous process on the Way; like steering a car, unless we keep doing it we get nowhere. It is a practice we apply to our inner and outer spiritual journey and which is cultivated so that, if we are in positions of service, it helps others discern the true from the false.

"This is what happens when soul talks to soul."

I never did engage with the woman of chance encounter I mentioned above, in this case a deep feeling of unease counterbalanced my wonder at the amazing chance and I chose to follow the former 'guidance'. I will never know the consequences of that decision. Did I miss out on a meeting with someone who could have been of great help to me or did I avoid what could have been a toxic relationship? And as to the experience of the 'inner voice' that led me to where I am now, I made a choice after due discernment - including taking the moment into prayer and meditation, seeking wise counsel from my loved ones and Soul Friends before acting upon it.

In Coming Home I place great emphasis on the need for our Soul Works, Soul Foods, Soul Friends and Soul Communities to assist in the process of discernment. I look at the many blessings in my life and can speculate that it is perhaps some sign of healthy discernment. Discernment helps us towards right relationship and right action; we may choose not to hang around with a person, but we do not judge them and put them from our hearts. The result is invariably life enhancing rather than diminishing, getting us closer to the Beloved rather than further away, our path of service fulfilled rather than lost. By such inner and outer fruits of the spirit we may know whether we chose the path of truth or not.

Here is another example of a challenge for discernment. While on retreat in Germany many years ago I would leave my hotel and walk in the forest and fields each morning. I was enjoying those lovely long days when the hours are your own, without need to be timetabled. Fasting and silence enhanced this, an awful lot of hours can be devoted to our inner life when we don't have to give time to buying, preparing, eating and clearing up after food. A fast carefully managed (it is not necessarily a case of not eating entirely – a little water or some seeds can help quell the pangs of hunger) can quieten the demands of the body so that all we have to do is rest and go deep within.

I left my room at dawn to watch the sun come up above the oaks and headed for a favourite clearing where I could also practise Tai Chi without observation. I passed along a low hedge by a rutted corner of a field. As I stepped into the open, before me stood an enormous wild boar. His massive head and shoulders must have been well above my waist height. He stood stock-still, stared at me and snorted loudly; I was rooted to the spot, both fearful and exhilarated to be so close to him. Those yellow-white tusks rising from beneath his arched snout could do an awful lot of damage. A wave of great calmness came over me, and so we stood for what seemed like an age, eye to eye. His wet nostrils twitched, the thick brown hair on his back rose and fell. I had the strangest feeling he was waiting for me as I met his intense gaze. By normal standards he should have charged at me or fled from me. He took a step closer; I did the same. He snorted; his wet nose twitched and glistened in the sunrise. Which of us would give way first? I could hear that inner voice telling me, "This is stupid, you're in his territory, he could kill you, run for it". But that fearful voice was subsumed by an overwhelming desire to stay with him. In my imagination (imagination?) I 'heard' him say, "Don't be afraid." I heard myself saying aloud, "Afraid of you?" I 'heard' him reply, "Afraid of anything." Then he snorted once more, spun round, trotted away and was lost in the undergrowth in seconds.

Such an encounter could be a random moment of no more import than man and beast colliding in the forest; the words could be mere projections from my mind onto a creature whose consciousness was far from my own. Yet I left feeling elated, that perhaps he had come to teach me something or to simply be there to mirror the voice of my soul to my self. What we do or do not interpret by such meetings is debatable; perhaps what matters is what they mean to us – and how they help us change our lives. Interpretation and discernment of events like this is problematic alone. The Soul Friend can hold up a mirror to such experiences and ask, "Is this true?"

I hold several questions or statements like this in heart and mind as guides to discernment, using them for myself or with others duly rephrased:-

"Is this true?" - can be brought into play with any experiences, thoughts and feelings before acting.

"Why am I doing this?"- a test of our intention, our motivations; hidden shadows can contaminate our actions. Am I meditating to 'get' something? Am I seeking spiritual experiences to avoid inner pain? Am I really seeking power to cover my sense of powerlessness? Deep exploration in reflection, prayer or with our Soul Friend will aid discernment.

"How do You want me to love You?" - when we get caught up in our 'stuff'. It all

"This is what happens when soul talks to soul."

becomes much clearer when we act from a place of loving the Beloved and 'seeing' what *the* Will is rather than our egoic will.

"It's not about me." - when we feel under attack or confused or we get caught up in trying to impose our view on others.

"Where is the grace in this suffering?" - to help seek out the light, the little jewel which may be there, in the darkness of our suffering.

"What does my heart tell me?"- when we are confused about what direction to take, we can frame the dilemma in this way and draw upon the guidance of prayer or visualisation to get clear.

"It is all One." - a reminder when we get scared and fall into dualism.

"There's nothing wrong with me." - when we are challenged or afraid, the ego trip can take us into that place of sabotaging our essential OKness; affirmation is needed to refute the inner critic.

"Who is at the centre here?" - without knowing it, we can find our egoic 'false self' has sneaked in and taken charge of our way of being in the world, sabotaging our sacred intent; inadvertently we have taken over from the Beloved, checking our intention helps us steer back to Source.

"Stay in loving awareness." - takes on the quality of a commandment sometimes; a helpful reminder when we have fallen into forgetting and become anxious or controlling and so forth.

"I Am." - being in roles and feelings can be a trap. The alarm bell rings if we can hear ourselves saying "I am a…. (add noun of choice)." An affirmation that *I Am* requires no addition, no accretion born of egoic needs for identity, role or experience at the time. In our uncluttered "I Amness" we are liberated (see also page 391).

"What is it that is frightening me?" – when we fall into disconnection and anger, invariably at root we have been touched by some deep seated fear that needs to

be seen, named and disempowered.

"What is really going on here?" – we may 'think' we know what is happening in a situation but this invites us to take a double check, to see if the unconscious is manifesting in some way, for example.

"Where is the Divine in this?"- sometimes we can fall into dualism, "God here, God not here", especially when we encounter things that are frightening and hurtful; this question invites us to return to trust that there is nowhere that the Beloved is not, that all is one, and that beneath our judgements and interpretations, the Divine is present whether we can 'see' or not.

Anger and Indignation

To develop the anger-fear relationship a little further, it's worthwhile noting that almost all anger comes from fear. The exception being indignation, although superficially it can look like fear-based anger. Examples are those of Jesus turning over the tables and driving out the merchants from the temple [Matt.21:12-13], the recent protests in European cities against the injustices of austerity or the treatment of refugees or individuals and pressure groups who persist against all the odds to right a miscarriage of justice. Indignation is rooted in a sense of outrage at a falsehood or injustice. It is more a 'demo' that may be short and swift or a persistent refusal to give way; a way of bursting through and transforming people's accepted ways of thinking and behaviour to shatter the status quo and upset the 'tables' that stand contrary to truth, compassion and the ways of the Beloved. Unlike anger, the indignant outburst is never personal or destructive and does not want to attack and harm others. It is ultimately a robust, creative act for it seeks to change things by piercing ignorance. It arises not from fear but deep trust in truth, that right will be done, in the essential good that is greater than the evil, in the Beloved.

The anger that we encounter in ourselves and others mostly arises when we feel under attack in some way – either directly because someone is threatening us or less directly because something in what they are saying or doing is provoking painful feelings in us that we would rather avoid such as powerlessness, shame or guilt. This form of anger is a striking out response so that we don't feel the fear source. The question we might ask when we feel angry with someone is not so much "Why have you made me angry?" but

"This is what happens when soul talks to soul."

"What has frightened me?" At the root of fear is invariably the loss of connection to the Beloved, or at least the fear of such. Anger reveals this fear when we explore its source, which in turn leads us into those places where we do not yet trust the Divine fully, where the work needs to be done to deepen that trust.

Anger is just another feeling (we will return to this subject a little more in part 9). It is to be judged neither good nor bad, it simply is. What matters is whether we react to it without awareness in a ping-pong, tit for tat way or whether, with awareness, we can see what is really going on in ourselves and the source of the anger. It's often assumed that letting rip with the anger is one healthy way of dealing with it, but studies have shown [110] that this may actually put us at increased risk of cardiac disease. What is needed, from a place of loving awareness, is to find a different kind of understanding of what anger is and how to respond to it rather than react to it.

Recently while working with a group on retreat one participant became very hostile towards me. I was watching in myself lots of buttons being pressed about not being valued or appreciated and feeling attacked by the violence of her language both body and verbal. I could feel my own angry response arising from that place of fear (of the hurtful feelings of unworthiness, the sense of physical threat) in myself and sought to gently hold it and sit with it, letting the person blow off steam and for me not to retaliate while being open to the Presence in what was taking place. It wasn't easy; there was a strong part of me that really wanted to give her a piece of my mind. But some degree of awareness allowed me to hold the conflict, to pray for my guru's presence, to feel the love that reminds (re-minds) me that I am loved and safe and worthy as I am – as is the person before me. I also began to see the fearful place in her from which the anger came, which softened my response into sorrow and compassion. Being thus with it I felt able to hold the gamut of feelings, and wait.

As the storm abated somewhat, I suggested that if she was so disturbed by the class and the way I was working it would be OK to leave, if she would feel happier and safer. She left the room in a huff, the group needed a little time to see how they could hold what they were feeling and then we took a break. She was there waiting for me as I came out of the room. More angry outbursts followed. It turned out she'd been 'sent' by her manager, did not really want to be there, found all the introspection and quiet unbearable and just needed permission to leave and follow up with some suggestions of help. Next day she was waiting outside for me as I returned to the group. She promptly apologised, wept while explaining her predicament (which included the fact that I reminded her of a psychiatrist she had worked with who had abused her) and asked to re-join the retreat. After a little 'work' she re-committed to the group process thereafter.

Callings and concerns

Another issue that arises in relation to discernment is how we make sense of a prompt-ing, a calling or a vocation (the roots of 'vocation' lie in the Latin *vocare*, to call). Rev-elation is rarely the total blast of the 'Road to Damascus' type. Experience suggests that for the most part the Beloved seems to move more gently in us, whispering rather than shouting, a gentle nudge rather than a big thump. We are usually 'spoken' to in ways that we can receive and at a level for which we are ready. There is no sense of the Beloved as a spiritual bully. Nor will we only hear what we want or expect to hear. True callings and illuminations are often challenging, seem to come from left field or ask us to step outside of our ordinary ways of thinking or doing things.

Such callings need careful discernment in our Soul Communities, with our Soul Friends and through our Soul Works to determine their veracity. As a general rule of thumb a true calling [111] feels deeply connected "to our nature, character and history." It comes from the Beloved and often asks us to look at something new and different about our work or ourselves. Thus it's not necessarily something we have to accomplish; rather it is a summons to express that which is already within us. Sometimes it can feel strangely related to something in ourselves that we have hitherto considered to be a wound or a problem. A woman I knew had a long history of domestic abuse. Despite the constant reminders which her 'calling' brought and the lack of resources and local support, she helped set up a refuge for victims of domestic violence. Another aspect of an authentic calling is that it causes us lots of difficulties and yet in our heart of hearts we really want to do it. There can be a risky, 'out of the box' element to it, feelings of 'not me surely, I'm not good enough?' and it might look financially tricky rather than a chance to make lots of money.

Here is another example of how the companionship of the Soul Friend can be es-sential to our working our way to truth. I often use some guided questions from the contemplative tradition that can be very helpful. Bringing the concern in a prayerful,

"This is what happens when soul talks to soul."

meditative way before the Beloved, these questions can be asked, reflected upon and made the grist to the mill of discernment with our Soul Friend. Thus:-

"In relation to (this concern etc. I have)…
                                   What is it You want me to receive?
                                   What is it You want me to know?
                                   What is it You want me to let go of?
                                   What is it You want me to do?"

Each question is taken slowly, in sequence, giving as long as it takes to be receptive to a response that occurs perhaps as thoughts, words, feelings or images; receptive that is to the promptings of the spirit in whatever way the Beloved speaks to us. It's important not to try to 'make' an answer if 'nothing happens' (sometimes nothing tells us something) or to fix things according to our (sometimes hidden) agenda or edit or make sense of things that are not clear. We can just sit gently with each question, notice what we notice and then let each response be taken into due discernment, through further prayer and reflection, with our Soul Friend and/or simply into a conversation with a loved one we trust. On balance I think questions like this are best used in personal work with a trusted guide rather than by solitary exploration, especially while we are in our early days along the Way.

It's in the relationship – unconditional love
The intention in spiritual direction is to help us find our Home by inner exploration and guidance through the minefield of spiritual awakening. The authentic Soul Friend does not turn our attention upon him or herself, but upon ourselves, holding the mirror up to us so that we may see and be transformed. The Soul Friend does not want to be our 'God', but for us to find the 'God' that we are. Through the process of testing and discernment, the spiritual director, the Soul Friend, helps us to see differently and ever more clearly. In many ways the relationship with the director can mirror our relationship with the Beloved, constantly calling us to go deeper.

Often people have asked me how do I get to know the Divine better? My response is, "How would you get to know me?" If we are forming a new relationship and want to get to know the person how do we do it? It's obvious, we talk to them, show up for dates, share a meal together, tell our story, talk about a book we have read, just hang out with them. It's just the same to a degree with the spiritual director and more importantly with the Beloved. Getting to know the Beloved requires as many approaches as getting to know a person. Invite the Friend round for a meal now and again!

Although the Soul Friend is a prophet, a truth speaker, such speaking is always done from a place of love. Having said that, just occasionally I might not speak of everything. A few years ago a very devout Roman Catholic woman came into retreat in the midst of a crisis of faith while terminally ill. As she readied to leave, she asked tearfully if I'd been playing music late at night, about 3am in fact. "No", I replied, "and even if I had the distance between your accommodation and mine and the thickness of these stone walls would have made it very unlikely you would have heard." She went on to say how regularly as clockwork in the early hours she could hear heavenly voices singing and felt that God was reassuring her, reminding her that she was loved despite the guilt, shame, doubts and fears that she had brought with her; she was returning renewed in faith and her relationship with the Beloved as a result. She felt she had been "visited by choirs of angels".

After her departure, I went to clean and prepare the sanctuary area, the place of our meeting each day. I noticed the CD player was switched on and more than that, someone had knocked the timer so that it was set to come on at 3am each day. The CD it had been playing was Hildegard of Bingen's "Canticles of Ecstasy" sung by Sequentia – heavenly music indeed if there is any. I had it in mind to 'phone her and tell her the real source of the angelic voices, but thought, "No, maybe somewhere in the Divine's busy workday if there are angels and they're fully occupied then maybe a CD would do just as well." I never did make that call.

Over the oracle at Delphi is written, 'Know thyself'. We might add, 'Then love thyself'. As we come to know ourselves through inner enquiry, through the work of personal transformation with our Soul Friend, counsellor or therapist the healthy response is not to move to beating ourselves up. We face up to our 'sins' – our weakness, the ways we have wounded ourselves or others or the world - all of which have come from that place in ourselves where we have lost contact with the loving Presence, the Beloved. The Soul Friend, while sometimes fierce in their presence with us, mirrors the unconditional love of the Beloved to us. Levine [112] writes, "Unconditional love is the experience of being, there is no 'I' and 'other' and anyone or anything it touches is experienced in love."

"This is what happens when soul talks to soul."

Although I refer often to 'unconditional love', the term is something of an oxymoron. Love simply is. We may experience it in many forms, but it is still the same thing. Unconditional love carries with it the assumption of conditional love, but love that is conditional is not love, it is something else – affection, addiction, attachment, call it what we will, but it is not love. Love, pure and simple, is the quality we seek in our Soul Friend and which my friend Sam so beautifully expressed in her letter to me, quoted at the beginning of this chapter. The loving presence of the Soul Friend can cultivate loving awareness for ourselves, helps us to see ourselves with compassion, with forgiveness, with the reception of the grace of the Beloved that bursts through our boundaries and changes us utterly.

The hunger in all of us to know ourselves deeply and our place in the scheme of things, to be happy, to love and to take that journey into loving awareness, into heartfullness, is not one to be followed lightly or alone. Knowing ourselves more deeply and our connection to that which is both part of and yet beyond the self, informs who we are in the world, what work nourishes us and how we must relate to others. Spiritual direction is one of the ways we can come to know and heal ourselves more deeply and heal our relationship to Sacred Unity. As such it is a pathway for us to become more well-rounded human beings. Ego, soul and Presence emerge as a renewed and integrated whole. As we deepen our relationship in the Divine under the sensitive and loving guidance of our spiritual director we find a wealth of love there to draw upon in our search.

Indeed it is almost as if we may, albeit temporarily, leapfrog some aspects of our concerns in the world or with ourselves. We can spend a lifetime picking over the wounds of the ego. But it may be that by prioritising our relationship to our Source we can look afresh at ourselves from a different perspective. While, as I have suggested, there is some strength in doing the psychological work first, the demands of the ego can be legion. While it is not possible to bypass the emotional work we can sometimes put it aside for a little while and dis-cover the transforming power of the Beloved that has been waiting for us. Thus strengthened and renewed we find we have a far greater resource of love to draw upon to heal and to give a different perspective on those old wounds. It might even be possible that the wounds don't feel like wounds anymore. After many years of spiritual practice I can safely say that my various neuroses are still around, but the gift of the Work is to deflate their size and importance, to set all their little dramas in their true context - merely aspects of my character. Embraced and accepted as an ever-present part of my story, that's all they are, just part of the story. They are not who I am. Their power and grip is diminished.

"I do nothing and nothing is left undone," Ram Dass once said to me. It has taken me some years to understand what he meant by this. Such words are rooted in the tradition of the *Tao Te Ching* [95]. It is the notion of *wei wu wei* ('do not do'). It is not a call to passive withdrawal but to action without clinging or attachment to outcomes, of surrender into the flow, the Source that works in and through us. Now, being with people I encounter for healing, in whatever forms it takes, I have learned that I do nothing. I may choose a word or use a guided spiritual practice or use my hands in a particular way, but these are all outer gestures of something deeper taking place.

The Soul Friend learns to let go of his or her agendas and other people's dramas, to get the ego out of the way and trust in the only One who heals. Having committed to and followed through the Work, the Soul Friend has become authentically available to others, 'seeing' into places where perhaps we cannot, then helping us to see too. As Campbell [60] reminds us "Freedom to pass back and forth across the world division, from the perspective of the apparitions of time to that of the causal deep and back…is the talent of the master…the Cosmic Dancer…does not rest heavily in a single spot but gaily, lightly, turns and leaps from one position to another." As we dance across our interior worlds in our search for truth, we are not alone, the Soul Friend dances with us. Not so much a solo as a 'pas de deux'. It's like praying together.

Spiritual direction is simply prayer in action; my work, if it is work at all, is to stay present with the Beloved, to open myself to grace and just let it do its work – I am not the doer, simply the instrument of the doing, the friend of the Friend. This is a kind of effortless effort. In this prayerful, heartfull condition the Soul Friend does not get caught up in the effort of trying to fix us, does not become exhausted trying to heal the world's wounds. "God heals, I make the tea". Soul Friend and seeker mingle mutually in the vast pool of friendship, the sacred waters of our becoming, but both ultimately flowing deeper into Sacred Unity.

"This is what happens when soul talks to soul."

In the loving relationship we can experience with the Soul Friend, a different level of conversation takes place that is less, far less, caught up in ego agendas. Our social functions, our roles, are no longer set to govern us; rather they facilitate a level of exchange so that we can communicate soul to soul. Sometimes that exchange is in deep silence when all words pass. I sat with Ram Dass once and for a long period nothing was said, just looking into each other's eyes. He said, "This is what happens when soul talks to soul." The Soul Friend offers us a safe milieu for our soul exploration, soul-to-soul conversations. The journey across the landscape where depth and transformation are possible, with our Soul Friend, is the terrain with which he or she has some familiarity, because they have walked at least some of the path already. It is a one-to-one demonstration of compassionate companionship along the Way. But that compassion and exploration takes place with others too, in community, and that is the subject of the next Part.

Startled by the thunderclap of Your voice,
in the 'ruhe sanfte' during a silent meditation,
sitting there perfectly still,
I move.
We all move.
A movement faster than the speed of light
or chocolate biscuits disappearing
off the plate at coffee break.
A time-lapsed sequence as we shift
from place to Place,
while remaining exactly where we are.
There is nowhere to go,
nowhere to be,
but here, now, always.
In our blindness we see much.
In our deafness we hear all.
Opening doors to a new room,
only to find it the same one
redecorated from chintz to new cool.
Moving in dreams from room to room,
only to find there is no door and no room and no walls.
We speak our truth to discover its lies.
And the shaman masked in eagle feathers
summons us to the party, or the funeral.
We are all invited, but the invitation comes,
(ah the invitation!) sometimes with a golden margin,
sometimes like the black-edged cards in the crematorium.
Some of us come dressed for dancing and Hafiz,
bearing the stretchers with Rumi in tow, calls
"Help me here!"
But Rumi, too busy dancing,
whirled and whirled and is whirling still.
We laugh until we cry and cry until we laugh
and sometimes if you pay attention,
(pay very close attention)

you can see God handing round the tissues
or making sure the kettle is full
or putting someone's hand into the hand of another.
For the laughter and the crying are all the same thing.
That's why the Buddha smiles, knowingly.
And the Mona Lisa.

Part 6

"Wisdom sees everything not in separateness but in unity."[100]

Soul Communities: colonies of heaven

Colonies of heaven - and hell

It's only a mile across, but the narrow stretch of jewel-like sea that separates Iona from the big island of Mull could be as wide as an ocean. As you cross the Sound it feels for all the world that you are leaving ordinary reality behind. In some respects you are, for this small island has few roads or cars and only 120 or so souls are resident. Thousands of tourists flock here each day in the summer – taking quick trips primarily to see the famous abbey and then most leave with equal speed. The rest of the island stays largely untouched by visitors who wander mainly within the short stretch from jetty to monument, or take the famous pilgrimage walk down to the southern tip to visit the bay where St. Columba is said to have landed.

Loved by painters and poets for generations, rich in religious history, difficult to get to, gloriously wild and unpredictable in its climate; Iona has called people down the years, especially to touch something deep within. Little wonder that poet Kenneth Steven [113] writes:

> *"Is this place really nearer to God?*
> *Is the wall thin between our whispers*
> *And his listening? I only know*
> *The world grows less and less –"*

Iona hosts a vibrant spiritual community, founded by George MacLeod early in the last century, which is influencing religious thought and practice well beyond its remote island base, its centre in Glasgow and its heart in the dispersed membership around the world. Among the tourists are pilgrims, some as day trippers seeking perhaps their Celtic Christian spiritual roots, others for longer periods to join in the spiritual life of the Iona Community with its many courses, and other religious houses on the island.

"In the spiritual life the last thing to go is fear."

The Christian community it offers is a world away from the fundamentalist, judgemental and sometimes vicious form that often gets the attention on the airwaves. Most Christians are not like this, and the Iona Community represents a thread of Christianity that is deeply embracing, loving, non-judgemental and inclusive. It is one of those places where people in community are working to make the essence of divine love tangible. They work to create what some have called 'colonies of heaven' (attributed to St Columba, the founder of the abbey and monastery in the 6th century, though probably the words of George MacLeod [114]) – a place on earth, in everyday reality, where the truths of 'the Kingdom' are lived out.

Soul Communities are gatherings of fellow seekers and can take many forms, as we shall see. They may be large or small, temporary or permanent. The former might be a week's retreat with a group of strangers, the latter a friary or ashram that is many generations old. In a sense, the Sacred Space Foundation, where I work as a spiritual director, is a Soul Community – a kind of ashram or monastery without walls. Many activists and friends support the work and are committed to the spiritual life themselves whilst funding our retreat houses that are places of reflection, contemplation, transformation, spiritual renewal and one-to-one attention. Some Soul Communities may be large networks hosting groups of people; others, like Sacred Space, are small and more individually focussed.

Soul Communities are more than groups of people, neighbourhoods or townships where such communities have economic and social purposes. The Soul Community (and we might be members of or participants in more than one) has the intention of expressly engaging in spiritual work and supporting others in the group in that work. The Soul Community may have other activities such as providing health care, education or running a business, but these are expansions from the central aspect of spiritual support. A Buddhist community to the north of where I live (the Tibetan monastery at Samye Ling) is an example. It has a shop, welcomes visitors, runs courses, maintains beautiful gardens and is engaged in social activism. But its central focus is teaching and holding a Buddhist community, who meet in prayer and meditation, have access to spiritual directors and devote the bulk of their time to learning Buddhism. Communities like this are specifically set up to support seekers and are well defined, but there are other perhaps more loose affiliations as we shall see where spiritual support is also a possibility and which can act as Soul Communities.

All religious traditions down the ages have sought to set up communities like Iona and Samye Ling (and I have visited scores in my time) in order to deepen their spiritual search. Sometimes this necessitates the community living by strict rules and being cut off to a greater or lesser extent from the rest of society. For some this cutting off is seen as essential in order to reduce temptation away from attention on God. Others saw their withdrawal as deepening their spiritual practice but to make it of service, for example in providing health care and hospitality.

A few years ago I had a week's retreat among the brothers at Worth Abbey, a Benedictine monastery made famous by a TV series called 'The Monastery'. From time to time, especially when my spiritual life seemed torn by other demands or in arid periods when I had lost that connection to the Divine, I would imagine how much easier it would be to live in such a community. How ideal it must be to get away from all the tensions of ordinary life such as paying the bills, dealing with conflict, problems in relationships or meeting responsibilities. Retreats into communities may sound idyllic and indeed they are – for a while. After experiencing Worth Abbey, Iona, Findhorn and others down the years both in the UK and abroad, I came to know that there is just as much struggle to stay focussed on the Beloved living in community as outside it.

Living in community, we still have to deal with interpersonal conflicts that arise (often!). Just because we are a saintly abbot or abbess does not mean we escape from the worries of paying the bills or following the boss's orders. Enjoying the remoteness of Findhorn or Iona does not mean that we avoid getting annoyed when someone has not done their share of the kitchen chores or has eaten the last of the blackberry jam. It has been my experience that living in community intensifies rather than diminishes the tensions of living together. We do not escape our shadows in community, we bring them with us and they are magnified there. What communities seek to create are more healthy ways of dealing with them. Those that do not are unhealthy groups to be among and just as risky - even dangerous- as the unhealthy teacher or guide as discussed in Part 5. The relationships themselves and all the joy and challenges they bring to us, are thrown into sharp focus. How we respond to them is just as much a spiritual practice as chanting or meditation, for they offer us countless opportunities for deepening awareness and compassion, for walking our talk.

"In the spiritual life the last thing to go is fear."

Being in a community, for long or short periods, can flush out some of our delusions and spiritual inadequacies, especially the inclination to project onto whole groups or people that they 'must have got it sorted'. We can load onto a Soul Community an almost dream like belief that it must be full of perfect people in perfect relationship. Go to any one of them and you will soon learn differently! A healthy spiritual community is like a normal family, sometimes we love them to bits, sometimes we can't bear to be in the same room as them – all this is grist to the mill along the Way.

Furthermore, we can risk extending this idealisation to whole social groups, indigenous tribes and nations. Tibetans, Hopi, Kogi, Australian aboriginals, Sami peoples and others can have idealised assumptions dumped upon them. This happens especially among naïf seekers alienated from their own backgrounds and cultures who cling to the belief that some other group has 'the answers' and a richer, problem free, more authentic spiritual tradition. This phenomenon is part of that inclination in us to transfer onto others our need for the perfect parent or family, to seek God outside ourselves and elsewhere rather than in the here and now. The spiritual work here is to attend to the places in our psyche where such distortions arise and to bring them forth for healing as part of the Work.

Living and working in community is like following a 12-step Alcoholics Anonymous programme – the processes are there to keep us on track, to push and challenge as well as nurture and encourage. In our searching, our healing, our whole-ing there is a need for discipline, guidance, community support and inspiration. The word 'companion' has French roots and means sharing bread with others. Our companions on the Way are ones with whom we share the bread of our food, the sacraments and other rituals, and also our shared lives as food for each other. Working together, healthy communities nurture us out of our various egotistic addictions into mature, soul-centred adults. Or rather the process is one of continuous refinement, as students of love, in the fire of relationships into ever-deeper connection to the Divine. Spiritual maturity on the Way Home is not about retreating from the world and having some sort of spiritual self-pleasuring life, but about expanding and full-filling our humanity so that we can engage more fruitfully with the world, not less.

There can indeed be times of retreat in solitude or in community as part of our spiritual work (see Part 8) but for most of us these are rarely lifetime commitments.

Thomas Merton [56] comments that the way of 'quietism', withdrawing from the world (consciously or unconsciously to avoid the suffering of the world, our frustrations and fears) is not the soul's way. To do so, as any monastery or retreat place will affirm, simply means that all the stuff we have stored up in ourselves leaks out there. Moreover, as Merton notes, "My soul does not find itself unless it acts. Therefore it must act. Stagnation and inactivity bring spiritual death." We are part of this world and for the great majority of us it seems that we must play our part in it.

Sometimes we might seek a community because we feel that we must escape the fog of our ordinary lives just to 'see' more clearly, and it may indeed have a quality of exile about it because we can feel like it is the rest of the world that has driven us away. But it is worth noting that living in 'Memphis', in exile, is not always a negative although it can feel like it sometimes. It can be a place of suffering, as the Jewish people experienced when captured and taken to Babylon. Sometimes the suffering of being away from home is balanced when exile provides safety from persecution, as when Joseph and Mary escaped Herod with the child Jesus by heading for Egypt. For forty years I was in exile from Christianity. Coming home to that faith, in retrospect, was the easy part; the tough part has been, and still is, staying there (a rich seam of spiritual work in itself!).

I refer not to the overarching faith rooted in the Christ and his message, but to staying with a tradition belonging to that faith such as (in my example) Anglicanism, which can leave you blossoming with wonder and joy while at the same time driving you crazy with its shadow side such as bigotry, rigidity and unlovingness. Like all faiths, all communities, all families, both light and dark are found in the same place. Healthy groups can handle difference and diversity; unhealthy ones can be full of threat and abuse. In exile we may have room to wander, to learn, to experiment, to see the bigger picture. We may return loaded with spiritual riches gathered along the way. Without the sorrow of separation, there is not the joy of reunion. I attended a Roman Catholic mass once in Dublin, and was profoundly moved by the simplicity and sincerity of the faith of the people I met, and yes indeed their certainty, although there was deep disagreement between us on many issues. I reflected that there was for me some envy there, some longing that I too could see the world so simply, so black and white. How much easier it must be, I thought, to live in a world of absolutes, no grey areas, as so many in that particular church seemed to do.

"In the spiritual life the last thing to go is fear."

Yet elements of the monastic community life can be found in many ways in our ordinary lives. Attending a yoga group, a study session focussed on a particular religious or spiritual text, a meditation course, participating in our religious community – there are countless situations in which we encounter others, some for short periods (perhaps the temporary community of a short course or retreat) or a permanent community with participation in our local meeting room, mosque, synagogue, church or temple. Then there are the endless opportunities for sharing our spiritual life that can crop up with friends and family and work colleagues. Each of these encounters may expose moments of sharing and learning. It is also worth remembering that we can engage with a Soul Community in many different ways; modern communications have opened up enormous possibilities for the 'virtual' monastery. We can commit to prayer groups, support groups and other communities large and small across the globe through video, email, shared meditation times, distant healing sessions, on-line support groups and so forth.

Many faiths have monastic traditions and provide opportunities for allegiance and participation through what are sometimes known as lay or third orders. Such 'monks' are not part of a permanent residential community, but live at home and are fully engaged through their shared values and vows in their local communities. To some extent, the Iona Community, for example, which is a 'dispersed' group of members, follows this pattern of commitment to a religious life of certain practices and values while bringing these into everyday life. While on-line groups can offer community to a degree, there's no substitute for person-to-person contact, relationship and action. What has become known as the 'new monasticism' of the last hundred years or so is seeking new ways of leading a spiritual life with the support of a Soul Community yet rooted in our ordinary domestic lives. The 'new monasticism' can be traced back to the writings of Bonhoeffer in the 1930's and onward through renowned spiritual teachers such as Bede Griffiths, Raimon Pannikar and Wayne Teasdale then into the work of Beverly Lanzetta, Rory McEntee, Adam Bucko and many others.

This search for new ways of creating and sustaining Soul Community is about more than organizational and relationship matters. It's worthwhile remembering what monasticism really means. 'Monastery' and 'monk' are derived from the Greek *monachos*, the movement that emerged in the early years of Christianity signifying those who led the solitary life or in close-knit communities as with the early desert fathers and mothers. They wanted to get away from the clutter of ordinary life as they saw it and focus entirely on God. The Greek word is a translation of the Syriac *ihidaya* - 'single one'. Syriac is closely related to Aramaic and both languages are rich in symbolism, layers of meaning and very influential in early Christian thought and practice. Thus *monachos/ihidaya* is not just about a person's solitary life, but about being single-minded, unified or at one. In the contemplative tradition this is what is known as unitive or non-dual consciousness. To be a 'monk' therefore is about a state of mind and not just a lifestyle.

Many times I have felt that pull to 'get away from it all' and just give myself over to the Beloved away from the troubles and distractions of the world. It's a feeling many have shared with me. The tough work is discerning whether such promptings are a true calling or mere escapism. I remember Peter who was beset by the troubles of the world and wanted to focus on his spiritual work and nothing else. He said that he wanted to go and live in a tent on top of a hill and have nothing to do with anyone. We laughed a little when he realised that he would still need someone to make the tent, to provide the transport and the roads and the food. Few of us are called or able to live in complete isolation and indeed this may be just an excuse for avoiding the difficult work in the swampy lowlands of the human experience. We can retreat for a while as a healthy spiritual practice, which informs and transforms us in ways that we can bring back into the world as we re-engage with our community. For most of us, the Way is one of being monastic, single pointed, within whilst walking the world with engagement and commitment. Eremitism (being a hermit) in this sense is an inner quality of non-dual consciousness; centred in the Self (not self-centred) whilst walking the world with practical feet.

A community of fellow spiritual travellers can be really helpful along the Way. Such a mosaic, such a gathering of persons, is packed with potential for spiritual maturation. Firstly, because it provides us with the milieu in which to practise what we preach, it becomes a container for our transformation from self-centredness to Self-cenredness. Secondly, because being among others we have the grist to the mill in our everyday contacts that refine us (participation in community is guaranteed to flush out our ego shadows!). Thirdly, because being in some form of community, temporary or permanent, offers the context for us to be helped ourselves. Fourthly, because in community we can be of service to others. Finally, being with

"In the spiritual life the last thing to go is fear."

others in community also provides opportunities for shared spiritual practice which have quite a different effect from going solo – the impact of a 'gathered' Quaker meeting, a shared reading of psalms, chanting in a group or dancing in a circle is very different in impact from Soul Work alone. Indeed some forms of spiritual practice are impossible solo, such as circle dancing or choral music. The collective experience brings new dimensions to our spirituality. Another aspect of being in community is the opportunity to be of service to others beyond it - perhaps helping locally those who are ill or disabled or in undertaking collective social/political action as expressions of our values. Lastly, our Soul Communities are also sources of friendship, fellowship and fun. Joy and pleasure are also part of the way Home.

Of course, not all communities are healthy; they can be just as toxic and dysfunctional as any society or family. Cults that emphasise complete surrender to their doctrines or leadership are best avoided. Seeking out the healthy Soul Community is part of the process of discernment, for just because it is tough does not mean it is unhealthy. As with finding a Soul Friend, we have to recognise that difficulty is itself a spiritual challenge and not necessarily something from which we must walk away. However, in general, communities in which we feel oppressed or threatened as opposed to challenged or stimulated are best avoided.

If we look again at some of the pointers at the end of Part 5, about unhealthy directors, then many of these principles can also be applied to the Soul Community. It is important, for example, to check in advance what the requirements are before signing up. Some, like the monastic traditions have tried and tested 'rules', possibly going back millennia, designed to nurture the soul and protect both the individual and the group, especially vulnerable individuals, children and minorities. A further good guide to a healthy permanent community is that its rules are in the public domain, indeed such a community would not permit us to join unless we are very clear about what we are signing up to.

Returning from exile: hard hearts and hard choices
Engaging with a Soul Community may not just mean finding a new one. It could be that we find it possible to return to one we left behind (but see and be present in it in a very different way). For the past decade or more I have been returning from exile and learning to participate once more in my local church. That, of course,

brings with it the challenge of not only being with people in community, my local community (but if we cannot serve on our doorstep then where?), but also holding the conflicts and contradictions that come with doctrines, liturgies and beliefs.

How far, for example, can we participate in a religion such as Christianity if we don't believe in virgin births, miracles, bodily resurrection or the absolute factual accuracy of scripture and many other assertions that might come with a tradition, or at least some parts of it? From personal experience I can say sometimes it's tough doing so, but not impossible, but then I think that everyone participating in a Soul Community will find things with which they disagree; it's a question of discernment, of under-standing priorities and what really matters. Personally I find language and doctrines much less bothersome than I used to, it's as if they flow on through me without trac-tion as I stay with the *credo* quality of my relationship in the Beloved as the priority. The Latin *credo* from which we get the word 'creed' is not so much about accepting certain statements as facts, for the roots of the word lie in the Latin for 'heart' (*cor*) and 'give' (*dare*), but in how we believe 'in the heart', it is a relational feeling quality rather than an intellectual one. This may help mollify some of the strong reactions we might have to certain words and requirements when participating in a tradition or Soul Community.

I'll explore this subject a little later, but it's worth noting at this stage that for some it is right to walk away from a community or belief system. I make no recommen-dation that we have to 'hang on in there' with an organisation whose beliefs and ways of working are anathema to us. Discernment of all our conscious and uncon-scious motives helps us to decide clearly our motivation and our intention for such decisions. For others to remain in a community with all its limitations may be the possible and right action, because we have come to what Liebert [103] called the 'interindividual' response of being able to hold such contradictions and paradoxes (see also Page149). A community rooted in a tradition draws on a rich wellspring of spiritual wisdom. It is possible to draw from that wellspring without being an active participant in the tradition, but being in community and working with it can ground that wisdom in our everyday lives.

One of the reasons I felt able to re-join the church was because I had been able to

"In the spiritual life the last thing to go is fear."

shed some delusions about community. Somewhere lurking in my consciousness was a dreamlike projection that someday I would find the ideal community where everybody agreed with everybody else, where we all believed the same things and where it would all be sweetness and light. It was indeed a dream. In my travels around many spiritual traditions and communities I have experienced each carrying just as much conflict, difference and diversity of view as any other – manifesting in different ways, but essentially the same.

A Soul Community is just like a family in which all kinds of polarisation, resentments and difficulties can be simmering away beneath the surface, and sometimes not very much beneath. And yet like all families, at least reasonably healthy ones, even when we have our differences we can still share a meal together. There seems no point in doing all this spiritual work and professing deeper love and compassion if we cannot express them with our own nearest and dearest. If we are not at Home in ourselves then we cannot be at Home with others. In the Soul Community all these qualities are thoroughly tested.

A task along the Way is to find one or more communities that mirror our journey and offer explicit support. It might be useful at this point to pause and consider what Soul Communities, if any, exist in your own life right now. Just asking around a few friends, apart from the examples I gave from my own life above, I found varied responses – some are involved in a meditation and support group for a Buddhist monastery, some active in Fair Trade or Make Poverty History groups rooted in their beliefs about justice and fairness, others meet to study sacred landscape, create gardens as sacred space, dowse for ley lines, walk labyrinths together, enjoy sacred dance or sing in choirs dedicated to sacred music. Among all these are Christians (8 different varieties), Moslems, Jews, Taoists, Pagans, Atheists, Hindus and one friend who insist he wants to be a Rastafarian. Some mix elements of different faiths in their lives. It seems that our Soul Communities can be overlapping circles of community.

The groups all have important social and enjoyable functions, but they are all directly and intentionally concerned with the spiritual life. Some are challenging as people report the difficulties of disagreement and not always getting on together, but these are overcome (a spiritual practice in itself) as the groups have evolved healthy ways of dealing with these. Groups that cannot develop right relationships invariably collapse, but may wound their members along the way. Being in Soul Communities is not about just being among people and ideas that we always like. When difficulties arise, what is the most compassionate response we can bring so that we bring in more light than darkness?

It's worth reiterating what to do when we are involved in something, be it an occupation, a faith, a group or a relationship (such as with a partner or Soul Friend) that gets stuck in unhealthy patterns. We have only four options really. Firstly, we resign ourselves to its stuckness and just carry on as best we can (with all the accompanying frustration and energy draining inauthenticity). Secondly, we leave with a lot of destructive anger, bitterness and hurt feelings. Thirdly, we leave with as much honesty, love and compassionate feelings and behaviour as we can. Fourthly, we make a conscious effort to transform things, working together to take the relationship(s) into deeper, more authentic, loving and rewarding levels. We must muster all our powers of discernment to choose which of these routes is the right course.

Along the Way I had come to learn that my resentment of Christians and Christianity, because of my sense of woundedness and exclusion, was harming myself more than any others. If I could not embrace my fellow human beings, including those with whom I might profoundly disagree or who might be very hostile towards me, then I was doing to Christians, at least some of them, what I had perceived had been done to me. My exclusion of others was a mirror image of what I felt had happened to me and was equally harmful. Part of our spiritual maturity is to see that if we put even one person from our hearts, then we wound some aspect of our own hearts as well as excluding the other.

This does not mean, of course, that it is right to submit ourselves to any community as some kind of sadomasochistic self abasement; we still have to be discerning and select groups that are healthy and nurturing to our souls. However, it does mean that in not participating with one group we do not put them from our hearts, from our compassion. We can still be loving and respectful of people, even those who might behave towards others and ourselves in quite horrible ways, while choosing not to hang around with them. When we close our hearts to another, that doctrinaire preacher, that treacherous friend, that untrustworthy boss, that hurtful abuser (and the organisations of which they are a part), then the only one we hurt is ourselves. The other does not get hurt by our

"In the spiritual life the last thing to go is fear."

anger or hatred, it burns painfully only in our own being. That is why Jesus said "Love your enemies" [Matt.5:44]; when we do not have compassion for another no matter how 'justified' we might feel, the only one we wound is ourselves.

The closing of the heart, however specific to another we perceive it to be, always becomes non-specific. That anger or unforgiveness or resentment, whatever fear has driven into our hearts, at some level contaminates every other relationship to a greater or lesser degree. That does not mean that we allow others to continue to attack us or wound or threaten us or drop all our boundaries and let them into our lives, but it does mean that we are called to hold them with compassion and let go of all the hard-hearted judgments that we have about them. In doing so, and yes it can be tough work, we set ourselves free. Recently in hospital one of my nurses was rather gruff and unkind when I was very sick. I could see a part of me that wanted to snap back, but I also saw the tired, overworked and scared being before me and chose instead a kind word of support. Her face lit up, she apologised, the tears came and I found myself in my sick bed offering her a much-needed listening ear. I smiled inwardly at who was nursing who here.

The queendom of heaven on earth.
Practising loving kindness, as with my nurse above, shifts the atmosphere around us. It's what it's like when the 'kingdom of heaven' comes down to earth. This 'kingdom' is not a place but a condition of consciousness. If the Way brings us anywhere it is to this point, which is of awareness rather than place. (Jesus: "The kingdom is within you" [Luke17:21] …"at hand" [Matt 4:17] …"everywhere" [saying 77b of Gospel of `Thomas [116]). Curiously, the Greek word for kingdom is *basilea*. The Aramaic, Jesus' everyday language, is *malkutha* [14]. Both have feminine gender and we therefore might better translate these and other sayings as 'queendom'. Yet, both Kingdom and Queendom fall short in describing what is really a gender-free Ultimate Reality.

The inclination to shy away from questioning the meaning of words that we take for granted seems to be part of the chronic denial, not to say suppression, of the feminine in Christianity and other faiths down the centuries, a subject succinctly addressed, for example, in Anne Baring's magisterial work [10]. Thomas Moore [117], while sticking with conventional language, offers a succinct explanation of the kingdom/queendom, "When you find yourself in the Kingdom, you will be in a different world, though at the factual level everything will seem the same. The Kingdom is translucent and empty. You don't see it in itself, but you see the world altered by it. Where one person sees competition and acts aggressively, you see community and act with compassion." This is the consciousness of oneness with All-that-is, it is the contemplative, mystic mind of non-duality. When we are in loving awareness like this we are in the 'kingdom/queendom', Ultimate Reality, and it is in us. There is no 'this' or 'that', there just is, Sacred Unity.

When we fall into forgetting, that sense of Sacred Unity is lost. I'm reminded of someone who experienced just that. To cut a long story short, she'd fallen into an angry, controlling, resentful place and had started spewing it out among work colleagues who she felt were having a go at her and undermining her. Her reactions to her situation were coming from a place of fear in herself. She'd 'forgotten' her core truth that she was loved completely and utterly safe in the Beloved as she is, without conditions. She recognised she had fallen into forgetting and how her egoic reaction had been to shore up her defences and/or go on the attack (in a sense much the same thing). Being angry and attacking others is a way of defending against the pain and fear of feeling lost, vulnerable, unloved. She spotted too how her reaction was exacerbated because she, or rather her inner ego critic, was also punishing herself for her 'inadequacy' – "I'm supposed to be spiritual, I shouldn't be getting angry with people"!

Her practice of re-minding herself, of returning to a place in herself (in this case through prayer and visualisation) where she knew deeply that 'I am loved' and 'There is nothing wrong with me' enabled her to reconnect with her Source of absolute compassion...and compassion for herself and others. Reconnecting with love of self and the love of the Beloved (arguably the same thing) helped her to let go of reacting and shift to responding from a place of loving awareness - an awareness rooted in knowing that there was nothing to defend, nothing to fear, that in her Essence she is deeply loved and loving. When we 'get' that kind of knowing it sets us free from the constant need to shore up the defences against pain and fear.

Such episodes are also teachers; in the spiritual life the last thing to go is fear. Where it still lurks around it shows us those places in ourselves where we have yet to trust, to have faith, completely. Being utterly fearless and defenceless and rooted

"In the spiritual life the last thing to go is fear."

in such deep trust seems like a tall order, almost insurmountable. It's a lifetime's work, but it does help us to react to fear less by punishing ourselves for our inadequacy and more as an invitation to go deeper into our relationship in the Beloved. It is human to fear, part of the fabric of our being, but the spiritual life can bring us the wherewithal not to be gripped by it. It's worth remembering that even mighty beings can tremble with fear. Consider Jesus when he 'sweat blood' in the terror of what he had to face the night before his arrest and crucifixion. Even he tried a get-out clause, "may this cup pass from me", only to surrender when he realised he must face it fearlessly and defencelessly…"Not my will but…" [Luke 22:42]. If it was normal for someone of his calibre to be scared, then we can be gentle and forgiving of ourselves when we fall into fear too.

The grasp of fear can seem almost choking and inescapable; it hurts us and those around us with its consequences. People who have come to full loving awareness do not behave harmfully towards themselves, others or the world. That's when colonies of heaven manifest the kingdom/queendom of heaven. We only wound others when we have fallen out of that consciousness, that place of full loving awareness, even if momentarily. Some people seem to live in a condition of almost permanent unawareness of love and under the governance of fear (not a few world leaders and notorious criminals come to mind) and thus wreaking havoc wherever they go. Yet those who are in loving awareness, who have done the Work and become at one with the Beloved, their response to such persons is not destructive, but entirely one of compassion for they see that behind the bravado is a person who is in hell, who is suffering deeply and unable to get out of it and is spewing it out on those around them. In this condition of loving awareness we are able to do what Jesus asked, to love our enemies even those 'enemies' in ourselves, those wounded, angry and frightened bits that we don't like and which from time to time, when we fall into forgetting, can erupt from us. The more we remain in loving awareness, the more we are able to love even these into forgiveness, wholeness and powerlessness.

Compassion can therefore be stirred even for those who are violent and hurtful, because we know that they would not be so were they not themselves hurt and wounded and scared deep within. Those who do not 'see' are thus, not because they are stupid, but because their hearts have become so hardened to protect themselves against reality. Our response, albeit often a tough call, has to be one of compassion rather than dismissal.

<u>Just when you think you're holy, try this; practising compassion</u>
It may be that at some stage we are called to work with unhealthy communities, but that calling is quite a different matter from seeking out one or more groups to nurture our souls, the former is the task of mature persons who are themselves healed before seeking to bring healing to others. One of the effects of the Soul Community is to bring all our shadows into the light, so they become available for transformation.

Being in a community aids the work of letting go of our attachments, encouraging us along the Way to more surrender of the self into the Self. There is indeed a sense of working at this sometimes, about discerning that we are making a commitment to saying 'no' to something in the hope of saying 'yes' to something grander, a bigger vision of who the uncluttered self might be, of Home. Discernment can get lost if we are falling into sacrifice, in the sense of striving, overworking, hurrying or pushing to make something happen, to reach a goal or to be pure. It is a subtle spiritual lesson to be learned - striving for a goal, yet giving up the goal; the energy in striving may be the very thing that keeps us from getting to where we want to be. We cannot 'make' ourselves surrender, we can only slowly learn in the everyday to turn our attention to the Divine, settling more and more into a consciousness of 'not my will but...'. It is a cultivation of humility where the ego, the self-will, gives way to the Will. We have explored much about humility and we will do so even more in later pages, but at this point a note of caution - beware of humility, at least false humility that is arrogance disguised. When we experience an authentic call from the Beloved or hear that we are loved and worthy, to deny the truth of these is an inversion of humility. It is a kind of blasphemy in the sense that we have set ourselves up as our own false god over and against the promptings of the One.

A Soul Community is a milieu where we can check out how far the egotistic will has truly surrendered to the Divine will. It is the test bed to see if we can be as authentically loving, inclusive and embracing of our fellow human beings as we seek to be of ourselves. When Jesus offered his two consummate prime directives, to love God completely and to love our neighbours as ourselves, he was not asking us to disconnect from the world to do so, quite the reverse. Thus the Soul Community provides

"In the spiritual life the last thing to go is fear."

us with the opportunity to put into practice what we preach and have learned. It may be simply helping out with the Soul Community's work – such as preparing the meditation room, sorting the finances, helping with teaching or befriending. Thus being connected into our own community of seekers, we may extend that compassion much wider.

In community, as well as in our private lives, we can offer the Soul Work of hospitality. Christianity, Judaism and Islam grew among desert peoples; hospitality could be a matter of life or death when food and shelter were needed. Hospitality (the meaning is rooted in the Latin *hospes* - guest, stranger, and *hostis* - stranger, enemy) is kindness or welcome for the 'other'. 'Hotel', 'hospice', 'hospital', 'host' are related words. In Aramaic we find *ushpiz* (guest). The importance of welcoming the *ushpiz* is found in numerous biblical references; we are reminded that even strangers may be aspects of God for us [Heb.13:2].

Jesus' wandering ministry depended entirely on the hospitality of local people. Soul Communities that are welcoming fulfil their mission of helping people to get to the Beloved; not least by being the very kind of human beings they want others to be; mirroring the Divine, embracing without judgement or exclusion. This can be tough work if we disagree with people or don't like them, when we have to discern where the boundaries lie at home (do we let every homeless person through our doors?) or in our Soul Community and its rules (e.g. who can/cannot partake in certain aspects of religious services) or when the language we use causes disconnection.

Hospitality applies also to ourselves; forgiving and becoming well integrated persons embracing all aspects of our character with compassion. We are thus better placed to be authentically welcoming to others.

Once, while studying at the Interfaith Seminary, I was plunged into a place of deep distress within myself. Old hurts and patterns were surfacing that made me feel bewildered, lost and in much pain. My fellow students had gone to lunch. I walked out alone with a head like thunder. Falling into this dark place was a familiar pattern to me and in my younger day I would drown such pain with drink or drugs or sex. Within 15 minutes of leaving the lecture room on an ordinary London street I was offered all three! "What is going on here?" I wondered. I returned to the classroom to find some solitude, to try and get my head together, because I knew that if I didn't I was about to give up and leave the seminary.

One of my friends on the course came back early from lunch. Linda said nothing. We were alone in the room together. But she went to the kettle, made me a cup of tea just the way I like it ('though heaven knows how she knew) and placed the cup gently in my hands. With a slight touch upon my shoulders she withdrew to sit silently and far off in another corner of the room. My tears came shortly afterwards and something long waiting to be healed finally surfaced into the light of day.

My friend could have fussed around, chattered mindlessly, ignored me or sought to advise me. Yet she wordlessly and kindly offered hospitality and withdrew as if knowing at some level just what was needed. She offered me a profound service that day, although a casual observer might have seen little of obvious significance taking place. Superficially, one person made another a cup of tea without speaking. But go a little deeper beneath the surface of this vignette and we see captured within it the very essence of conscious service that comes with the blessing of the Soul Community. Hospitality is one dimension of service that can only be manifested in community, in sharing with others. Hospitality, welcoming and caring for the stranger, the distressed or the excluded is an expression of love for the other that encourages the transformation of the other. To encourage – from the French *coeur*, heart – is to bring heart into something, someone. Hospitality with others is a spiritual practice where we extend our boundaries to embrace and include the other.

Hospitality if practised consciously may affect far more than our immediate circle and ourselves as is the case with all our Soul Works. One person's transformation and enlightenment tends to transmit outwards like a spiritual domino effect. Here is but one personal example. Alnmouth Friary in the North East of England stands high on a hill overlooking the sea. It is one of my regular places of retreat. After a recent visit I wrote this to the Brothers:-

> *"Thank you once again to you and all the Brothers for the mighty*
> *work of hospitality that you do. I can't emphasise enough how*
> *important it is - this sacred space that you hold. People like me*
> *who run retreats need retreats! So does everyone on the Way in*

"In the spiritual life the last thing to go is fear."

*fact. In my brief conversations with others this week, there was
not one who was not gaining something.*

*I wonder if you and the Brothers always appreciate the holding
power of prayer and hospitality? How important it is to someone like me to feel held and unjudged while I have the blessings
of silence, being untimetabled and the freedom to go deep at
my own pace. The pattern and rhythm of worship creates a kind
of resonance, a kind of embrace, that permits the inner work
and R&R for the body at the same time.*

*When someone takes up responsibility for worship, for creating an
environment that is clean, comfortable, homely and with attention
to beauty of house and gardens amidst fine scenery, to providing
food, a glorious library....well all these provide a powerful, very
powerful, milieu to meet the needs of whoever turns up and whatever level they seek.*

*I have deeply nourishing work and know how to take care of my-
self, but that doesn't stop me sometimes falling into forgetting or
even when pretty centred still needing that time and space when
it's just me and God. When someone lifts off your shoulders, for
just a little while, the labours of the everyday it offers a kind of liberation. Your spiritual practice of service permits an opportunity for
others to go deep, for the Spirit to be at work without the clutter
of everyday concerns for a little while.*

*Of itself, this is a great gift, but look how it ripples out? I spend a
large part of my life with my colleagues picking up the pieces of
broken people on our doorstep and venturing out there teaching
and offering retreats. What touches me touches them and onwards and outward to who knows how many others? The service
of hospitality at the Friary not only affects the lives of those who
come there, but spreads out way beyond the building.*

When we're busy doing something, as you and the brothers al-
ways seem to be, having our noses to the grindstone and elbows
to the wheel a lot of the time, well, this is not a good position to
look up and see the world around us and appreciate the results
of that work. Please be assured the results are deep and wide.

So, may this note of appreciation from one grateful retreatant offer
a little encouragement for your holy work. God bless you, one and
all."

If spirituality were only a private matter, then we would remain caught up in our private selves. When we are not drawn into relationship with others, then spirituality is
just a kind of self-pleasuring; avoiding the hard work of transformation that practising what we believe demands. To some extent the spiritual search can be distorted
and become a way of staying where we are, not facing up to the incoherence of
our experience of ordinary reality, having fun with transcendence to avoid worldly
suffering.

Furthermore, the subjective relativism in post-modern culture and the New Age
movement – 'one truth for me and one truth for you' - may take us away from the
possibility of transformation because it avoids relating and connecting; we each
remain in our own little truth silos. We can do the same with theology of whatever faith, studying it intensely yet not grounding it in relationship with others. We
can easily embrace the great teacher's guidance on, say, the self-evident goodness
of compassion. Putting it into practice with real people might pose many difficult
challenges. Indeed it can be argued that getting hooked on theory and our own
spiritual insights can be a way, unconsciously, of avoiding the messy business of
engagement with the world.

Yet being with others is one way we get to know the Beloved in the now. The fullness of the Beloved is essentially unknowable as I explored in the introduction. In
the Kena Upanishad [88] are these words of wonder about the Beloved, "There
goes neither the eye. Nor speech, nor the mind: we know It not; nor do we see how
to teach one about It. Different It is from all that are known, and It is beyond the
unknown as well." Yet *knowing* is what we long for and through our spiritual work in

"In the spiritual life the last thing to go is fear."

community we can find a Home in the world that is knowable and through that draw a little closer to Sacred Unity. Approaching an everyday activity, such as hospitality, consciously we may find that we shift from the shallow experience of it to realisation that it is full of lots of buttons to be pressed and potential depth for personal insight and connection.

From the known we can connect to the unknowable that lies beyond any definition no matter that we flail around in all manner of theologies. Barth [118] wrote of the "prattle of theology". In the Lord's Prayer Christians say, "Hallowed be thy name" not "Analysed be thy name". That is not to suggest that analysis and inquiry are contrary to faith or the spiritual search. But we are called to know the Divine ourselves not second hand. Sometimes theological exploration is a way of staying in the intellect, avoiding the personal encounter with the Divine, other people and our innermost self. It may be an unconscious drive to keep us from that encounter and all that it would entail.

Theology provides an interesting route for intellectual debate, keeps a certain kind of temperament content and might spark an inquiry that leads to the Beloved. It maybe helps some organisations to decide the 'rules' – and certainly provides many courses, publishers and libraries with employment. Yet I know of no one who ever got to the Beloved through theology. Some people do indeed get very het up about it, but I have sat alongside thousands of people in my time as they approached death and no one ever wished that they'd studied more theology or decided upon the finer points of doctrine. Regrets about not loving enough, yes, but not about learning more theology.

I remember watching a grainy black and white TV programme about the run up to World War II. I was only maybe 10 or 11 years old and someone called Prime Minister Chamberlain was saying something about why Britain should not get involved in a war over a quarrel between peoples far away about whom we knew nothing (and by implication cared even less). I remember especially my dad's snorting reaction and him saying something about trouble far away always coming home if you don't stop it. That moment must have impressed me as a child because it is with me still, and maybe my dad helped to pass on to me then some inkling that my responsibilities while I am here do not stop at my garden gate.

The Chamberlain excuse holds no water anymore. Modern communications bring instant reports of what is happening even in the most remote parts of the globe. We cannot say any longer that we do not know; our awareness of suffering in the world demands a response. The fearful person looks at the world and is inclined to disconnect – "it's not my problem, there's nothing I can do, it's their fault anyway..." The loving person wants to help, but often feels powerless to do something about it. Pressing the guilt button that we *should* help is an unhealthy approach to the problem. (As an aside, shoulds make me shudder! They invariably come from the egoic guilt or punishment part of our conscious- ness. The soul needs no 'should'.)

Few of us have the power and influence of the culture 'stars' or a president or a prime minister to sway the opinions of governments and agencies into action. That sense of powerlessness can encourage us to switch off. Yet millions of people are inclined to the opposite – witness the tremendous global response, protest and petitioning manifest- ed in campaigns against famine, war, poverty, injustice and environmental degradation. The first lesson from this is that individually we may indeed be able to do very little, but collectively we can move mountains.

Feeling sorry for people or situations is not enough. Sympathy is when we feel pity or sorrow for someone else's suffering and misfortune. We can find the sorrow difficult to hold, but the person remains 'someone else'; to some extent we feel what they feel but we remain essentially detached. Empathy is when we step into the other's shoes and feel what they feel, but this can drain us as we enter into their suffering (thus risking becoming overwhelmed and exhausted by it ourselves). Compassion is a 'fire' word; it suggests that we are with the other in their suffering, feel what they feel, but are impelled to action. At the same time we are called to retain non-attachment and safe boundaries so that we do not exhaust and burn out ourselves in the process. We can help the other while retaining our authenticity, our sense of self. It is spiritual practice and its fruits that enables us to 'see' clearly what is going on and engage with the world of suffering but within safe limits.

But why bother at all? Surely other people's poverty is not our problem? In a global market this no longer obtains. The food or clothing or electronics I buy are woven into a fabric of interdependency where these goods directly affect someone else's wage packet and conditions of work in a far off country. We can make choices to buy goods that are fairly traded that are produced with respect for the workers and the environ-

"In the spiritual life the last thing to go is fear."

ment. The choices are not always easy, but we can easily check that label and choose whether to buy something from countries and companies that exploit and impoverish their workforce. These are some responses to material poverty. There are other forms including spiritual poverty, which we will explore in part 8.

Meanwhile, the National Health Service (NHS) in the UK is an example of the principle of community support. I was born into the newly formed NHS and my mother was very sick and nearly died. Access to health care that was free at the point of delivery kept both of us alive, as it has millions of others. The NHS system, indeed our taxation system as well (however flawed} is predicated on everyone giving something to lift people out of ignorance, ill health and poverty, with the expectation that some will take out more than they pay in. Why should we do that? Because poverty breeds violence and crime, so we all have an investment in getting rid of it.

A friend of mine, who did not have children, once asked why she should pay taxes that go to parents with kids. Yet those kids grow up to be plumbers and shop assistants and doctors and nurses – all of which were essential to her. We are all interconnected. In giving we also receive. Our Soul Community, large or small, is a place of giving, and as suggested earlier, there is some evidence that people who feel they are giving more to their community than they get out of it are happier and healthier.

Community has no walls.
Let us not underestimate the power of the compassionate heart that lies in each of us, although sometimes buried deep, willing to help others in trouble. All sorts of genetic and psychological arguments can be put forward, but perhaps it is very simple. It is the very essence of what it is to be human to care for others and we can all do that in ways big or small. Individually it can sometimes feel hopeless, but collectively we can change things. Indeed, looking at the many recent studies on the non-locality of consciousness (e.g. those on prayer, heart energy or distant healing) it is clear that human consciousness transcends the body. Our intentions in themselves can influence wider reality. We might not be able to feed all the poor, but simple actions and healing intentions do have an impact.

Witnessing the monks at Worth Abbey, in their daily round of worship and prayer,

I was reminded of a communist friend's dismissal of them as parasites. However, monks and nuns are not withdrawn from the world, rather by being in their communities and their own interior solitude at the same time, they engage more deeply with the human condition. Apart from the fact that the monks I came to know were offering a very useful service to the community (running a school, a church and various development programmes) I felt they were doing something else, invisible but vital. The vital (*vita* - Latin for 'life') of Soul Communities, wherever they are, in their prayers and meditations while seemingly inactive are bringing life to the world, holding compassionate intention in their consciousness.

Where other parts of the world may have a warlike consciousness, perhaps by holding a peaceful one those who apparently are 'doing nothing' may in fact be offering a powerful counterpoint of consciousness, preventing ordinary reality from a complete descent into darkness. Across the world, Soul Communities of all shapes and sizes are, I suspect, contributing along with individuals to a force of prayerful love that may be helping to hold the whole of the creation together.

Individual acts of soulfulness are of value too, for in an interconnected cosmos the one is part of the all. There is a story of a man walking along a beach after a storm; thousands of starfish had been stranded. He picked up one starfish after another and threw each back into the sea. His neighbour laughed at him, "You're wasting your time, there's millions of them, nothing you are doing matters." "It matters to this one," he replied.

The Soul Community provides the context where we can walk our talk and in doing so it moves us into greater spiritual authenticity; the impact ripples out way beyond the immediate group. It is also a place where we can get taken care of. Not long ago I was quite ill and my consciousness was knocked sideways by a combination of pain, anxiety and medication that seriously disturbed my consciousness. Spiritual practice such as simple prayer and meditation was not possible. I was touched that so many in the local meditation group, fellow interfaith ministers, friends in far off places in email contact, my local church – all these included me in their prayers (and it is worth remembering that there is compelling evidence for the power of non-local healing [119]). This is another example of the benefits of the Soul Community. The spiritual search can sometimes be a lonely and frightening place. The Soul Community can

"In the spiritual life the last thing to go is fear."

step in to help us in that distress when we need it. Others can pray for us when we cannot do so for ourselves.

We are called to love our neighbours as ourselves [Lev.19:17-18; Mark.12:31], but I am struck by how many people seem to miss the second part of that statement. We seem ever so willing to help others, unwilling to ask for it. Loving ourselves is part of the equation in the Soul Community, because we deserve it and because, not least, to do otherwise denies others the blessing of giving. It is just as important to ask for help and prayer as it is to offer it. When we cannot participate in this way it shows that we have much to learn about the mutuality of caring, our own self worth and humility. Indeed "compassion starts with ourselves, although this can sometimes be seen as gratuitous self indulgence. No, it is much more than that. Unless we love ourselves first, loving others comes from an effort-full place of woundedness within. Loving ourselves first unleashes the boundless love that lies within, the source of the Beloved. Once we heal our way into that, it is set free then to love our neighbours and the world" [120].

We are all in this together
Ram Dass and Paul Gorman [121] write, "At times, helping happens simply in the way of things. It's not something we really think about, merely the instinctive response of an open heart. Caring is a reflex. Someone slips, your arm goes out. A car is in a ditch; you join the others and push. A colleague at work has the blues; you let her know you care. It all seems natural and appropriate. You live, you help." This "naturalness" of helping, of being of service to others is a deeply affecting human response. It is not the sole province of professional helpers. Some have argued that it may be genetically determined – a Darwinian process where humans and their communities who helped each other were more likely to survive and therefore passed this trait on down the generations. Others see psychological processes at work, an extension of natural parenting or the result of patterns imprinted on us in childhood, where the child who helped the adult got rewarded with approval and satisfaction.

The major religious faiths have added their influence, for each in their own way espouses the duty of human beings to be of service to each other if we are to attain enlightenment, heaven or divine approval. Whatever the cause of our desire to be of service, it remains one of the most powerful forces binding human beings together. Mutual support is the essence of the Soul Community; without it relationships, communities, societies fall apart. It is not insignificant that some of the most powerful stories to emerge from any natural disaster are not just about the suffering, but about how people share what they have and help each other even in desperate and life threatening times.

Yet in these times of the 'subjective turn' [3] conventional organisations are in flux. We are having to explore new ways of community and connection. Some New Age thinking suggests that riding on the back of the Age of Aquarius has come the shift into individual expression. The age of Pisces associated with structures, bureaucracies and authoritarian hierarchies and authorities – in work, education, religion, politics – has had its day and slowly we are emerging into a new culture where the locus of control of our lives (driven in part by social media) facilitates connection at levels and in ways undreamed of by our ancestors.

More and more we see organisations and political movements shifting away from models of centralised and bureaucratic control and into models of social engagement: - crowdfunding, petitioning, pop-up stores, communities or spontaneous events, for example. This has impacted no more than on religious organisations where the individual spiritual search demands bespoke solutions rather than 'here's one I've prepared for you', where the inclination is against clustering. Each unique soul, it seems, is bent on finding its own way Home and one-size-fits-all no longer obtains especially in the 'developed' countries. These have met, to a degree, most of the material and social needs of their populations, which then seek more than material satisfaction.

Despite the promo' material, religions often reinforce the ego's agenda. The latter can adapt to either rigid systems or freewheeling individuality; it's clever like that. Religious organisations still tend to cling to needs for certainty, security and black and white views of the world. Even when stimulated to service, they may wrap this up in faux humility and generosity – not really geared to substantively helping others but more geared to inculcating a sense of goodness for the participants. A small example has been the rise of giving to food banks in the UK. All well and good, and lots of people do indeed get food who would otherwise miss out, but this merely

"In the spiritual life the last thing to go is fear."

keeps the poor where they are, food banks without active campaigning for food jus-tice – challenging the very roots about why so many people in a prosperous country like the UK (and many others) need them in the first place.

Thus the religions, or any Soul Community come to that, fail if through their work they do not produce substantive transformation of the world we live in. That cannot be done without substantive transformation of those who participate in those spir-itual or religious communities. The real work of the spirit (which unconsciously or otherwise religions sometimes avoid – it would be too challenging to the status quo) is a deep personal transformation of their participants, nothing less than a complete re-seeing (over perhaps many years of work) of 'who I am' and 'how I may serve'. The transformative work of the spiritual life, the deep and authentic transformative work, sabotages the accretions of the ego and changes us at a profound level.

For some it stops at the individual; both Old Age and New Age religions or spir-itual movements sometimes just focus on the personal experience and leave it at this self-gratifying level. But there is more. The authentic transformation not only changes who we are, it changes how we function in the world, how we question injustice, work for change and engage with the relief of suffering in all its countless forms. This is precisely the model offered by spiritual masters such as Jesus or the Prophet or Krishna or Lao Tzu or Moses and many others. The Beloved does not call us into relationship so that we can just have a feel good happy-clappy time, but draws us into complete engagement with ordinary reality that we may participate in the healing of its brokenness in whatever way we are called.

Religions tend to have a tension between moralism and mysticism, between telling people how to live by the rules and encouraging the relationship with the Beloved that produces such transformation that we live morally anyway. It's no good trying to do and be good under our own steam; that can only take us so far and can lead to exhaustion and anger or fear that we are still not good enough. Getting into relationship with the Beloved (including through our 'guru') and with our Soul Com-munity opens us to the transforming power of love, from which we become and do good in the wider world.

There is a deeper level of consciousness at work here too. Every single major spiritual teacher down the ages drew the attention of his or her communities to poverty. All the various holy books that followed had something to say about the poor and the responsibilities of the not-poor. Their teachings offered a profound wisdom long before the modern science of quantum physics began to suggest it – that everything is connected to All-that-is; that we are all bound to each other by an awesome intricacy and complexity in the cosmos. Try as we might to make the other's problem just that, the other's, there is in reality no other, we are all one. From scientists (Einstein [21]:"A human being is part of the whole, called by us, the 'universe'." to poets (Tennyson: "I am part of all that I have met…" [122]). We find a unity of thinking about the connectedness of all.

Mystics and scientist here meet on common ground. Bohm's [123] 'implicate order' rubs shoulders with Sheldrake's [124] 'morphic fields'. Shifting scientific perceptions of reality are not that far removed from the mystical descriptions found in all traditions. Namely, that the cosmos is alive, conscious and connected – everything is whole, nothing is separate. In the quantum/fractal universe the small affects the large, our own connection, action and awakening assists the awakening of all. The Soul Community is not just our meditation or temple group. As we expand our consciousness we see that the whole is our community.

More than enough for all
Divine love by definition is superabundant and can never be exhausted. If the Beloved, who is love, is infinite then the love is infinite. The Work cultivates a consciousness of abundance. When we fall into egoic mean-spiritedness, fear or lack of compassion it is usually because we have forgotten that abundance, perhaps because of a painful experience or anxieties about health or money or other things. Our Soul Works are our aide to drawing us out of that consciousness of lack and back into the essential abundance. Our spiritual work teaches us that love is not that perceived by the ego, which sees it as a cake where if one person gets a slice another gets less. We come to know the true Love that has no limits, wherein we find we can live in the world with greater generosity because we know that we are not in lack and never could be. Authentic spirituality mirrors in our relationships with others what we experience of the boundless love in Sacred Unity; a unity where everything is connected.

"In the spiritual life the last thing to go is fear."

Ram Dass and Gorman [121] add, "When we join together in this spirit, action comes more effortlessly, and everybody ends up nourished...We take pleasure not only in what we did but in the way we did it. On the one hand the effort was so natural it might seem pointless or self-conscious to make something of it. It was all what it was. Yet if we stop to consider why it all felt so good, we sense that some deeper process was at work. Expressing our innate generosity, we experience our 'kin'-ship, our 'kind'-ness. It was 'Us'. In service we taste unity."

In community whether temporary, permanent or virtual, we find the opportunity to give and receive service. To be neighbours to each other, and this is service rooted in *agape*, compassionate love for one's fellow human beings and such communities are embedded in helping each other and not in seeking power or profits. Each caring relationship is also pregnant with spiritual potential. Countless opportunities to deepen our understanding of who we are and why we are here are presented to us; the Soul Work for expanding our consciousness and connection to Source, whatever we perceive that to be. In every helping relationship we may ask honestly of ourselves not only "How can I help?" but also "What is this doing to help me?"

I have suggested that the Soul Community is also a place of testing and discernment, and a recent news report reinforces this truth. A man felt he had been guided by God and told to kill his sister. Leaving aside the elements of possible psychosis here, this is an extreme example of what can happen when we have what we think are spiritual experiences, but they are not questioned. The presence of a Soul Friend and a Soul Community might have asked that man some serious questions about the veracity of his calling.

Reference to the Soul Food of scripture about killing, to the Soul Works of meditation or prayer before action might have added to the discernment of the truth of his 'revelations'. Another example comes to mind of Julia, who had just completed a series of workshops at a well known New Age retreat centre and reluctantly returned home. She was about to leave the country and had planned trips to pursue her spiritual goals, including a trek to India to Sai Baba, to see Mother Meera in Germany, to seek out the Dalai Lama and to work with a shaman in South America.

I felt uneasy about what was going on with her. While honouring the wonderful insights she had received on the course, which had been life transforming and the spur to get to the Beloved, I sought to query with her the implications of packing up and leaving. She became rather cross with me when I did not offer my whole-hearted support for her journey. She was indeed distressed and struggling to make choices, but the passion following her discoveries seemed to have quite knocked to one side awareness of her responsibilities. She could indeed set off, but she would be leaving behind three very young children, a husband and two business partners to whom she was deeply financially and morally committed. Her personal journey, it seemed to me, included accepting some difficult lessons that included meeting re-sponsibilities and not just abandoning them. Her desire for freedom seemed simply reckless and damaging for others. Perhaps her spiritual practice at this time might equally be found in dealing with her relationships and responsibilities as in jetting off and leaving them behind. Finding ourselves does not mean that we have to lose and wound others.

The history of religion and spiritual awakening is littered with stories of men and women who abused their calling, themselves and others when their convictions were not challenged. Soul Friends and Soul Communities are prerequisites to guide us along the way, to test out whether what we are experiencing is the stuff of in-spiration or delusion. Too many people have been wounded because they had no friend or group alongside them offering spiritual accompaniment and, through dis-cussion and prayer, providing checks and balances; opportunities to sort the wheat from the chaff, the authentic from the bogus.

In the Soul Community there is no 'other'; we are all in this together, and in coming together we experience the ever-present origin, the Presence that knows us as we are known. We do not exist in the world just as an "I" but as a "we". In community we express mutuality in the giving and taking between each other along the way to our personal and spiritual maturity. When we come together we may do more than meet as persons, for there is a transpersonal quality to it. When we gather to consciously and prayerfully care for one another we are mirroring, indeed inviting, the divine presence. Then we may shift into recognition that it is not so much us but the very consciousness of the Beloved at work among us, doing the discerning, feeding the love and guiding the "way of seeing".

"In the spiritual life the last thing to go is fear."

Different faiths have different concepts and names for it, but it is essentially the same, the inbreaking of the Divine into community. The Soul Community is the opening for the Beloved to pour into the world, communities of heaven to be established and where that which is above is manifested below. The Soul Community is a community of companions, recognising that we each bring our unique struggles and our unique gifts, and many of them may be tough gifts – for there it might be argued that it's not much of a discipline where we only have to love people that we like or who love us. Those who are our 'enemies' (including our own ego 'enemies') also have something to teach us about love, for love is the only thing that drives out fear. All those gritty bits between us grow out of fear. "Heaven on earth comes when we respond from love not fear", as Gary Zukav [125] wrote.

In this sharing we draw strength from each other and for ourselves where our spiritual search can find anchorage and minimise the risks of spiritual waywardness. New insights, ways of seeing, and healings emerge. No community is perfect, in the sense that it is free of problems and conflicts, but in a way these imperfections are perfect, forming the grit for the oyster of the Soul Community from which a pearl of great price may emerge. Our Soul Community is a sort of family, and like all families they can be dysfunctional. Being in family we need to be alert, through loving awareness, how we and others may fall into unhealthy parenting or child-like roles... more grist to the mill! Nevertheless, our Soul Community is a place where we can come to be the best we can be. As we draw closer to Home, that divine light in us shines more and more. Without needing to do anything or be other than our loving, aware selves, we hold the possibility of transmission. Who we have become and are becoming, without us lifting a finger, allows others to be transformed through our transmission of the radiant Presence within.

No community is ever 'there'; it is in an endless process of becoming; each member and the whole is vital to that process. Each person's enlightenment contributes to the other, and until all are free none of us is fully free. The Soul Community is another milieu for our awakening on the Way Home.

You can arrive at a hotel, one you have seen before,
and sit in the same chair with the same covers
with the same view from the window and the same staff
and the same people from last year
like Michael who remembers you and you say,
because you feel,
you feel,
"It's like we've never been away!"
And the space between now and then
was the frame for a work of art.
Like a dark room suddenly and momentarily
illumined by a camera flash.
And in between,
life sandwiched between life; grown ever thinner.
God pours down the windowpane in a summer storm
And drips down to the cut grass
(eyed by the corncrake in the bushes)
a holy libation; God watching God falling against God.
And so we sit like children, caught twixt cradle and coffin,
staring out at the window to the ocean,
feeling the repulse of the sea air rushing
beneath the wings of disappointed terns
diving again and again and again
into the fire, the remorseless fire
taking flesh from flesh, flesh from bone,
and wailing "I am, I am, I am!"
Stripped of change and chance;
ashes to ashes, dust to dust, dust to nothing,
for there was nobody there.
Only the facing of the ocean,
the endless watching.
Waves now fall and rise and retreat
and rise again; a momentary identity
in eternal shuck and draw, rising from the universe,
falling back into unfathomable unblemished depth.

You could hear this and hear nothing,
read it and read non-sense,
smudge your fingers in the ink to find no word lives there.
For this you can only feel, and to feel must experience.
And going through it you know,
know,
because you have gone through it.
There is the Way and there is not the way.
My words slip and slide once more
sucked into the vacuum of a receding wave
broken like these shells on the rocks of time
glistening in the memory when the wave has gone.
For there we have been which is every place and no place.
There we have been where there is no have and no been,
only the now left floating in the ocean
like a driftwood barge or
a child's yacht lopsided in the surf.
In a moment, in the twinkling of an eye
all seas, all eyes, all words caught and held.
Caught and held only to be lost again
left behind in the corridors of memory,
empty now and windblown through the cracked plaster.
No memory,
for no one was there.

Part 7

"In Nature's infinite book of secrecy,
A little I can read." [126]

Soul Foods: inspiration and perspiration

'There' and 'not there'
It's no coincidence that this book begins with a quote from poetry. The arts can feed us on our journey simply because they can touch us deeply in ways that discussions about facts or theories along the Way cannot. It's no coincidence that all religious traditions engage with words, imagery, movement and sound as ways of connecting to the Beloved. Spread out all around is a vast smorgasbord of nourishing options that can help us on our way, inspire us.

Mother Meera draws thousands of people each year to meditate with her in silence and to step forward when ready to receive her blessing. She is one of the few New Age 'gurus' in Anthony Storr's [86] searing analysis who is not condemned for exploiting or abusing others. I went to her home in Germany many times down the years in the quest for truth. The evenings were devoted to silent time with her, but during the day I walked the dark forests south of Limburg or spent time in solitude in my hotel room. In these weeks I would dedicate my time just to the search, avoiding that temptation to bring the mobile phone or computer with me 'just in case'. There would be time to fast and pray, to reflect, maybe work with the Tarot or the Enneagram and most of all to read. I would go with far more books than it was possible to read in a month, let alone a week.

Yet in books of poetry, great literature and scripture from different faiths we can find inspiration. Some of those that have influenced me I have listed at the end of this text. Many books have fed me down the years. The same can apply to music, theatre, film, art and all the other creative human endeavours where depth of inspiration is sought and shared…all Soul Food. The same applies to that which is not part of human creation – the beauty of nature, the experience of the elements, the wonder of the night and day skies…all about us is an abundant banquet for the soul.

"Coming Home is not escapism, but a plunge into the moment and eternity at the same time."

To be inspired is, literally, to be in-filled with the spirit. When we read a book or look at a piece of art or listen to music we enter into the thoughts indeed the being of another person. All about us a vast work of art is available to us – the night sky, a winter storm, the light on a hillside, the rustle of leaves in the breeze, the burgeoning of life all around us…everything is singing an enormous song of inspiration to us, if we but listen and see and touch. Perhaps, in some way, when truth that we read or see or hear touches us deeply, we are entering into the mind of the Beloved. Sometimes while on retreat I would read a passage or go to a piece at random and it seemed to fit perfectly with what I was seeking or experiencing at the time. The words and their meaning would be so wonderful as to make me want to literally take a deep breath. We breathe in, in-spire, books of truth and they feed our souls as can the output of all the arts and in the presence of nature.

Then, whilst on those long days of 'time out' from my usual routine I might take a long walk in the forest, pausing often just to take a deep breath in the earthy air or just find a spot to meditate. Sometimes I was on a spiritual high after some profound insight or still moved by the impact of Mother Meera's blessing. At other times it would be a real spiritual low as I struggled with some painful blockage, aridity or the sense of being in a void. Some people claim Mother Meera is an avatar, an enlightened being and a manifestation of the divine feminine in the world. They are devotees and worship her and ascribe great powers to her. I don't know if all that is true, but I do know that those weeks in Germany were often deeply moving and replete with rich teachings. Was it her working some magic, was it me willing to bring my 'stuff' there and work on it, was it simply the act of stepping aside from ordinary life that made the liminal space for these things to happen spontaneously? Perhaps all or none of these.

These times also reinforced the need to take time out as a spiritual practice, a subject I will develop more in part 8, away from ordinary life. They gave me many lessons in the pitfalls of spiritual duality. I could return from Germany feeling blissed out and at one with the world, arrive in Manchester and begin the drive home only to have someone cut me up on the motorway and I would feel enraged! There can be times when we feel spiritual and times when we do not, times when we feel connected and at Home and times when we feel exactly the opposite. Spirituality here has become reduced to whether we feel good or bad. Part of the work is getting beyond the perception of 'this is spiritual and this is not'.

In a busy life with many demands on our time and attention, the spiritual life can get squeezed out - and look at what I've just written, that the spiritual life is somehow separate from the ordinary. The Hindu concept of *aduaita* is relevant here - oneness or non-duality (in fact the word duality is derived from the Sanskrit *duaita*). We can find it relatively easy to 'be spiritual' when we are away on retreat or during our quiet time at home when the family is away, but then we can 'lose it' when we are caught up in the pressures of getting on with life. All the Soul Care suggestions in this book guide us to a different plane of consciousness, no splitting of the 'spiritual' from the 'other' but a recognition, a re-cognition, that it is all one in Sacred Unity. This is the mind of the mystic, the contemplative and the non-dual witness-participant.

'Losing it' is an ego concept, a thought, a very powerful one but an ego thing none-theless. It is a fear-based idea that separates and conflicts. We cannot lose what is our essence, rooted in our very being; all we can do is (temporarily) forget that truth. Thus, if there is a reason for our Soul Works (Part 8) such as prayer or meditation, it is to cultivate an awareness (a loving awareness), it is to keep hauling us back to re-membering who we really are and what is really going on as the many planes of reality play themselves out inside and outside us. Our little egos (bless 'em, and remember not to get in a fight with 'em, that just feeds the little beasts) will find umpteen routes to hang onto their power. They also tend to get more sneaky as time goes by and they're getting sussed out, including telling us we're rubbish for not being spiritual enough or taking time out to retreat or getting angry and fearful in the everyday buffetings of life.

The voice of the inner critic (q.v.) can be mighty powerful. "So, you think you're getting spiritual? Huh! What kind of spiritual are you when you can't decide whether to sleep or pray in the middle of the night? What kind of spiritual are you when you didn't do your meditation this morning because you had that deadline to make for work? What kind of spiritual do you think you are when you are mightily furious with your neighbour who's just trashed your car?" and so on and so on and so on..... The watchwords here are patience, persistence and perseverance. First of all when we catch ourselves thinking that we've 'lost it' or we're not good enough, at that moment of awareness we can, instead of beating ourselves up, re-mind ourselves

"Coming Home is not escapism, but a plunge into the moment and eternity at the same time."

with loving awareness and with compassion for ourselves in our struggle and invite the inner critic(s) to take a back seat. When we 'see' we can then 'feel' (sorrow, pity, compassion - for ourselves and our struggle) and from that place gently remind ourselves that we're just doing the best we can.

After a while we may find that the times of disconnection diminish and there's less of 'Now I'm aware/meditating/being spiritual' and 'Now I'm shopping'; more 'Now I'm aware while shopping'. This perennial tussle in our consciousness is par for the course. Don't despair. With the Work the times of dualism do get less and we become more kind to ourselves when we fall into forgetting. The compassion for our yuckyness and ourselves softens our response from 'Look at you, you never thought about God or held loving kindness for 95% of the day.' to 'Well done, I had 5% of my time feeling connected today.'

Those who work with others on the Way seek to cultivate non-duality as much as we can, so that we can be there for others who are also wading their way through it. Embracing and deeply integrating the essential Oneness of All-that-is, getting free of the delusion of separation, holding the cosmic interconnectedness of all things that modern physics is demonstrating and which the mystics have always known - all this is a quality we develop as our spirituality matures. I have never met anyone so possessed all the time. The track record of all the great teachers from Jesus to the Buddha from Lao Tzu to the Prophet and onwards to modern day acknowledged holy persons and wisdom teachers…they all show that they too encounter(ed) this challenge. In fact I'd be very wary of anyone who doesn't own up to it. It is the human condition, it can be the catalyst for the determination to continue and it teaches us humility.

There is a story told of Guru Nanak – founder of the Sikh faith. Dismayed by the warfare in his country between Moslems and Hindus, he sought to find the common ground of truth to unite his people in God. He journeyed to Mecca and rested in the street with legs outstretched. People remonstrated with him, for the soles of his feet were uncovered and by chance facing the direction of the holy city (an unpardonable insult). His response was to challenge his tormentors: "Show me where God is not and I will point my feet there."

If the Divine is all and everywhere, in all things yet contained by none and all things are contained in the Divine, then separation from the Beloved or the possibility of the Beloved being in one place and not another are just thoughts, very powerful thoughts, but thoughts nonetheless. We may actually be Home all the time, we just have not yet realised it. The good witch of the north in the Wizard of Oz comforts Dorothy, who is weeping that she wants to go home, by reminding her "But you are home, all you have to do is wake up!"

Our true Home is within us all the time, all we have to do is become aware of it. The kingdom-queendom is within and spread out all around us. All our Soul Care is designed to cultivate that truth. Our path is not found outside us, in the light of some other spiritual career or some other person. As Jesus reminded us "You are the light of the world" [Matt. 5:14]. That which we seek, and the way to it, is present in the here and now, ready and waiting in the depths of our own being. False teachers and practices lead us away from this into creating idols of themselves or their ideologies. Spiritual materialism leads us into adherence to, acquisition of and dependency on (false) spiritual things and experiences, because we cannot believe that everything we need is already inside us. Investing the power of wisdom in external things is a kind of idolatry, taking us away from hearing the whisper of the Divine within who is already calling us Home. Soul Foods help us to hear that whisper.

The inner critic and the power of love
If there is Soul Food, we also have good ways of trying to starve the soul. One of the most powerful is the voice of the inner critic.

We can't stop thinking; that is what the mind is for. It starts when we're were born and continues until we die, perhaps with the exception of certain altered states of consciousness such as anaesthesia, sleep or shamanic journeying when it is either temporarily switched off or gets used in different ways. So, given that we cannot stop thinking we can relax and stop trying to make it stop. Getting into battle with the thinking mind, sometimes from a delusion that there is some serene state without it, just sets us up for struggle and disappointment. Of course there are deeper questions, "Who is it that knows I am thinking?" or "If I'm not my thoughts and feelings who am I?" – subjects we will explore in Part 10 page391. Meanwhile, recalling our exploration of the Heartmath work and Psychoneuro immunology in Part 1, we can see how thoughts and feelings are connected and they directly affect our health and wellbeing.

"Coming Home is not escapism, but a plunge into the moment and eternity at the same time."

Neurological studies show how repeated patterns of thinking and feeling tend to get programmed into the very structure of the brain itself. Suppose we believe the idea, for example, that "I am afraid that I am going to die and I will become nothing". If thought and felt often enough this becomes a kind of default wiring in the brain. As far as the brain is concerned, if we're thinking it an awful lot it must be important, so it does its job embedding and protecting it in the very structure of the neurones themselves. Now, if we've had years and years to learn that "God doesn't love me" or "I'm going to die and be annihilated" then every time we get anxious our brain will go to these default thoughts - very strong it's true, overwhelming, but thoughts nonetheless. This process applies to all kinds of negative thoughts and feelings about ourselves; they work like uncontrollable voices causing us to react and undermining our ability to really see, feel and hear alternatives. Our capacity for loving awareness can be shut down and we become unable to find more healthy compassionate responses. The inclination is to try and fight, see off or avoid these thoughts - all of which simply feeds them.

Different planes of consciousness interact. The patterns of thoughts and feelings we have acquired become part of the inner critic, one of the primary weapons of our egoic nature. It (indeed 'they' – some of us seem to have whole armies of inner critics!) conducts a relentless assault upon the psyche to keep us under control and the ego in charge. Such 'negativity' suffocates our longing for love and our ability to connect, which in turn affects out immune system, our physical condition (especially the heart), the networks of neurones in the brain and our emotional intelligence. What we think and feel about ourselves affects our bodies and our whole way of being in the world. The inner critic has the power to sabotage and subvert almost anything we might do should it get the merest whiff the false self might be losing control. It is a master at keeping us afraid, self-limiting and even making us emotionally or physically dysfunctional.

I recall one woman, working as a nurse, who arrived at the Sacred Space retreat exhausted and burned out, caught up in patterns of over-giving, doing her best to make it all OK, trying be kind and caring, going the extra mile, missing those breaks or getting off work late. Then the complaint came in from a patient – was it a misunderstanding? Had she got it wrong? "I'm always caring to my patients, I treat everyone the same, how could he say such things?"

The thought that someone had something bad to say about her, justified or otherwise, had cut her to the quick. It seemed like the world had turned against her, not just the outer world of the patient who had complained or the boss who had to suspend her or the colleagues who were asked to provide statements, no, but her inner world as well. Suddenly she was plagued with self-doubt, racked with thoughts that she was 'wrong' and 'bad', that she wasn't 'good enough' to be a nurse. Her inner critic, a voice we all hear from time to time, rooted in our upbringing and the forging of the ego, was having a field day on her. Whatever punishment she felt she was getting from the world around her was nothing compared to the interior voice of blaming and shaming.

Here's the paradox. In a job where she was required to express her compassion for the suffering patients she encountered day by day, she was incapable of extending that compassion to herself in her time of trial. The destructive inner critic had taken over her consciousness, and when we hear a voice telling us we are bad all the time, that keeps us stuck and stops us seeing clearly what has gone on. It inhibits forgiveness, the expression of loving kindness and acceptance of our humanity and our limitations. Whatever the world might be throwing at her for her misdemeanour, real or imagined, it was nothing compared to her ability to beat herself up. Most of us have been in this place at some point in our lives and some of us can feel like we live in it all the time.

There are many ways in which love plays itself out; some have familiar Greek names such as *eros* (romantic or sexual love) and *agape* (love for humanity). Less well known are *storge* (love of family), *ludus* (playful affection), *philia* (love of a shared experience) and *pragma* (enduring love). One other has sometimes had a bad press, *philautia*, love of oneself. It's largely interpreted in the negative – a narcissistic, self-congratulatory kind of love. But there's another side to it, a recognition of our fragility as human beings, the possibility that there is good planted in us more deeply than all that is judged wrong, an acknowledgement that while we may mess up, we are equally deserving of respect, forgiveness and compassion. No one flourishes when they are told constantly they are rubbish, whether that telling comes from inside or out. A big part of the work of my nurse in this story was for her to start with compassion and forgiveness for herself so that she could embrace

"Coming Home is not escapism, but a plunge into the moment and eternity at the same time."

the difficulties she faced with acceptance and equanimity, ungoverned by a sense of attack and defence. The inner critic can be sent packing when we bring in new voices, stronger ones, that tell us the opposite of its demeaning rhetoric.

If we allow ourselves to be subjected to the relentless attack of the inner critic, we block out the capacity of our own hearts to express compassion for ourselves. A compassion that takes the form of a willingness to respect, value and take care of ourselves – to feed our very souls. A compassion that enables us to look upon ourselves with gentleness, softness and an inner embrace that forgives, welcomes and accepts us as we are with all our human frailties no matter how many times we err. A compassion that accepts "I am just doing the best I can". All the main religions place compassion at the centre of their belief systems.

If we repeatedly pay attention to affirming thoughts instead of the critical ones, then the brain begins to learn that these are more important than the old ones and the brain, being very efficient in its use of resources, begins to change its structure. It's as if it is saying to itself, "Oh, I've got all this lovely copper and steel and plastic fixed in my wiring that's no longer being used as much. Another part of the junction box is being used a lot more and needs some more wiring, so I'll strip out the old stuff and use it to help build the new," …the new wiring being... "The Beloved loves me", "I don't need to be afraid, my soul is immortal", "I deserve to take care of myself" and so forth. As we move more to our 'I can-ness', our 'Yes' rather than 'No' way of thinking, the impact of the fear based voices diminishes not because we have fought them off, but simply because we have re-wired ourselves to have more powerful, truthful, default thoughts and feelings.

Another one of the ways the inner critic can get to us is to play the reverse card by donning the voice of inflation – telling us that we are more enlightened than or superior to or above the common run of other men and women, that whatever's wrong its someone else's fault, that we have a special mission to save the world, display magical powers or insights that only we posses, that we can outrun mortality. Seeking to seduce him into his power, the 'devil' sought to try these tricks on Jesus during his 40 days in the desert. Incidentally, it's worth noting how Jesus acted here as an exemplar of how to deal with our own inner (critic) demons of whatever sort. Notice in this story [Matt.4:1-11] that Jesus does not put up a fight, he does not ignore the temptation, he does not pretend that this seductive voice does not exist, he does not threaten to kill it. What Jesus does *not* do is of interest here. He simply says 'no' to it, by referring to what is true instead and simply refusing to give that tempting voice authority. Just as negative feelings may diminish when we do not fight them, so those inner demons of our ego temptations and the inner critic may give up and go away, lose their power, when we acknowledge them but refuse to give them what they want.

The 'energy' of the negative thought/feeling is not ignored but used, turned against itself, as a wake-up call to a deeper truth. These inner critics/demons are always liars. This is a good place to bring in that basic question of discernment we explored in part 5. 'Is this true?' This question, asked of ourselves or of our Beloved or of our Soul Friend or Soul Community, helps us discern more ably what is true and what is false. Whether the inner critic is sneakily playing ego inflation with us or tapping into our wounds of shame, unworthiness, unlikableness, weakness and so forth, a referral to 'Is this true?' is a useful countermanding strategy. If we hear that inner voice telling us we are bad or wrong in some way, we may hold that (not fight it) and at the same time draw our attention to the truth – that actually we do have people who love us, that we have been successful in something, that we have helped others, that the Divine loves us and so on. These and myriad other affirmations can counter the snide voice of the inner critic. When we are under attack like this we tend to feel small, dark, cold helpless, fearful. Affirmations help us to expand our loving sense of self, bring warmth and loving light into our consciousness.

Deprived of attention the inner critics become like small children, inclined to give up and go away of their own accord. While holding them but letting go of our attention upon them we thus shift our attention elsewhere – to remembering love, re-membering it. A simple process to feed the soul and not the beast of the inner critic when it moves in on us is to breathe deeply and slowly. With each breath to think of, re-member, those who love us, places that are dear to our hearts, times of affirmation and success, moments and relationships and people that re-mind of us of the love in our lives, indeed how perhaps the love and the light is far stronger and greater than the shadow of these dark feelings. We may find then that those 'negatives' diminish, get more settled and in proportion. Hence they are 'defeated' without engaging with them in a battle (of wills) at all.

"Coming Home is not escapism, but a plunge into the moment and eternity at the same time."

One of the commonest phenomena I encounter in the role of Soul Friend is the heavy feeling of worthlessness and insignificance that so many people carry. We can absorb these signals from family, work, culture and religions and it becomes a 'truth' that we are useless and pointless in the vast scheme of things and the awesome magnitude of the universe. One night with a friend who follows the Buddhist path we looked up, awe-struck by the Milky Way on a crystal-clear Cumbrian night. He said to me "It makes you realise, looking at this, how insignificant we are in the cosmos." "No!" I replied. "Consider this, we are each of us unique. Nowhere on the planet is there another exactly like you or me, nor has there ever been in its billions of years of history, nor will there ever be again. Not only that, we are each of us unique in the solar system and as far as we know among billions of solar systems in the galaxy there is no other me and you. And further, our galaxy is one of countless trillions of others in which it is pretty certain there is no other you, and further still, all the galaxies of this universe stand among possibly many other universes – and still there is no evidence that there has ever been in all this vastness a you quite like you or a me quite like me. Whether you see this reality as random or purposeful, whether the Beloved is real to you or not, the fact that you and I are here, seeing this for whatever reason in our own unique and unrepeatable or unrepeated way, the very fact that we are here at all and conscious of being here, well, does that not make each and every one of us, make you, make me, pretty damn special? How awesomely magnificent is that, are we?"

Our fear of being weak, of being swallowed up by fear in ourselves and the world, our apparent insignificance in the mighty scheme of things, the vast unfathomable sweep of evolution, the enormity of the expanding universe (perhaps one of many universes), the view that we are no more than animals processing large amounts of other forms of life to stay alive and pass the detritus out of the other end...all this can understandably sink us into apathy or despair. Yes we have animal natures, but we also have a capacity to embrace that and commit acts of transcendent wonder, creativity, compassion and imagination that despite this nature and perhaps because of it, our consciousness makes us awesomely special.

Stuck in our ego identity, our creatureliness and the pseudo-heroic paths we take to deny our death and insignificance (Succeed! Procreate! Dominate! Keep busy! Numb out!) – all this is just an egoic counsel of despair. Perhaps simply because we know our death we can live and fulfil ourselves, love and be creative, perhaps these are precisely why we in our awareness are not quite the same as other life forms, why we are somehow special and gifted of the Divine within each of us.

Yes, the reach for the transcendent could be just another delusion to make us feel good in a meaningless world. But no, there is worth and meaning and purposes *simply because we are here.* And beyond that the wonder of our capacity to *know* that we are here, to know the here and now and that which is beyond it!

Braking the power of the self we transcend the self and discover the reality that the 'something more' we hoped for is real. As we break through the power of ordinary reality we can surrender ourselves to infinity, an infinity that is neither unaware, un-real nor unfeeling. We plunge into the love of the Beloved; it is real and present. Millennia of human history and countless documented experiences of the enormity of this truth cannot be dismissed as mere psychological tricks to avoid our mortality and our inner demons. Our work to get free of egoic limitations and dis-cover "I Am" justifies us, transcends death and illuminates our essential immortality.

When we live from this wisdom we let go of the belief that the vast life force around us is indifferent to us and our search for meaning. That view only holds while we see ourselves as separate from the world, from ordinary reality. Embracing the transcen-dent does not place us outside of nature, but plunges us ever more deeply into it. We are part of life and may come to revel in that participation. *Coming Home* is not escapism, a feel good retreat out of ordinary reality, but a celebratory plunge into its glory into the power of the moment and of eternity *at the same time.*

Heart songs
The soul does not have needs; it is perfect unto itself. Yet food for the soul along its journey Home helps nourish that reunification and reassures the false self. Arguably it's our ego-selves that really need this nourishment, helping them to let go, change their way of seeing things, let the soul take command and even collaborate with it. We can find this kind of nourishment in our relationship with our Soul Friends, Com-munities and Works, but it is also available to us in each moment, among friends or alone, for the books and other things of inspiration are all around us.

"Coming Home is not escapism, but a plunge into the moment and eternity at the same time."

Our Soul Works, Friends and Communities can only take us so far; at some point there is the time of the solitary quest too, alone in a book or on retreat. They are the books on our library shelves, the ones handed over to us which, by chance if chance it be, just seem to offer us the perfect words we need at the time. They might be the holy books of the great faiths, books written by wise spiritual teachers, prophets and poets. But beyond them there is another holy book; it is the book of life, the book of creation. All around us life buzzes and blooms to a thousand songs, every moment pregnant with inspiration, food for the soul. It may be in the arts, music, sculpture and theatre and so on that we find new insights and ways of seeing that refresh and renew us.

It is perhaps no coincidence that the waste land of our culture has also witnessed a burgeoning interest in sacred music such as monastic chant or the arts in the form of icon painting. It may be in the beauties of nature and all that the creation has to teach us as it unfolds around us. It may be in things that are serious, but also in the lightness of a novel or the hilarity of a TV programme that new insight can arise as well. A limitless store of wisdom and truth is all about us, which may provoke an awakening to the wisdom and truth within ourselves. It may be in our path of service where we have the gift of getting out of the way, as my friend Sam described in Part 5. When we are busy being there for the other, we forget ourselves and our 'stuff', including our inner critic, for a while. Paradoxically that creates a space that may permit new insights, blessings and grace to come flooding in.

Great spiritual teachers down the ages used stories or parables to illuminate truth. Written or spoken they offer us insights into a deeper reality. Sometimes these Soul Foods can be troubling, disturbing, making us feel conflicted because they chal-lenge our established way of seeing things. Some of the most important Soul Foods can seem unpalatable at first, sabotaging our set ways of thinking. "Let him who seeks, not cease from seeking until he finds; and when he finds he will be turned around and when he is turned around he will marvel and he shall reign over all." – these words of Jesus in the Gospel of Thomas [116] suggest that being turned around, troubled, made to think again and re-frame our perception of things (in Greek, *metanoia*) can be the catalyst of spiritual awakening.

Soul Foods are firstly those things that make our hearts sing – songs of joy and re-lease, songs of sorrow and trouble. I have mentioned some above which I have in my own life, but there are many, many more. In a recent workshop with a group of hospice staff we looked at what our Soul Foods were. That feeling of being open hearted, full of life, in the moment or being 'blown away' by some new insight or inspiration is what Soul Foods can provoke. We can experience these in our own individual ways in our everyday lives. The group mentioned things like being with grandchildren, gardening, diving, running, sitting by a lake, walking by the river, knitting, painting, mountaineering, having an aromatherapy massage, going to the theatre, friendship, preparing a meal, dancing, helping out at a community centre, visiting an ancient yew grove. These are all examples where we can feel that our soul is being fed and strengthened, full-filled. Many as we shall see overlap into Soul Works (Part 8) and Soul Communities (Part 6).

Entheogens

One theme has been omitted from the list in the previous paragraph and that was the suggestion from one member of the group that drugs could be used to open us up to the Divine, a subject discussed at length elsewhere [34], and about which extreme caution is needed. People have been trying for millennia to transcend or-dinary reality and get to the Beloved (arguably successfully) using what in modern usage have become known as the 'entheogens' – substances that induce an altered state of consciousness associated with an experience of the Divine. Many drugs now readily available to us, from the legal (alcohol, caffeine, tobacco) to the illegal (cocaine, cannabis, mescaline) were once used by initiated individuals, rarely and sparingly, in tribal cultures. They were not the stuff of mass consumption and were regarded as possessing great spiritual power. These substances, which induced al-tered states, became sacred; the holy of holies for what they offered in breaking through the doors of perception [127]. They were therefore restricted to special occasions, people and places.

Modern synthesised substances such as LSD and Ecstasy (MDMA) are entheogens and are consumed on a massive scale for leisure and pleasure. Making available cheap agents of consciousness change is fraught with dangers and one of the rea-sons for strict legal controls. Some might argue that, at last, access to the numinous is (more) available to all and might be of service in the world to wake us all up to a

"Coming Home is not escapism, but a plunge into the moment and eternity at the same time."

deeper reality. Thus we might appreciate and take care of the present one better than we currently do. Yet if we look at the way the early plant-based entheogens were used and controlled there are some important lessons to be learned, for the context matters. Taking Ecstasy along with alcohol, boosted by amphetamines and driven by rap at a wild party will have a hugely different impact (as some of the arrivals in any accident and emergency department amply demonstrate) than ingestion after fasting and ritual preparation, inclusion in a sacred ceremony and environment and guided by an experienced Soul Friend.

Even so, a glimpse of enlightenment is not enlightenment itself and there seems to be no way of bypassing the long-term discipline of spiritual practice, even if there has been an initial opening of the doors of perception. There are no short cuts around the emotional work and the spiritual labour if we are ever to approach healthily, for ourselves and others, the true essence of our being. Furthermore the drug induced experience may leave the user wanting more to repeat it or failing to trust it simply because it was chemically influenced or it fades away in the dusty and unused filing cabinets of memory.

Words and books: reading between the lines
To return to the non-drug Soul Foods; it may be that we approach these things without conscious effort, or it may be that we see the blessing they bring and set our intention to be open to what new offering might emerge from them each time. With Soul Foods, wherever we find them, there are added dimensions if we approach them consciously and in seeking thus we feel moved and inspired. By and large our Soul Foods are those sources where we seek, mostly as an individual interior experience, to draw closer to the Divine, and it is an explicit seeking. There are many pleasures in life and there is no reason why we should not enjoy these to the full, but a different conscious approach to them can reveal new dimensions if we are actively looking to connect with our Source.

All the Soul Care themes mentioned in this book can be approached joyfully and lightly; spiritual work is not all about suffering. In fact if we see the Way as one of pain, labour and sacrifice, then there is an unhealthy consciousness here that is itself worthy of exploration for example in our Soul Community or with our Soul Friends. However, as we have mentioned in the story of Isa (page136) neither pushing away the difficult nor pulling towards us only the enjoyable is advisable. Both such ap-proaches, while understandable, are forms of attachment that obstruct us on the Way.

We are naturally drawn to places and things of beauty. *Philokalia* is the love of spiritual beauty, (which also happens to be the name of a wonderful collection of writings for spiritual guidance [128]) that we seek to inspire us. The *via negativa*, the way of renunciation and letting go of theology or trying to define the Beloved, also takes us into the dark places in ourselves and the world as well. We can find it easy to read a piece of scripture that does not conflict with our feelings or look at a beautiful landscape, and these are all part of Soul Food. Yet words and other things that we find difficult have something to teach us too. In being thus stretched we can go deeper by making the difficulty itself the stuff of spiritual practice, a Soul Food that might be indigestible at first but ultimately nourishes us as we learn to be more understanding and compassionate and at ease with conflict and diversity.

Once we get past obstructions, say in our interpretation of scripture, we may find jewels of wisdom there that we had not seen before. I once found Bible reading, for reasons like these, very problematic. Years of work later, I can now find great depth of insight in, say, the psalms that I had not seen or felt before. Words in scripture can burst with new meaning that we had hitherto overlooked as we heal and mature. There are many scriptural exhortations to help the homeless and poor and those in prison. Reading with more depth we see that words like this take on new meaning – are we not homeless who seek? Are we not in prison who are not free, because of our ego traps, to go Home? Are we not poor who do not know love? When scriptures write about driving away enemies, these can be seen not only literally as rather cruel exhortations, but also metaphors about driving off the power of the ego. Healing the old wounds that blinker our spiritual vision opens us up to new horizons of thought and insight. Things which we once saw as sim-plistic or unrealistic or unpleasant may still yield wisdom especially when we see them from a *mythos* (a subject we will return to shortly) viewpoint, that is, reading symbolically rather than literally. This way of overcoming blockages and using ev-erything available to come to know the Divine does not imprison, it sets us free in unfettered exuberance to full-fill the soul's intent.

"Coming Home is not escapism, but a plunge into the moment and eternity at the same time."

There is the story of the Buddhist monk who received enlightenment by observing his own faeces flush down the toilet. Indeed it can be one of the toughest spiritual practices to contemplate something in the world that repels us and say, "This is of God too"? Florence Nightingale had a short phrase written on cards and placed in each room of her house 'Be not afraid, it is I' (*Ego sum noli timere*). These words of Jesus (he tells people many times in the gospels not to be afraid) to his disciples amid the storm as he comes to them across the water are perhaps in part a teaching that the storm and the miracles are of God too, the wonderful and the terrible are both sides of the same coin. It is easy to repeat those words of Jesus as we watch a beautiful sunset. Can we say the same when we watch a destructive flood wash over the land destroying all before it? Julian of Norwich [17], whom I cited in Part 1, offers us the deep insight of the mystic who moved beyond dualistic conceptions of the creation and saw God wonderfully and unfathomably in all things, even in things that most of us might see as evil or repellent.

Thus, in studying the words in Soul Foods, we learn how to read again, read differently, *mythos* rather than *logos*, that which may hitherto have been hidden to us because we tried to read the words only as facts. A difference in response comes when we read, in what is known in the esoteric tradition, the black letters and the white letters. The black letters are the printed words on the page, the obviously readable. White letters lie between them, full of subtle meanings and possibilities. The task of the seeker is to learn to read both.

However, interpretation can sometimes be a struggle. Some, especially those whose faith is rather brittle, can get stuck in literalist interpretation of holy books. Most people in most traditions see such works as Soul Food to be chewed over and digested slowly, not swallowed quickly and uncritically. People whose faith is fear-based or lacking strength and in whom there is difficulty dealing with paradox, controversy and grey areas will tend to stick to absolutist understandings [103] which does little to nourish the truth in our own souls. *Mythos* sees scripture as rich in metaphor and allusion in which truth rests, *logos* sees facts and literal interpretation as truth. Both can appear in the same holy text, but *mythos* offers us access to a deeper truth. It does not mean that the facts are necessarily wrong, rather it is what they mean that matters.

I don't imagine that when Jesus told the parable of the sower and the seeds that people in the crowd interrupted to ask him the sower's name, or what sort of seed was being sown, or what time of year it was. Jesus, like all great teachers was telling a story, a *mythos*, but what mattered was the meaning; that is where the truth is found. Something can be truthful without being factual, for the story of the sower and the seed, for example, tells us a great truth about the outpouring of love from the Divine, broadcasting it to all, and how individuals may accept it or not. Symbolism helps because the teachings are hidden from or incomprehensible to the intellectual realm. In falling into relationship with the Beloved we look for an encounter with the Beloved. In symbolism, the language of *mythos*, of spiritual truth, of parable, we draw closer not just because we *know* it is right but also because it also now *feels* right. We know the Divine differently thus.

I have encountered many who have difficulty even looking at a book or attending an act of worship that does not belong to their own faith. At a Christian meditation group recently, one parishioner reported that she had to attend in secret as her church saw meditation as a route for Satan. Deep and real faith has no fear, it is open to enquiry; scepticism does not undermine faith but strengthens it in the faith-full person for it permits questioning, uncertainty and exploration without fear that the underlying faith is under attack. A fear-filled person will tend to unconsciously shore up their faith with absolutes. A faith-full person is less fearful, for faith is more than a belief, a hope in certain things; it is a deeper level of knowing.

Several of the prominent and recently well-publicised atheists I cited earlier tend to pooh-pooh faith as something foolish and irrational, the province of the stupid and venal. In their own way they are being as fundamentalist as the thing, religion, they condemn for faith is not about a hope that something is true or hoping that something clung to is not a lie, faith is a knowing of something that transcends rational explanation, it is something deep in the soul, like Jung's quote in Part 2, about 'knowing God' rather than 'believing in', that offers a different dimension to knowing.

Scripture can be read at many levels. So can other books, in a metaphorical sense not just the paper and binding kind, yet equally sacred. John Philip Newell men-

"Coming Home is not escapism, but a plunge into the moment and eternity at the same time."

tioned, at a retreat I attended some years ago, how the Celtic tradition saw the Bible as a main (little) book of learning, but also saw the (big) 'book of Creation'; the Beloved present in the unfolding reality all around us, offering teachings as rich as any of those in scripture.

Jesus offers us some lessons here. First of all he does indeed regularly refer to scripture (though often to challenge it) and we have at least one account of him reading in the synagogue from what we now call the Old Testament. Secondly, he offers us the Book of Nature. Many of his stories and parables are peppered with examples (the lilies of the field, foxes with holes and so on) drawn from nature to illustrate his teachings. Third there is the Book of Humanity. He offers many stories of the human experience (the sowers in the field, the prodigal son, the labourers in the vineyard) as well as the stories around him of the human encounter with him (the rich man, the centurion, the blind man, the haemorrhaging woman etc.). All of these present us with enriching examples of the human condition from which to learn, all the joys and struggles of seeking to follow the Way. Lastly there is the Book of the Heart, the way of contemplative prayer, the going inwards to that 'inner chamber' [Matt.6:6] where we open to a direct encounter with the Divine. Jesus prays regularly and the accounts especially tell of his seeking solitude and silence. It is in the inner chamber (as I have explored in a companion volume on contemplation [52]) that we come into the loving Presence in intimate relationship, the soul in union with the divine splendour.

Thus we might read scripture and other spiritual books, from whatever tradition, and pause to reflect on what is being said to us, then sit and appreciate the natural word we live in, then reflect upon and integrate a human story we have read in the paper or encountered with family or friends, then slip quietly into contemplative prayer and open to the One in whom 'we live and move and have our being' [Acts 17:28}. So many books are available to read.

In Part 5, I mentioned wariness of teachers who advocate uncritical use of scripture and it is wise to approach all words of Soul Food with the same qualification. They can be subjects for rumination and contemplation, to challenge and motivate and can be part of the material we take to our Soul Friend(s) and Soul Communities as a source of reflection and discernment. It has been my experience that an interfaith or interspiritual dialogue and exploration can strengthen and deepen commitment to an existing faith rather than diminish it. We discover that the food of Truth can be found in all faiths and there is far more in common that unites rather than divides. The *mythos* space between the truths and guiding principles of the great faiths is really paper thin.

Body food

A puritanical and absolutist position can sometimes be found along the Way in relation to the food we eat. Extreme dietary requirements, sacrifice of pleasures (which I will touch on more in the next Part) often say more about the person than they do about a particular spiritual practice. There are, for example, very good reasons for eating only vegetarian food (I almost wrote there, 'being a vegetarian' – quite a different issue as we will explore later). However, it is possible to get caught up in a kind of fundamentalist, Pharisee approach where we convince ourselves that by making this sacrifice and following these rules we will get to heaven. I have never met a vegetarian or someone with some other dietary attachment who was any closer to the Beloved than anyone else. I have met some people whose diet and lifestyle choices left a lot to be desired by some standards yet they are holy and wise beings.

There is no evidence that 'heaven' is only full of abstainers from certain foods or those who dress or behave in a particular way. The desire to be good and pure can be the undercurrent that really drives the diet rules, which implies that the person has not really given them up in their hearts. The strict adherence can become a cover. Seeming to be 'good' in something may be a mask to hide deep-seated feelings that we are not already full of essential goodness within. Repression like this, which is another form of punishment, suggests more spiritual work of healing is needed. Restraint, however, offers a more healthy approach for it suggests that we forgo certain foods or drinks (however enjoyable) because they affect our wellbeing or our consciousness. Abstinence helps our conscious attention to our spiritual work and helps body and mind to be healthy and receptive. Dietary restrictions such as vegetarianism may or may not be necessary, but what does appear to be necessary is eating and drinking with reverence and respect for all life and our own bodies. Other reasons include using restraint to help to break the will of the ego or because we are genuinely seeking to adhere to part of a religious tradition that is dear to us or as an offering to the Divine where by the virtue of saying 'no' to some things we give space to say 'yes' to the Beloved.

"Coming Home is not escapism, but a plunge into the moment and eternity at the same time."

Paying attention to our diet and such things as smoking, drinking and exercise that affect our bodily health is itself an aspect of Soul Food. By eating and drinking wisely and healthily we honour our bodies and strengthen them in the service of our spiritual work and our way in the world. Surrendering some things to be spiritually healthy has quite a different consciousness than constantly sacrificing and depriving ourselves of things that really in our hearts we are not willing to do or let go of. What comes out of our mouths, how we speak authentically in the world, is as important as what goes into them.

Refinement

It's my experience that as we become more sensitive spiritually we become more sensitive emotionally and physically too. We can't get drunk or smoke or fill our bodies full of junk food as we used to, even if we ever did. We can't hang around in toxic environments or relationships in the same way. Old friendships, habits, customs, routines may have to pass away. Some relationships forged, for example, when we had much the same worldview as each other may be difficult to sustain (but not impossible) as we transform. Discernment is needed to see which relationships still nurture others and ourselves and can still be held and which need to be let go. Likewise we may find that our bodily tolerance to substances like alcohol, tobacco or processed foods that we once consumed with impunity now changes and we have to reduce or avoid their intake.

We may also find ourselves becoming more emotionally sensitive. The Work takes us past our defences. Some people can think that spiritual practices can help inure them from the pain of life (mindfulness is currently often 'marketed' as a cure-all for stress and turmoil). But authentic commitment to the Work opens our hearts. As we do so we feel the love more, but we feel the pain of the world more as well.

Once, let's say in my 'early days', I was driving home after a wonderful weekend of inner work. I'd read the paper before I set off, nothing unusual in that. Two hours into my journey I had to turn off the motorway. I was sobbing. At first I was perplexed; where was all this sorrow coming from? I'd seen a colour picture on the front page of the paper and in my usual hard-as-nails way had not paid much attention to it. It was of a woman in a floral dress hanging from a tree. She'd killed herself after the loss of her loved ones in the massacre at Srebrenica. Hitherto I would have shrugged this off as just another senseless tragedy, but out of the blue the enormity of what I had seen hit me. I realised then, among other things, that my usual way of bypassing the emotional challenges of life was no longer tenable. The work of awakening into loving awareness makes us more sensitive not less; yes more hurt, but more joy too – and quite simply to feeling more fully alive.

In the past I have enjoyed the role of trustee of Penny Brohn Cancer Care (formerly the Bristol Cancer Help Centre), an innovative cancer charity in the UK. Currently I serve as a trustee for a leading Glasgow charity TheWel. Participants in the wellbeing pro-grammes of both of these Trusts are encouraged to make significant changes to their diet that will improve their nourishment, based on the research evidence for dietary connections with many health problems including cancer, asthma, ME and depression. Diets rich in alcohol, refined sugars, wheat/gluten based foods, processed or non-or-ganic foods are all very suspect based on the most recent research.

There's nothing wrong with having treats, but foods and drinks that make us feel unwell, limit our physical vitality or affect our state of consciousness are risky options if we are seri-ous about our spiritual work. Part of our Soul Food's initiative may be to make some clear decisions about what we will or will not put into our bodies. Our selection of Soul Foods in terms of our diet may entail moral decisions, such as what is good for the workers who produce it or the environment from which it comes. But we also need to beware of the neo-Pharisee, puritanical approach that suggests having these laws will of themselves save us. Only what is in our hearts will save us. A judgemental, holier-than-thou attitude about our diets is spiritually unhealthy. Being a vegan, tobacco and alcohol free, who gets plenty of fresh air and exercise (also Soul Foods) may be enriching for the spirit, but being smug or obsessed about it certainly is not and a sign of more inner work to be done!

Meanwhile, as the deepening of our spiritual seeking gets under way, it is right to take care of ourselves and to seek out the beautiful, the aesthetically pleasing to nourish all aspects of our lives – physical, emotional, mental and spiritual. Soul Work is heart work and it is right to nourish our hearts in every sense. As Thomas Merton [129] reminds us: "The concept of 'the heart' ...refers to the deepest psychological ground of one's personality, the inner sanctuary where self-awareness goes beyond analytical reflection and opens out into metaphysical and theological confrontation with the Abyss of the

"Coming Home is not escapism, but a plunge into the moment and eternity at the same time."

unknown yet present – one who is 'more intimate to us than we are to ourselves.'" The spiritual work of opening the heart to these depths needs to be sustained by honouring body, mind and spirit in all the ways we are able to encounter the Unknown-yet-Present. We cannot see the One with our eyes; they would surely burn out in the face of such radiance. But we can 'see' in our hearts, with our feelings, with that overwhelming sense of fullness and oneness that can arise in those moments when we feel inspired and connected. Anything that nourishes the heart, physical and metaphorical, is Soul Food for the way Home.

Into the desert
Nothing is sometimes a kind of Soul Food too. As I write, the rain pours down on the green fields of Cumbria. There wouldn't be a Lake District without an overabundance of the wet stuff we so often complain about. It is hard to imagine anything less like a desert than this beautiful place where I am blessed to live. But the landscape of the fells evokes some of the qualities of the arid deserts I have traversed in my life – the sense of enormity and of massive indifference to our presence. The high hills, perhaps on a bleak winter's day or in summer very early in the morning before life stirs and the silence is so deep and solid you could almost touch it – they too have that sense of eternal brooding presence oblivious and uncaring of our existence. This place even though the wettest in England, can be its own kind of desert, any situation where we go inside, to an empty place, is a place where we confront God.

"The desert is within you", wrote Jung [99] in his Red Book. The desert on the outside, a place of solitude, of distraction from the everyday, of challenge to the senses may be what we need to mirror our interior terrain.

The desert profoundly influences our cultural landscape, for the great faiths that have forged our recent history in Western Europe after the early Pagan traditions - Christianity, Islam and Judaism - were born of desert peoples. We may not follow a particular faith, but in our laws and conventions and ethical codes, for example, we are profoundly influenced by desert-origin religions. The sociological evidence that I have cited earlier points to an ongoing decline of religions in the UK. Fewer, and falling, numbers of people may be religiously Christian – that is accepting the core beliefs and participating in the life of a Christian religious community, but huge numbers of us remain culturally Christian through the dominant influence this faith has had upon our individual and social mores.

Retreating to the desert was an early tradition of the Christian Church – to deepen understanding of the self and the relationship to the Beloved. I remember a song from the 70s, something about a long trek through the deserts of the US, and a line that says, "In the desert you can remember your name." I sought out many deserts in my own spiritual awakening some years back – spending time in the bleakest of places such as the red desert of central Australia or the desolation of northern Arizona. In Death Valley, California, a dangerous, night-time ride in a world of deep darkness and silence without the comfort of reference points brought me closer to death and my fear of it. Desert landscapes can open us to the wonder and majesty of the Divine. They can also strip us of our significance, summon the ghosts of our deepest fears to haunt us, face us with the terror of our essential nothingness – re-membering our name only to lose it. Everett Ruess, an American explorer of deserts disappeared in Utah's Zion National Park in 1934. Later his boots were found but nothing else [130] and nearby in his handwriting scratched on a rock was "Nemo 1934". In Latin, *nemo* means no one.

Death Valley in the USA is a vast saltpan of a dried up lake deep in the desert below sea level. I have a vague childhood memory of a black and white film of settlers in their wagon trains coming to grief and dying one by one as they attempted to cross this barren, waterless wilderness. However, an unusually heavy rainfall had caused the desert to bloom when I visited with Jeannie. We had been exploring Egyptian mythology at the same time and as we paused in the mountains overlooking the white-baked valley bottom, I said that it felt like the "womb of Isis", the great earth goddess, but she disputed this. The womb was a place of water not the dry heat of this sun-baked bowl.

We descended to the valley bottom, to discover that the lakebed had acquired a thin film of water that had run off from the surrounding hills after unseasonal overnight rain. The water was warm and salty like the waters of the womb. I walked half a mile out across the shimmering lakebed, just wanting to embrace the silence and the solitude and to tai chi in this wondrous place. As I returned, a small knot of tourists had turned up and I noticed they were excitedly laughing and taking

"Coming Home is not escapism, but a plunge into the moment and eternity at the same time."

photographs of me. The water covering the salty lakebed was no more than a few millimetres deep, but it gave the impression on my return that I was walking on water. How deserts can stretch the spirit and the imagination, but also our sense of humour!

Deserts are therefore not just the hot barren places. They can be anywhere, such as the wide moors where I live, that conjure up that same sense of diminution of self, of absence of the usual things that keep us orientated in space and time. The outer reflects the inner, that interior soul landscape where, stripped of its ego identifications, our personhood is left bewildered – if not this, then who am I? The excellent BBC2 series The Monastery, showed what happened when five men entered the Benedictine Worth Abbey. Leaving behind all their usual sources of identification – jobs, relationships and mobile phones – these five entered their own kind of desert filled (or perhaps more accurately emptied) by long periods of silence, reflection and prayer. They arrived with names, but this particular desert soon left them wondering, "Who am I?" - a core question of the spiritual search.

Few of us have the time or inclination to subject ourselves to a desert encounter. Yet the deserts are not only in remote places or the monastic retreats bereft of everyday identification. All of us, consciously or unconsciously, are familiar with the desert and arguably the most terrifying of these are found on our own doorsteps, our day-to-day experiences. There are the deserts of grief, loss and suffering of others and ourselves when all the securities and trappings of our ordinary lives and identities are carved away, such as when sudden and traumatic illness or death strikes. We encounter soulless workplaces and families where we are left wondering why we are there and made fragile by environments and situations that leave us feeling disturbed, barren, bereft. Often our deserts are familiar, more intimate, in which who we are, or who we think we are, is regularly, sometimes constantly, pushed to the limits. They are the arid places of the sick room or the heaving pub, the loveless home or the meaningless church service. They are the cracked plains of our communities where we encounter the drunk or drugged or deprived. They are the baked canyons of our prisons and hospitals where relentless fear burns the psyches of those who must confront pain and loss.

The contemporary desert of our culture, the waste land, is as much a place of potential awakening as any retreat or sojourn in the desiccated Sahara; if we approach it consciously. It is the place where the assault on our humanity occurs at every level – physical, social, psychological, spiritual. It is the place where our personhood is forged, broken, and re-forged. Joy and suffering, sometimes merged within moments of each other, are the undiminished scorching heat of our Soul Work when Soul Food does not seem to be present. Deserts are also cold places, especially at night, where the chilly winds of solitude and the freezing air in the darkness of despair or desolation can push us to other extremes. The desert heat and cold causes expansion and contraction, splitting the ego just like frost shattered stone.

Sometimes we may retreat to our own form of desert, sometimes it comes to us and sometimes we may realise we are already living in one. But to retreat is yet another way to feed the soul, to enter solitude and stillness so that we may hear, what? – the still small voice within. It is the *hesychasm* - the way of uncluttered stillness and repose that draws us into deep contemplation. I've lost count of the number of people who have visited the Sacred Space Foundation's retreat spaces in rural Cumbria who ask "But don't you get frightened and lonely?" or "Doesn't the silence freak you out?" Yet in the absence of other distractions, there is no better place to encourage the reflective turn into the interior realm where that still small voice can be heard. Sometimes there is more truth in silence and this is no more so than when we attempt to speak of the Beloved. No matter what words we use, they never even get close. All we can do is try, and then give up and sit in silence before the wonder of the One who calls us Home. The practice of listening is food for the soul that draws us into Being further and further. More and more of the time we becomes attuned like a radio to a single (Divine) station.

On retreat
There is a tradition in all faiths that to get to know what it's all about there is a need for times away from other people and ordinary life. Some might take to desert or mountain, some to monastic cloister or isolated Buddhist temple, some to solitude upon the sea – countless ways can be found to seek the space that enables us to escape the constant stimulus of ego-orientated daily life. It may be that we will do so for long periods, or it may be that we seek a brief retreat or respite by spending our break time in some quiet room or chapel. This is the sacred space [53] which I have explored at length elsewhere. It is the seeking out/creating/opening to places

"Coming Home is not escapism, but a plunge into the moment and eternity at the same time."

that remind us of and hold a sense of the holy. Such places draw us to the interior *temenos*, the inner temple, the sacred space where we reconnect with the sacred within us and around us in each moment and which never leaves us.

Opportunities to turn within are many, but the pressures of the modern world may crowd them out. We have moments of longing for that space then blink and another month or year of life has gone by and we wonder where it went to so fast? For lots of people nowadays, the car is the only place of solitude we have! It can be very difficult to block out that time for ourselves in the diary and hold to it come hell or high water unless an absolute crisis intervenes. Setting and keeping to the priority of our sacred time can itself be a spiritual practice exposing all sorts of ways in which we can easily be pressured or seduced away from our Soul Work.

When we make that break we find our shadows may stalk us. One summer on retreat at Alnmouth Friary on the North East Coast, I could see everyone playing on the beach. In the town people were enjoying a beer, fish and chips, companionship, laughter – and here was I stuck in this monastery in silence, fasting and alone. I felt the strong pull to give up and head outside, then I realised what all those temptations were – perfect spiritual practice about seeing my inner demons, the willingness to discern what is really important and stick with it.

We need moments of retreat, quietness and solitude to feed the soul and re-mind ourselves of the presence of the Presence when we have become disconnected from our Source – often a time when the inner critic sweeps in to tell us we've got it wrong or we're weak or bad. We can therefore experience this disconnection from the Beloved in many ways, perhaps as loneliness, abandonment or punishment, for example. I've noticed down the years that many people I have worked with have felt times of disconnection from their Source, initially thinking that the Beloved has left them or is not real. Invariably upon deeper examination they have discovered that it was not the Divine who walked away from them, rather it was they who had wandered off.

In the concept of *Tsim Tsum* (Hebrew for the experience of the Divine withdrawing) we see that sometimes the Beloved can indeed seem to pull away from us, to create space between, but this is never to punish, rather it is to create the space in which the new can emerge, in which transformation and expansion of consciousness can happen. Here it is not so much the Divine abandoning us as giving of Self so that we can change, draw closer to Home and know the Beloved and All-that-is more deeply.

Everything is sacred. Everywhere we stand on sacred ground. Yet some places and things can seem more sacred to us, either because we have prepared ourselves to pilgrimage (part 8) to them for worship, like praying in a great cathedral or stone circle, or because of what we project onto or draw from it, like a sacred icon. Or perhaps we simply feel so because so many people have prayed and worshipped there, maybe down many centuries so that we perceive an intense sense of the holy lingering there more than other places.

Going on retreat is a kind of pilgrimage, consciously turning inwards and away from distractions to explore the interior landscape and our relationship to the Beloved. This can itself be a forbidding desert for nothing seems to be there but ourselves – perhaps the most frightening thing in the world we can face. Some would find this temporary drop out from the busyness of ordinary life too much of a stretch. As well as bliss, we may find fear there too. It is also the landscape of the shadowed and un-reconciled, the broken and fearful, the wounded and unresolved. Beyond this may lie the nothingness, the loss of self or memory or identity and only what Dionysius the Areopagite [131] called the "dazzling obscurity of the secret silence outshining all brilliance with the intensity of its darkness". We will explore more about the "darkness" of the Divine in Part 9.

Despite, perhaps because of, the challenge that silence and solitude can bring, retreating from the daily grind for a while seems increasingly popular. Some do so intentionally as spiritual practice, some for temporary relief from the stress of ordinary life. Some, in assuming they only seek the latter also find elements of spiritual awakening creeping in. One friend said, while on retreat in Greece, "I'm only here for a rest and to get me taken care of for a change." Two weeks later her whole life had been inverted as she found herself questioning the very meaning of her existence. I said to her, "Sometimes the reason we come to a place like this is not the reason we think we come for!" The swirling realm of the unconscious, the movement of grace, call it what we will, has a knack of creeping up and mugging us and

"Coming Home is not escapism, but a plunge into the moment and eternity at the same time."

running off with us into the night just when we thought we had it all sorted. "I didn't come here looking for God" another participant said, "and I don't expect him to be mentioned here." And I thought of the words of Jung's tombstone – '*Vocatus atque non vocatus deus aderit*' ('Bidden or not bidden, God is present'). The Absolute, the mystery, grace, however we think of it, seems to have a knack of hanging around and working away at us whether we think it's there or not.

The great spiritual supermarket of much of the developed world has lots of temptations for the spirituality shopper who wants lots of options, but to stay superficial rather than go deep. The shoppers still get something out of it, if only a general feel-good factor. There is nothing wrong with this *per se*. Spirituality as stress reduction or pleasure may have valid wellbeing benefits. Yet if it is spiritual depth we seek then such practices must be approached with a different intention. We can embrace tai chi or meditation to enhance health and wellbeing or we can draw upon them to aid our profound transformation.

I discussed this with friends who had put themselves (or been put!) through many years of the fierce discipline of spiritual practice. I wondered if we were turning into grumpy old seekers having a bit of, what – spiritual envy? Maybe sticking with the fun of the superficial is not such a bad idea. What does it feel like to someone who has put in many years of hard graft, commitment and discipline in spiritual awakening to see some fly-by-night person do a quick introduction to meditation and suddenly hit the spiritual jackpot? Of course, after all our years of spiritual work if we feel like that then there's more work to do! But perhaps more importantly, glimpses of enlightenment are not enlightenment. A session of meditation may put us on the first rung of the heavenly ladder, but in the long term there is no bypassing the tough commitment to spiritual work (which of course can also be light and joyful) if we are to climb higher and dive deeper.

In contrast, the exquisite 'Monastery' programme, which I mentioned above, illuminated what can happen at a deeper level when more serious commitment is made. For 40 days in retreat in a Benedictine monastery, five men put themselves in the hands of wise spiritual counsellors and long periods of silence, meditation, prayer and contemplation. Capturing spirituality on TV is extremely problematic. Whoever had the courage to broadcast the silent moments in the programme deserves an award. TV tends to avoid stillness and silence. One of the most powerful moments of spiritual awakening I have ever seen in the media took place when one of the participants, Tony, finally rolled his head back in the deep silence held so beautifully by his spiritual director. It was almost possible to see the lights coming on in a perfect example of deep listening. You could have cut the silence with a knife in that intuitive moment when Brother Francis knew that no words needed to be said. Sitting before Tony's dawning realisation, the sweeping grace of understanding that was flooding Tony's consciousness was almost palpable. I held my breath then, in anticipation, wonder and awe, and the joy of witnessing a magnificent demonstration of midwifery of the soul, you could sense something being born.

It also had something to say about the rigours of the monastic life, which the participants endured…and endured is not too strong a word. They were engaged in the community life of the monastery and none was left untouched by it. Here there was abundant discipline (a subject of Part 8). There was no swift ascent up the heavenly ladder, only a relentless climb, sometimes exhausting to witness. I do not know if these five men, having left the monastery, maintained their climb, but I trust that something of that fierce discipline informed and strengthened and encouraged them. They arrived in the retreat each heartsick in their own ways and none left unhealed; a fine example of healthy spirituality being part of health as a whole. The wellbeing of each was transformed, perhaps forever. This was no New Age fluffy retreat – these men went with loving guidance into the interior desert and all were burned and fed from a bottomless basket of Soul Food in the times of silence, stillness and ritual. And thus burned to varying degrees of their superficial selves, they found the communion, the brotherhood, of a deeper Self within - and with each other.

Retreat time seems to be calling more and more people, it is one of many Soul Foods that nourish us on the onward search, and spiritual work needs the energy like any other work. The arts, poetry, literature, music, nature, beauty, healthy eating and drinking, good companionship – all these and more feed the soul in what can be tough work sometimes.

Spiritual work can in fact seem like the hardest task of all when we really commit to it. I have been amused by those who say that 'God seekers are just looking for an

"Coming Home is not escapism, but a plunge into the moment and eternity at the same time."

easy time of it' by bringing a sweet comforter, a panacea, an opium into their lives that helps them cope with the world. I have never yet met a serious spiritual seeker who has not found their work the hardest and most challenging (and most wonder-ful) experience in their lives. Indeed it could be argued that those who do not seek have in some ways the easier time of it. This is not work for the faint hearted, it takes a lot of effort and regular nutritious meals of Soul Food are needed to sustain us.

The darkest hour is not before dawn,
it stands in the lonely moment
when all others appear to be in light.
Oh brothers. Oh sisters.
Let the heart speak then.
It shall trustfully pray, even in sleep.
The angel comes to sit upon your bed in the night,
hold you with her eyes,
embrace you in her gilded wings.
We are not alone.
We are never alone.
The ocean forever reaches out for its own,
waves found sent in search of waves lost.
This is not the lover who disappears
down the long empty corridor of death or separation.
This Beloved, this boundless ocean is faithful.
Faith full.
Practise remembrance,
oh my brothers oh my sisters,
until we forget forgetfulness!
I asked the birch trees, "Which way?"
and they pointed graciously to the west
where the grey mountain drew the clouds around her,
tucking herself in for the night.
Under a pewter sky, I turned indoors,
retreating from the impossibility of night
and watched a promise in the candlelight;
in the silence, in the rhythmic recreating silence,
and the stillness disturbed only by the angel
as her feet thudded upon the ridge tiles
(a bumpy landing).
And from time to time
I caught a glimpse of her feathers
slipping across the windowpane.
I knew she was here to take care of me,
though the demons pouring down the chimney stack

had other ideas.
But I watched them, paying particular attention,
very particular attention,
to the flickering gleam in their eyes.
I couldn't help thinking of all those little figures
trapped in celluloid like an overwrought Spielberg work
or the gargoyles of Notre Dame.
You see, I was quite safe with them
because this silent sacred space was an echo
of the holy of holies.
Not the altar or the tabernacle,
curtained from the world,
but the global search for the perfect spot,
found in the eternally present,
between womb and tomb. No.
As above, so below.
When the search is complete,
when all the signs have been followed
(which always point the same way, wherever you are)
the retreat into retreat finds fullness in emptiness,
vacancy in occupation.
My mother would come home and throw off her hat,
with the shopping done,
and stick her hatpin in the waiting box,
"Put the kettle on, love.
Home is where the heart is."
Mothers always have the right answer,
even if they do not know it at the time.
The angel swept her soft wings around the room
wafting the demons; my little pointy friends
fell swiftly into the cracks in the floorboards,
dissolving into rust and dust.
She turned before she left and, winking,
pointed to her heart, offering a re-minder.
Whether here or there,
I am at Home.

Part 8

"When I gazed out, I found it beyond all that was outside me; when I looked in, it was further in than my most inward being."[132]

Soul Works: digging deep and digging long

It's a question of the way you look at it

Working with a Soul Friend, getting involved in a Soul Community and choosing our Soul Foods are full of all the fun and struggles of getting relationships right. They help us check ourselves and our motivations to ensure they are authentic and not excuses to avoid the difficult and demanding. Soul Works take us into the challenging realm of prophecy, that is, learning to live the truth. To become a prophet (often misunderstood as a predictor of the future) is really about a willingness to examine our deepest selves, to let go of all that is false, to commune deeply with the Divine, speaking and acting in service from that foundation of veracity and sincerity. It's tough work. Seekers of Home experience just about every feeling there is in the endless unfolding and discovery of our relationship in the Divine. The fear that 'there is no end to it' [1] is replaced by the excitement and joy of limitless possibility.

As we look now at Soul Works, the spiritual practices we pursue, I am going to introduce some tough words – discipline, duty, devotion and dedication – all words, which those of an individualist turn of mind might find challenging. What, in order to get Home, do you mean I actually have to work for it? OK I'm willing to do what my spiritual director tells me, yes I'll make an effort to stick with a bunch of people with whom I've got a lot of 'issues' and I can just about apply myself to making sure my soul gets some decent meals, but now you say I've got to do some real work? Apply myself? Commit?

Yes! To some extent these four 'd' words apply to all the subjects we have explored thus far and they apply no less to the hard labour and enjoyment of applying ourselves to spiritual practices. There are so many Soul Works and I have explored some of them elsewhere in more detail [52,53]. It is not the scope of this text to give complete guidance on different spiritual practices. Rather, what we will seek to do here is explore

"As we expand our consciousness beyond ego power, we may begin to experience the infinite."

some of the key principles that need to be applied to our Soul Works if they are to aid us on the Way.

It is not necessary to have a huge range of Soul Works; sometimes 'less is more'. Applying ourselves with greater depth and intensity to a few is of more benefit than spreading ourselves thinly. If we feel we have to try everything for fear that we might miss something, then that kind of thinking is itself the stuff of deeper enquiry. Furthermore it may well be we already have some in our lives yet are not fully conscious of them. A switch of awareness around them may help us to integrate them as Soul Works more fully. For example, I am often told that "I'm not like you Stephen, I don't do anything spiritual, I don't pray or meditate or anything like that". My response is sometimes to ask, "Do you have a job? Relationships? A health problem? A hobby?" All these and more, the material of our everyday lives, are rich seams of spiritual mining if we look at them differently.

Spiritual practice is found in the everyday if we approach it consciously as well as the myriad opportunities open to us in the spiritual supermarket. The number of options is positively dizzying; we could probably spend several lifetimes trying them all. This has the advantage that we can select from a huge range, but the disadvantage of choice overload or hopping from one to another or abandoning one when it gets tough. A disciplined attention to a few seems to be what works best. In fact a Soul Friend once told me we can probably reduce all Soul Work down to two things – prayer and fasting. The first, prayer, is taken in its widest sense of simply turning our attention to the Divine. Fasting is not so much about food, although that might be part of it, but giving up distractions of all sorts that get in the way of that relationship. Soul Works are a means through which we pay attention to *relating* to the Beloved, rather than something we do to achieve some sort of spiritual target.

Our Soul Works also keep us grounded when we might otherwise go awry, reconnect us to the Beloved and to others when we might otherwise drift into separation, re-mind us when we fall into forgetting our route Home. They bring us deep pleasure too, in the fascinating and often exciting relationship of ourselves in the world and in the Divine. Spiritual practices help us integrate our spiritual life and diminish the sense of duality. They draw us closer to Sacred Unity and perhaps point us toward being of service to others. Just by bringing our perspective to a meditation group, for example, someone else in the group might hear, learn and be reassured. Soul Works are not all about growth and getting something, but about being and becoming, giving rather than taking. They can engage every aspect of our being: body, heart and mind.

I have several Soul Works in my life, from those which might be seen as obvious spiritual practice such as meditation and prayer, to the more mundane things I have to do around the house or things that are not particularly satisfying that I have to do to earn a living. Approaching them prayerfully and consciously can also enlighten the latter. In other words, just about every activity and relationship can become integrated with our spiritual life. Maybe after a while we may notice that there is indeed no spiritual life and other life, but simply life where it is rolled into one. The sacred and the secular are dualistic illusions, everything is in and comes from the same Source and all separation is drawn together, in part aided by our Soul Works. Our life becomes, is, a prayer, a meditation.

Waiting
Our Soul Works lead us into a place of waiting, where we seek re-connection. All of us, even the most 'expert' practitioners fall into forgetting and become self-indul-gent or just plain silly. There is no problem with 'feeding the beast' now and again; a treat to sweeten the ego and take some time out from the Work for a while. The problem can be if such treats draw us back into old habits and addictions, keeping us from staying the course. In addition our Soul Works are not all about hard labour. We can lighten up and indeed make fun and laughter spiritual practices in them-selves, a subject I will return to later.

The moments of forgetting, when they happen, are opportunities as we become aware of them to be led into more spiritual practice – of being in silence, of wait-ing. This waiting is not as in a queue, but being open to the Divine and allowing the Presence to be revealed. It is a patient if sometimes difficult waiting that allows intimacy in a relationship to develop, a shift from ordinary time (our will) to sacred time (Your Will). It is the cultivation of a different attitude that makes us aware of how much pushing we might be doing, relaxing out of this and evolving the quality of waiting without attachment to a goal. Yet there is also a quality of knowing, in the faith sense, that there is a goal of sorts, a different way of seeing. This know-

"As we expand our consciousness beyond ego power, we may begin to experience the infinite."

ing-not-knowing waiting is pregnant with possibility and not fixed in time or space or specific outcome. It is worth remembering that we should not expect an immediate response from our waiting. Divine timing is always perfect timing and is not the same as the ego's timing. Like a medicine, it may take quite a while to feel the effects.

The quality of non-attached waiting applies also to what we might experience in the pursuit of our Soul Works. Past lives, precognition, premonition, spirit guides and all the panoply of New Age and not so New Age thinking are often grasped by the ego and made personal, puffing up our sense of power, pride and importance. I remember my disappointment during a study day on 'finding your angel'. Everyone else was hanging out with Archangels Gabriel or Michael or the names of famous saints. Mine was called Kevin. Now there's nothing wrong with the name Kevin, but somehow it didn't quite resonate with a member of the pantheon of mighty beings I had hoped for. Whether I do or do not have a guardian angel called Kevin is somewhat beside the point. The spiritual practice, of course, was my response to him and all the little judgments and ego niggles it flushed out.

I suspect all spirit 'guides' are merely faces of the Beloved presenting to us in a way that is acceptable to us, or they might be fakes, slivers of our unconscious moving in to bolster the ego. Past lives and other such things can be part of this ego agenda, psychic phenomena that, willed or not, bubble up before us along the Way. They are not themselves the Way. As we expand our consciousness beyond ego power and liberate the soul from its tight corset, we may begin to experience the infinite. It is the world of quantum physics, the universal energy field [133], the realm of the mystic, of All-that-is.

Mad or mystic

When we come to know ourselves in this All, then All is available to us, but our minds, in order to get a grip on it, may select only parts of it (the parts that usually are attractive to us in some way and tap into our unconscious desires). If the soul is of the One that is All, then we may have intimations of that All, past present and future. We may feel we see or know things that are beyond the ordinary and our egos can latch onto these things, attaching us to visions or spirit guides or endless past lives. Our fragile minds are flooded with the enormity of a glimpse into eternity, like a million TV channels being received all at once; they crash with the overload or get hooked on one bit of it. We may personalise them, perhaps rooted in an ego need for identity or specialness. Or we may go crazy with them.

Nothing is lost. In the many planes of consciousness that are possible everything is held like some vast computer back-up memory. To some it is the 'mind of God', to others the Akashic record, to others the realm of eternity.   Some people, as we explored in Part 2 when we considered spiritual emergence, can download the enormity of this and can hold it. For whatever reason, perhaps because they have done the Work or it's their particular 'karma' or perhaps because they just happen to have a particularly resilient neural network, such mystics can swim in this oceanic wonder. Others can unravel, their minds 'blown' into becoming psychotic. Some get attached to the specifics leading them to become ego inflated and to believing that they are somehow special or singled out. Without a strong internal structure of consciousness that in which one person swims, another drowns.

I suspect that large parts of our mental health services are dealing with people who have had such experiences and have been unable to handle the download. They wander the corridors of our institutions (or running B&B's! – consider the story of Isis and Osiris in Part 1) believing they really are John the Baptist or Napoleon or Chief Red Cloud. Or, having sussed out how to not get trapped by psychiatric services, they absorb these inner experiences uncritically and without due discernment turn into often dangerous false gurus, demagogues and snake oil salesmen/women of all sorts. Of course, in the eternal ocean of consciousness we are all connected to all these beings, and more. We are all, as Tennyson [122] wrote, "part of all that I have met." But absorbing a revelation of this truth, for those beings too fragile to cope with it or without the wherewithal to filter it and make sense of it, may cause collapse into chaos. The problem is not that I might believe that I am a reincarnated saint, it is that I believe others are not. It may be true that we are John the Baptist but that is because in the holistic realm of the vast connected and universal con-sciousness we are *all* John the Baptist. The mistake is to filter out one bit of it and make it our own; that is the path to ego-inflated omnipotence and madness.

The phenomenon of 'channelling' is a related issue; a person appears to be select-ed to receive messages from what are believed to be other planes of consciousness

"As we expand our consciousness beyond ego power, we may begin to experience the infinite."

or from someone no longer in physical, human form. I have met many channellers down the years, and books arising from the guidance they feel they have received are hugely popular. Some I have found to be full of great universal truth and wisdom – I have in mind the 'received' works of Pat Rodegast with Judith Santon (*Emmanuel's Books*), Neale Walsch (*Conversations with God* series), Helen Shucman with William Thetford (*A Course in Miracles*), Eileen Caddy (*God spoke to me* series) and the *Seth* works by Jane Roberts (*The Nature of Personal Reality*). I met Pat Rodegast and was profoundly impressed by her humility and authenticity. The groundedness of these authors and the support they have received appear to be important factors in enabling them to 'hold it together'. Others might find themselves plunged into madness by such experiences.

I've touched this sense of being guided and 'spoken to' myself – very often. I remain open to the possibility that beings from other realms really are trying to guide us, that we can be spoken to by God in that quiet inner voice. But it is also possible that, unable to grasp the magnificent magnitude of our individual consciousness and its home in the vast ocean of consciousness, we sell ourselves short and believe that it must be something 'other' that is guiding us. The truth and wisdom we hear seem so great that it could not possibly come from within 'little insignificant me'. I can imagine the reaction of the audience when Jesus said, "The Kingdom of God is within you" [Luke 17:20-21] – astonishment and disbelief at such a possibility, maybe anger at such a 'blasphemy' or maybe a sudden burst of joy as this awesome truth hit home. Perhaps he was encouraging people to see how wonderful and divine each of us is in the depths of our being, if we would but open to it.

During a workshop some years ago, Michael Harner (who has done more than many others to reintegrate shamanism into the modern world) [134] had some wry words to say about spirit beings. He reminded us that, just because something is in the spirit world, we must not assume that it is any wiser than we are! In the ocean of consciousness, all of the water can become available to us as it is available to every one who seeks, but it is important not to get side-tracked or ego-inflated. When these experiences happen, simply embrace them as interesting gifts of grace then let them go, unless it is the Will that they should be shared as part of our path of service – a subject requiring deep discernment on the Way.

Psychic or mystical experiences can tempt us into the predicaments of spiritual materialism and ego inflation. We can come to think of ourselves as special, above the common run of other people. We may become hugely attached to the experiences, seeking more and more of them because we want the excitement or to get enlightenment, but falling into disappointment when they are not repeated. As a general rule no matter how wonderful the experience, for example a blissful vision in meditation, it is unwise to attempt to repeat it or to seek more. This is getting seduced into attachment that distracts us rather than nourishes us along the Way. Authentic spiritual experiences expand our consciousness, not our egos. They deepen us in love not in addiction to the 'highs'. They liberate our souls rather than have us fly off into fantasy. They edge us closer to the Divine rather than the acquisition of the shiny trinkets of spiritual 'highs'.

Interesting as these psychic/mystical phenomena might be, they are best regarded with extreme caution and subjected to testing and discernment with our Soul Friends and Communities and in our Soul Works. (A little later in this Part we will visit a good abbot with some sound advice on this.) I could fill this book with my tales of fantastical, mystical times, but that would be pointless, for their point is not that they are tales to be told so that we or others think we are wonderful, but teachings to be integrated and accepted with humility. When we treat them as possessions rather than temporary gifts, then they possess us. What would we seek, the fullness of Home or a long rest in the cul-de-sac of an interesting and fascinating temporary accommodation? Remember the guidance of St. Paul [1Cor:13:1], that when we become adult we must put away the things of childhood. We have to be willing to set down the experiences and artefacts of our spiritual work along the way if we are to integrate them and mature beyond them. A spiritual identity is just another identity; we need to be ready to let that go as well, to become impoverished of spiritual possessions of whatever sort.

Poverty

'Poverty, chastity, obedience' echo through the teachings of many traditions as Soul Works; these are more than simplistic interpretations of rules for sex and money. Poverty can mean reducing the clutter and distractions from our lives so that we can give more attention to the Divine, not just material poverty; we are not asked to live in penury and starvation. In fact in my experience the Beloved does not 'ask'

"As we expand our consciousness beyond ego power, we may begin to experience the infinite."

in the ordinary human sense. Being beyond asking, it is the nature of the Divine to draw unto itself that which came from it, that irresistible attraction is a kind of asking. Most creation stories, such as Genesis, begin with the creation of the material world, coming out of the Divine, not out of nothing. It is a theophany; the intrinsic nature of the universe is of the Beloved and therefore good ("and God saw it was good" [Gen:1:12]) – and the words God and good have the same linguistic root. Those creation stories also tend to include a 'fall' away from this perfection; the history of the universe is then a relentless reclamation of that which was lost, a returning of the lost children to Eden.

The material world, ordinary reality, has all that we need for the journey Home. It is, as we explored in part 7, a Soul Food. The Presence is not remote from us, but in the very here and now, unfolding in all its possibilities right now in and all around us. That is not to restrict the nature of the Divine to the created world, but rather to emphasise its essential goodness and opportunity (again the mystics like Julian of Norwich reinforce this), its existence from and in this divine goodness.

Although I have often used the word 'creation' in this text, I do so with caution. If there is a creation then there is *de facto* a creator, suggesting a separation or dualism. The dance between the Beloved who is separate from us and with whom we can be in relationship waltzes to the rhythm of the essential oneness of All-that-is. As we explore such oneness and creativity I am reminded of the time at school when I sang in the choir. One year when I was 13 years old we performed Handel's *Messiah*. As the great *Amen* chorus soared to its conclusion, I glanced at my best friend, Nick, at my side. We were both in tears while singing our hearts out at the same time. I understood something then about the creative act. We were not just singing the music of Handel, the music *was* Handel. We were participating in some-thing of ourselves and beyond ourselves. I've felt the same looking into a Rothko painting, reading Eliot's *Four Quartets* or sinking into a film like *2001* into which a great director has poured all his talents. Countless acts of creativity are imbued with the love of art in which the creation and created are at some level the same.

When we see the world as a co-creative work of art, as an emanation from or a face of the Beloved, as an outpouring of grace from the One, our heartfelt response can only be one of profound reverence. Environmental activism, for example, flows from a place of deep love for the world, because we have been 'saved' by the love that loves us and All-that-is. This is contrary to the activism that comes from a place of fear and in which we seek to control or destroy the opposition. When we no longer see ourselves as separate from the creation, we know that we are immensely wealthy in the midst of its abundance. We are part of All-that-is, which is part of us. We do not need to shore up our place in the world by the acquisition of material wealth and power, but become more content with the requirements to meet our needs and to share generously with others. People who have become more spiritually awake rarely seek high power-driven roles with *power over* others as an ego-feeding end in themselves, for they feel more at peace and unattached to such things. To them the world at some level beyond surface perceptions and judgements is whole, holy. Holy people are less interested in themselves or stamping their view on the world, more interested in *power under*, service for the wellbeing of others and the planet. If they are socially or politically active they tend to do this from a place of egoless service. They come to know that one way to change the world is to change their own response to it and to help others do likewise.

It is often said that religions or politics cause wars, but people cause wars. Religion and politics are merely the vehicles for human consciousness and behaviour. Without the attention to soul, bringing unconscious shadows into light and deep personal transformation all belief systems will be corrupted by shallow egoic drives for power, control and the need to transfer onto other persons or systems a god-like capacity to save us and make the world OK. That is why so many revolutions fail and become as destructive as the regimes they seek to replace. That is why so many religious movements intent on saving people or producing perfect societies according to God's laws become stuck, oppressive and murderous. Intentions, however 'good' the reformer 'thinks' them to be, are not enough. Thinking that we know how the world ticks and that we know how to put it right (or we know someone else who can) is profoundly suspect.

The raising of consciousness, the nurturing of loving awareness and the cultivation of deep insight are essential precursors to healthy movements for reorganising the way we live. These only come about when all our ego agendas are made transparent, transformed and healed into forgiveness and humility so that the only power we exercise is *power under* in authentic service. Otherwise the best of intentions

"As we expand our consciousness beyond ego power, we may begin to experience the infinite."

will continue to be broken into the soil of the waste land. Our spiritual maturity is a prerequisite to action rooted in loving awareness. Those involved in the work of that maturation, through personal commitment to transformation of themselves and by transmission of such soul wisdom to others are the real revolutionaries.

To embrace and serve the presence and goodness of the Divine in the All-that-is is not to suggest that to become 'spiritual' is to become a Pollyanna of the soul, passively resigned to the condition of the world and its inhabitants. Quite the reverse. We become more, not less, engaged, but from a place of trust and non-attachment within ourselves. When Arjuna is faced with the great battle on the Kurus Field in the Bhagavad Gita [135], he wants to opt out. His divine mentor, the Lord Krishna, advises him that he cannot *not* participate. If he does something, then there will be an effect. If he does nothing then something will still happen. He goes on to guide him to act, but to do so with peace in his heart. He tells Arjuna also to keep his mind, his eye, turned to him and do what he has to do but put no-one from his heart.

Thus being constantly reminded of the Divine he will not disconnect, lose that peace at his centre and become trapped by attachments and ego agendas. He will see the real reality behind ordinary reality, the interplay of the creation, the essential immortality that is veiled by limited perceptions of life and death. Keeping our eyes on the Beloved helps us to see through the veils of ordinary perception, to stay attentive to what matters and let go of illusions, distractions and the inconsequential. It helps us stay alert to where our own will creeps in to sabotage our serving of the Will. This is an example of 'prayer and fasting' in action; Arjuna stays single-minded (an equivalent from the Christian tradition is 'keep your eye on the cross') focusing on what really matters, his connection to the Divine from which right action flows. All our Soul Care approaches are at their root intent upon this purpose.

If we approach the world thus, the response both for ourselves and from others is very different than if we do so with an egoic desire to control or change it. The spirit is like a beautiful butterfly to be appreciated and accepted as it is, to let it do its work through us, to serve it. Try to make it bend to the will of the little egoic self and we distort and corrupt it. In trying to pin it down to our agenda we may capture it in a way, but it's like pinning down a butterfly – beautiful, but it is dead. By trying to control the spirit, the Will, in this way we bring into the world the very thing we seek to condemn and change, the corruption of power and all its consequences.

When we have liberated ourselves, coming Home to a deep trust in the love of the Beloved, then that love and trust naturally radiate through us. The effects great and small are all around us, but in a flow that is life enhancing and co-creative. One person's shift in consciousness always affects the whole, as does the practical actions we may take from that place in ourselves. Just as Buddhists may work to bring enlightenment to others, on the basis that no one is free until all are free, so Christians may work to bring Christ-consciousness (and parallels can be drawn from all the great faiths) into the world as a manifestation of that same universal harmony, that non-duality, that is the ground of the creation. Thus poverty as Soul Work is not about giving away all our material support and having nothing, for most of us living in the world and in community that is not possible or even required. Some people may feel called to the extremes of denying all worldly goods, but that is rare. Rather it is about becoming 'dispassionate' [22] or letting go of attachment to them, about poverty in things that distract us from the Divine, about sharing what we have with generosity of spirit, about living simply and lightly on the earth. Thus we do not impoverish our earthly home or gain so many attachments that we have too much clutter between the Beloved and ourselves.

Poverty includes reducing the wealth of noise and interference, setting aside indulgences like TV or chattering so that we can give priority to hearing what the spirit is saying to us. It asks us to be more still when our lives are rich in movement. Poverty is saying "no" to some things in order to say "yes" to the Beloved. Waiting, silence, absence of things, staying power, solitude, time in the desert and so on - these and others are the Soul Works we practise when we embrace poverty. Some say "I do not have time", "I have children to raise" or "a sick relative to care for". Perhaps a more helpful way is to change the way we think about these. Caring for another, if approached consciously can be just as much spiritual practice as any of the more obvious ones like prayer or attending a communal service. In fact, with attention to spiritual practice, we may find that we can approach our task with more time, energy and compassion not less. It's not so much what we do as the consciousness with which we do it, as we saw with the story of Martha in Part 3.

"As we expand our consciousness beyond ego power, we may begin to experience the infinite."

Poverty and emptiness

Being quiet and still, in all senses, may not just lead us into the peace or presence of the Divine. It can also become a blank space, a void or a place filled with things that trouble us. This is not meditation or contemplation but one of the reasons why the soul guidance is suggested in this book. Emptiness might guide us to the Beloved, but it may also be a place where we encounter suffering and the painful shadows lurking in the unconscious. Furthermore, teaching emptiness, which is part of many traditions on the Way, without the support of Soul Foods, Soul Works, Soul Friends and Soul Communities may just lead to nihilism especially in the person who has not yet matured spiritually. I am very wary therefore of DIY packs for meditation and other spiritual practices. Soul Work can summon up states of consciousness where we need the personal help of a Soul Friend or Soul Community to support us.

Jung [99] illustrates the fierce struggle that can be involved when we seek to be still and listen. In the Red Book, a set of personal journals published after his death, he writes, "When can I order my thinking to be quiet so that thoughts, those unruly hounds, will crawl to my feet? How can I ever hope to hear your voice louder, to see your face clearer, when all my thoughts howl?" Those who seek along the Way the path of silence and awareness know well the struggle with the "unruly hounds". One approach to dealing with these beasts is not to fight them as we explored in Part 7. As time goes by we come to see that the Way lies with what Jung called the "spirit of the depths", our inner being which is boundless and immortal, rather than to place our efforts in the "spirit of the times", the attachments and extrinsic things which seem to govern our lives but which are superficial and transient. The Way shifts us from seeing ourselves through the reference points of extrinsic factors to the intrinsic valuing and knowing the depth of the Divine in ourselves to guide our lives.

In the poverty of silence and inactivity we can experience a deep fear, a dread as we realise that aspects of ourselves might be deeply inimical to the Beloved. That this illusory superficial transient thing we have called ourselves is, at its core, antagonistic to the Divine and we are left wondering, perhaps fearfully, what the response of the One might be to that enemy. In our dread we can withdraw, consciously or unconsciously, pulling back from the Way, disconnecting from the Beloved as we come to know deeply how part of our nature is false to life, false to the Divine. Perhaps the magnitude, as it seems, of the task of surrender can overwhelm us. As our limited interpretation of the possible consequences sinks in we may retreat or rebel. We can struggle to bring back the intimations of peace from our spiritual practice, those nice experiences of sweetness and light so that we can feel better again. We can project the fear outwards and see the Beloved as the enemy or we can become an enemy to ourselves, anxiously dragging ourselves off the Way.

Paradoxically, it is not possible to seek emptiness even with the apparently 'good' intention of wanting to be filled with the Divine. In a sense we do not seek surren-der, meditation or any other spiritual 'state', for to target any of these with purpose is an oxymoron. To aim for emptiness for example suggests that we are already full – of the seeking, the ego desire to accomplish, reach or obtain something. All our works of prayer and fasting may contain the hope of something 'more'. At some point these (often well hidden) desires are to be put down, even the thought of the 'more', even the hope of it. Arguably this is one of the most taxing of predicaments along the way, to do the work yet let go of attachments to outcomes from the work, to have concepts yet release them, to want something yet allow the dissolution of that wanting.

The sense of loss or separation from the Beloved does not arise because we have been abandoned. It is not the nature of the Divine to reject that which love calls Home. The sense arises because at some level it is we who have turned away from our Essence. It may be that we have become full of expectation of rewards for the spiritual life, got hooked onto concepts of 'God', become presumptuous about the Way – all of these and more can subtly and sometimes not so subtly worm their way into our consciousness, building barriers between us and the One for whom we long.

All of these dread-full experiences are also hope-full, for they are signs that the work is going on, that the transformation is indeed under way, that in the suffering, grace is at work. They are not punishment but purification. The desire to engage with Soul Work, no matter how much we despair or mess up, is a sign that the Beloved is already at work in us. In a sense, when we want to do the work, we already are! It is going on in us beyond the conscious realm. We are being turned inside out so that the surrender of the false self can be completed. This is the time to persist with prayer when all might seem lost, time to seek help when we might wish to go our

"As we expand our consciousness beyond ego power, we may begin to experience the infinite."

own way, time to rest when we might feel panicked into action, time to embrace love when we might want to give way to fear.

If these are sometimes hard ideas to grasp, they are even harder to experience. They strengthen the need for the four Soul Care approaches proposed in this book. Without them we may give way to despair, give up or return to old habits or harden our hearts so much that we may seem to become almost impenetrable to the spirit of the Divine itself.

Christine gives us an example of some of these concerns. She led a busy life. Sixty or seventy hour weeks, meeting after meeting, papers to work on at home then squeezing the family and a social life somewhere in between. This is the common lot of many people's working lives today, driven by social expectations to succeed, make money and keep a roof over our heads as well as deep unconscious needs to deny death, feel worthy, powerful, helpful, loved and so on. So many of us engage in a kind of inverse heroism like this, throwing huge amounts of energy into suc-ceeding in the world to avoid the dark heart of our unconscious fears. As I listened to the long tale of her packed schedule, I was feeling exhausted just at the thought of it. It was not hard to see how someone could keep up that pace, because after all I'd been there myself, what seems now to be another lifetime ago. She was in that arid phase when something inside her knew her life was all out of sync, knew it had to change, but couldn't envisage how life might be otherwise. She was in a trap in part of her own making for the job paid for a lot of things – the big house, the flash car, the private schooling - all of which now kept her bound to the treadmill, or at least she thought they did, to keep the money coming in.

She was looking for something deeper, some way out of her current debilitating and disconnecting impasse but was trying to apply the same process to the search that she had learned to apply to her 'successful', driven personal life. "How do I get 'there'"? She often asked. "How do I find that inner voice to guide me that I've heard about?" She wanted the checklist, the action plan and the boxes to tick to "get in touch with my spirituality". In time she came to see that the busyness was also a way of avoiding being still, afraid that she might not like what she might feel and see within if she did so. Yet, some drive deep within her was pushing her in a direction that she was unsure of, but felt she must respond to, even at the expense of a break from work ('though strictly limited and the mobile phone was at first constantly on hand and the car was full of files "just in case"!)

She saw Eileen Caddy's book (*And God Spoke to Me*) in the sanctuary at the Sacred Space Foundation's retreat house. "I've read bits of that," she said, and I wondered where she ever found the time, though the "bits" was the clue. Her brother had given her a copy and she'd treated the book to the rapid read techniques she used for executive meeting papers. "Lots of people tell me that God spoke to them", she said and chatted away about how that never happens to her. In the brief silence as she gulped her tea I was able to add, "I'm not surprised, I doubt if 'he' can get a word in edgeways!" "Funnily enough," she said, "people at work have told me the same thing, and my mother says what a good job it is that my husband is such a quiet man." So we had a good laugh about our own ridiculousness and began to explore how a bit of stillness and silence might come into her life. What she might need to be able to do so and feel safe. Then she might be able to 'hear' those messages from her deepest self, that which has been given all kinds of names down the aeons. This voice is the song of the heart that calls us to do what is right and meaningful for us in the world, even if it demands a shift great or small in the current way of living. When we do not pay attention, dis-ease and disease in one form or another inevitably ensue.

The Sufi mystic Hafiz [136] says in one of his poems that everyone gets an invitation Home, so that narrows down our choices to just two, "to come dressed for dancing or be carried there on a stretcher." When we follow what has heart and meaning for us, life can feel joyful and fulfilling. When we do not, it's an accident waiting to happen. Of course that can be easier said than done if we have both time and money to make that search. When we are young, time is spent rightly in defining ourselves – establishing roles and doing all those things like earning a living, building a career, making relationships, setting up home and maybe raising children. Indeed for many people these are what feel deeply right for us in our lives, at least for a while if not the whole of life, but sooner or later the voice of the call Home can get more insistent.

Christine found it tough to learn to be still, for paradoxically doing nothing and just learning to be can be hard work, at least at first. After a year, life was differ-

"As we expand our consciousness beyond ego power, we may begin to experience the infinite."

ent. She changed jobs, downsized many aspects of her life, moved to a cheaper house, spent more time with the family, and with herself. She wrote, "I don't have as much of what I used to have, but I and all the family have more of what we didn't have – happiness". She had a life that was materially wealthy, but in so doing she was impoverished - in time, human relationships, happiness and love. When she learned to let go of so many attachments and saw what poverty really meant, she then discovered the meaning of wealth.

Chastity

Chastity is not just about giving up sexual relations. Chastity might mean being faithful to our chosen tradition, and sticking with it when times are tough. It means not being a spiritual dilettante and practising our Soul Works superficially just to get them out of the way or indulging in spiritual bed hopping in search of the next spiritual high. It means applying ourselves to the discipline of going deeper into few practices rather than many. The serious Soul Work cannot be undertaken without discipline, an unpopular concept in libertarian cultures where 'doing your own thing' is seen as a hallmark of freedom. But it is worth remembering that the root meaning of discipline is the Latin *discere*, to learn. Discipline is about applying oneself to learning and not, as it has come to be interpreted, as subjection to rigid authority and loss of freedom. Freedom includes making the choice to learn from someone or something no matter what the cost and voluntarily giving up things – time, money, luxuries for example – for a greater reward.

It is not freedom but spiritual promiscuity when, in the spiritual supermarket with so much on offer, we continually try out different things and move on when going deeper is what is needed. We can dig a well to find the water of life, but give up when it gets difficult or rocky or muddy and the digging gets tough, then try and dig another well somewhere else [137]. So it can be with the spiritually unchaste; trying a bit of Buddhism, then a bit of Islam, then a bit of... moving on usually when it gets difficult or boring rather than cultivating tenacity to faithfully reach the rich rewards of the water of life (the same water at the bottom of all wells) in the depths. Part of the discipline of working with any religion is having the insight to see that we have to keep digging even when it gets hard. No religious tradition or spiritual practice is full of sweetness and light all the time. No matter how much we idealise a Soul Community it is never without conflict. Sticking with a discipline, a community, a tradition is in part tested by our willingness to include the spiritual lows as well as the highs, the nice people as well as the not so nice people.

Chastity means honesty and integrity and discernment in relationships, being faithfull to the Beloved and ourselves when other things might tempt us away. Since chastity is often assumed to be entirely about sexual propriety, let us explore a few things around sex and spirituality.

Sex and spirituality

I grew up in the 60s on a council estate to the North of Manchester, and like most teenage lads of my age we bluffed a great deal about sex, more than we actually knew about it or practised. A deeply embarrassed teacher explored the mechanics and little else with world-weary bluntness in two sessions in the science lab. Beyond that the landscape of sexual awakening was largely without map or compass. I was 13, maybe 14, and wrapped in some daydream when I had my first sexual epiphany. It hit me like a flash - my mum and dad must have had sex. More than that, they must have had sex when they were old, I mean old! My mum was in her mid 40s when I was born – ancient!

At 15 I met Janet, my first serious girlfriend. School was about to finish and it was to be that last summer of devotion to my bike and my mates. I met the usual gang at the fair, but she was new in the crowd. I caught her eye momentarily and held it and had the feeling that I had never in all my life looked someone in the eye before. There weren't exactly violins in the background, but for a while all conversation around me became muffled, the fair disappeared, the bike no longer existed. There was just Janet and that lingering moment. I was lost for the first time. The second time occurred that night. Janet and I shed the gang and the rules, and were alone on a bench up Cemetery Road. Hesitant every step of the way, somehow her hand found its way into mine, then my hand across her belly, then our necks entwined, then our lips met. That volcanic first kiss shot me into another realm of consciousness; I imploded, exploded, dissolved into intimacy. It became the classic summer love and I was never the same again.

In a recent TV programme a participant appeared to have sex in full public view. The head of factual entertainment for the channel responsible for the programme said,

"As we expand our consciousness beyond ego power, we may begin to experience the infinite."

"Sex is no different from property. Millions of people buy homes just as millions of people have sex." [138] I think he was wrong. My youthful awakening is common to many and it tells us something about the power of intimacy. Yes, sex has a reproductive function and yes it is powerfully pleasurable and often bought and sold. But to reduce it to "property" is a kind of desecration, a commodification of something profound in human relationships. To dumb it down to entertainment, public entertainment or display being the antithesis of intimacy, is to debase the very essence of loving relationships. Loving relationships are one of our pathways to the Divine [139] for in loving the other we learn about and receive love, a mirror of loving the Beloved. Relationships are just as much a spiritual practice as any other if we approach them consciously as I have explored elsewhere [53]. Sexual promiscuity is proscribed in many faiths for reasons more than judgmentalism or disapproval, but because it can be an abuse of love, a means of exploitation (especially of women or children) an ego self-gratification that boosts pleasure, power and desire but keeps us away from really connecting with another person and with the Divine. At the same time sexual promiscuity can be a sign of our unconscious longing for God – endlessly searching for the perfect lover we are perhaps expressing the desire for the Beloved in whom rests that perfect eternal love.

The response to promiscuity does not require, and this book does not advocate, puritanical, oppressive and repressive rules around sexual expression, rather the encouragement to see sexual activity as more than self-gratification. Sex for pleasure is fine and normal, but if we want more from life and relationships it is another aspect of human behaviour that we need to approach consciously. Gratification for its own ends often accompanied with a lack of respect for the other and ourselves does not seem to be compatible with spiritual maturity and personal transformation. Desire can be renounced; restraint is not the same as repression. Spiritual work is not about the gratification of the false self, but about reducing its power and that does not happen if we keep feeding it. Indeed there is another effect of such gratification and that is to increase the ego identity with sexuality. Sexuality is an aspect of our personhood, an important one for sure, but it is not who we are. When we elevate it to a primary aspect of our identity, indeed make it our identity then this too becomes just another ego trap.

For example feminist, gay or manhood movements can only take us so far. They may free us from social oppression or a sense of lack of self worth, but at some point even these identities must be let go as we explored in Part 1. For, in spiritual terms, the cultivation of an identity is only a partial journey, the whole journey leads us into the surrender of that identity, into the *fana' fi-l'Ilah* if we are willing. That identity is important to our function in the world, and of course we have to have one in order to surrender it. Further, this is not to say that there is no such thing as gay or straight or any other sexuality, rather there is a world of a difference from saying "I am gay", for example, to saying "I am experiencing being gay." The former is attachment to an identity; the latter creates a little witnessing space between our I-Amness and that identity. With the former we are trapped by an identity (as with any identity thus attached) and we see the world and ourselves through its lens; it becomes our life. With the latter we celebrate an identity simply as one of the ways *through* which we live our life and dance with it rather than something that *is* our life; we look at the world with loving awareness through the lens of the soul. We have an identity but it is not who we are.

Meanwhile, we rarely see in our media the alternative of deeper relationships. In a utilitarian culture, sex and relationships are for what we can get out of them, to be abandoned when no longer fun. Yet relationships, including their expression through our sexuality, can be a spiritual practice like any other. In the high wire act of joining and separating, balancing 'my' with 'your', learning to move beyond ego and see that what we can bring to the other rather than what we get from them is what matters – this is the very stuff of spiritual maturity. Our sexuality can be a glorious medium for intimacy, made the more glorious when two people choose to deepen and practise it as a loving dimension of the awakening of each other.

Furthermore, in a culture that tends to conflate sex and love, we can find fierce challenges in relationships when sexual desire and libido diminish. If sex has been a part of the bonding in a relationship, that bond can continue because it is the love in the relationship that is the real glue holding it together. Hugs, affection, loyalty, care, kindness, intimacy, remembrance, being told we are loved and honoured – these and many other qualities sustain, strengthen and deepen a relationship long after sexual desire has abated in importance.

Sometimes it's right to let go of a relationship. But there is also a case for per-

"As we expand our consciousness beyond ego power, we may begin to experience the infinite."

sistence, patience and perseverance that can lead to an ever-deeper connection (see also part 6 page 195 on possible responses when a relationship gets stuck). Such is the spiritual discipline of love. Sexuality is part of spirituality, because it is part of our humanity. For some people the path to Truth may embrace celibacy. But it is not the only path. Loving intimate sexual relationships where depth and maturation can be encountered are also a path to the same goal. Sexual union, that blissful state when all boundaries fall away is one of the means by which human beings can experience a sort of union that transcends the ordinary - a state like the mystics report in their relationship to God. It is one of the means by which we can fall in Love, from self into Self. No wonder we like it and pay so much attention to it!

All faiths have histories of 'issues' with sex, but none seem to have taken it to the level of some branches of Christianity, that sex in any form is bad or sinful. The devastating effect of Augustinian theology on Western Christendom (and through much of Western society) is that it saw the body and its works as sinful and separate from the Beloved rather than something to be celebrated, divinely infused and available to us as the medium for our path of relating, discovery and service in the world. This deep wound, argues Baring [10], plays itself out in all kinds of neuroses and the acting out of often lethal fears from the unconscious e.g. the torture, mutilation and destruction of our own or others' bodies as a means of getting 'clean' or rid of something in ourselves that is seen as bad or unworthy of care and compassion.

Augustinian thinking sank deeply into Christendom and led people like Pope Innocent III (1160-1216) to state that "the sexual act is so shameful that it is intrinsically evil" and another Christian theologian maintained "the Holy Ghost is absent from the room shared by a wedded couple"[140]. The publication of the *Malleus Maleficarum* [9] in the late 15th century was the nadir of Christendom's hatred of sexuality and women in particular. Linking the "sin of Eve" in the Old Testament with the belief that women were inherently evil gave foundation to witch-hunts over a period of 250 years. By some estimates up to nine million Europeans, the vast majority women, were tortured and killed in a prolonged holocaust. Linking sex, heresy and witchcraft was a potent weapon of terror and orthodoxy. By the time the Inquisition left some towns and villages the whole of the female population had been wiped out.

Few modern Christians or come to that people of other faiths, would agree with these mediaeval perspectives – at least when applied to heterosexual sex in wedlock. Step outside these parameters, however, and the doctrinal ground gets shakier. The waiting rooms of the modern priests – psychotherapists and counsellors – are replete with people who still bear the burden, straight or no, of repressed sexuality. Meanwhile some religions continue to tear themselves apart over differences of rules on sexuality. Sometimes they persist in various oppressive forms of misogyny and homophobia permitting exclusion or discrimination (on the most 'well argued' scriptural grounds). Millions of girls across the world continue to have their genitalia mutilated on the basis of religious and cultural norms. In recent times we have seen almost identical beliefs to the *Malleus* applied to women and men in the Islamic extremist controlled parts of Syria and Afghanistan. The deep wound in the male psyche continues to be manifested by the fear of and need to control the sexuality and power of women especially, but also over anyone who challenges male heterosexual authority. We live in times of expanding liberty for women and sexual minorities in many countries, but also contraction in a great many more.

Few belief systems, whether theist or atheist, are therefore free of problems with sex. It might be outright hostility (e.g. Roman Catholic doctrine currently defines gayness as 'objectively disordered', Islam in some countries condones stoning of female adulterers) or more subtle suggestions that sexuality and its expression inhibit enlightenment. I worked with a Hindu priest who was adamant celibacy was a prerequisite to a relationship with the Divine. "You cannot have ice cream and fire together", he told me, but I wondered; "In the heart of God, are not ice and fire one?" A Buddhist teacher I met asserted it was not possible for women to become enlightened until they were reborn as men. Sexuality and sexual expression are not barriers to enlightenment, what matters is the consciousness with which we approach them.

It's little wonder that we live in a world of sexual hang-ups when the signals from so many sources of authority are negative. No religion, Old Age or New Age, has escaped the distortion of sexuality. Fear, provoked when patriarchy and its values are threatened, still leads to abuse especially of women, children and those it picks out as 'other'.

A classic psychological trick, when we are unconsciously fearful about some aspect

"As we expand our consciousness beyond ego power, we may begin to experience the infinite."

of ourselves, is to find another person or group to condemn. That way we avoid facing up to our own shadow by instead pointing the finger at the perceived shadow of the other. Religions and people that 'other' or exclude people from their love are not whole, and a religion that is not whole is not holy. Non-duality means not excluding others from our 'club'. It is rooted in the notion that beyond superficial differences (sexuality, class, roles, race, age etc.) we are all essentially the same in the One. This is the mystic or contemplative mind, which does not 'other' people. Sexuality divorced from spirituality is unhealthy and is trapped in the old dualistic paradigm that sex or the worldly creation is inherently evil. Our sexuality is part of the sacred; spirituality is in the physical and sexual too.

Obedience
We turn now to obedience, which is not just about blind surrender to rules or to persons. There is a process of discernment at work here too. It does not mean that we must obey everyone and everything if, for example, the one we obey abuses his or her power over us, as in the case of sexual abuse by a false and unhealthy Soul Friend or Community. Obedience is rooted in the Latin word *oboedire* [141] meaning to listen as well as to obey, to incline one's ear towards someone for guidance. "Listen to me" is a summons commonly used by great spiritual teachers, which carries with it a call to pay close attention, understand and act or change accordingly. It is more than hearing the words, rather it is the kind of hearing that touches us deeply producing transformation in our way of seeing and being.

The discipline of obedience tends to fall foul of the individualist cult that is wary of letting others have authority over us, yet we all live by rules, even ones we create for ourselves. Rules provide us with structure, ways of holding our lives so that we can explore wider realms healthily. Obedience as a spiritual discipline (discipline and disciple are closely related words suggesting a willingness to take notice or follow in order to learn) urges us to pay close attention, to understand and integrate something deeply and to transform the way we are in the world. Thus we might be a disciple of a particular religious leader or school of thought and there is a quality of discipline/discipleship/obedience in our relationship with our Soul Friend (not least when he/she challenges us), in our application to our Soul Works when we might feel tired, bored or disheartened or in the call to a particular religion. We stick with it not as a form of self-punishment or willingness to surrender to abuse by others, but because we are committed to going deeper, knowing, perhaps in faith, that it is necessary to keep digging deeper if we are to reach the water of life at the bottom of the well.

Paradoxically, obedience is not a labour or loss of choice for at some level of course we have freely chosen to obey. This discipline of obedience also has a loving quality to it because of our love for the Divine and a desire to get closer. Thus there is a degree of willingness to surrender things which would distract us e.g. forego a lot of alcohol in order to remain clear headed to commune, to fast (not just food as suggested, but that can be one way) in order to pay closer attention to our relationship to the Beloved, to give way to a regular practice or to our Soul Friend because of the spiritual authority he or she holds. Discipline implies self control, the diminution of ego desires and trivial comforts that otherwise distract from the Work, the reining in of the thoughts and impulses that take us away from what is True, our heart's desire. The discipline of love has an essentially gentle and kind quality to it, even though it can be incredibly tough at times, but that is not because the discipline is tough, it is because the ego is tough - seeking to haul us back from the Beloved's love that is drawing us magnetically, inexorably Home. As awareness of this Love deepens the battle-like quality diminishes as the ego begins to accept who is in charge (although it will always search, often more subtly, for ways to be the boss again!).

One of these subtle ways, incidentally, is the ego trick of returning us to old patterns and engendering hopelessness - that we will never be free. I am reminded of Geoff, who in his struggle to heal his relationship with his father would regularly sink back into blaming himself. "It's my fault again - It's always me that's wrong", was his default position. We can probably do very little to change the ego and its inner critic scripts, the pattern of this aspect of our personhood may be pretty well set, but what we can do is learn to witness it and its power tricks and respond differently.

Geoff was like a man who would leave home every day and fall into a hole in the road. He kept on doing this every day until one day he was more aware of the hole, and learned to walk around it. Thus it is with some of our personality traits. They are there, they have become part of our identity and our inner landscape, but they are not who we truly are. We are not our scripts and histories. We can catch ourselves before we fall into such traps by disciplined attention to soul work that raises our

"As we expand our consciousness beyond ego power, we may begin to experience the infinite."

awareness of them. Thus aware, we are less likely to be trapped by them once more. And it's worth remembering that such persistence pays off, the brain (see page 224) is capable of 'rewiring' itself so that new patterns of healthy thought come to predominate and older critical ones are diminished. The holes have not necessarily gone away, we have simply learned how to respond to them differently, not allowing ourselves to be dragged into them, but accepting their presence with compassion rather than getting into a fight with them. Geoff's self-blaming was a form of self-discipline, but it was a punishing ego discipline trick to keep him stuck in his old way of being. It was a means of keeping him from the One, from the very awareness he needed that would subvert the power of the little, egotistic, false self.

This discipline that is not discipline, whose real name is punishment, comes from the inner critic, the ego - the desire to hurt ourselves because we feel bad, the need for pain or suffering because we feel we are not worthy of the Beloved. Or we have projected our unworthiness onto the Divine, who becomes one whom we demonise and who demands pain, one who says we will not be loved because we don't love enough. It is a chthonic force seeking to keep us from the Beloved by locking us into suffering; an inverse discipline that keeps us thinking we can only be enlightened by suffering. It's a trick of the mind/ego that keeps us from asking the question, "Is there love in this?" Are we involved in spiritual discipline in order to get closer to the Beloved, even though some of the tasks are hard e.g. by reading difficult books or fixing a prayer time when we'd really rather sleep? If the motivation is to wrestle control from the ego so that we can be free, beneath that tough reality we know there is a hope worthy of it and which will persist; in time the opposition diminishes. This is the discipline of love. The discipline that is really punishment on the other hand is the discipline of fear. The discipline of love draws us closer to the Beloved, fear-based discipline separates, dualises, keeps us away from the Beloved.

The discipline of love is the foundation of the contemplative way, which I have explored in detail elsewhere [52]. Contemplation is found in all faiths with many different names and is arguably at the root of all Soul Works as we deepen our commitment and discipline in them. Contemplation is, literally, to be *con templum* (Latin), to be in the temple, in unity with the Presence. To summarise here, one author [142] from a Roman Catholic background sees it as "The heart of the Christian mystical element since its beginning is *contemplatio*, that is, the contemplation of the soul on the presence of God through the inspiration of the scriptures. The Desert Fathers and Mothers of the first Christian centuries saw in *contemplatio* the vision of the 'pure in heart' mentioned in the Beati-tudes [Matt.5:8] and tried to live this through their solitary contemplation."

Analysis breaks things down into parts in an effort to understand things. Approaches like contemplation help us to see the elements as part of a whole, to see the relat-edness in things, the Sacred Unity. The contemplative has to concentrate first, to pay attention to preparing him or herself and then may be drawn into a prayerful state, which may involve approaching the Divine with our list of requests. But this too pass-es as we move into a meditative awareness; the mind settles and the heart begins to open to the Divine beyond which the contemplative state awaits, the state that is no state, the "condition of complete simplicity costing not less than everything" [1]. In contemplation, we move beyond our methods, our Soul Works, our mental constructs, definitions or efforts and enter a deep and simple form of receptivity, a Sabbath for the soul when the 'work' of prayer and meditation is let go and we simply are in the Presence, open to God being at work on ourselves.

Beyond the method
Is this what all our Soul Works bring us to, the *contemplatio*? Once we get past or set aside the 'method' in our Soul Works, all that remains is pure awareness in the Presence. They teach us how to 'be here now' [57] for past and future do not exist no matter how much our minds like to wander into them. Through our Soul Works we are encouraged into sole attention upon the Beloved, helping us to set aside all distractions – the result of poverty, chastity and obedience. Often these Works are pursued with others, encouraging connection and community. They help us to transform our consciousness and hence our actions in the world; as agents of change they nudge us into ever deeper humility and service.

Whatever Soul Works we engage in, and there are many, they are therefore not ends in themselves. They engage us at every level – physical, emotional, intellec-tual and spiritual - opening us to the Divine. Practitioners are miners for Truth, ex-plorers in search of the One. Through our Soul Works the mind and its entire works are relinquished, for what it stands before is ultimately incomprehensible to it in the conventional sense of knowing. Here there just 'is'; *contemplatio*.

"As we expand our consciousness beyond ego power, we may begin to experience the infinite."

This is a movement beyond prayer, a stillness attitude or posture of consciousness where faced with the all-knowing Beloved "Prayer is really a waste of time" [143]. "The incarnate form of our prayer may be concerned with getting something done, forwarding our plans, and the generosity of God is such that He will let Himself be incarnate even in these ways. But the very heart of prayer is not getting anything done. It is a waste of time, an even greater waste of time than play… For a real absolute waste of time you have to go to prayer." If prayer is really only asking the Beloved for things, entreaty, then arguably it really is a waste of time before the One who is all-knowing.

However, there are other aspects to prayer - bringing ourselves into a space of worshipful intimacy with the Beloved where we might be transformed. It is the place of being open to, experiencing and expressing our allegiance to the Beloved. It is the sacred space where we draw close to the Beloved and our various methods of Soul Work are transcended as we shift our consciousness into the unknowable, indescribable Presence. Furthermore, the scientific studies on prayer are also revealing some intriguing results that cannot be explained by conventional science [119]. An increasing body of research into prayer and non-local healing, points to the possibility of physical reality, not least health and wellbeing of those prayed for, being changed by our prayerful intentions.

One of the reasons that we pray for others is that we do so when they cannot pray for themselves. This applies especially to those who are ill or distressed in some way. This is not just concerned with the possibility of prayer as means of non-local healing, but also as an expression of compassion. We may find it very hard to pray or meditate when our consciousness is knocked sideways by fear, drugs or pain. I have been impressed by how many people, in times of difficulty, have appreciated that others were praying for them whether or not anything 'happened'. Prayer then becomes a kind of love for someone. Perhaps the theological arguments are rather pointless; it's probably best to simply pray as we can, not as we can't…holding a loving attention for the wellbeing of others, and letting the Beloved do the work.

Prayer may therefore not be a waste of time even before an all-knowing deity. It is a means by which we are drawn into a deeper relationship with each other and the Divine, one more method the point of which is not the method itself but what it leads us to. As Thomas Merton [129] says, "We should not look for a 'method' or 'system', but cultivate an 'attitude', an 'outlook': faith, openness, attention, reverence, expectation, supplication, trust, joy. All these finally permeate our being with love in so far as our living faith tells us we are in the presence of God, that we live in Christ, that in the Spirit of God we 'see' God our Father without 'seeing'. We know Him in 'unknowing'."

This "knowing in unknowing" is found in all religious traditions. Although the words used to describe it may differ, the experience is essentially the same. Whether we rest in deep silence or whirl like a Sufi, whether we surrender into the moving meditation that is tai chi or pray at sunrise, the practice at some level is not important, it is merely the opening of the gate to something more, a glimpse of Home. Thus what our method takes us to is not an add-on which we fit in now and then in order to achieve something - bliss, communion with the Divine, insight or relaxation - but a purpose which becomes purposeless, where we let go of expectation, wait and just be. God's grace at work, not our will.

It is the waiting on our part without hope or love or faith [1] where all agendas are set aside. The kind of serious faith "of breathing when you're drowning" [144] for "Once we recognise our nothingness and helplessness before God then we can begin to pray. From such a perspective, even a coldness or impossibility to begin prayer is in itself a sign of this helplessness" before the Beloved. For, as McCabe and Merton remind us in their own ways, ultimately there can only ever be one teacher of prayer - that which emanates from the Beloved. Thus we are also reminded in humility of our dependence upon it. Such a prayer, such a *contemplatio*, is "not a *fugit mundi*, a flight from the world, but leads us back into life, into the arms of the world" [142].

Back into life
Our Soul Works are not vehicles for escapism, a means to retreat from the world and avoid its challenges although we can be tempted to use them this way. Rather they urge us back into life, a life in which we step into the unknowing in every encounter from a restful place of being in the moment, for we have been fed by the unknowing of the Beloved, where we know that we know very little. The thought that we can bring expertise and control to every nook and cranny of our lives, work

"As we expand our consciousness beyond ego power, we may begin to experience the infinite."

and relationships is exposed as an illusion. This contemplation as the embodiment of all Soul Works is not a flight from the world but *eros*, a willingness to engage with it at every level - body, mind, heart and soul - but from a completely different place within ourselves free of ego neediness and attachments. Here Krishna's advice to Arjuna is fulfilled. Here we discover the peace that surpasses understanding. Here we discover the sacred interior place of enlightened consciousness from which we can fully participate in the world.

Spirituality is thereby no longer disembodied from our 'ordinary life' in a dualistic way, for there is no spiritual life and ordinary life, just life lived completely and fully integrated. It is not a matter of the Divine or the world but the Divine in the world. In such a life we do not burn out, in whatever social activism engages us [54] for we have abandoned the idols, the addictions, of our own goals, our (often unacknowl-edged) pride in them, our desire to make everything perfect and just. Instead we relax into being humble servants not ego-driven controllers.

A spirituality engaged with the world does not deny political power; rather it knows its limits. Power rooted in the will of the ego, no matter how benevolently masked, always leads to corruption and abuse. The spiritually aware person is alive to the tricks and deceptions of this kind of power, which is incapable of humility although it can try Uriah Heep-like to appear humble in order to gain power more subtly. Spiritually-based political power is power set in *power under*, in service of others, of the Beloved, not *power over* others, which seeks to dominate for its own ends. Dictatorship in all its forms is always about power over (although the authoritarian can cleverly and corruptly use the language of 'serving the people'). Power under is not rooted in our will but the Will. The Jesus story of the towel and the bowl, which we will explore in a moment, is an example of this. Politics, like science or any other human endeavour, without heart and surrendered to the Will is inevitably oppres-sive, even deadly.

Authentic Coming Home does not detach us from the world, we walk both cos-mically and locally; engaged with but not captured by the powers and seductions of material gain. "Where else but here and now can we find the grace-bestowing, inexhaustible presence of God? In its light, all our hopes and fears flitter away like ghosts. It is like a treasure in a buried field; it is like a pearl of great price; it is like coming home. When we find it we find ourselves, rich beyond all dreams, and we realise that we can afford to lose everything else in the world", writes Mitchell [145]. We find a new understanding of riches; our work in the world *is* Soul Work

As spirited social activists, however great or small in scope and in whatever arena of life, we are in the 'war' but with peace in our hearts [135], the peace that surpasses all understanding. Being indifferent to the world or striving to perfect it according to our standards are different sides of the same coin. Both hold a kind of energy of fighting (either the struggle not to or the struggle to participate). The contemplative has spotted this trap [146] and "Therefore, merely abstaining from affairs which we are unable to accomplish or complete, even if we wanted to, certainly does not prove that the disease of worldly ambition does not dwell in our minds. The same is true of despising those things, which, if we affected them, would make us look important among both spiritual and worldly persons. It is rather a matter of our also rejecting with unwavering strictness of mind those things which cater to our power and which have the appearance of a kind of goodness." Looking for the 'true action' behind the appearance of goodness is rooted in our capacity for discernment in ourselves and with others.

The way up is the way down

When Jesus washed the feet of his disciples [John 13: 3-10] he offered a profound teaching on the nature of obedience, service and spiritual awakening – that the way up is the way down. We do not become more spiritually mature by worshipping delusions of grandeur and status, but by the humility of recognising our own lack of self-importance (the opposite of many New Age teachings and the 'get rich' mentality in some Old Age teachings too). In washing the feet, a taboo part of the body in those days, he lowered himself to the ground. He used a bowl and towel - the kinds of things that only a slave would carry, not 'important' people. In fact it could be argued that the bowl and the towel make an interesting symbol of an important aspect of Christianity, and for that matter for any faith that seeks to get to the core of what it is to be enlightened/liberated (*moksha* in Hinduism). In what others may dismiss as dirty or low level work, the highest element of service can be found. In many traditions the path of service (e.g. in the Hindu *Karma Yoga*) is a path to the Beloved. Service too is a Soul Work; it all depends on how we think about it. Consider again the story of Martha in part 3.

"As we expand our consciousness beyond ego power, we may begin to experience the infinite."

As a youngster my school motto was rather meaningless to me. Not many of us understood Latin anyway. On my school cap and blazer were the words 'Sto ut serviam' (I am here that I may serve). I thought such words pointless at the time. I was young and wanted to get out there and get something. It's funny how along the way things come back to haunt us with new meaning with the benefit of greater awareness. Decades later, what better words could I pick to include in the vow taking ceremony at the Interfaith Seminary?

To accept the burden of the towel and the bowl with deep appreciation we come to see that it is light, no burden at all; if the source is from the Beloved not ourselves then it is no effort. The burden, if any, is staying with that consciousness and putting aside ego desires for control and status. Our culture floods us with images and rewards reinforcing values that to be materially wealthy, famous and powerful are the main goals of life. Happiness can be found in designer clothes, homes, food, bodies, babies. This heroic energy thrusts us deep into ordinary reality and is escapism from the deep-seated fears in the unconscious of isolation, worthlessness and mortality. A life of style is for winners; a life of service is for losers.

Yet, every spiritual teacher down the ages has offered a counter-argument to this. We are not required to live in material poverty if we are to mature spiritually. However, the calling does ask us to divest ourselves of attachments to the superficial including the denials and power trips of the ego, which distract us from getting to the truth of our own essential nature and that which respects that nature and the rest of creation.

In lowering himself to the ground, to the earth, Jesus humbled himself before his disciples. Humus (Latin: the earth, soil or ground) and humility are closely related words, so too is humour). He demonstrated his lack of ego attachment to a position of power. In doing so he offered a supreme model of the leader as the servant and the deep spiritual teaching of the nature of enlightenment. For the way up (to greater awareness, expanded consciousness, enlightenment, the Beloved) is paradoxically the way down – away from attachment to material gain, worldly power and personal prestige.

Humility symbolised by the towel and the bowl changes our approach to the world.

We do not encounter people and situations from our own perspective but from the perspective of the other. From a built up ego to a demolished one, that old power is broken and placed under the authority of the soul so that we may draw closer to Home, to worship, to service, to right living. No other 'God', be it money or status or control can be worshipped on this altar if we truly wish to come Home. The "jealous God" [Ex 34:14] is not jealous in the human ego sense of desiring what another has, rather in the sense of not being approached, loved or worshipped as anything but a unity with no false distractions or idols getting in the way.

Strength, power and freedom are found in surrender to the will of the Divine, of moving from our will to the Will, from doing our work to the Work. Individualist, ego-driven societies and temperaments do not like this. That is one of the great paradoxes of the spiritual search, by surrendering our power and our desire for power, we lose ourselves, in losing ourselves we find our true Self in the Divine, in service, in the power of humility.

To illuminate this further, a few hours later towards the end of Jesus' life, the towel and the bowl make another appearance. This time [Matt.27:24] Pontius Pilate, in an effort to prevent a riot, gives the crowd baying for Jesus' execution what it wants (and neatly absolves himself and Rome of responsibility) he calls for the bowl of water and famously washes his hands. Signifying that he thus took no responsibility for Jesus' crucifixion, he used the towel and the bowl as symbols of power – they were probably brought to him and held up by a slave. There is no indication that he lowered himself either physically or otherwise. He had the power over life and death as an ambassador of Roman governance.

The towel and the bowl here are about power over others, not power under others in service, that is living in the world in such a way that we remain aware of our own essential transience and powerlessness and that real power, when we are empty of such precepts both flows through us and in us. That power is one of love, for oneself, for others and for the Beloved. Liberated from such ego attachments we are set free to be full-filled in the world.

More Soul Works
Working as a Soul Friend, I am often asked to give some suggestions for Soul Work

"As we expand our consciousness beyond ego power, we may begin to experience the infinite."

to pursue, or to say what I do myself. I have some reluctance in sharing my own approach for reasons that I will explain shortly. As to suggestions for practice, there are so many! Space does not permit a full exploration of them here, but a discussion I had recently with a small group of eleven seekers shows the enormous range that is available to us (and this just in one small group). More information can be found elsewhere [52,53] and in the suggested reading after the reference section. I have added some extra notes to a few that are part of my own life. Soul Works, whichever we pursue, are pathways to initiation, to new ways of seeing truth, expanding our consciousness and knowing ourselves and the All-that-is more deeply.

Pilgrimage: There are mountains to climb, deserts in which to lose oneself, oceans to sail and long journeys to travel. Sometimes along the way Home we may feel called to undertake arduous challenges in order to 'get' spiritual rewards, mature and transform. I've certainly found this in my own life; often a great challenge is accompanied by a shift in perception of self, of the relationship in the Beloved and with the world. Yet these may also be projections of the inner needs in the search, for within each of us there are indeed the heights, depths and deserts of the self, of the conscious and unconscious realms to explore. Pilgrimage is one such possibility.

My first (forced) pilgrimage was at school – made to read Chaucer's Canterbury Tales. The elements of the classic pilgrimage (from the Latin 'peregrinus' - stranger or wanderer) are found therein; groups or individuals journeying to a religious shrine in search of healing or spiritual guidance. The film 'The Way' [147] exemplifies the contemporary combination of a tough physical journey, prayer and worship, encounters with persons and places - all of which challenge us inwardly, shaking and shifting our perceptions of self, others, faith and the Divine.

Pilgrimage of all sorts, long or short, has become hugely popular again. Well-known, traditional routes like that to Santiago de Compostela (requiring resources and ability to walk many hundreds of miles) contrasts with the trend toward self-created routes. Almost invariably 'walked' or wheelchaired (the physical, earthbound effort seems to aid the shift of consciousness) I have recently met people going from Durham Cathedral to the Angel of the North to lay a wreath, another group walking the stone circles of the Isle of Lewis, yet another following ley lines to Glastonbury Tor.

It is not so much the nature of the journey that matters, but the *consciousness* with which we do it. If we travel to any sacred site to marvel, photograph and gather facts we will have a very different experience than if we take a reverent approach seeking to deepen our relationship in God. As the former we are mere tourists, the latter true pilgrims.

A couple of years ago I pilgrimaged from Iona to Glasgow. Over 13 days and 155 miles I passed through bucolic idyll and industrial wasteland, stayed in nurturing B&B's and some awful ones, traversed mountain and valley, sailed across sea and loch and tramped through bog and along city streets. I met folks of all sorts along the way, had conversations rich or shallow, and was often asked "Why Iona *to* Glasgow? Surely it should be the other way round?" Such judgements create dualism; the Divine in this place but not in that place. Lately pilgrimaging around Cumbria, creating a circuit connecting the Mungo/ Kentigern churches around the Northern Fells, I found myself again questioning the notion of some places as sacred, others not. Certainly it can seem easier to see the Beloved in beautiful landscapes or loving encounters. But can we also find God in the people we meet along the way who challenge us, in places that are not glorious or in the detritus in the street?

As I have grown older I have come to appreciate that the sacred is everywhere. There is nowhere that the Beloved is not. Perhaps that is one of the 'products' of pilgrimage – an evolution of consciousness, of realisation that it's not about where we are in place and time, but our awareness of the Divine wherever and whenever that matters. Thus, we do not necessarily have to endure some arduous journey over great distances and at great cost (in many senses) – even the thought of that can put people off. Pilgrimage isn't just for the 'holy' or those who feel the need to struggle. A short walk to church, the effort to find time and place at home to meditate, walking the labyrinth of our interior realm as well as a labyrinthine journey in physical reality; this everyday interplay of one with the other creates transformation in our relationship with self, the world, the Beloved and is the essence of pilgrimage.

We do not have to suffer on pilgrimage – to travel half the way on our knees or stretch our bodies beyond limits. The thought that we only gain something if it hurts is suspect. The consciousness with which we approach pilgrimage – the surrender of the will, the intention, the desire to make the effort – is of equal if not greater importance. It's not so much *where* we pilgrimage, but *that* we pilgrimage. Through

"As we expand our consciousness beyond ego power, we may begin to experience the infinite."

prayer and effort in faith, working through scripture, opening to the guidance of spirit, all these and more, we come to know that the sacred we seek is within. The outer journey however long or short paradoxically takes us deeper inwards. The place to which we pilgrimage and encounter God most readily is in that "inner chamber" to which Jesus pointed [Matt. 6:6].

Pilgrimage stretches us at every level, physical, psychological, spiritual. That's what pilgrimage does to us, yes does *to* us. Although we do all the walking and organising, it may become clear to us that it was not so much that we take a pilgrimage, but that pilgrimage takes us. On my own journeys I realised I had not so much sought the Beloved, but that the Beloved had sought me.

Silence: Making time in life to be quiet, perhaps going to a place reserved for it or bringing it into daily life e.g. having a silent meal or reserving a place in the home for quiet. In silence, when the world around us and our inner world are quiet we may truly 'hear'. Silence is an accompaniment to many practices, such as going on retreat or meditation.

Meditation: Quietening the mind, often with a repeated phrase or mantra, which may or may not have a particular meaning. This is sometimes seen as a halfway house to contemplation. I have explored both contemplation and how to meditate elsewhere in detail [52]. Information is also available on the Sacred Space website.

Just about every spiritual tradition refers to the breath as a medium for transformation, as an adjunct to meditation, as practice to quieten the mind or be receptive to the 'holy spirit'. Indeed the word 'spirit' can be associated with breathing – respiration, inspiration expiration and so on. From the most ancient times the breath has been associated not just with physical life, but the very essence of the life of the soul itself. Beyond the breathing exercises associated with spiritual practice, there are two types of breathing. The first is horizontal, the in and outward movement of the air to and from the lungs that keeps the body alive. Symbolically it also represents our connection to the wide world around us. The soul is nourished by vertical breathing, the rise and fall of the 'spiritual' breath from the highest self, the Beloved into and out of the depths of the soul.

Vertical breathing is sacred breathing, communion with the Divine, meditation and prayer. Indeed some practices include combining attention to the in and out of ordinary (horizontal) breathing with attention to the spirit soaring up to the Beloved and back into the soul again. "Breathing should be linked with the remembrance of God; we should breathe with reverence, with the heart so to speak" [148]. Breathing in remembrance of the Divine is vertical breathing.

I am reminded of a childhood experience of breathing that changed my perceptions and alarmed not a few people. Our school class would be taken for swimming lessons at the local 'baths'. The swimming pool had a deep end, which scared me when I swam over it, but at the shallow end I used to like diving to the bottom (contrary to the teacher's orders). Once, I seemed to have eluded her gimlet eye and everyone but me was out of the pool to receive instructions. I'd been able to avoid her by the simple trick of keeping close to the edge and sinking to the bottom of the pool. It was but a moment or two, but I fell into a kind of reverie as I lay on the bottom, slowly flapping my arms to stay down, and watching the bubbles trickle gently, gently to the surface. I was astonished by the silence, by bearing witness to the rising bubbles.

I felt I could have stayed there and never surfaced, a kind of ecstasy set in as I just watched. It didn't last long…my peace was broken as the teacher crashed down upon me to pull me to the surface. She was enraged, I had frightened her; red faced with fury she hit me over the head and roared her disapproval at me. But the experience stayed with me, and there is a parallel today with meditation. We rest at the bottom of the pool of consciousness, paradoxically "breathing while drowning" [144] from a place of peaceful observance, watching our thoughts forming and floating away; watching the phenomena of the world rising to the surface of the boundless pool of consciousness.

Meditation, particularly mindfulness meditation associated with the Buddhist tradition, has spread across the world (often divorced from its Buddhist roots) where the agenda is concerned with de-stressing or building resilience in the face of life's difficulties. Mindfulness and resilience have become buzzwords popping up all over the place in popular literature, conferences, workshops and coaching opportunities. Building resilience, a person's ability to survive in difficult times, along with the

"As we expand our consciousness beyond ego power, we may begin to experience the infinite."

benefits of mindfulness, would seem self-evidently good. Yet I have some cautions to offer here.

First of all, mindfulness approached solely as a health benefit buys into the zeitgeist that 'it's all down to you' – that whatever is going wrong in life and work is the result of your own moral or other weaknesses that, with a bit of work, you can put right. Thus, stressed workers get asked, "What's wrong with you?" rather than, "What's wrong with the circumstances that have made you stressed?" Responsibilities (and costs) of making sure the workplace has the right resources get bypassed if we can dump the problem on individual failings. Many of the resilience building/mindfulness website and self-help tools are breathtaking in their lack off attention to the responsibilities of employers and governments.

Secondly, mindfulness is not value-free and cannot be divorced from its underlying Buddhist philosophy, not least what 'mind' is. I do not think the promoters of mindfulness have always been candid about this, and its implications. There has also been an inclination to separate 'mind' from other aspects of being and teach 'control' of it as an end itself, but in some Buddhist teachings 'heart' and 'mind' are one and the same. Mind cannot be separated from the All-that-is of being.

Thirdly, mindfulness is a spiritual practice of profound implications for liberation, healing and personal transformation. 'Using' mindfulness as a technique to make life easier may not set us free, but keep us stuck in existing ways of seeing things. Reducing it to a stress reduction/self preservation (these are side effects of mindfulness, not its core intent) technique debases it; akin to disembowelling a rich faith tradition.

Fourthly, using mindfulness to medicate life's pain can easily confuse non-attachment with detachment (see the discussion Part 1) without careful teaching (they are not the same). The former helps us to be in the world and to act with compassion while not getting sucked into stress and burnout, the latter is a way of cutting off from things as a defence mechanism. Authentic spiritual practice is not a way of avoiding the suffering in the world but of engaging with it more deeply and safely. Without care, mindfulness becomes just another way of keeping people quiet instead of encouraging us to question and challenge.

Fifth, we can come to see stress as 'bad' and mindfulness a cure all. It isn't and it isn't.

Sixth, embracing oriental mindfulness ignores indigenous options. At an audience with the Dalai Lama a few years ago in Manchester, many present were surprised that he was not acting as a salesman for Buddhism. Indeed he questioned whether Westerners should be embracing Buddhism at all when there were already rich spiritual traditions embedded in their own culture. Furthermore, he wondered if these God-centred traditions offered different avenues for support and transformation that might be of benefit.

Seventh, although often used interchangeably, mindfulness and awareness are not necessarily the same. The former, to some, is a means of developing the 'witness' in our consciousness. It is often assumed to have a neutral 'observer' quality to it that can keep us separate from the pain of the world – a quality sometimes used to seductively 'market' it. The contemplative tradition and lineage, to which I belong, sees the cultivation of awareness as a primary focus of inner work, but it is not a neutral awareness, rather a loving one, a quality of consciousness that awakens the heart to fully engage in the pain and joy of the world.

Lastly, any kind of meditative technique can profoundly disturb the psyche as all manner of things lurking in the unconscious can surface. We must be very wary of quick fix courses, on-line learning or self-help books. Insight practices such as mindfulness should never be practised alone or without support, especially in the early stages.

Contemplation: We may concentrate first to pay attention and plan our time for a session, then meditate to quieten the mind, there may be included a degree of prayer moving beyond entreaty to where prayer is then (and this process cannot be controlled, for to make it a goal is to create an obstacle – the goal gets in the way) we may enter a consciousness of waiting, as discussed above, where we simply sit utterly in the moment, before the Divine. Words cannot describe it for to use words is to fix the unfixable and name the unnameable. Contemplation is often regarded as one of the deepest spiritual arts. It is not a method, but a unifying experience of the Beloved in the Christian tradition and similar to ways in other traditions such as *jnana yoga* in Hinduism. A full account of contemplation is provided elsewhere [52].

"As we expand our consciousness beyond ego power, we may begin to experience the infinite."

Lectio divina: Literature focussed on the Divine, the Latin means literally divine or godly reading. This is one of the Soul Foods mentioned earlier, developed here as a practice to stir up spiritual awareness, and to draw us deeper into contemplation. For example a short piece of scripture or other inspiring words may be read and we then sit with it, reflect upon it, use a phrase as meditation, let the words and meaning of it roll around and shift our consciousness and understanding to draw us closer to knowing the Beloved, what the Beloved is 'saying' to us. Lectio divina is a completely different way of reading from our usual goal orientated method in which we try to get something or somewhere, whether it be some new fact or to the end of the plot line. We are invited to resist such an inclination to productivity and instead tune in with "reverential listening"[149], attuning our ears to the sound of the Beloved in our lives. We allow words to penetrate deeply and open to layer upon layer of meaning, not so much the words speaking to us as the Divine. This is slow reading, stepping out of ordinary time to touch the eternal.

Tai chi: A Chinese discipline of body movements, which are carried through like a moving meditation. Apart from the joy of practising alone, it is usually learned in groups through which we may experience another Soul Community. There are many forms of Tai Chi but all nurture qualities of stillness and being in the moment, as well as having overall physical and mental health benefits.

Yoga: In the west yoga has come to be associated with a group of mental, physical and spiritual practices originating in India. Like Tai Chi it is often learned and pursued in groups as well as alone. Yoga practices are associated with all-round benefits to physical, psychological and spiritual wellbeing. In the Hindu tradition yoga embraces deeper and more complex approaches to enlightenment than body-mind work. Yoga means 'yoking', originally concerning the tethering of draft animals to war chariots and came to refer instead to the reigning in of ego and unconscious drives and the exploration of inner space.

Body prayer: A series of movements associated with certain prayer words with the body moving in rhythm and depiction of the words.

Prayer: Is often seen as just asking the Divine for things, but it is much more than that. It is a coming before and making time for the Beloved, offering our hopes and fears and as well as asking for help. Prayer (see further notes above in this chapter) is a form of being intimate with the Divine. In prayer we draw close and may pass beyond words into contemplation. Intimacy with the Beloved is perhaps the essence of prayer. All prayer is the creation rising up to the Divine. The true work of prayer is to open "our latent capacity for God" [24]. We see the power of this uncreated love in the life of Jesus. Invaded by love of such force and such magnitude that it poured out of him in his service to others. When we are so invaded, everyone else around us is affected too. Love does not stop at our skin but ripples out to those around us in all that we say and do. Prayer is a means, perhaps the primary one, to becoming open to this boundless love. Prayer takes us into the swampy lowlands of our psyches, prepares the soil and harrows the ground for the invasion – that's about the most that is in our power to do. So much of modern spirituality assumes we can fix it all ourselves if we work hard enough at it, but eventually we (may) learn that we have little power ourselves – thus the nature of surrender, of prayer, of coming to the essential nature of our own powerlessness then opens the gates for the invasion of love. When this happens, as Torkington summarises [150], "Nobody can experienced being loved and remain the same".

Prayer takes practise and time, like anything else, it is a skill to be learned and deepened. It may start as something we do at set times, but after a while and with continued practise it seeps into every aspect of our day – our life becomes a prayer.

Prayer also takes us into community with others who pray. The oneness of all is accomplished in transpersonal reality. As we open ourselves to love, through prayer, we become possessed by it. Prayer takes us out of ourselves and into eternity.

In prayer we join in the breathing of the cosmos. We breathe "in and out at the same time" [52]. Just as the universe is currently breathing in, expanding, someday it will stop and contract (breathe out). Our breath is like that, a constant expansion and contraction, a universe in microcosm. Our ordinary breathing is horizontal – taking in the world and responding to it. Stretching the chest and relaxing back again. Then there is the other form of breathing – vertical, as we pay attention to that which is highest and deepest in us, above us and in our depths, prayer. Thus in prayer, we are breathing in and out at the same time.

"As we expand our consciousness beyond ego power, we may begin to experience the infinite."

Prayer is a way of coming into direct relationship with the Beloved. It is the love of the Beloved and more, for love for someone is a kind of prayer. In these times so many of our places devoted to the sacred are closed, how much more so therefore must we work to find the sacred in the "inner chamber" [52] and all around us…there is nowhere that the Beloved is not. In prayer, no matter what we think we are saying or doing, at some level we are opening up to the Beloved and being worked on in the unconscious beyond our ordinary awareness. The impact may not be discerned until much later if at all. Prayer opens us up to that possibility in the Absolute, Ultimate Reality.

"I felt you and I knew that you loved me" – this Tracey Emin sculpture hangs in the Anglican Cathedral in Liverpool. I remember being nervous, having paraded down the aisle behind a bishop, a vicar and several other dignitaries. I was to lead the prayers for the Royal College of Nursing annual congress. I stood up and looked to the great west window and the pink neon sculpture beneath it, at once incongruous and perfect with words that could have been written by any mystic. For the primary focus of the relationship of the mystic with the Beloved is just that, in the relationship, the felt bond between lover and Beloved and All-that-is. I read those words and was instantly re-minded of whose Presence I was in and was in me, and the nerves went.

The traditional translation of the Lord's Prayer does not quite fit with all that we have been exploring here about the gender-free God. The early gospel writings were mainly in Greek and Latin, and both the Greeks and Romans it seems were incapable of conceiving of the 'top God' as being anything but male. The common translations into English are also rather restricted in their meaning:-

Our Father, who art in heaven,
Hallowed be thy Name,
Thy kingdom come,
Thy will be done,
on earth as it is in heaven.
Give us this day our daily bread.
And forgive us our trespasses,

as we forgive those
who trespass against us.
And lead us not into temptation,
but deliver us from evil.
For Thine is the kingdom,
and the power, and the glory,
for ever and ever. Amen.

This ancient prayer has a beautiful poetic rhythm to it, but the words and their meaning are now lost to so many. Those who have dug deep in the Christian faith are not alienated by words and can get past their limitations, but many others can find masculine language a blockage to spiritual awakening. Making God male may draw us into all the problems of patriarchy and the pain and disconnection that arise from the wounding actions of some men and fathers. In the original Aramaic Lord's prayer we find the word *abwoon* translated as father, although its derivation suggests a more subtle interpretation as divine origin, source or parent. (I would encourage anyone seeking more information on the Aramaic roots of Christian and Middle Eastern spirituality to pursue the excellent works of Neil Douglas-Klotz mentioned in the references [14] and bibliography). Even so, to use parent or father in prayer was a startling revolutionary act by Jesus in its time. Hitherto, God was almost universally depicted as remote and separate. Suddenly we see a words being used, *abwoon* or *abba* for short (like saying 'daddy') to suggest an intimacy, familiarity, bond, kindly guidance and availability of the Beloved.

For mystics and contemplatives who do not experience a solely 'Father God', a less fixed version is possible, and I have found this useful with groups of mixed faiths:-

Beloved,
Source of All-that-is,
Soul of all souls,
You in eternity, eternity in You,
the One in whom we live and have our being
and who lives and has being in us.
Sacred and honoured are You to us
holiest name of all names.

"As we expand our consciousness beyond ego power, we may begin to experience the infinite."

May we know the truth
of Your perfection in the here and now.
As Your will prevails,
help us surrender our will into Yours,
uniting the eternal realm with
the earthly realm of time and space.
Nourish our loving awareness
of Your presence each day,
and help us let go
of all those inner and outer distractions
that separate us from You.
Help us to see and heal
that which is broken and wounded
in ourselves so that we do not fall
into fear and separation.
May we live as trusting, faithful servants
of the radiant presence of Your love.
Help us to know You, the One beyond knowing,
yet closer to us than our own breath.
Draw us into the realisation, wonder and joy
of Your true nature, its glory and power,
the eternal in each moment,
You in all
And all in You.
So be it.

Retreats: Time for the practise of community or in solitude to be alone with God and to be free of distractions for inner exploration.

Enneagram: At a superficial level it is a form of personality assessment, but it goes much deeper than other types. As a means of in-sight, it teaches us not only about our personality, but also about the very essence of our being and our connection to All-that-is. It is one of the most potent sources to emerge in recent times making the bridge between psychology and spirituality. I have found it immensely helpful both personally and with clients. Unlike many other personality inventories it does not put us in a box, but it does tell us the box we are already in and how to get out of it. It guides us in how to transform and become healthier at every level. We offer it to retreatants at the Sacred Space Foundation and we have found it to be universally helpful. It can be regularly revisited and studied in depth alone or in groups as a spiritual practice to deepen our understanding of our nature and the Beloved. An excellent basic introduction can be found in Riso and Hudson's text [151] and there is guidance on their website (the Enneagram Institute).

Walking a labyrinth: There are many forms of labyrinth, with probably the most refined being that in Chartres cathedral, now replicated and available in many places and often offered at courses and conferences. It is possible to make one in home or garden as we have at the Sacred Space Foundation (more information including a video is available on the website). It is a pathway with one way in and one way out, not a maze with blind alleys, designed to permit walking meditation and prayer. There has been a great revival of interest in labyrinths in recent years assisted not least by the ground-breaking work of Lauren Artress [152] and the art of Cindy Pavlinac [153].

Work and relationships: Conscious exploration of these on a day-to-day basis to enrich our capacity for being more loving in the world, healing old wounds, practising walking our talk and so on. The Beloved is not relegated to the place of worship. A maturing spirituality is engaged with every aspect of our lives. I can usually guarantee that just when I'm getting a bit spiritually complacent, then someone or some situation will turn up that will really expose where I have yet to learn not to give way to the reactions of my false self. Feeling very loving of the world? OK, watch this news report about that venal politician and the murderous mayhem he's unleashed. Feeling quite spiritual today? OK, here's your partner to press one of your buttons. Feeling like you are at One with the Beloved? OK, here's your co-worker challenging the way you're doing things. Everyday encounters are replete with the material for our personal transformation, for living in loving awareness and recognising when we are not and for the practice of service to others.

Working with dreams, I-Ching, tarot and astrology: Seeking meaning and understanding through interpretation and symbolism. In the holistic cosmos where everything is connected, there is possibility of transformation through the power of symbol, syn-

"As we expand our consciousness beyond ego power, we may begin to experience the infinite."

chronicity and the archetypes in the unconscious [154,155]. Dream work can be one of our Soul Works, for its exploration and insights that come from them can lead us to deeper illumination and the drawing out of things that lurk in the shadows of our consciousness. Jung [99] describes dreams as "the guiding words of the soul".

Sacraments: Participating in worship and holy rituals alone or in our Soul Communities. Ritual draws us into that deeper connection, alters our state of consciousness and draws out the mythic archetypes in the unconscious, takes us out of time into the timeless [60, 99, 156, 157].

Shamanism: Probably the most ancient form of religious practice. It has seen an enormous revival of interest in the past few decades, not least through the influential seminal work of Michael Harner [134] and Carlos Castaneda [158]. Shamanism requires deep training and involves, among other things, the skill of journeying in altered states of consciousness in 'other worlds', to seek the guidance of the spirit realm in search of personal awareness and service to humanity.

The practice of generosity and compassion: Doing things that involve sharing and giving, for example tithing part of our income to our religious community, becoming active in social enterprises that work for the wellbeing of others, fundraising and making donations, giving rather than receiving. Being involved in peace and justice movements. The practice of virtue is as much a spiritual practice as any other, being a truth speaker and authentic agent of love in humility at work in the world to aid others. It's also worth remembering that 'free giving' has benefits for the giver.

Sacred song and dance: Such as circle dancing, hymns and chants. The patterns of sacred song and dance tend to be rhythmic and repetitive, guiding us in an altered state of prayerful consciousness toward the Beloved. The approach is ancient (for example the Coptic chants of Egypt, the Syriac communities, the Gallic psalms of the Western Isles, the chanting of shamans and first nations peoples, Buddhist chants and the Hindu sacred songs) and stretches through to the present with many modern compositions across traditions now available.

Creating 'sacred space': Perhaps not so much creating as holding, by helping at church, mosque, meeting room or temple and/or creating a special space in the home dedicated to spiritual practice [53]. The physical space becomes 'holy' and helps re-mind us of the sacred space in our relationship to the Beloved that is not visible. It contributes to ritual and sacraments that shift our consciousness towards the Beloved. Setting our intention to visit a sacred space is a kind of interior pilgrimage as we ready ourselves to go deeper in meditation and contemplation.

Journaling and reflective diaries: Keeping notes about our spiritual unfolding, and re-reading them to discover new insights, perhaps taking them to the Soul Friend as food for discussion. A journal can be a Friend in whom we confide and 'see' truth by reflecting our experiences to us.

Icon painting: As a devotional practice in itself and to work with the rich, sacred, mystical symbolism that icons contain. There has been a great revival of interest in icons in recent years. The painting (more accurately 'writing') of and/or prayerful reflection upon one stills the mind and draws us into contemplation of the Divine. We do not worship the icon *per se*, rather that to which it points. My personal experience of icon writing, proved to be deeply illuminating. I offer a full account of it here as it illustrates so many issues of Soul Work condensed into one practice. Icons are found in almost all traditions, what follows is a practice drawn from my experience of being taught by a Roman Catholic nun, Sister Petra Clare, a deeply gifted icon teacher, at a Benedictine Skete in Scotland. Other traditions may have different methods and imagery, but the elements are essentially the same.

I thought I could learn to paint an icon; it looked easy. All those pictures I'd seen in those Greek and Russian churches, well, they were beautiful and deeply meaningful, but the art, those almost childlike, cartoon-like pictures, well, they must be simple to do mustn't they? And although it was donkey's years ago, I was good at art at school – won the art prize two years running and my art teacher wanted me to study it. But working class kids from Manchester didn't 'do' art; you needed a proper subject to get a proper job, so art got dropped in favour of science. I'd dabbled years later with watercolour, after moving to live in the Lake District it seemed the natural thing to do. But I never quite found the time to really get into it. Now icons - this seemed the sort of painting that I could get into in no time.

"As we expand our consciousness beyond ego power, we may begin to experience the infinite."

Sometimes in life we look back on an event and think, "How did that happen?" Knowing ourselves and our daily pattern, somehow we seem to take a turn that seems out of character, to say, do or be something that stands out of the ordinary run of our lives, something to which we would not normally turn. A decision is made that seems to be out of our hands. That decision sets us on a different course, brings something into, or sends something out of, our lives that had we thought about it, had we *really* thought about it, we would never have done it. Something in us, not quite in the region of conscious control, calls us into something which while it may not quite fit, is prompted by some inner 'yes'; some ungovernable response standing outside of logic that makes us want to go for it, even though it seems out of character, out of place, out of synch.

To some people this is 'going with the flow', surrendering conscious control and just going where intuition or the spirit takes us. To some it is hearing that deep inner voice calling us to places and times and things against which we might normally rebel. To some it is acting on the promptings of an invisible command, the power of an angel unbidden and unseen summoning us into what is right for us, though we may not see it as such at the time. It can happen suddenly and without notice – that right turn on the street when we normally go left and we bump into that long lost friend, or miss a catastrophe had we gone our usual way. Sometimes it's a series of synchronicities and coincidences – an article we read in a newspaper suddenly resonates and days later a friend raises the same topic with us. We casually open a book and there's a quote that fits. Then something arrives in the post on the same subject and we turn the TV on and there it is again. Chains of clues pointing always the same way and we have to choose – do I follow this?

It happened that way with the icons. A slow drip of fascination down the years, a gift from a friend, a visit to a church, a postcard from abroad, an 'accidental' trip over a website, the coming into life of the space and time when something can happen – all compounding a strange feeling that something is to be followed, some inner urging or vocation of the heart that whispers over and over, "do this, do this, do this". So we may summon up some rational reasons to follow, or not follow (and in choosing the 'not' – somehow it seems harder, like walking against the wind – a sign that we should choose differently?). My surrender into the icon course was something like that.

I arrived for the icon course cocksure that I could learn this skill. Then Sister Petra Clare gave the first slide show and I sat with jaw dropping awareness for the first time of the sacred depth and beauty and intricacy of the icon. Of its ancient traditions, its high skills, its devotional intents. I was overwhelmed with the thought "I'll never be able to do this". Spiritual practice even before the brush dips the paint – sitting with that defeatist, doubting part of my consciousness (an old friend I have come to know well) and not giving way to it.

The whole course became spiritual practice. The moment by moment encounters with the teachings, with the teacher and fellow students, the silent meals, the movements into the church, the halt to work for the primacy of Offices, the loss of time and space in the utterly focussed attempt to enter my first icon. I watched my impatience and frustration when I couldn't get it right. I watched my joy and satisfaction when something suddenly just seemed to work.

Painting, or writing, an icon is prayer in action. The bringing together of body, mind, heart and soul in the single pointed attention, the utter mindfulness of what is before us. And not as a task as an end in itself, but a task underpinned, infused with the absolute desire to surrender to, pay attention to, listen for, approach, sit by, feel the presence of, serve…the Beloved. Not many of us get to the Divine with sudden Damascene blasts, for most of us it's a lifetime of slow cooking, veering between simmering and boiling point and sometimes feeling like the power is off altogether. And thus in the icon, all human response is here – the continuum of emotions as we lurch from pleasure to pain, from impatience to attentiveness, from energised to exhaustion.

I had to learn to slow down, that getting to my Beloved, writing an icon, can only be accomplished by patience, persistence and perseverance. My fiery, rapid results, instant gratification personhood had to take a break. The process had a momentum and trajectory of its own. There were no short cuts, no quick fixes. The gesso could only be prepared in a certain way, water can only boil at a certain speed, paint can only dry at a certain pace. In writing the icon we are not governed by our own will, but by the inherent will, pattern, nature of the ingredients. The egg yolk of the tempura determines its own lifespan, the ochres mix precisely to their own inevitable colour, the wood has taken its own time.

"As we expand our consciousness beyond ego power, we may begin to experience the infinite."

The ingredients are governed by their own unhurried nature, and the design is followed down an ancient lineage and not freely expressed – so how can this be freedom? Why paint the way a hundred generations before me have painted? Where is the individual expression, as in much contemporary art and culture, without which surely we become choiceless and purposeless? There is freedom here too. The freedom comes in being, paradoxically, liberated from choice. There is a certain pattern to follow, a tradition to fulfil, a pace to work at, prayer and meditation to be practised before, during and after painting, a design to follow, the principles of sacred geometry – immutable and inviolate to be incorporated. Freedom comes in the surrender of self to Self, from indiscipline into discipline, from "not my will but….". Getting that tone quite right, that line just so, that movement perfectly captured – the choices and freedoms and individualities are there, but all of them entirely attentive to what has gone before. In the explication of the perfect personally created icon, is the replication of the perfect collectively created tradition. *I* become *we*. The one is in the all and the all is in the one.

Iconography is meditation in action. In each mindful attentive moment we are lost in what is simply before us, that single pointed timeless moment when brush and paint and board, a holy trinity, come together under the guiding hand. The guiding hand sometimes flows with ease and grace; sometimes it is wired and trembling. Every muscle in the body is holding this point – from tip to toe, the whole body is held in correct posture to bring that hand at the exact point at the exact pressure at the exact angle. Little wonder that a spell of painting can feel exhausting – it's not just the concentration of the mind, but the concentration of the body too that is being called upon. Movement may be minimal, but holding the body with minimal movement takes energy and effort too, yet forgotten in the greater remembering that is going on where hand and eye and brush work in harmony.

Iconography is a spiritual journey. What appears on the gesso is a manifestation of the interior journey into ourselves. Every brushstroke represents the state of consciousness at the time it was created. Every bit of attention and inattention, fun and fear, frustration and forcefulness – all states are found here, buried in the layers of tone, the line drawn precisely or carelessly, the bit of garment worked on and worked on until it comes right, that hand worked on and worked on and given up on because it could not be gotten quite right. In following a tradition, who I am is contained in this painting too. And there is more to the journey. For a spiritual journey, when it begins can seem big and blank and empty – unknowns more than knowns. It is the creation itself – beginning with emptiness and from the void the solid and material emerging – yet resting always on its original creative source – itself mysterious, unfathomable. Starting the icon is like this, first a blank space, then shapes are formed – a design becomes clearer. Then blocks of paint, the shape is there, but lost again. The endless repetition of losing and finding, the application of prayer and attention to summon up what is already there. Layer upon layer of effort and tone is bringing what is already there into the world. Like the spiritual journey, it is not so much discovering the new, but a true dis-cover – removing the cover from that which is already there. We do not so much find our soul path as re-mind, re-collect, re-present that which is already there within us.

And as the face of the icon rises, brought up through time and colour, we bring the face of the Christ back into the world, of the saints, of the holy Mother. I found as the face of Christ Pantocrator took shape in the layers of paint, gradually emerging from nothingness into somethingness, that I was also forming a personal relation-ship with it. Talking to it, telling it stories, apologising when the brush went wrong, asking for help when I seemed to get stuck, seeking guidance on choices of colour or shape. This and the preceding prayers, stopping while working to pray and med-itate, enhanced a sense of the whole process as spiritual practice – losing myself, being absorbed, connecting, becoming more whole in the whole (holy). As we stare into that picture that we have realised, we stare at the face of the one we seek, which is the holy one, which is our Self. As that face, those eyes, those garments, those hands are brought forth patiently, only patiently, it is like a new birth, the endless interminable birth of the Christ consciousness coming into the world. As above, so below.

Iconography is a deep Soul Work and a reminder that our life is a work of art. The birthing of the icon mirrors our own enlightenment as we come Home. Every bush stroke perfectly placed if it is an icon or word if it is a poem or note if it is a symphony – these are like our own life. A work of art; stand back and admire it.

Sabbath time: Maintaining a day of the week (not necessarily a Saturday or Sunday) dedicated to our Soul Work, relaxing, being attentive to spirit, putting aside the

"As we expand our consciousness beyond ego power, we may begin to experience the infinite."

distractions of labour or chores. Being in the moment and relating and connecting as fully as we can to our Source. If a full day is not possible, then holding some time each day as a miniature Sabbath.

Writing poetry, haikus, painting, composing: As acts of prayer focussing on the Divine and the inner creative experience. The attentiveness, the attention upon the Beloved, the birthing of words, internal conversations, images or sounds into the world echoes the original creation. Like iconography, we can become 'lost' in the process, lost in the Beloved.

Fasting at regular intervals: A common practice in many traditions, to put aside bodily needs for a while as a preparation for approaching God and as a discipline to rein in the power of the ego. Fasting gives us more time to pay attention to our inner life – not needing to shop for, prepare or eat food liberates a surprising amount of time in the day.

....

The above are just a few suggestions from my own experience and that of a small group of people. I am frequently asked, "Well, what do you do, what keeps your 'eye on the cross' (that is, attention focused on the Beloved)?" I hesitate to offer my suggestions as this can set us up for disappointment, when we can't 'do' what someone else does, or competitiveness or doing what someone else does for fear otherwise of 'not getting it right' or not seeking alternative and more appropriate Soul Works. These responses are of course grist to the mill of further spiritual practice in themselves.

As a member of the Iona Community, I have to make a commitment to daily prayer and other rules that bind our community together. I find this strengthens my personal commitment to my daily practice and it is also an example of how being part of a Soul Community is such a blessing. The solo journey is not for most of us; the support of others is a real source of strength and encouragement along the way.

It is important to choose what works for us. Given that there's also no need to reinvent the wheel, much of the Work along the Way has been tried and tested down the millennia. Across the traditions there is a great deal of common ground. However, with these caveats in mind, here are some suggestions of what 'works' for me. It's not so much the individual action that I mention here, rather what they bring collectively. Although there are differences, it is the consciousness with which they are approached - they are all just prayers really. By coincidence, they all begin with an 'S', forming daily practice with varying amounts of time to each every day, some as constants, some at intervals:-

Service: Doing the work in the world to which my Beloved calls me, wherever and whenever. With this is the requirement to being open to discernment that these callings and promptings are true. The path of service is a Soul Work (*Karma Yoga* in the Hindu tradition], a way of expressing compassion in the world and of translating all the work of inner enquiry into action. This action is vast in its possibility and we need to be wary of judging it by quantity or fame. We do not all have to be chaining ourselves to the railings in protest, feeding the starving millions or changing the governance of nations. Small acts of invisible service, the everyday kindnesses, putting our own wishes aside and others first, a little generosity here, an ego efface-ment there – these and countless seemingly tiny acts have their own intrinsic value and make up the mighty expression of compassion that is the collective.

Service has the beauty of being good for others and good for us – providing it is authentic, heartfelt and of right intention. The place of service may be with my various Soul Communities such as the Iona Community or my local church, or while teaching on courses and retreats or with individuals in need who come to the Sacred Space Foundation. I find all this helps me to keep the Beloved at the centre. When I'm working with people 'I' disappear ("God heals, I make the tea!"). That is one of the gifts of mutuality of spiritual direction; 'I' gets out of the way. There's just the Beloved, the stillness within the movement of thought and feeling, simply being 'in the moment'. Service also distracts us – look at that word 'distracts' – to dis-tract; take the traction or grip out of something. We can be caught up in the grip of ego distractions. Attention to Soul Work helps us break the traction of the ego and set us free to Come Home to the Self and 'be here now'. In time, perhaps one of the 'fruits of the spirit' of years of Soul Work is the evolution of a consecrated person-ality. The dualistic struggle between the longing of the heart and the desire of the ego is diminished; all that we are is subsumed into an ever-greater loving awareness in service to the Beloved. The whole of our personality becomes integrated and turned to the One for more and more of our day.

"As we expand our consciousness beyond ego power, we may begin to experience the infinite."

Socialising: Relationships are a spiritual practice when we approach them consciously. I've emphasised in this book that for most of us complete withdrawal from the world is not our path. I offer an engaged spirituality where every encounter with another person is replete with the potential for loving awareness. I include here participation in the life of my various Soul Communities. The fierce tests invariably come not among the kind of persons who make us feel loved, valued and appreciated, but among those who challenge and who 'press our buttons'. There's a gift here, we may not like it but it is a gift nonetheless, of humility. Just when we think that we are being ever so spiritual and 'getting there' it's as if the universe conspires to say, "Oh, right, getting a bit spiritually smug are we? Well try this one." And along comes someone in person or in the media who nudges us into being judgemental or raises feelings of anger, frustration, fear or whatever. Then we may realise it's not so much 'them' that's the problem as our reaction. More work to do then!

Sacrifice: That is, putting aside other interests and distractions no matter how tempting and committing to daily practice and all that helps me keep my core attention upon the Presence of the Beloved. It is an offering to the Divine. Sacrifice is not about shedding the blood of animals nor is it a puritanical denying of life's pleasures. Such a consciousness of sacrifice is really about acquiring power or escaping guilt by scapegoating, making something else carry our sense of wrongness. Sacrifice as a spiritual practice concerns a willingness to bring a gentle resting of attention upon what really matters and to forego things that are shallow. The true meaning of sacrifice (from Latin *sacra facere*) is to make holy.

Surrender: Cultivating a quality of "Not my will but Thine". These happen to be the words on my mother's gravestone and have been a meditation mantra with me for many years. It is a quality of watchfulness of those places where my ego desires sneak (or sometimes crash!) in so that they cannot gain purchase. It brings with it a quality of constant discernment in pretty much everything that is said and done…"Am I really putting the Beloved at the Centre here, or myself?" It involves regular contact with my Soul Friends to examine my motives and intentions. It also includes my 'daily drudge' - spotting something I really don't want to do such as some aspect of housework or some task I've offered to help with. It involves exploring the whys and wherefores of that, what ego stuff it is flushing out - then doing it!

Study: Having some time each day of attentiveness to soul foods, and the holy books (see Part 4 on the 'Four Books') and all they contain and offer each day – inspiring words from many sources and including *lectio divina*, appreciating art, nature, the unfolding world of humanity around me and so on that inspire and nurture evolution and transformation. It includes regular reflection on insights from the Enneagram.

Silence: Finding time for long or short periods to be quiet and in quietness, a turning of attention to the deep silence that lies at the core of All-that-is if we open to it. In the depths of our being we discover the 'sound' of love and how it reaches all. How this silence permits that still, small voice within to be heard. Silence is the place of communion, the sitting in relationship to the Beloved and simply feeling – love, gratitude, peace as acts of worship. Silence, along with stillness, permits insight and inquiry. In fact, a maxim I sometimes use with retreatants who want to know what the spiritual life is all about is, "Sit still, shut up and listen". In listening, we might then discover the 'ears to hear' – the voice that speaks to us with answers to questions asked and not asked, that whispers of wisdom. All of which we can bring out into the world and our relationship with our Soul Friend for discernment, to nudge us ever more deeply into truth and awakening.

Sensation: Although the body gets short shrift in some traditions, even to being thought of as bad or evil as we have explored, I live in and through my body. It is the medium of my service and through which I relate and connect to others. Let us celebrate the body rather than hold a consciousness of punishment or denial. I love to engage in sacred circle dance, chanting, singing, walking and appreciating the feel of the earth beneath my feet and the weather against my skin. I practise tai chi, get a regular massage and love wild swimming. I include doing/being something everyday that brings joy and creativity, often writing, icon painting or poetry. I have some form of physical exercise or labour each day be it long or short, perhaps a walk to a neighbour, a few moments in the garden. I also include here paying attention to physical wellbeing; my attention to foods and body maintenance with various health practitioners (a lot more as I've got older!)

Stillness: Seeking this in myself amidst the movement of body, mind and the world. Resting in that stillness as a template or tuning fork for others in my path of service, being attentive to the great stillness that lies at the heart of All-that-is and perme-

"As we expand our consciousness beyond ego power, we may begin to experience the infinite."

ates every aspect of ordinary reality whether acknowledged or not. Stillness of body, heart and mind drawing on heart and breath meditations, centring prayer, prayer for my community/others.

Simplicity: Of worship, lifestyle, living lightly, ethically and honourably on the earth as best I can. Simplicity of attention upon the One and remembering that it is all very, very simple – just keep still, listen, see, feel and act; all with the same loving awareness rooted in the ground of being. I seek to remember one particular expression, 'keep your eye on the cross', from the Christian tradition. It means to pay attention to what really matters, to stay centred on the Beloved and let all our thinking, feeling and acting emanate from that place. After a while I have found that all debates, discussions and disputes fall away, there is little or no need for explanation or theorising or theologising (or even writing books!). The Work brings us to a simplicity of doing and being – in Love.

Sabbath: Time set aside to be free of distractions and just be with the Beloved. During the day, during the week and some weeks each year. Times when it's just Me and the Beloved hanging out together that nourish an awareness that really it's always just me and the Beloved hanging out together. It's all a matter of awareness. Still, those special 1-1 moments when nothing but the sacred is in my attention are needed. I particularly hold to keeping Sunday a non-work day.

Solitude: Time to be alone, away from people and things to do, which supports Sabbath attention, insight, reflection on the Way, whether actions and thought are authentic and so forth. Solitude is another cultivator of awareness, a drawing into the sacrament of the present moment; everything is holy.

....

Thus, with some hesitation, that's my list. I trust it may offer some suggestions and reflections. I emphasise again we don't have to 'do' a lot; sometimes less is more. The trick is to integrate them into our lives, to make them everyday and ordinary. The Work is not done alone and we can only do so much ourselves. Through our commitment and our practices, we show up, present ourselves, pay attention, do the work; the rest is up to the Divine at work in us. The former makes space for the latter. The list is a long one, both my own and that which arose in the group I mentioned above, and we could go on a good deal longer. Notice how even such a small group has thrown up a diverse range of options. Staying focussed on a few and giving them time seems to be the important feature.

As the practice grows we may find ourselves ever more yoked to love; what was once seen as spiritual and non-spiritual becomes more at one. Being part of a religious tradition can mean that we embrace many of these as part of a coherent whole. Our Soul Works of choice, with practice and discipline can become as natural and everyday so that eventually we may begin to realise that we are always on pilgrimage, always in meditation or prayer. Our practice provides the milieu for us to be in a place where remembering has become part of our lives, we have started forgetting to forget. This is the principle of 'as you sow, so shall you reap' – the fruits of the work when applied diligently are the thing we seek, Home.

<u>Presence in absence</u>
Sometimes, perhaps often, we can feel hopeless or stuck, that is why the four key elements in this book offer us the context that will bring us out of such an arid place. The spiritual practice of *contraria contrariis curantur* (Latin: literally, the opposite is cured by the opposite) is an intriguing one to pursue when we are feeling like this. It suggests we do the opposite of what we are feeling at the time to shift out of the stuckness. Feeling mean? Give some money to charity. Feeling sad? Go for a walk and seek the joy in nature's beauty. Feeling without time or inclination to meditate? Stick to the routine anyway. 'Sticking with it' even though we might be feeling hopeless can of itself lead us out of that stuck place, and as we move out of it we can feel encouraged, simply because we feel we have succeeded in doing so. In the Aeneid, Virgil [159] noted how success encourages success: "Success nourished them; they seemed to be able, so they were able." But beyond approaches like this are the gifts for the soul of remembering our Soul Friends, Foods and Communities as well as our Works and grace itself are there to nourish us. We are never alone and need never stay stuck for long.

Soul Work does not rule out the gift of grace, of the inflowing of the Divine directly into our lives, awakening us to the presence that is already there, helping us to see who we truly are and not fuelling the search for a new 'me'. The treasure we seek is where the heart is, right under our own noses. What Soul Works do is prepare the ground that encourages this re-turn, this re-awakening fired by the gift of the spirit,

"As we expand our consciousness beyond ego power, we may begin to experience the infinite."

of the Divine energy pouring into our lives. Like a dam slowly undermined, any ob-struction in us must eventually give way to the water that has built up behind it. And in between times, what happens? Moments of joy, moments of sorrow. Arid times when we feel the Sacred has left us, blissful times when we can see that which we seek and it almost overwhelms us. The abandonment when it happens is not real, no matter how harsh and long it seems. Theresa of Avila wrote [160] of having "arid years" when she could not feel "the presence of God". Yet often this dryness, this darkness, this sense of absence is a prelude, a refinement in preparation for being drawn closer.

Sometimes we can feel we are in an empty place, a void where there is neither up nor down often accompanied by an absence of feeling. If there are feelings, they are usually disappointment, despair or hopelessness. Sometimes there are power-ful thoughts like "I'm not getting there" or "I've failed' or "This is a waste of time" or "Why have You abandoned me?" Other arid experiences can include finding or-dinary life – sights, sounds, people – to be amplified, jarring and disorientating. Our five senses may seem to be hypersensitive or dulled to the other extreme. These experiences are part of the process of refinement and sometimes ego tricks and attempts to dishearten. They are just part of a phase that must pass. Often these experiences follow a period of illumination.

They can be moved through by 'prayer and fasting' and taking them to our Soul Friends and Communities for guidance and support. An arid phase can be changed positively to a waiting time of integration and settling. Sometimes we can feel blocked or stuck because we have got caught up in goals or hurrying or because a period of rest and integration or renewal is needed (not least of physical energy). If we find we are in such spiritual inertia we can take heart, for it is a sign that the spir-itual refinement process is working not the reverse. Sometimes this is mistaken for the dark night of the soul but that, entering the unknowable mystery of the Divine, is quite different from the spiritual ache of feeling stuck or in spiritual pain because there is something we are not seeing.

Eventually we evolve an attitude of equanimity, but in the meantime spiritual highs and lows are a common feature. There are rich spiritual practices here too – learning not to seek just the highs and avoid the lows, for the highs can seduce us into a relentless addiction and the shadow too, as we shall see, has purpose in teaching us. The teaching of Isa ibn Maryam (page 136) is worth recalling here. Both spiritual highs and spiritual lows (*consolatio* and *desolatio* in the spirituality of Ignatius of Loyola [161] are places of surrender into a closer relationship with the Divine, they are to be neither pushed away nor pulled towards us.

Sometimes we can feel the flip side of the hopeless 'never going to make it' and fall into grandiosity that we are 'there'. Both phenomena are ego constructs - thoughts, very powerful thoughts coming from the inner critic, but thoughts nonetheless. Patience, persistence and perseverance in 'prayer and fasting' is a response to free us from being captured by such thoughts. It may also be a time to set Soul Work down for a little while, to reflect upon and celebrate how we have transformed and relax into life's simple pleasure – fresh air, the company of good friends, sleep, a good meal or giving ourselves a pat on the back.

Distance or depth
While we may feel that we are stuck or have made progress on the journey, all of these - stuckness, progress and journey - are themselves illusions, for none of them is permanent. Being stuck is always temporary. We may just need to take a break from spiritual work and lighten up or work with our Soul Friend, Foods, Community or in prayer to discern the right response. 'Progress' too is a false premise. While we see ourselves as getting 'better', or making 'advances' or 'growing' we need to recall that these are all ego concepts of judgement. Spirituality is not about growth in the egotistic sense and 'getting something' like power or aggrandisement, rather it concerns lessening, surrendering, merging, losing the self until we find the Self. Our religiosity, our spirituality is not something we create to make the sacred; rather it is a response to something that is already there; our Soul Works help clear the way to that truth.

Perhaps it is better to see 'progress' not in the linear sense of moving from A to B, but as an expansion of awareness. In mediaeval times the King's progress around his kingdom meant travelling around with his court from place to place returning to where he started but knowing his realm more. The progress here was a procession, a circular ambulation of knowing, not of attaining a distant goal. The 'journey' while being a helpful metaphor to some degree, does not capture the essence of what

"As we expand our consciousness beyond ego power, we may begin to experience the infinite."

is going on. This 'progress' is not smooth, it often lurches between *consolatio* and *desolatio*, between moments of bliss and moments of feeling stuck and cut off. It has to be remembered that even disappointment contains the seeds of hope.

As Meister Eckhart [162] succinctly notes, it is a journey that is "only an inch long but a mile deep". We are not really going anywhere but here and now, that is where the journey brings us, right back to where we started and yet we know it as Eliot [1] reminds us more fully, perhaps for the first time.

Are there then any distinct stages of spiritual development or is it a flowing process, back and forth? Can we say along the path that there is some sense of 'progress', some measure of movement from A to B? Some authors [103] as suggested in the discussion under Soul Friends (Part 3) intimate that a kind of 'progress' is indeed observable that might be called spiritual maturity – an expansion or *hierarchos* of consciousness that parallels the changes in the body from child to adult. But perhaps it is better to see these as phases rather than as checklists to monitor our maturing. Arguably the desire to monitor maturity is itself a sign of immaturity! As our consciousness expands, rises and deepens towards Sacred Unity, then there do indeed seem to be some 'mores' as suggested below. But there are some caveats here too. Firstly, just because we feel we have 'advanced' or 'expanded', this does not mean that we cannot fall back into forgetting or even corrupting all that we have learned. The latter is especially easy when spiritual knowledge outstrips inner transformation and the person has not acquired the accompanying humility, for example in doing the emotional work and submitting to the checks and balances described in this book. Secondly, just because we fall into forgetting, does not mean that we cannot remember through 'prayer and fasting'. Thirdly there is another paradox that in becoming more we also become less; more soul-aware is less ego-full.

More or less
Getting lots of spiritual highs is not the goal; indeed there is no goal at all. Goals are the labels of the ego. To meditate with a goal is a spiritual oxymoron. I recall a story told in a class by Jack Kornfield. Two monks approach the abbot, excited to tell him of their meditations. "Master," said one, "today in my meditation it was amazing. I saw lights of many colours, felt surrounded by love and felt at one with

the whole of creation." "Hmmmm," murmured the master, but said no more. The other monk said, "Oh master it was so ecstatic, so beautiful. I saw the entire universe unfolding around me and felt drawn into the very presence of God himself." "Hmmmm," the master eyed them both again, paused for a while with his eyes closed. The monks were puzzled; they had expected his praise and approval. After a moment the master opened his eyes and smiled, saying, "How interesting, but maybe tomorrow your meditations will be better!" Surrender not acquisition is what we are about. Goals have to be renounced so that the Divine can be revealed in us. The intensity of our sense of connection ebbs and flows and wanting the highs and avoiding the lows are both ego temptations to be dissolved. As striving declines we learn to be more docile, more receptive. Rather than trying to make things happen, we are emptying and opening to All-that-is.

A few years ago I spent a couple of weeks teaching on a gloriously seductive Greek island where holidays are organised with a focus on personal growth and awareness (with a bit of Ouzo and sunshine thrown in!). As with so many 'growth' experiences I wondered what was being grown, what bits of the psyche were simply being re-arranged to keep the participants feeling happy about the status quo rather than transforming them?

The agenda of the ego is legion and we can spend our whole lives in endless processing of experiences, relationship problems, co-listening, group sharings, having spiritual highs and countless other treats. Is this just another neat trick to get surrounded by the personal comforters of unlimited exploration and attention, keeping us in that cycle forever? Does the modern day dance of so much counselling and psychotherapy succour that relentless appetite for self-exploration (the false self?) – thus avoiding the deep Soul Work and the loss of ego power this would entail? For in all spiritual traditions, the ego is not to be grown, it is to be rendered powerless. 'Personal growth' holidays and retreats seem to have the potential to keep us stuck in ego exploration and gratification, but they also have the potential to open doors and invite us into deeper work.

A recent television series, the tellingly titled *The Spirituality Shopper*, highlighted some of these issues. Could people really be steered to deeper spiritual insights through a seemingly superficial personal growth agenda, a pick and mix approach,

"As we expand our consciousness beyond ego power, we may begin to experience the infinite."

a sampling of spirituality without the disciplined, long-term attention that all the great spiritual teachers have advocated if we are really serious about spiritual awakening? I suspected the programme would sacrifice the serious to the televisually superficial, but a friend watching with me pointed out that while the participants' experiences may have lacked depth, they were still "getting something".

Doors were being opened for people who might otherwise not even knock. My initial reservations were misplaced. The participants certainly got a feel-good stress-reduction factor - worthy in itself. But who is to say that a peep through the crack of the door of perception [127] does not eventually lead to a walk through? There has to be a willingness not only to take a peep, but also let go of existing fixed ideas through which we look. As Thich Nhat Hanh [163] notes, "For things to reveal themselves to us, we need to be ready to abandon our views about them." Perhaps that little look through the niche can sometimes encourage us to seek a bigger view.

Furthermore, the desire to be whole and to come Home works in such mysterious ways in each of us. The ladder that connects heaven and earth is everywhere present – we may simply not always see it, but once we step on that first rung, who knows what might happen next? Much of the New Age fluff and come to that Old Age fluff we see around us may yet be the ground for seeds to grow in some circumstances – "you never know" as we shall explore in Part 9.

Even so, while it is wise to not limit the way the Beloved is at work, a trick of the ego can be to trap us in the endless search for who we are, for one identity or another. In seeking answers to the question "Who am I?" we can spend a lifetime in analysis, group processes, courses and one practice upon another. This cycle of self-interest can look on the surface like spiritual seeking, but in reality it is just another ego trip. Authentic spirituality breaks free of this cycle, dives deeper and deeper into the Beloved, realises that the search for identity is just another trap and surrenders into the divine Will where identity is no longer a goal. Paradoxically, it is in this consciousness of humility that our true nature and purpose in the Divine is revealed to us; all identities used in the world become useful tools for functioning, for service. Had this occurred while we were still attached to our ego, then our ego would have grasped it and corrupted it. The answer to the question "Who am I?" is that we realise the redundancy of the question; not so much the answer that matters but where it leads us. The question played its part in spurring us to seek, but its relevance dies in the face of the annihilation, the *fana*, in the Beloved.

However it is disguised, the ego lusts for power – to be special, to be attractive, to be invincible, to be immortal. If we do spiritual work but without the emotional work to understand our ego's desires, unconscious tricks and wiles, whatever spiritual insights we receive will become distorted. We can even fool ourselves that we are seeking to surrender so that we can serve the Divine, but ego shadows of seeking to 'possess God' or 'be like God' lurk in the background, ready and waiting to mug the soul of its birthright. Surrender into the Divine is just that, surrender, there are no half measures and that includes surrendering the notion that we are in charge of this process in any way at all. For a while we may think that we are contributing and with the best of intentions doing the work, indeed we must, but at some point we come to know that it was not we who took the Way, but the Way that took us.

Our egos, our personhoods, have 'being in charge' as their raison d'être. Does it, do we, unconsciously keep picking over the wounds and seek out new questions only to maintain the distraction and avoid the surrender, the extinction, the annihilation of the self before the Self? It may be that there a point where enough is enough of ego exploration. Perhaps we break free of its seductive power and engage with the discipline of various spiritual practices that ease or push it out of the way so that the soul can be set free?

Spiritual work is not about self-actualisation, but about self-surrender. Once we have found the self then we can see it for what it is and dissolve its power until it serves the soul and no longer masters it. Meditation is one good trick, among many, to keep the ego occupied while the soul sneaks in. Like some computer seduced into an unwinnable noughts and crosses game, all its energy gets distracted into it, leaving the soul free to slip round the back and pull out the plug!

"Know yourself" (Greek. γνῶθι σεαυτόν or *gnothi seauton*) was inscribed in the fore-court of the temple at Delphi. To know ourselves we must plunge deep into the unknown realms of our interior castle, as Theresa of Avila [160] called it. And it seems we have two choices. We can go there willingly, that is consciously, to explore and become more whole, or we can bumble along through life hoping and trusting that

"As we expand our consciousness beyond ego power, we may begin to experience the infinite."

somehow we will get it all together and learn to be a better person. Our conscious application to our Soul Work helps to inform and understand, to clarify and to heal (and none of us is unwounded) so that we may know the self and that in which the self has its being.

Our Soul Works draw us into an expanded way of being – more whole, more loving, more aware, more compassionate, more at ease with the world with more equanimity. These 'mores' and others like them are the "fruits of the spirit", the very stuff of becoming a more fulfilled and fully conscious human being. We become suffused with the divine light in more and more of our being; the divine consciousness becomes embedded in us. To ascend to a higher consciousness we also descend lower, to unpick the ties that bind and restrict us, our fears and angers and resentments and hatreds, many of which are lurking away in our unconscious, limiting us from being more at ease with the world, catching us in ping-pong reactions over which we seem to have no control and which hurt ourselves and others. In other words we break through our previously accepted view of what 'life' is and discover real life. The former is a kind of living death that leads only to death (however delightfully sweetened by that life's seductions), the latter is deep life rooted in the touching of eternity and coming to know our essential immortality.

In summary, the fruit of the Work helps us to:

1. Be expansive rather than contracted; the experience leads us to be more present, more available, more authentic, more appreciative, more functional in the world - and more joyful. In short, being more alive in the true life and the not the false life we once 'lived'.

2. Be more loving, increasing our capacity for compassion and non-violence towards ourselves and others and diminishing any desire to harm.

3. Be more forgiving, accepting, inclusive and embracing of others rather than judging, shaming, punishing or excluding.

4. Deepen our capacity for discernment rather than judgmentalism.

5. Encourage a sense of trust that enables us to work collaboratively with others and to be at peace in the unfolding of the universe.

6. Foster humility and the possibility that we are not always right, that we do not always have to be in control (indeed the realisation that we have very little power at all) and that having our beliefs tested and challenged need not be threatening.

7. Draw closer and closer towards Home, into relationship with the Beloved.

8. Experience a sense of coherence, harmony and equanimity in daily life including being comfortable with the particular individual personality that we have.

9. Hold loving awareness for all around us and that within us.

10. Strengthen our willingness and commitment to the spiritual life and service.

Our Soul Works are also to be enjoyed, but we need to beware of satisfaction becoming self-satisfaction and falling into forgetting (of the Divine). Work becomes art when we put our [he]art into it, when we feel we can be creative and find joy in service. I have use the word 'work' a lot in this text. Often I am asked why 'at your age' I don't just retire and enjoy the fruits of many years of labour. But work, or for that matter any activity or spiritual practice, ceases to be work when it is play, when I enjoy it, when my heart is in it. Part of that shift from work into play is brought about by the feeling of creativity – as a spiritual director, for example, participating in people's unfolding is joyful. It's not that different from my time when I worked as a nurse in the NHS. Nursing is essentially a creative act, a work of art, an engagement with people towards healing and transformation. When work becomes a creative playful act it ceases to be work. There is no duality or differentiation between work and play, it is all the same, a continuous flow of participation, of co-creation.

Again this reinforces the view that being spiritual is not just allocated to certain times of the day, but a constant turning towards the Source-of-All and drawing on the rhythm of and commitment to our Soul Works to aid that. Our whole lives thus become a prayer, a sustained willingness to be alert to the movement of love in the world and ourselves.

One aspect of this discipline, of normalising Soul Work in our lives, is about becoming authentic.

"As we expand our consciousness beyond ego power, we may begin to experience the infinite."

That authenticity extends to our "attitude of learning" [164] with which no techniques or forms can ultimately help us, we just become dependent on them. That longing for the Beloved and the willingness to commit demand a condition of "complete simplicity costing not less than everything" [1] which must permeate every aspect of our lives. Hanging on to roles or practices for whatever reason raises the spectre of hypocrisy in us. All the great spiritual teachers homed in on hypocrisy wherever they found it. And hypocrisy - not living authentically, not walking our talk - can creep into our spiritual lives ever so easily. The checks and balances that Soul Friends, Communities, Foods and Works provide help keep us in the way of authenticity, which is also the way Home. The way we live our lives through our Soul Works is a demonstration of its authentic fruiting. Please consider these two passages:

"Love is patient; love is kind; love is not envious or boastful or arrogant or rude. It does not exist on its own way; it is not irritable or resentful; it does not rejoice in wrongdoing, but rejoices in truth. It bears all things, believes all things, hopes all things, endures all things." [Cor.1,13:4-7]

Now replace the words "Love is" with "I am" and the word "It" with "I" amending the verb tense accordingly and read the passage again. Consider: just how loving, patient, kind, willing to bear all things and so on we really are? Now try a similar approach with this passage from the Hebrew prophet Micah:

"...and what does the Lord require of you, but to do justice, and to love kindness, and to walk humbly with your God?" [Micah 6:8]

Sitting with these simple words, we can also let their meaning roll around in our consciousness and apply them to ourselves. Can we say that we always act justly, love kindness and walk humbly?

These two passages offer benchmarks for our authenticity and we cannot become authentic without doing the emotional work along with the Soul Works – otherwise our egos can sneak in and capture even our best intentions. We can't *make* ourselves be more loving. That's using ego power to change ourselves even seemingly for the better; it's still about power. Instead we look at those places in ourselves where we are unloving and own up to them, our powerlessness in them and the pain this brings. Here is where we open up to the Beloved, in acknowledging our essential powerlessness to change we surrender in humility to the only power that can change us.

If by engaging with all our Soul Care and spiritual work our consciousness really is expanding, what are the fruits by which this is known? Have we really become more loving and just? Have we really grounded our interesting spiritual work in the world by being more sincerely engaged with it and not less? If there is any test by which we can measure the fruits of our Soul Work, it is to set them against values like these. Thus, in humility, we can see where we might fall short and recognise that we are forever 'work in progress'. The fruits of the spirit are not so much fixed states or goals reached, but integrated into our being in ways that are always being renewed. That is why our four Soul Care themes are so essential to support us in our spiritual awakening, our constant becoming of the true Self in the world.

"As we expand our consciousness beyond ego power, we may begin to experience the infinite."

Judgment that grips and will not let go.
Judgement that deploys its forces
in relentless pursuit of comparative existence.
Sometimes while in time we up periscope
and peer into it, from the depths,
and see that it is all on the surface.
Judgement knows only the surface right now,
sees nought of what lies beneath.
Beneath is a place and time which is
no place and no time and where
beneath has no meaning.
In eternity, in aeternos, where 'in'
has no meaning and words have
no existence; an eternity not neutral,
the boundless isness, has a nature,
it is a radiant compassion, what a
surprise, a love beyond any definition
or concept or fixity where words even these
words are rendered redundant, where
knowing and loving are the same thing,
where all potential awaits in the void
where waiting and potential have no grip,
where seeing and not seeing drown in
the abyss of glorious possibility and
the watcher watches with exquisite clarity,
no this no that, oneness, one reality,
and one yes even one drops off the edge of
relevance.
There are no turning points, only the endless
journeying in and out of time;
perception locks us into them, perception mine,
perception yours, doing exactly what it is
supposed to be doing, everything,
every thing doing exactly what it is
supposed to be doing.

And the eye of the soul, clouded by
tears of joy, tears of sorrow,
watches out of eternity in
the ecstasy of its own being.

Spaceless and timeless we come to serve You
we all come to serve You.
In welcoming our birth, in revelling in our death
as each little birth slips into the next little death
into the next new life Into ……
there is no end to it, our endless becoming,
then unbecoming, rising and falling.
Waves crashing, identity and oblivion,
filling and emptying.
For when all is said and done,
All said, all done
and the slip into knowing
nothing was said, nothing was done.
Beyond the stagger of the new born lambs
and the collapse of the aged ram,
only You,
and the restless waves upon waves,
the bedrock of being,
everywhere and nowhere, always and never.
The clock ticks and the universe continues its silent prayer,
for You are the prayed for, the prayer, and the pray-er.
We set aside fear of the emptiness of Thee
and find the fullness of Thee.
The tectonic plates, binding the soul in place, crack.
The slow drip on stone completes its inevitable history,
extinction of self in Self, we become Light
extinguished by Light...

Part 9

"I said to my soul, be still, and let the dark come upon you which shall be the darkness of God."[1]

And let the darkness...

<u>Heaven and hell</u>
The rich, spicy smells hit us as we walked into the restaurant, and the headwaiter rushed to meet us to offer a table. We were expected, my distinguished friend and I; all the waiters seemed in a flurry to help out. My friend was wallowing in the special attention for he had been here many times before and loved to have the staff acknowledge him and treat him as someone important. I recognised this feeling, I had felt it myself before and recognised also that I now noticed it and no longer wanted that feeling, finding it now both vaguely amusing and discomfiting. We sat down to talk and the waiters hurried back and forth seeming to compete to be each more obsequious than the other.

I spotted one waiter who was a little different, hovering around as if desiring to speak rather than serve. He seemed overly nervous. Eventually he plucked up courage as he hung back with a few empty dishes, and turned around to speak. "Excuse me sirs, professors, may I ask you a personal question?" he said almost bowing. My friend looked annoyed and tried to get the attention of the headwaiter across the room to summon. So I quickly replied, "Of course." and I saw the look of consternation on my friend's face. "Please can you tell me," he pressed on, swallowed and said, "if you believe in God?" The look of sheer panic on my companion's face was one to treasure, I had never seen him speechless before. "Of course," I replied, "though I think the word *know* rather than *believe* is what I would use."

The waiter seemed relieved, scurried off and brought the next dish while my friend looked sour and apologised, saying he would complain to the headwaiter. I stopped him before he could do so and our questioner returned with the next dish and promptly asked a whole stream of questions, but I noticed he focussed a lot on the subject of hell. He was clearly agitated and deeply troubled by something. For the

"Loving awareness enables us to make more healthy choices and act with compassion"

rest of the evening he scurried back and forth with various dishes, coming back with new questions and listening attentively to my response. My friend became strangely quiet and I could tell that he was now getting grumpy with me.

The headwaiter had by this time spotted our own waiter's unusual attention to our table and asked if all was well. I interrupted my friend who sought to complain to say that I was more than happy to converse and was enjoying the excellent service and did not wish him to be admonished. The conversation continued, our waiter spent longer and longer each time hanging around. When he asked, "Do you believe in hell?" I replied, "Yes of course in a way, because are you not in it now?" His face changed and his agitation subsided. "Hell, to me can be here and now, it is feeling separate from God, fearing punishment from God, that is hell enough is it not? The fire and brimstone stuff is not real to me. Heaven and hell can be here in each moment."

Between the clatter of dishes, the increasing noise of a busy restaurant and the sullen looks of other waiters who were not party to the discussion and thereby carrying extra work for their colleague, our waiter somehow secured moments for interesting philosophical discussions. There we were in this ordinary scene having the most incongruous debate about the loving nature of the Divine, which seemed to lighten his spirits. In contrast to my friend's sulky gloom, he was positively radiant by the time we left.

As we did so I asked our waiter a question. "Do you mind if I give you some advice?" He beamed and said he would love it and I sensed he was expecting some profound and wise professorial statement to be uttered. But I just said, "Please remember, my friend, that just because people have fancy titles like professor, it doesn't mean that we have an inch of wisdom more than you do. The very fact that we have had this conversation shows you to be a truth seeker far more than many clever men and women I know." He laughed and we took our coats and left. My friend never went back to that restaurant again and our relationship was to gradually dry up thereafter.

I got the impression from this man (who it transpired was a Moslem, but could have been from any faith in view of the subject matter of our conversation) that he had done something 'wrong' and that he feared he was going to suffer 'punishment from God' for it. He was in torment, but something of our exposition and exploration perhaps helped him see a different face of the Divine, not least a reminder of the one that in his suffering he had seemed to forget but who is mentioned in the very words that open the holy Qur'an – about Allah being the merciful and compassionate.

In the previous sections we have examined where this shaming and judging 'God' arises and why. Yet this little vignette in a restaurant brought the false and the true Divine into sharp focus. In the popular press, the rather nasty character and 'His' (and 'He' usually is a 'He') followers seem to get a lot of attention. Religion, however, is a bit like a public swimming pool; all the noise is at the shallow end. Meanwhile, that kind of 'God' paradigm brings huge suffering to people across the world, when the world is already full of so much suffering, as all kinds of unconscious drives, neuroses and projections can be loaded onto it. We often brand this 'evil'.

Light and dark
I have been in places in my life and met people who would be described as evil, but I have never felt comfortable with the idea of pointy-tailed little beasties running rampant inside and outside our bodies. Describing people or places as evil may sidestep the responsibility to look at what makes people behave badly or to see what projections from deep in our own minds we are placing on the world around us. Evil can be a spiritual experience too in the sense that it can teach us what is false, but it can also seduce us without the presence of our soul practices into believing that it is true. It can draw us into a passionate desire for power and self-perpetuation. We can find a kind of inverse meaning in it. After all we have created something to fight, a devil, an external force that we can heroically battle and defeat to justify our earthly existence and divert attention from our deepest fears.

I remember reading an account [165] of the life of a serial murderer who described how by killing he felt life had a meaning, a purpose and gave him a sense of connection 'beyond'. These are qualities that fit with some definitions of spirituality as discussed in Part 2, but unless we have the insight and guidance from outside ourselves, the shadows in the unconscious (some would see these as demonic by definition) pervert the search for love into the way of destruction. Perhaps some

"Loving awareness enables us to make more healthy choices and act with compassion"

persons are so wounded, so dark, so 'evil' that they might not be capable of love. My heart tells me that in all human beings that same core of love is there, but there are many in whom it is buried so deep that we may wonder if it could ever be free at all. But then, maybe quite suddenly that person can surprise us when some glimmer of light in the eyes or a loving action makes us hope once more.

Is there, then, a separate evil one? A devil? A broken aspect of the Divine intent on subverting the Beloved? In the Upanishads [88] it is asserted that, "There are demon-haunted worlds, regions of utter darkness." But it is open to question whether these demons have their own independent existence or whether the only devils, as Gandhi [166] remarked "are running around in men's hearts". On this basis evil arises from the dark place of woundedness in ourselves.

I know many people who believe evil and devils to be real entities and see a Manichean struggle in the world between light and dark. There is indeed a struggle, a constant push and shove between the boundaries of shadow and light; fear and love at opposite extremes with all the gamut of the human experience sandwiched in between - anger, hate, resentment, kindness, compassion, forgiveness.

We may see three levels of possibility. First there is the divine Will, the spirit, the power, the energy behind all things moving everything into wellness, into wholeness. Then there is a second aspect of will, that of our own ego consciousness, which even if seemingly intended benevolently, is essentially self-will and about seeking self-satisfaction and power over others and the creation. (Extremes of this, which we might see as evil, would be black magic and negative prayer - wishing for harm to come to someone). Just as there seems to be a capacity in us humans to affect physical reality through our consciousness e.g. non-local healing or prayer [119], then the reverse might be the case that we can bring harm to others by applying our consciousness as negative prayer or cursing. Such psychic energy is contrary to Soul Work, for it stands against surrender to the will of the One; the ego wants to *be* the One. A third dimension of this 'evil' might be that mass of swirling unconscious energy, individual and collective, that can result in individual and collective acts of great harm. Some traditions have it that anything that is not aligned with the will of the divine must ultimately come to grief or is an opening for the personification of evil known as the devil, Satan, the enemy.

At one level and embraced in psychoanalytic theories, evil is a social construct driven by power. Elites, demagogues and dictators control their own fears (of mortality, vulnerability and difference, for example) through power over the masses. Systems of control are created and designed to keep people ignorant of the causes of their own suffering and deflect it further by creating 'otherness' – alien races or social groups who are 'different' and onto whom we can project our deepest fears of the 'enemy'. While busy giving attention to annihilating the 'alien' outside ourselves we can avoid and suppress those aspects of ourselves – fear, shame, otherness for example – that we would rather not see. Those demagogues who employ all their wiles and the instruments of state, even war, to keep people looking to others as evil aliens can then successfully retain power and wealth for themselves.

If the 'other' is not the same as us, then we can judge them as not fully human. If they are not human, we can do anything we want to them. All wars thus become 'holy wars', for we are the people of God (whatever we decide this God is, be it the idols of territory, nationality, belief system or simply ourselves). QED anyone 'other' must not be of our God and must at best be controlled by all manner of actions, at worst exterminated.

Peace in this scenario cannot be permitted, it's too dangerous. If the war stops our attention moves from an external enemy to internal reflection – on our inner lives, the way our society is organised, how we wound ourselves and others and where power really lies. Then we might see the repression and injustice and want to change things. At times of peace we may unleash psychic forces that cannot be permitted. Sadism is a way of keeping attention on the outside world so that we avoid reflection on what we see as a fearful inner world. The danger from the demagogues and the mass neurosis they exploit is not just what they let rip when in power, it is what happens afterwards when the project has failed and scapegoats must be found. Thus in the Nazi era we saw vast suffering unleashed on those seen as 'other', the cause of all the nation's problems. When that project had exhausted itself through war, the evil turned inwards as its leader killed himself and showed no pity for his nation. In his eyes, the German people had not proved themselves worthy of the task and thus their own ruin was deserved.

It is therefore necessary to look first for evil at the contents of our own conscious-

"Loving awareness enables us to make more healthy choices and act with compassion"

ness. There is more than enough shadow there to deal with. The shadow side of us, all the ignored, fearful and repressed aspects of woundedness in the unconscious is the source from which all our dark behaviours are drawn. Of this darkness and personal shadow, James Hillman [167] observes that there is collectively "the archetypal darkness, the principle of not-being, which has been named and described as the devil, as evil, as original sin, as death, as nothingness." The alchemical process of transforming the darkness into the light is the only way it and its power are resolved and made whole. By illuminating it rather than fighting it with its own weapons of violence or destruction the shadow, the place of not-being, is made light.

We do not overcome evil by using the very same weapons it uses, but by the opposite. Zukav [125] writes, "The remedy for an absence is a presence. Evil is an absence and, therefore it cannot be healed with an absence. By hating evil, or one who is engaged in evil, you contribute to an absence of Light and not to its presence. Hatred of evil does not diminish evil, it increases it". The response to evil has to be its opposite. This is the principle of 'loving our enemy'; we defeat evil by extending compassion even to the evildoer. This does not mean that we let them do as they will. Sometimes restraining them is an act of love. For example, I've often worked with people who have committed terrible crimes. Making sure that they are in a place (such as prison) where they can no longer harm others or themselves and may yet be rehabilitated can be an act of compassion. Compassion does not mean letting someone do whatever he or she wants.

I was once confronted by a person with what I can only describe as great evil, in whom the shadow was intimidating and strong; probably the most terrifying experience of my life. There was an 'energy' (one scientific explanation [69] for such intuitions would lie with our receptivity to the electromagnetic field of the heart, see page 103) about him that I felt to be deeply disturbing. I just wanted out of his presence. It began with a pleasant enough evening, then hints and suggestions of a very dark sexuality. I was with Jeannie and I became aware that she was feeling it too. Our attempt to leave was literally blocked when our host placed himself in our way.

Bypassing my English inclination to politeness I insisted on leaving. It was a long drive through pitch black in heavy rain back to our accommodation. As we got there the access to the drive had been locked and I had no key. In the deep night and through the rain I was aware only of a motorbike parked by the gate and in the car lights I could see that it was all black and had no number plates or any identification. I could feel the fear rising and was trying not to show it as I gripped the lock, which despite being of thick brass, snapped cleanly in my hands in my efforts to wrench it open. We got back to our rooms and I was telling myself that this was like some scene from a horror film that I was cooking up or that our drinks had been spiked or that the bike was just probably broken down and I couldn't see it clearly in the dark or that the lock was probably already cracked. Picking through these rationalisations, however, did nothing to diminish the fear or dispel the visions flowing in of this man in such deep darkness and a profound sense of being under attack at some level.

I sought to fight this 'absence' with all the conscious means at my disposal and with Jeannie's support, yet its grip was relentless and seemed to grow after moments of respite. It is difficult, indeed impossible to put into words here what happened then, for words would reduce it and would not make sense and after all it is just a story that could have been entirely a delusion. All I can say is that after much discernment, even years later, that I felt and saw the palpable presence of a malice I had never known before.

Suffice to say one thing I learned that night about evil was that we cannot do battle with it on its own terms. Jesus warns us not to "fight" evil [Matt.5:39], which seems perverse unless we see how fighting it, as in this example, merely feeds it. Instead the struggle against evil must be in the opposite terms, by turning away from it, refusing to engage with it in like manner, preferment of love and surrender to the Beloved. Thus it and its methods are rejected and given over to the power we do not own, surrendered instead to the Love and the source of that love in whose hands the evil is dissolved.

When bad things happen in the world – terrorist attacks, wars, poverty, disease and so forth - we can see a natural response to develop a consciousness of attack, retribution or revenge. Such a consciousness is rooted in the judgmentalism of the fearful false self; it separates and disconnects. It is its own evil, merely feeding the beast. An alternative is to confront evil by renewing our efforts to become more loving, truthful, compassionate and caring in our work, by increasing the potential of love in action rather than reducing it.

"Loving awareness enables us to make more healthy choices and act with compassion"

That is the choice faced by people and nations in the face of terrorist atrocities; to stand against the hatred, isolationism, exclusion, racism and revenge consciousness and instead strengthen and renew compassionate efforts. When we become angry, hateful, vengeful – who does it hurt most? Only ourselves. All this in turn comes from that place of not trusting the Beloved in humanity and the unfolding of the cosmos. When we get scared it can thrust us into evil thoughts and actions ourselves and it flushes out that part of our consciousness where we are fearful, unhealed and do not yet fully trust the Beloved. We stand against evil by standing against it in ourselves first of all.

So when faced with evil the right response is not to dwell on it ("Depart from evil and do good" [Psalm 34:14]) but to resolve to participate in healing where there is disease and brokenness, to redouble our efforts to seek justice where the roots of suffering lie in injustice, to cleave to the Beloved and draw upon the boundless love rather than force our own fear-based will into the place of darkness. We do and be the opposite of evil. We connect - with others, with the Divine with our hearts and resolve to act with even greater compassion and service towards non-violence, peace and wholeness.

If there is shadow in us there is also great light, a light greater indeed than any shadow once it is set free. I believe that light is there in anyone and have not yet given way to cynicism despite the years in which I have encountered human suffering in all its forms inflicted on ourselves and others. It informs my work now, sometimes with people who have done terrible things or who behave in ways that seem so very dark and evil. Yet still I trust that light is in there somewhere, longing for release, that in all persons no matter how depraved or evil we may judge them, redemption is always possible if we could but find the right way through and the right one for them, the way Home.

The Beloved we can come to know is All, is One, Sacred Unity. There is nothing that is separate from the Source of All. The great minds of theologians and philosophers have wrestled with the problem of evil for millennia, all I can do is address it where I can in myself and my sphere of influence, see it clearly with help and engage in its transformation. For even in the darkness, the Beloved is there too and even the shadow has its own part to play in a consciousness both personal and transpersonal; the 'plan' of which our egos can see but a small part, while the soul at Home sees it all. The shadow is full of potential but there is no spiritual maturation without going down into it.

Disconnection into connection

Diabolic and symbolic are related words, both with Greek origins. They have more subtle meanings than the general use of them. The symbolic is that which draws things together, connects and makes things whole. The diabolic is that which splits apart, disconnects and destroys. In both we can find meaning, but only in a consciousness firmly founded in the heart, in the Divine, can we ensure that we follow a symbolic rather than a diabolic path.

When Jesus taught in parables, as did so many founders of the great faiths, he rarely used literal truth but spiritual truth. He used the *symbolic* approach (see also page 234 and *mythos* and *logos*) to draw ideas and people together with each other and in themselves into a new unity of understanding and connection of and in the Divine. The scriptures of all the great faiths are full of stories packed with symbolism, with spiritual truth while not necessarily being factually true. Authentic teachers use such stories symbolically as instruments of love.

False teachers and gurus corrupt this approach. They use stories (usually about themselves) as factual truth to draw attention to themselves or their view of the world. In so doing they separate people from truth rather than encourage them towards it. When Jim Jones led his people into massacre in the jungles of Guyana [86] in the name of God, he did so in a *diabolic* way, splitting them off from their common sense, from their love of their children and the Divine and into subservience to himself and his version of 'God'.

His unhealed personhood was projected onto others where he used fear not love, the desire for power not surrender into the Divine, his own unchallenged view of the world instead of a deep and reflective experience of the Divine. This led him ultimately to destroy himself and his followers. Such is the familiar pattern of narcissism that the false guru, the false community, the false teaching can weave. We see exactly this same process behind terrorist organisations and individual dictators across the world. It is the same consciousness of 'otherness' that separates rich from poor, weak from strong, healthy from sick.

Much that is wrong in the world stems either from our egocentric belief that we are separate from the creation and that bad things like natural disasters should not hap-

"Loving awareness enables us to make more healthy choices and act with compassion"

pen. Or it occurs through people who are in the shadow of disconnection from the love of God and who act it out on the world in destructive ways. Or perhaps, in the Jungian collective unconscious sense, a kind of vast negative prayer emerges that manifests in the world wearing many faces according to our projections, unravelling the connected threads that love weaves.

The shadow of evil that emanates from human consciousness is not in the Beloved I know, but somehow in some way I cannot quite comprehend, the Beloved is there within it ultimately making all things whole. Evil does not have the victory for it exists only at one plane of consciousness. In the consciousness of the eternal, its entire works are resolved and made whole. For those who awaken, their transformed consciousness brings the eternal into the now, into this moment against which evil does not prevail. As the psalmist sang "If I make my bed in hell, you are there... even the darkness is not dark to you" [Ps139:8-12]. There is nowhere that the One is not and all things are contained in the One and that includes the paradox of evil.

Holding light and dark

Then there is another kind of darkness, not that of the shadow of suffering and evil, but the darkness of God of which the poets [1] and mystics [52] (such as Julian of Norwich) write, which has a very different quality to it and perhaps serves a different purpose. This sense of equanimity about good and bad, also reflected in the parable of Isa (on page 136), is also found in a short story of a man who was poor and lived on a small farm on the edge of a forest. One day he was in the woods and he found a beautiful big horse, brought it home with him and was looking forward to its help in ploughing. His neighbour came by, saying how fortunate the man was, how his labour would now be much reduced and he could become much wealthier. "Well, you never know," smiled the man. A few days later his son took the horse for a ride, fell off and broke his leg. The neighbour came by again this time to say how sorry he was that the man had now lost his main help on the farm, how he would now struggle to get the crops in to make ends meet. "Well, you never know," said the man once more. A few days later the army came through the village and forced all the young men into service and marched them off to war – except the son with the broken leg. The neighbour came by once more, full of sorrow for his own son had been taken. "How fortunate you are, had your son not broken his leg you too would have lost your son like the rest of us." But the man replied knowingly as before, "Well, you never know".

I wrote in Part 2 about the person with cancer who had seen her disease as a spiritual journey, in which the search was not just for a cure, but to find meaning and purpose in it. As a follower of the Christian Way she had revisited many aspects of her faith and found them wanting. How could Jesus in the beatitudes talk of those who mourn or are reviled as being blessed? Her cancer had certainly plunged her into grief about the loss of her old lifestyle, her body image and the possibility of death and perhaps there are more ways of feeling reviled than personal insults. Cancer or any serious illness for that matter can feel like a revilement upon one's own body. In his poem "A sleep of prisoners" Christopher Fry [168] writes how even times of dark and cold are filled with potential, where we might take "the longest stride man ever took".

The notion that suffering can be pregnant with the possibility of transformation is a spiritual truth. Yet it can be a real stretch to see this at the time when we are in the midst of it. Some persons do indeed seem to be able to embrace, transcend and find meaning in suffering and, arguably, those who have done the Work are more likely to be able to do so than those who have not. Certainly, from the studies I have mentioned earlier, it seems that those with some sort of religiosity are more likely to cope with life's vicissitudes than those who are without.

Nelson Mandela showed how a man can come to fullness as a human being rather than diminish into resentment and bitterness despite a terrible prison sentence. Victor Frankl [169], Dietrich Bonhoeffer [170] and Etty Hillesum [171] were unbowed by the concentration camp nightmare. Florence Nightingale [172] used the horrific experience of war and disease and her own ill health to go ever deeper into her faith and fuel her passion for reform of nursing and public and military health.

The Sufi mystic Hafiz [136] seems to positively welcome suffering, using it as a means of releasing his attachments to ideas of body or personhood and thus set him free on the path to enlightenment. "Pour on more oil", he writes, to bring yet more flames to the place of suffering until all that keeps us from the Divine is burned away. For most of us, suffering is something that we just want to go away, but our Soul Care approaches can help us reframe that and find the light, even a small one, in the darkness.

"Loving awareness enables us to make more healthy choices and act with compassion"

Maya Angelou [173] wrote, "If you can't change a thing, change the way you think about it." It's perhaps not just a matter of 'thinking', but she has a point. These words came to mind when I lay in my hospital bed readying myself for a dose of radioactivity. In a brief quiet moment, I noticed I was unaccountably scared. I was facing a lot of pain and even risk to life in surgery, but also I noticed a dimension of the fear that hung around that word 'radioactivity'. I found my anxiety level rising the more I associated the word with the many negatives through my lifetime. My father-in-law was a prisoner of war in Japan and witnessed the bombing of Nagasaki in 1945. I grew up in Lancashire and remember the scary news when the nuclear power station at Windscale (now Sellafield) leaked over a vast area. My teenage years were filled with the threat of the nuclear arms race. Later came the catastrophes of Chernobyl and Fukushima. My consciousness around radioactivity was entirely negative, yet here I was about to submit to a sizeable dose of it being injected through numerous needle piercings and seed plantings through my perineum and into my prostate.

Maybe reading this makes you a wince at the thought...I know I did. Sitting with this deep inner programming for a while I noticed the anxiety intensifying as I sought to hold in balance the fearful attachment and word association with the healing potential. At that point I found myself thinking about my mother. She died when I was 21. I have childhood memories in my working class culture of being told not to get "above yourself". I might come happily bouncing home from school to report I'd got a gold star next to my name only to be told, "you'd think the sun shines out of your bottom." (People other than my mother would use a stronger word than 'bottom', but I'll spare you that in print). So I sat there with my mum and a thought stream went:– radioactivity=nuclear power=the power of nuclear fission=the power of the sun. Then I burst out laughing. The location of the Iodine125 seeds was about to make my mum's prophecy come true! The sun really was going to shine out of my.... I laughed more, and the fear dissipated.

The development of a capacity to hold opposites in equilibrium and integrate the light and dark of life is the Work along the Way. To do so requires a turning around of our assumptions about things and seeing where our attachments might be keeping us stuck in certain ways of thinking, feeling and being.

Repent!

The word 'repentance' has been rather reduced in meaning in some circles to saying we are sorry for being bad in the hope that the Divine (usually the masculine, authoritarian God) will forgive us and fix our life for us. However, the original Greek word is *metanoia* and it means much more - to 'turn around', to 'transform'. That is, to turn our way of seeing what was once judged bad into good, to change our way of being in the world, to make something that is fearful and threatening into a catalyst for change.

In Soul Works terms, this might mean looking at something that we see as bad or unforgivable in our lives and finding new dimensions to it, without which we might be stuck in our old ways. I have worked with so many people down the years who, much to my admiration, have taken some form of suffering that hitherto they had fought to push away and instead embraced, explored, understood and integrated and indeed found that they could change their lives with it; yes, even be grateful for it.

That is a tall order for many of us, yet I think as I write of Mike who burned out and went through the pain of leaving his job but who is now glad of the experience because he is so happy in his new life with more fulfilling family relationships. Of Christine, abused as a child and who now has turned her victimhood into a force for change and for helping others. Of Annie who has taken the suffering of the loss of her son and deepened her capacity to care for others so wounded. A wound may also contain a blessing. Suffering can be a source of what my teacher Ram Dass called "fierce grace" [174] as he passed himself through the shadow of having a life-threatening stroke. It is interesting to reflect in these terms what kind of 'life' is being threatened in the light of the discussion in Part 2.

How we receive fear and suffering in our lives depends upon our level of awareness, of awakening. Someone who has done the Work can see a grace in their woundedness, as with Christine, Annie, Mike and Ram Dass. Others may only receive suffering as an attack, a source of victimhood, anger, shame or the desire for vengeance. We have to be careful how we use this understanding; otherwise it can make things worse for some people. Telling a woman with cancer that she would feel better if she could find the grace in it, asking a man who was abused as a child to see this

"Loving awareness enables us to make more healthy choices and act with compassion"

wound as a gift, suggesting to the heroin addict that his problem would be relieved if he forgave his parents - these are beyond the pale until our consciousness is ready for them.

The heroin addiction, the cancer, the abuse are not the gifts, but gifts may be found *within* them at some point when the person is ready, but not before. I have lost count of the number of people I've worked with who have been made to feel guilty or weak or ashamed because they have not been able to make the adjustments of forgiveness and integration of their suffering, and felt thus because some well meaning helper has told them that this is what they 'should' be doing. It does not help us to heal if we are made to feel that our failure to do so is all our fault.

The gifts in fear and suffering, often hard to see at the time when they hurt so much, may sometimes be visible instantly, but more often take some time to make themselves known, perhaps once the fear has passed. Such gifts include the flushing out from those places in our psyches where we do not yet fully trust the Beloved. That is not to give way to the inner critic and beat ourselves up because "I'm not good enough, faithful enough, done the work enough, strong enough…". Rather it is to be received as a gentle insight, an offering to help us see where further work has to be done to deepen faith and have compassion (rather than the harsh voice of the inner critic) for ourselves.

Within the space of a few months, a year or two ago, I was faced with real fear in the run up to treatment in hospital, with deep anger at some suffering in my family and with irritation at the abusiveness of an organisation. Being Mr. Angry gets me nowhere, I know, but gently embracing my ego responses to some of life's challenges allows a compassionate response: "Ah, there I am again, I can see I'm not trusting You here that 'all shall be well'". This does not mean that we become passive and do not act in the face of an injustice or suffering of some sort, but it does mean that we can re-frame ourselves from reacting to responding. The latter is possible when we can 'see' what is going on inside and outside ourselves. That 'seeing', that loving awareness, enables us to be more likely to make more healthy choices and act with compassion for ourselves and others rather than fear.

Honour thy father and thy mother

My dad spoke with pride of one thing in his life, his Royal Air Force (RAF) wartime service. Mention of it was sure to animate him with fond reminiscences and end-less stories. I learned much later that the picture he painted was not entirely true. My relationship with him was a long and difficult one. Mine was a family where emotional intelligence was limited and would probably nowadays be classified as dysfunctional. But it was solid working class and I got 'good enough' parenting I guess, if somewhat limiting and loveless. Overt signs of affection were few – so few that I can count on a few fingers moments of loving physical contact and no one in those years ever said, "I love you". With all its limitations it was, paradoxically, a rich grounding for life in so many ways. I look back on it now entirely with acceptance, affection and respect. It was not always so.

The anger I had for my parents took a long time to heal, but when it did I set about learning more about my father and my mother although both were long gone. I had always until then rejected the biblical admonition to "Honour thy father and thy mother" [Ex.12:20]. I have worked a great deal with people who were abused as children and had far more damaging childhoods than mine – how on earth could they be expected to honour, let alone love? Yet I know that the wounds of childhood persist and at some level the abuser still abuses, until we have come to forgive and let them go. The kind of forgiveness I mean takes us beyond statements of right or wrong, rather it requires us to stand back and see our histories from a grander perspective, to see ourselves in the long chain of the generations where each plays its part in making us who we are, as we do the next generations.

Honouring the father and mother is more than accepting everything our parents do as OK simply because they are our parents. It is about having the humility to see ourselves not as products of our individuality, but of the endless process of gener-ation and that sometimes things that we think of as black or white may in fact be much more mysterious and unfathomable. Purpose and maturation in life are not always arrived at in ways that are obvious to us.

My childhood could be classed as deficient in so many ways, yet I bless each mo-ment of it, yes even those parts that were filled with suffering. Why? – Because I

"Loving awareness enables us to make more healthy choices and act with compassion"

feel now at this point in my life profoundly OK, and the emerging picture of my life would not be as it is if everything had not been as it was. Judgements like good or bad are simply no longer relevant, they are the diabolic efforts of the ego to self justify, to separate and make unwhole that which seeks to be whole, holy. Stepping outside this way of thinking we find that integration and forgiveness are possible and that they set us free. The emotional shackles of unforgiving bind us and continue to wound us long after the original source of that wound. Until we come to forgiveness, the soul itself is not free.

I have worked with cancer patients who in the midst of their horror, as I have suggested above, have found immense peace and even come to appreciate their disease for its transforming effect on their lives, with women who have been beaten and years down the line almost been grateful to their ex-partners for the part played in ultimately setting them free. Countless situations where what seems like a life tragedy at the time ultimately (and especially with the benefit of nurturing guidance) can be part of the *metanoia*.

Forgiveness lies at the root of *metanoia.* Through it we are able to let go. This does not mean that we forget harm done or condone it or pretend that it does not matter or passively accept it as 'God's will'. What forgiveness does bring about is liberation from all the feelings that bind us to our story in ways that continue to feed the beasts of anger, resentment, hatred and fear. We realise that all such feelings wound only ourselves and keep us stuck in a sense of victimhood. As we have explored already, such closed-heartedness affects our ability to love and be loved. Closed heartedness tends to be non-specific (although we might think we've got it boxed away concerning one person or thing), it leaks into every aspect of our lives. Forgiveness is an act of loving self-interest. It's not so much about letting the other person or situation go as freeing ourselves so that we can choose to be different and more loving of ourselves and the world.

Forgiveness is also about changing our view of the past, recognising that it has gone and lives only in memory; it does not exist. How can something that does not exist continue to trouble us? It requires us not only to let go of the thing and our diabolic splitting feelings around it, but also to let go of hope or attachment that the past could have been different than it was [79]. Thus by the process of forgiveness, that which was once deemed harmful paradoxically make us whole, one of the catalysts for the search for Home.

Honouring the ancestors has another dimension for it does not just refer to our biological parents, for we have parenting in many spheres of life, including those who built society before us. (In my youth in the 60s I fashionably took part in denigrating everything that the older generation stood for!) Bright young moderns of every generation tend to see themselves as more scientific, more skilled and more knowledgeable than their ancestors. If we have a grand view of our world, it is because we are often standing on a giant's shoulders. Then there are the symbolic fathers and mothers, sources of teaching and inspiration, the countless organisations and helpers along the Way, the work we have done in different traditions – all these are our parents too who have helped the formation of our personhoods and the birthing of our souls into the world. Honouring and accepting their contribution to our becoming grounds us in deep appreciation of the interconnectedness of all things. When we do not honour our roots, they shrivel; a rootless community dies, a rootless person wanders lost in the waste land.

My sister and I took the trouble to investigate more of my dad's wartime life by contacting the RAF. We got access to his records and found among other things that the rosy picture he painted included more than a few spells in the military prison. My sister and I suspect he must have been a difficult man to manage, wilful and disobedient to authority. "I wonder who he reminds me of?" she said. Perhaps sometimes we have 'issues' with our parents because we are more like them than we care to think!

I have come to honour him now, and made the simple gesture of ensuring that his name is now written into the book of remembrance at St Clement Danes in London, the RAF church on the Strand. When I visited the crypt lately and saw his name in the big book in its glass case I was profoundly and joyfully moved. And I had the strangest feeling that my dad was too.

My mother holds an equally honoured place in my life, although she was ever an enigmatic presence to me. She was a woman born into material poverty and impoverished too in education and, like so many women of her time, in expectations for herself. I remember her as forever cooking, cleaning, knitting or mending things,

"Loving awareness enables us to make more healthy choices and act with compassion"

or reading romantic novels, the Mills and Boon type. I wonder if the books were her escape from a life of limited horizons. It may also be that through her I came to love books and words. Books in our neighbours' homes were as rare as hen's teeth in those days and indeed anyone who was bookish was suspect in some way.

I must have been a challenging kid to raise as well. At a time of life when most mums had done with childbearing, I was born when she was 45 years old. She was in her fifties when I was passing through junior school and her sixties when I visited the horrors of my adolescence upon her. I don't remember her complaining. She just seemed to get on with life, deferred always to my dad, accepted what money he offered for housekeeping and dreamed a dream forever unfulfilled of living in a bungalow. "I could have had one but your dad sent it up in smoke or down the drain." His daily diet of 60 Capstan full-strength cigarettes and many a pint of beer took a lot of resourcing.

Perhaps I inherit from her too a love of the land, of the countryside, of things that grow and especially the cherry blossom tree in our back garden which she so admired. Its radiant pink flowers buzzed with the sound of bumble bees each spring, and its petals would shower like confetti across the back doorstep. She loved her garden and the outdoors, the long walks through the fields up Cemetery Road or to my aunt's farm a mile or so away; little escapes from the industrial red brick all around. She would adore where I live now with its wild hills and green fields and not a factory to be seen.

She left me with so many mysteries about herself; she is forever veiled to me now by death, but I planted a cherry blossom tree and I watch it grow as she must have watched the one grow in our garden back in Radcliffe, growing in tandem with my life with her. Perhaps my attempts at wordsmithery are also in part her legacy and her inclusion in my work is her epitaph. I looked for a particular shrine to the feminine where I might remember and honour her. My dad has his place in the RAF church in London. But whither the feminine? She has her place too, not in one place but in all places, in the eternal unfolding of the creation that surrounds me, the cycle of the seasons and of birth and death. My mother's shrine is not in a book of remembrance or building, but in the creation I see bursting all around me, town or county, field or factory, she is there. I see her and know her more as the years pass, both as her own person and as a representative of that primordial mother impulse, Isis, Mary, the Great Earth Mother, the divine feminine.

Whole into holy

In forgiveness we draw all strands of our lives together, into the whole. Sometimes that unwillingness to make whole is manifested in our spiritual work, a diabolic tendency to split ourselves into parts we judge good or bad, light or dark. But the Whole draws the whole unto itself.

I am mindful of Julie, a woman with some years of spiritual experience and an episode of visualisation we shared. She felt estranged from the Divine and during the course of the session she became distressed, seeing herself forever on the threshold of a doorway into the light yet unable to step through it. In exploring this she described herself as standing by the door wearing a tatty hat and an ill-fitting coat and socks that did not match. She had with her lots of polythene bags from upmarket shops, full of what she thought were the good and admirable bits about herself. Stashed well away from her in a darkened corner of the room were old bags from cheap stores full of the nasty parts of herself she did not like. She became aware of what kept her from stepping through the door. She was holding back part of herself she judged bad and unworthy. She realised that actually nothing less than all of her was called and loved by the Divine. Julie, my spiritual 'bag lady', was able to gather up all that she had been and step through the door.

Another person I encountered in more recent years also had some lessons for me about forgiveness, suffering and shadow. The Keswick Convention attracts thousands of Christians every year to its three-week gathering. My friends encouraged me to go along to one of the meetings one evening, and we packed into the giant tent with several thousand others to hear one of the speakers.

Long years of spiritual seeking and training, including interfaith ministry, have brought the blessing of being with people of many different faiths and feeling comfortable with different ways of worship, although there are some in which I am glad I do not have to participate. This particular event had a decidedly fundamentalist element and some of the speakers were pretty quick to identify whose 'side' of Christianity they were on, not least by deploying those classic means of reinforcing group identity by suggesting that their beliefs were the only true ones and that they were under attack from 'others'. These are some of the oldest tricks in the book among fearful people for polarising society and excluding some in order to feel safe in the special group 'in the know'.

"Loving awareness enables us to make more healthy choices and act with compassion"

The main speaker got into his stride, drawing on Psalm 22, the one later used in the New Testament to substantiate the view that the manner of Jesus' death was fore-told. By the time he had finished I felt I'd done twenty rounds of heavyweight box-ing. I heard nearly an hour in which blood, nails, suffering, guilt, shame, punishment, sins, broken bones, more blood, more punishment poured out from this man. I think the love of the Divine got squeezed in a couple of times, but only in the context that the son was sacrificed as a token of that love for humanity. Encouraging people to believe by making us feel guilty is not a healthy approach to spirituality and faith. This child-sacrificing, punishing, angry, sadomasochistic deity is not the One I know although I accept that He (sic) is very real to some people. It also occurred to me that if the preacher had used the word sex in his talk instead of the word 'God', he'd have been arrested on the grounds of promoting sadomasochistic pornography.

The overwhelming impression I gained of this man was that he was a deeply wound-ed and angry individual who was projecting his stuff out onto the world. You didn't need a degree in psychology to see that maybe somewhere down the line this man may have had the kind of parenting or other life experiences where love and pun-ishment, shame and affection, suffering and attention somehow got horribly mixed up. He seemed to be a classic example of the spiritual teacher who has done an awful lot of theological work and can quote and spin the holy books with great skill, but has not done the emotional work on him/herself to become a more whole and well-rounded human being.

Part of me wondered if he is like this with his religion, what on earth would he be like without it? And I shuddered to think of the options – for history is littered with the damage and mass slaughter done to others by those who have not resolved their woundedness and instead have projected it onto the rest of the world. I got the sense that religion had provided this man with a kind of anger management course. It kept his woundedness well repressed, but had done nothing to resolve it. Anger and hatred come from fear, as we have explored, for they are responses to feeling that we are under attack, responses that can help us feel powerful in the face of it. Revenge is likewise a use of ego power – the desire to get others to see us, how they have hurt us.

Angry men (and women) can be the most destructive beings on the planet, especially when they get into positions of power over others. 'Anger management' (arguably something of an oxymoron – can one really manage anger?) programmes are somewhat suspect if all they do is give us the tools to control/repress the anger as opposed to finding ways to acknowledge its existence, heal it and channel the fiery energy in more positive ways. For example, many great spiritual teachers expressed a kind of anger at the human condition, but channelled that energy into working for public good. Gandhi, Martin Luther King, Aung San Suu Kyi , Malala Yousafzai and Mary Robinson are modern examples who offer a model of a healthy response to anger. They demonstrate a workable pattern - acknowledge it (as opposed to repression, denial and bottling it up), work with it to see where it comes from in ourselves (usually a situation that provokes feelings of being helpless, unloved, unworthy, attacked etc.) and transform it. As we explore this anger we often see in such leaders not the attacking form that comes from fear, but indignation. The former is an egoic response to defend against pain, the latter a heartfelt, energised expression seeking transformation of suffering and injustice.

The emotional energy of anger can be changed into something positive in our actions in the world and in changing parts of ourselves seeking to be healed. For example we can use all that fiery energy of anger to fuel our commitment to peaceful protest or integrate it into meditation practice. Jesus encountered his own demon, but refused to give way to it [Matthew 4:3]. Notice he did not ignore, fight, repress or pretend that it did not exist but chose not to let it hold sway over him (restraint). When we fight evil on its own terms we feed it and it grows as suggested above, even when we do so with good intentions. Those who 'fight' cancer can bring an unhealthy imagery to their attempts to be cured, those who 'fight' bullying risk becoming bullies themselves, those who 'fight' crime may sustain the very violence they seek to neutralise.

Thus the kind of response we bring to suffering can enhance or diminish it according to the violence or otherwise of the consciousness with which we approach it. So many opportunities arose for transformation in suffering as I look back on my life. And I look back on them now with wonder, and compassion - how on earth did I miss that one? Where did that one come from? Why did I react to it 'that way' and not this way? Why did I not see the options? Thus the ongoing struggle to be ever more whole, more healed, more loving and more compassionate is part of our spiritual life and there is no end to it. This includes struggles with the shadows that come into our lives in the present and the revisiting of those that arose in the past. I had a delusion that someday

"Loving awareness enables us to make more healthy choices and act with compassion"

all that was in my past would be perfectly healed and whole. Yet, here I am, seventy years down the line and I still find myself revisiting parts of my history, old hurts and old joys and with that seeing new facets of them, new teachings, new understandings and integrating them into the trajectory of my life.

This is not a morbid dwelling on the past or picking over old sores, rather a conscious appreciation that our life experiences, even ones we think we have long left behind, are a rich seam to mine for yet more knowing about ourselves and the Divine. To know ourselves more deeply is part of the essential teachings of all the great faiths and all modern psychotherapeutic approaches. Jesus, for example, taught the need to "bring forth what is within" [116], drawing out from our shadow selves that which needs to come into the light to be healed. Otherwise we cannot be fully healed and truly know ourselves for "if you do not know yourselves then you are in poverty, and you are the poverty".

It's not just about us
Jung's [48] understanding of the shadow has provided us with the landscape for interior exploration, for the bringing of the darkness into the light of full conscious awareness. Consciousness, as we have explored, is more than personal cognitive processes in the brain; we are embodied in it, it radiates out from us and into us connecting us to All-that-is and the very source of life, the Ground of Being itself. Through the process of what Jung called 'individuation', we are called not to just break free of our 'animal' nature, but also to accept and enter into our divine nature as well. Through individuation, the essence of our spiritual life on the way Home, we fulfil that potential and promise in each of us. We stop expecting 'God' to rush to the rescue like some exterior 7th cavalry and fix things for us, but mature into the fullness of our humanity that enables and empowers us to take responsibility for the world and ourselves.

Knowing ourselves includes knowing the nature of the reality we live in, the ordinary reality of the created world and its continuum into the invisible world of spirit, of expanded consciousness. I watched the horrific pictures of the Tsunami that devastated so many lives on Boxing Day 2004. Men (and they usually were men) of varying religions preached and pontificated about God's role when the wave hit. Some tied themselves in theological knots trying to squeeze out a rational explanation. Others lapsed into duality of good and evil forces, thereby inadvertently making the best case for atheism – if there is an all powerful 'God' and 'He' (and this God usually is a 'He') permits evil to exist while 'He' has the power to prevent it then 'He' is not worthy of worship; if 'He' is not all powerful then 'He' is equally unworthy of worship. Still others lapsed into harsh judgmentalism - it's "God punishing us for our sins", but what a strange divinity it is that appears to punish innocent and guilty alike. We can observe responses like this emerge with any natural disaster and they are all egocentric distortions arising from the struggle to find reason in the un-reasonable.

Equally, in many traditions old and new, is heard the regular refrain that these are dangerous and special times and that a particular movement, person or belief system has emerged or needs to be made by 'us'. Each age seems to produce its own spiritual demagogues and egocentric worldviews. Times have always been dangerous, movements and ideas of humanity come and go, nature has always seemed indifferent to us (although the essence of the very Ground of Being is not, as we have explored) and natural disasters are part of the cosmic order. We are part of All-that-is, not its centre. The planet has taken care of itself without us and will continue to do so. In the long view of geological history, we are but blips on the horizon. No matter what we do, even destroy the ecosystem, life will more than likely still find a way, the universe will continue to unfold with or without us.

In our egocentrism, our dualistic attempt to set ourselves apart from the natural world and the Beloved, we can forget that we too are of the cosmic order. The elements, earth, air, fire and water are just being themselves apparently without regard to what we think of them. The primary forces in the world – creation, destruction and maintenance - are forever shifting and unfolding. That is the evolving nature of the cosmos, the creative process and we are part of it. We are in a reality where suffering and bliss exist side by side; some beliefs would say we have chosen to be here. So, all we can do is accept responsibility for the bits we can and work to relieve the suffering wherever we encounter it and where it is in our power to do so.

All the great spiritual teachers put this among the foremost of their teachings. Jesus, the Buddha, the Prophet, Guru Nanak, Krishna, Lao Tzu, these and others of all faiths urged us to spend less time judging people or trying to pin down the divine Will and rather more in being active compassionate helpers of others – at every

"Loving awareness enables us to make more healthy choices and act with compassion"

level of life. Most of us could not help those involved in the Tsunami directly, but we could look at where our money and our lifestyles cause suffering in other ways. We can address the attention-commanding crisis when it arises, but we can also (perhaps more difficult) give ongoing attention to those sufferings, which are lower profile yet equally relentless and tragic as well as the suffering in ourselves. Individually we can probably change very little, but it is important that we try nonetheless and Mother Theresa [175] reminds us, "In this life, we cannot do great things. We can only do small things with great love."

Not long after the Asian tsunami, my own locality was hit by flood and storm. We lost just a few slates and thirty fine old trees. Not far away many lost homes and livelihoods and a few their lives. Once again the judgements of 'God', or otherwise, were trotted out. But one man just turned to a TV interviewer and said, "It's nature isn't it? Simple as that. Get on with it." I was visiting a hospital at the time and watched nurses and doctors deal with the endless river of suffering. It rolls up the corridors of our hospital wards and clinics; spills through the doorways of our homes and health centres. I turned from the TV in the waiting room and went back to the bedside and was deeply grateful for nurses and doctors and paramedics who just got on with dealing with what was before them. No judgements or attempts to rationalise or explain away the suffering, just dealing with it and seeking expertly, compassionately, the relieving of it. But against death, even they must at some time give way.

Dying into life
A death in my family caused me to reflect on this cycle of suffering. When death comes to the home it knocks us into another reality; ordinary life with its passions and priorities is put on hold. Western culture generally does not prepare us well for death. It is invariably seen as something to be denied and associated with loss or defeat. The spiritual search is about dying into life, in a sense, for we may awaken out of the sleep of one plane of consciousness, the consciousness of the false self that is really a kind of living death. The life as lived in our early years is not life as it might be and waking up to that can be a gentle emergence or an emergency as we discussed in Part 2. This new vision of life is urged upon us by all the great spiritual teachers, a revised understanding of it that is completely different from that limited by biological processes and 'existence'. It concerns another plane of consciousness present in the

here and now as we return Home, into the Beloved. Spiritual practice in all traditions has at least one common thread [176], the preparation "for our eventual encounter with death and what follows, whether this is conceived and experienced as heaven or some form of paradise, transcendence of the human condition subject to samsara or rebirth, or some other ultimate state of realisation." The mettle of our faith and practice, of whatever tradition, is tested when we encounter in others or ourselves that point of crossover into the ultimate mystery. Religiosity and spiritual work contain the groundwork for that encounter.

Readying ourselves for our own death may be a lifetime's process, not a subject of morbid fascination, but a conscious exercise with both practical and spiritual implications as I have discussed elsewhere [34] and on page 52. Doing so in order to make death and bereavement less painful for others and ourselves, such as sorting out practical things like finances or living wills, seems one level of approach. Doing so in order to deepen our awareness and annihilate the illusions of the self or mortality quite another. We may come to live in each moment as if it is our last embodied moment that can make life seem supremely precious.

The disciples asked Jesus about death and like all great teachers he did not provide a straight answer. In so doing he completely subverted their existing notions of death [116]: "The disciples said to Jesus: 'Tell us in what way our end will be.' Jesus said, 'Have you therefore discerned the beginning since you seek after the end? For in the Place where beginning is, there will be the end. Happy is he who will stand boldly at the beginning, he shall Know the end, and shall find Life independent of death.'" He challenged and sabotaged the whole basis of our understanding of life itself, the contrast between the egotistic life and the soul life asserting that we have to lose our lives (i.e. the limited way of life) in order to discover true life, life lived in the Divine, eternity.

Life lived from this point takes us to a very different view of reality, indeed we see the real reality. We are no longer trapped by attachments to past, present or future – time and space are the realm of ordinary, egoic awareness. Meister Eckhart (162) says, "The person who lives in the light of God is conscious neither of time past nor of time to come but only of the one eternity...Therefore he gets nothing new out of future events, nor from chance, for he lives in the Now-moment that is, unfailingly,

"Loving awareness enables us to make more healthy choices and act with compassion"

'in verdure clad'". This is the Christ consciousness, the Buddha mind, the Tao, the Hindu "knowers of the real"; a 'seeing' of the world through new eyes, the eyes of the Beloved that sees through us. This "Now-moment" is the single point of the All-that-is in which all time is present, having its equivalent in the *ekaksana*, the 'one moment' of Buddhism or the *bindu* of Hinduism. The followers of the Way learn to walk with feet in both realities with equanimity, clinging to neither, dancing in both.

Jesus in the beatitudes offered a further glimpse, specifically about how an encounter with bereavement, however painful it might be, can also be a blessing. He said, "Blessed are those who mourn, for they will be comforted." [Matt.5:4] His announcement that eternal life dwelt in every person was reinforced by the gift of mourning. How can this be so – those in the midst of mourning and its agony can hardly be expected to see a blessing there? Mourning is not just an experience we have for a dead person, for our lives can be full of so many deaths – of expectations, roles and so on. Mourning can thus affect us at many levels, but the poet reminds us that in an ending there is also a beginning [1].

Sahajananda [177], synthesising a Hindu-Christian perspective, writes that those who mourn may be brought to realise, if they do not already, that much of their happiness is a passing happiness when it comes from others or material things – all these must pass away. People who "lose their earthly source of happiness may realise its passing nature and so find eternal happiness." Thus the gift of death can be paradoxically not just terrible loss, but also the potential for a shift of consciousness, a *metanoia* of our way of seeing the world that moves us from attachment to the transient nature of life in this reality, to the possibility of life that is lived fully 'in the now' coterminous with the life at Home. It is not a life to be found after death, but a life that can be lived fully in this moment.

Resurrection does not have to wait until we (physically) die; it can happen in each moment as we take a deep breath and come fully into that moment. We live again free from that 'dead' place of 'forgetting' where we are caught up in the relentless distractions of ordinary reality. The more we just live in this moment rather than caught up in that which does not exist (the future, the past) the more we are at peace, watching with absolute compassion this reality as it unfolds around us. Only being fully in the moment can we be resurrected into life as it is fully lived. The Kingdom or Queendom is here, now, all we have to do is wake up to it.

To see death and loss as a gift, as having potential for more and not just less can be superhumanly difficult when we are caught up in the midst of them. That is why the presence of wise persons, such as Soul Friends, at the time of death can be so profoundly healing through the pain. That is why so many spiritual teachings in many faiths urge us to prepare for death now as part of life, not as means to avoid suffering but as a way of approaching it with greater awareness and equanimity.

<ins>On the existential edge</ins>
We teeter always on the existential edge. At any moment our quietly ordered lives can fall apart as we are robbed of all those things in which we invest certainty. Like thieves lurking in the night the forces of chaos are ever present, waiting for the right moment to slip up behind and mug us of our precious possessions. I witnessed this after a delayed flight to Australia when, veering between resignation and fury, my fellow passengers sought to handle the countless disorders, missed moments and scuppered plans that now filled our lives.

The shambles at the airport mirrored the chaos into which my own body slipped a week later, when an unexpected health problem laid me low, dangerously low, and I found myself in the Cairns Hospital emergency department. Far from home, exhausted, sick - I watched my fear shifting ground constantly as the twin poles of the terror of non-existence and the humour of the ridiculous pulled in opposite directions. Sometimes I felt my body giving way and my heart failing and I was plunged into a gut-stuck tremble, at others I lay there thinking of the utterly futile like "If I die and have to be sent back to England in a box, will somebody remember to cancel the meals on the plane?" or "Have I got clean underwear on?" (Mother, oh dear mother – what memories you have left me with!)

I was knocked off centre, into the abyss, into the place of forgetting by a combination of fear, pain and drugs. I was helpless and facing the helplessness and, during the long wait as machines clicked and hummed to tell me more than I knew myself of my own inner workings, sometimes quietly furious with the Beloved for letting me down. The possibility of death after decades of joyful and painful conscious spiritual awakening seemed damned unfair, I wasn't ready to die; it just wasn't in the plan! It

"Loving awareness enables us to make more healthy choices and act with compassion"

had taken me years to awaken and to transcend the mortal trap (or so I thought) and escape my ego nature - only to die? All that work, then so what? Shouldn't there be some reward, at least a few years to enjoy the benefits? What's the point of waking up from my neuroses only to find that life really is short and miserable after all? So, not much ego stuff going on then really!

I'm sure I lapsed into unconsciousness for a while. I opened my eyes at one point and the clock had silently ticked by an hour or more and I had no idea where that time went. I cannot say it was to sleep. It was some other plane of consciousness, where the 'dream', if that's what it was, had a searing intensity of colour and sound. In this place I watched myself dying, the slow deconstruction of muscle and sinew, the cracking of bone, the falling of flesh from flesh. The accompanying miasma of terror suddenly dissolved when a flashing thought burst in. "If I am watching myself die, who is the 'I' that is watching?" With the benefit of hindsight, I can see an element here that is often reported in the Work; the dismemberment of the body in a vision of some sort in order to learn that 'I am not my body'. When I looked at the clock I noticed I was feeling strangely hopeful while every other part of me seemed to be demanding I get a grip and realise I had reason to feel anything but hopeful.

As I lay there waiting for whatever was to come next, I reflected on this health crisis, I realised I was not surprised. For, weeks before, I had been having strange and disturbing death dreams. The lecture tour, when requested over a year before seemed like a good idea at the time, but as the moment of travel drew closer a steady and increasing series of mishaps occurred – emails going astray, arrangements falling through, problems arising one after another. Moments of prayer and contemplation were spiked with grim words and imagery. I had an overwhelming urge to make out my will, settle some affairs and phone the kids to say I loved them – all of which I did. When people said, "You must be looking forward to it", I said, or thought, "My heart is not really in it." - words that rang with many meanings as I stared at the erratics on my monitor in the emergency room with the madness and distress of a busy department roaring around me. Somehow I knew there was something I had not paid attention to here, some synchronicities missed, yet inevitable and unavoidable.

My interior struggle was not mirrored in the affectionate discipline of my doctors and nurses who were universally kind, attentive and practical. They were superb chaos managers – keeping all those forces of disorder inside and outside my body at bay by the quiet concentration on what needed to be done. One nurse with an unusual degree of spiritual intelligence held my gaze and said, "You need to be alone don't you? This kind of place doesn't lend itself to quietness, but I can tell you need some time to make sense of it don't you?" I was astonished by her sensitivity, not to say possible telepathy and her practical response of shooing people away, partially drawing the screens to permit observation without obtrusiveness and leaving me to drop within.

It was then a loneliness came upon me, the intensity of which I had never before known. Something deep and dark overwhelmed me as I passed from rage at the Beloved, to suddenly feeling a profound abandonment. Despair welled up. A feeling like drowning. An absence of breath. A lifeless, hopeless void. In this interior shadow I could 'see' only one thing, a great black hole that was growing bigger by the second and turning into a vast vortex. Whirlpool-like it was drawing me in, to a place beyond terror, for this was death and it was headed my way and there was nothing I could do about it and I was on my own and the Beloved had left me and I didn't know which if any of these frightened and desolated me most. As I lay on that trolley that vast black vortex was set to overwhelm me. In the depths of my being I cried out within after the fear and the fury were dissipated, "Where are you now, where are you now when I need you most?" And felt the wetness of tears.

After what seemed like a long age, but must have been no more than seconds, from the heart of the darkness came a still, calm, quiet voice – "I am here, I am here". The nurse returned behind the screens, the doctor arrived to do what he had to do. I opened my eyes to them and was at peace; ready to surrender into the hands of my carers and the unknown. Perhaps those last words from the darkness were part of my nervous system seeking to reassure me, perhaps some conjured up voice I needed to make it all OK, perhaps a sudden chemical or electrical discharge I had triggered to make it all feel better and give me courage. I did not experience it that way. That loving 'voice' was real to me, a new dimension of the Beloved in the dark as well as the light, something about God though perhaps not God that is beyond words or identity.

"Loving awareness enables us to make more healthy choices and act with compassion"

In the first part of this book I summarised some of the various explanations for 'God' as a comforter. Some people get the 'God feeling' from drugs and I can agree from my hospital experience that there's something to be said for them! As I slipped effortlessly into unconsciousness as the white liquid slipped equally effortlessly down the intravenous line, I recall thinking, "This is just like God", as the anaesthetic and relaxant took hold. That same bliss swept over me that I have felt so many times before as I fell into mystical union. And another thought came – that underlying addiction (to drink or drugs) may be that same desire to fill the empty space, to drown the pain of existence, to seek the rapture that paradoxically is readily available within if we learn to receive it.

As Paul Tillich [29] observes, belief in the Divine or something else is what holds at bay the unconscious fear of non-existence. He writes, "The anxiety of meaninglessness is anxiety about the loss of an ultimate concern, of meaning which gives meaning to all meanings. The anxiety is aroused by the loss of a spiritual centre, of an answer, however symbolic and indirect, to the question of the meaning of existence." As I lay in that emergency room, a collapse into uncertainty, anxiety and meaninglessness was more painful than anything that was going on with my body. Nurses kept apologising for sticking needles in me or scraping off my chest hair and all the other pokings and proddings, but I have no memory of physical pain.

I have instead a memory of watching everything happening, feeling everything happening, but in some oddly detached way as if it was happening to some stranger who was yet vaguely familiar to me – that 'haven't I seen you before somewhere?' feeling. Even the fear that swirled between body and mind neither possessed nor was possessed by me. Some 'I' was experiencing it all, the suffering, in a way that was curiously liberating and interesting even though death was stalking around; an uninvited and invisible though not necessarily unwelcome guest. In fact a kind of dying seemed to be happening as some aspects of myself, or who I thought I was, became ensnared by all manner of little humiliations and fears. The witness or the watcher of all this, in contrast, seemed ever more free, blissful and expanded – and I hadn't had any drugs yet! I wondered if this was some trick of the mind, a disassociation in order to detach from the pain and fear. Or perhaps it was a sign of mental collapse and irrationality. Then again, maybe it was indeed the deep peace of letting go of who I thought I was and being at One. But the theorising soon fell away; the drugs took hold…and oblivion.

Science or spirit?

I love science. It's really useful. I like drugs, ECG machines, aeroplanes, roads, water supplies and countless other things in life that work because of science. Some aspects of New Age and indeed Old Age thinking envision a world without science. In this model we dream of going back to some happy, pre-modern, primordial condition. In this harmonious, natural state we are at one with the creation and all is bliss. A reality check, based on the archaeological evidence, indicates that our ancestors never lived in such a realm and life was often tough and short. I suspect the idyllic arcadia is really a reflection of our desire to get away from the difficulties of living in the present, or perhaps it is a collective unconscious urge to return to that lost, imaginary Garden of Eden. Spiritual work teaches us that we cannot return to such a garden in historical terms, but must seek it in the here and now in the liberation of the soul. In any case, I think it was Gore Vidal who, when asked for a good reason for not wanting to live in a past age replied, "Dentistry!"

To the Navajo the Beautyway is the discovery and living out in ourselves of the essential coherence of the universe, of All-that-is. The Garden of Eden in this philosophy is not somewhere else in time and place, but in the condition of our consciousness in the present moment. That requires a cultivation of harmony between our interior world and the exterior, the holding together of opposites. It is similar to the esoteric tradition of 'as above, so below'. It has parallels with the 'colonies of heaven' we explored in part 6. Coherence, integration and harmony - these are the elements of the Beautyway, the Garden of Eden and Coming Home. The Garden of Eden is not a place of science *or* spirit, but science *and* spirit. Serious minded searchers after truth such as Einstein [21], "are religious in that sense and therefore have common ground with those who would see themselves as religious…we are all in this together." Science and spirit do not have to be in conflict and many organisations (the Scientific and Medical Network is one example) are doing sterling work to explore the common ground.

The tendency, however, to split science from spirit has another consequence. It's common in the culture of developed countries to see physical symptoms as some-

"Loving awareness enables us to make more healthy choices and act with compassion"

thing going 'wrong' with the body. In an holistic universe, everything is connected and no less so are body, mind and soul. It may be that the sense of restlessness, tiredness or a high temperature are signs of an underlying physiological illness. But they may be also signs of inner dis-ease that is calling for our attention; wake-up calls that indicate we are ready to make a shift (of consciousness).

A headache between the eyes may be a sign of too much alcohol the night before or it may be a sign of pressure from the need to 'see' things differently and look within. A sore throat may be viral infection or it may indicate that there is some truth to be spoken. A pain in the belly may be a sign of constipation or it may be telling us something about our need to explore our gut feelings and discover our true power. It is important not to act on one without full consideration – too many people have ended up dead because they insisted on seeing only spiritual solutions when surgery was really needed or more confused because biological solutions were applied when deep psychological or spiritual matters needed attention.

I'm blessed to have networks of conventional and unconventional carers in my life. As I develop more health problems with ageing it is curious how each may tend to look at me through their particular lens. My physiotherapist looks at back pain and sees pulled muscles, my nutritionist questions some dietary indiscretion, my psychotherapist friend wonders at some inner burden I might be carrying, my shaman sees the need for soul retrieval, a 'past life' believer thinks it could be due to some karmic connection. One, all, none or more of these may be true! We have to be careful that we do not squeeze people into our particular model of perception. Holistic practitioners and patients can work with them all. With due discernment we can pay attention to the options and decide whether medication or meditation is needed (or both). Solutions can embrace both science and spirit. As with all these phenomena, discernment is the key and the kind of experiences we take to our Soul Friends and Soul Works as well as to our doctor or other health care practitioner.

Science, then, is not something to be rejected from the spiritual life. It is part of reality to be embraced, what matters is the consciousness with which we do so. Just as some spiritual seekers insist on rejecting science, so there are scientists who are hostile to the realm of the soul. Unlike Einstein, there is a will for power among some in modern science, however it is dressed up (to know everything, to be certain, to find a solution) that is sometimes rooted in very reductionist views of human beings and a very irrational attachment to a faith position (that "There is no God"). The scientific creed (and I use the word creed advisedly for it is just as absolute as any religious creed) goes something like this:

"I believe in a single substance, the mother of all forces, which engenders bodies and the consciousness of everything, visible and invisible.

I believe in a single Lord, the Human Mind, the unique son of the substance of the world after centuries of evolution: the encapsulated reflection of the great world, the epiphenomenal light of primordial darkness, the real reflection of the great world – evolved through trial and error, not engendered or created, consubstantial with the mother substance – and through whom the whole world can be reflected. It is he who - for we human beings, and for our use – has ascended from the shadows of the mother-substance.

He has taken on flesh from matter through the work of evolution, and he has become the Human Brain. Although he is destroyed with each generation that passes, he is formed anew in each generation following, according to Heredity. He is summoned to ascend to comprehensive knowledge of the whole world and to be seated at the right hand of the mother-substance, which will serve him in his mission as judge and legislator, and his reign will never end.

I believe in Evolution, which directs all, which gives life to the inorganic and consciousness to the organic, which proceeds from the mother-substance and fashions the thinking mind. With the mother-substance and the human mind, evolution receives equal authority and importance. It has spoken through universal progress.

I believe in one diligent, universal, civilising Science. I acknowledge a single discipline of the elimination of errors and I await the future fruits of collective efforts of the past for the life of civilisation to come. So be it."

This somewhat tongue-in-cheek creed epitomises a little of the hypocrisy of some contemporary scientists – believing themselves to be rational and objective, yet deeply rooted in their own articles of faith and dogmas. It says something once

"Loving awareness enables us to make more healthy choices and act with compassion"

again about the egocentrism of human beings in placing ourselves at the centre of the universe and the creative process. We lay claim to all that is known and knowable, to an essentially materialist and quantifiable cosmos with no room for mystery or the possibility of creative and conscious forces at work that may be beyond those produced by the human brain.

In claiming to be the *summum bonum* of human endeavour, it omits one significant human quality – humility. It is noted [177] that, "Man's freedom requires a religious basis. Freedom only grows from participation in absolute truth, from the human being's bond with the divine mystery in life." Public spats between prominent theists and atheists shed more heat than light on the debate, and often both parties just look polarised and arrogant. To seek the teaching of creationism alongside evolution, as is happening in some of our educational institutions under pressure from the religious right, is nonsense. Faith comes from another domain of what it is to be human and is not part of the scientific realm. What we believe in, rather what we *know* deeply, is not provable in scientific terms yet we believe in it because is not provable. Faith rests in the heart, a completely different way of knowing than through the intellect although spiritual maturity brings a capacity to bring both into harmony.

To match creationism with evolutionary theory arises from the error of mixing *mythos* with *logos* which we explored in Part 7, to confuse the nature of literal truth of facts and spiritual truth in scripture. This attempt to root religion in facts reflects once again not only a misunderstanding of factual and spiritual truth, but also perhaps a brittleness of faith that needs to feel something must be factually true in order to be believable. To seek to put them together demeans both the value of science and all that it brings us and the precious Beloved that simply transcends definition. Science is debased by attempts to equate the faux science of creationism with it and scripture falls foul of scientific rationale, reduced to fairy tale instead of its rightful place as the poetic, mythic, inspiration towards the Divine.

Knowing and believing.
When Jung [99] said that he did not "believe" in the Divine but "knew", he touched on a fundamentally different approach to knowing. Thomas Merton [56] writes of a kind of faith, a *gnosis*, which is not rooted in the kind of false-hope beliefs that defend us against existential despair. Instead he points to an authentic hope arising from the

kind of "knowing" that we feel when truth touches us deeply (and certainly does not require or is indeed accessible to scientific validation).

Faith seems to come from a 'force' that is beyond the grasp of our mind or our feelings, yet is interpreted by both. Needleman [164] suggests this is why so many religious traditions proscribe images of or attempts to conceptualise the Divine. Unwilling or unable to embrace *neti neti*, not this not that, we may find ourselves obstructed from cultivating a deep relationship with the Beloved if we hang on to theological definitions, pictorial representations or emotional responses to the Beloved when faith is something much deeper. Yet this elusive concept of faith is seen as the essence, the root, of our capacity to find our Way Home in all religions. I am reminded of a scene in the film *Jurassic Park* when, in response to the possibility of dinosaurs being recreated, a palaeontologist says 'I'll believe it when I see it." To which a child replies, "No, first you have to believe, and then you'll see."

Belief is a surface dwelling cousin of faith nudging us towards truth, not least because it is not constricted by rational discourse. Indeed the word 'belief' derives from the Teutonic *belofen*, which is in turn related to 'beloved'. Belief in these terms suggests a non-rational acceptance of something, a different way of comprehension and more a heartfelt connection.

What we do or do not believe and the depth of it in our consciousness has a profound impact on our lives as we have explored in Part 2. Thoughts and feelings shift our state of psychological, spiritual, social and physical wellbeing. Some things 'work' for us simply because we believe they do. Consider for example the placebo effect in medicine or the impact upon the degree of trust we have in our doctor and the success or otherwise of treatment. Hippocrates [34] noted that, "sometimes the patient gets better simply because of the goodness of the doctor."

Different spiritual 'ways of seeing' thus affect our response to suffering. Some call it part of the process or cosmic pattern, some call it karma, some call it fate, some call it the soul's path – it has a thousand names but the key thing is where we place our belief and trust in these different views. In the Buddhist tradition suffering stems from *attachment*. The Work, and it sure as hell feels like work sometimes with all the essentially solitary efforts to fix the mind, is to see these and get free of them. There is another option. That suffering stems from *detachment* from Source (which then creates fear leading to attachment to the world of possessions in all senses). We may open

"Loving awareness enables us to make more healthy choices and act with compassion"

to the possibility that the Beloved is at work in and for us often beyond our conscious control. If proof be needed we can look at all the synchronicities and blessings in our lives, those countless occasions when we 'know' something deeply not least that we are worthy, safe and loved despite the buffetings of life and that somehow 'all shall be well'. Our differing relationship to the Absolute, as indifferent or involved, affects our response.

Yet what of my own experience in that emergency room, that stalking by death, the sense of a presence of the Divine even in the darkness? Was this to be distrusted because I could be loading it with all kinds of psychological baggage or the effects of drugs or the fear of the moment? If the evidence of religious experience has any meaning in the world, then surely it is in its transformative power – to make us more loving, more conscious, more socially engaged, more connected to the world, more healed and whole, more able to relate to others, more empowered to relieve the suffering of others, more able to see clearly to truth. This 'more-ness', an expanded state of consciousness, of being-ness, is the product of these extra-ordinary human experiences. Indeed for many years now these moments of being 'touched by God', as David Torkington [179] describes it, have to me not been extraordinary but ordinary. They occur so commonly amongst human beings [50] that to *not* have them is extraordinary!

Whenever I tried to explain the mystical experiences of my youth, I was told that it was "just my imagination". I couldn't find the words to explain this intense 'oneness' and what it felt like, an overwhelming 'loving'. But what are we if not our imaginations? And what is our imagination if it is not processed with due discernment to truly sift out whether what we experience is madness or mysticism? The discernment process is measured by the 'fruits of the spirit'; the 'mores' that we become if the experiences are authentic and we are properly nurtured through them.

Once we really 'get' that there are many coterminous planes of consciousness, that we can embrace all of these and trust in the deep OK'ness of this vast work of art of which we are a co-creative part, then we may live in the world with greater coherence, harmony and willingness towards compassionate action. These are some of the fruits of this spiritual work. We seek to relieve suffering, to make the world a better place, but without clinging/attachment to outcomes. And maybe, just maybe, being that loving presence and agent of change in the world we may touch the lives of others and in some way also contribute to their awakening.

This longing to help does not come from the fearful ego, whose apparent helping is loaded with its many attachments to feeling good about itself and being in control, but from heartfelt compassion. It is the "love that loves to love"[180] yet does not feel the need to impose itself on others or feel rejected when its offerings are not taken up. A simple soulful word or gesture may go ignored or it may spark a whole new level of conversation and connection, which may become an 'open sesame' for that person's awakening. I find myself less willing than before to engage in butterfly conversations. Once at a gathering I dropped in some words like 'sacred' and 'spiritual'. Most ignored them and the conversation drifted along its superficial course. Later one guest took me to one side, the words had sparked an enquiry that made him want more and which later contributed to his awakening. We have been friends ever since.

On another occasion a woman spoke in a group about her anguish at a situation in her family. Others present tended to dive in with comforting platitudes and practical suggestions ('Job's comforters'). One person held his counsel, asked for some silence so that we could all listen more deeply and suggested we all listen rather than speak. As she was given space to tell her story, allowed to express her feelings, given the option of whether to hear suggestions or not, she found herself validated and able to work out solutions for herself. The group felt more deeply connected to her and each other as a result.

The more OK and aware we are in ourselves, the more we live our lives as a kind of offering. We feel no need to proselytise our truth or fix everyone's problems. Service becomes a way of life, just being among others in open, authentic, loving awareness without attachment to outcomes. Each encounter is pregnant with possibility; we offer and rest in trust that any outcome is to the good without judgement or expectation. "You never know".

The last thing to go
The Way summons us to integration, to embrace the left and right brains of ourselves, the masculine and the feminine, the scientific and the spiritual, the ordinary and non-ordinary realities, the animus and anima, the perishable and imperishable

"Loving awareness enables us to make more healthy choices and act with compassion"

worlds. The Beautyway is thus fulfilled in the harmony of seeming opposites that are actually heavenly twins. Thus integrated we do more than serve ourselves; we are available in service to others and the world as well. In this Beautyway, this integrated way of being in the world as we come Home, one thing becomes less – the way fear governs our lives.

Paul Tillich [29] writes, "The courage to be is rooted in the God who appears when God has disappeared in the anxiety of doubt." It is said that in spiritual work the last thing we let go of is the shadow of fear. Our lives are full of opportunities around fear and perhaps we unconsciously summon them up, where we must confront it, and like confronting the enemy in the darkness, we may learn how to respond to it, embrace it, love our enemy and work with it. If fear was a herd of buffalo, death would be the biggest one that leads the lot and yet Joseph Campbell [181] wrote, "One thing that comes out in myths is that at the bottom of the abyss comes the voice of salvation. The black moment is the moment when the real message of transformation is going to come. At the darkest moment comes the light." Many of the people I have mentioned in this book tell their stories of such moments – stories of feeling hopeless, spiritually arid, and suffering from terror, disease or loss. Each in their own way experienced that darkness, but each too saw a light there at some point.

Thomas Merton [56] writes of "the God Who is God and not a philosopher's abstraction, lies infinitely beyond the reach of anything our eyes can see or minds can understand. No matter what perfection you predicate of Him, you have to add that He is not what we conceive by that term. He Who is infinite light is so tremendous in His evidence that our minds only see Him as darkness...to find God we must pass beyond everything that can be seen and enter into darkness." When I spoke of my time in that emergency room, a friend said, "I'm surprised you were afraid – I thought you were supposed to be spiritual." I have often heard this from fellow seekers, taking on board some delusion that in the spiritual search we somehow lose our humanity. It is human to fear, to be spiritual is to know that we are not our fear and not be imprisoned by it.

The soul, being of the Beloved, does not know fear. Fear is the province of our small, false self. Our life experiences hold the grist to the mill of losing the governance of fear. The toboggan of fear I rode on that occasion in hospital, down a long dark slope, took me to a place I had not expected or would probably not have gone willingly. Certainly it took me closer to the One in whom I live and move and have my being and who lives and moves and has being in me. It flushed out fear, as so many moments have, from which I might run or which I might embrace that I may trust ever more deeply. And oh those angels, those doctors and nurses who rode down with me, those accompaniers in shadow, and those warriors against chaos - they stand with us like our Soul Friends and Communities, on the existential edge being there with ropes and hooks to haul us back when it looks like we might teeter over. And what hidden, unknown power works its way in them too we might wonder?

"Loving awareness enables us to make more healthy choices and act with compassion"

We rave at mountain views
or the sun losing itself over Skye.
We see in the eagle's brief shewing
a high spot worthy of recounting,
or perhaps it is the perfect womb
the sanctuary offers, which is
cause for comment. But this
mighty crumpled landscape
comes into its own when
enfolded by night, the time
that Mars owns and insists
upon attention, the time Orion,
naked and belted calls to us
to seek under the moonlight.
If we were to overturn convention
and let the balcony feel our flesh
under starlight, let the wet boards
hold us while a passing cloud
prophesies the content of our dreams.
Then and only then stripped to the
bare essentials like we were at the
changing of the guard, then, if we
forget just a little, we may remember.
For this is a hall of remembrance,
the place of dis-covery of something
we already know and having hidden
once in a secret place for safety,
safely hidden, even from memory.
Here lies the eternal invitation
finally gathered up from the reading
room floor, the one we always knew
we would receive. In the house of
remembrance, past sense and sensation,
there is a kind of elevation.
Above the rocky cliffs climbed

perhaps over many decades,
a history, walled and pacified,
in that solitary point beneath
the procession. The world turns,
the stars turn, but on a quiet night
by a solitary candle we may find
that we are simply Here.
There are only three kinds of
People; those who are awake,
and those who are asleep,
and those who are at some point
of transition between the two.
The bridge is the metanoia,
where meaning and experience
collapse in transcendence.
Bell, book and candle, incense,
calling Home.
My mind is like Tarzan,
I swing through the jungle,
from experience to experience,
from thought to thought,
I grasp and swing, until someday
I guess, I swing slap bang into some
big trunk, really big, and cry out at last,
"Me Tarzan, You God."

Part 10

"Home is where the heart is."

Testimony

<u>Where the wind takes us</u>
In my desire for finite goals some years ago, a woman of deep wisdom and mighty Soul Friend, Janet Swan, said to me as I moaned about wanting a clear endpoint that, "If you really knew what it was you wouldn't do it." She was right and in more ways than one. If anyone had said to me a couple of decades ago that in this spiritual pursuit my value system, my way of being in the world, the work I do and the religious path I would follow would end up where they are now I would probably have told them they were crazy and opened another bottle of wine.

And who knows where the next step might be, for we never know which way the wind, the spirit, may take us? Coming Home is a call to a dynamic relationship with the Divine where we must learn to trust deeply and abandon our egoic needs for certainty. Our need to know is often rooted in our basic drives such as wanting power, worthiness, safety and the deep-seated desire to escape death. The Way Home takes us into the 'cloud of unknowing' [182]; each moment we know to be full of uncertainty and yet we have learned to trust and act, to be, as Hildegard of Bingen [183] described it, as a 'feather on the breath of God'. Just like my encounter with that young fulmar described in Part 3.

Ecologist and philosopher Brian Swimme [184] saw that, "The great mystery is that we are interested in anything whatsoever. Think of your friends, how you met them, how interesting they appear to you. Why should anyone in the whole world interest us at all? Why don't we experience everyone as utter, unendurable bores? Why isn't the cosmos made that way? Why don't we suffer intolerable boredom with every person, forest, symphony, and seashore in existence? The great surprise is the discovery that something or someone is interesting. Love begins there. Love begins when we discover interest. To be interested is to fall in love. To be fascinated is to step into a wild love affair on any level of life." The exquisitely composed poem that is the creation calls us into love for it, cannot do otherwise and in loving, falling into love, we participate co-creatively in the writing of

"The authentic spiritual life helps us to go ever deeper into truth."

that vast poem. As we participate little is known to us; the fullness of it is a mystery.

There is nothing new under the sun [Ecc.1:9]. For a moment, holding Rose my new granddaughter I felt this very intimately. I suddenly seemed to see the long trajectory of her ancestry of which I am but a small part. She lay in my arms at peace, unaware of how deeply moved I was and just feeling her presence in the world. How she will live her life I do not know, but what I did feel then was that her unique life will be only an image of her true life, that beneath surface impressions, the whole of creation is an endlessly repeating pattern. There is, was, nothing new. All newness, innovation is but a surface impression, waves upon the still waters from which they arise only to return whence they came. The pattern is beautiful, rich and eternally shimmering and shifting in form, but the pattern is repeated, change is only part of the perception of time and space.

Spiritual experiences are unique to every individual [185], yet there is an order to this down the ages and in all traditions…of a longing for the soul to be free, sometimes precipitated by a crisis when we have not responded to that longing, a shift in perception and priories in life, many trials as we go through the changes that tend to lead to being "strong enough to be humbled and wise enough to surrender." Through this we are guided to the ultimate surrender (death), the wonder of life and the possibility of renewal.

Beneath the surface the eternal now is as it always was, *isness* is the constant, in which time and space are contained. Rose as a baby is born into that *isness*. Somewhere along the way she will surely lose it, only to find her Way Home. It is an inevitable course. The *isness* of my beloved granddaughter and the exquisite journey of life she will make is made all the more exquisite by the constancy of what lies beneath superficial impressions of change and chance. And thus we come to know ourselves fully as we are already known by the Source from which we sprang.

It begins and ends with the Beloved, where the beginning and the end are one. When we rediscover our Home we have a new place, a liberating deeper plane of consciousness, from which to bear witness to and participate in the world. Witnessing is not creating a separate entity, a duality, it is a quality of being of the Presence, it is the Self looking at and knowing the self. Psychiatrist R D Laing [186] comments that, "…there is a mystery in the reality of God. That when the search for the divine begins, the first step is towards a deeper way of relating, of understanding the dimensions of the mysterious, of seeking evidence of truth, and trusting in the "presence that exists". "

We can return to Memphis (Part 4 - the metaphorical place of exile) and embrace it with love, breaking through the dualistic perceptions of reality and work in and with and for the whole. All perceptions of this and that become one. *Aduaita*, the Hindu teaching of non-duality, becomes a reality not a taxing concept to be grasped. We can approach with contemplative, non-dual awareness our joys and difficulties in life with greater equanimity, wisdom, compassion and peace as Isa, Jesus, taught us (page136). We are less likely to be caught up in those countless tricks of the ego that can pull us away, that cause us to fall into forgetting where we came from and who we are, into the delusion that the Beloved has 'left' us.

This Divine, this Absolute, this One, this Sacred Unity, this Great Friend whom we come to know is ever present no matter what thoughts or actions might pull us away from time to time. If we do fall into forgetting, our disciplined attention, our Soul Friends, our Soul Community, our Soul Works and our Soul Foods are there as helpers to bring us back into remembering. We live, move and breathe in the world with greater compassion, ability and willingness to serve without feeling that we are sacrificing ourselves; we love without grasping or feeling lacking, needy or unworthy. We shift from a splitting, diabolic perception of reality where 'now I'm being spiritual and now I'm doing the shopping' to the non-dual, symbolic, contemplative consciousness where everything is one, unfolding in perfection. We are participant-watchers of this Sacred Unity, this cosmic consciousness.

These are the authentic fruits of the spirit by which we are known, unto the Beloved, ourselves, others. The Divine, Home, Ultimate Reality becomes our 'still point in the turning world' [1]. We fall in love with the One because we come to know that the Beloved is love (know it deeply, not as a hopeful belief or a theological deduction). How could love not love to love? We are liberated from the concerns of our false self to the concerns of the Beloved in the world and all of humanity. We learn to live in the eternal now, less buffeted by the insatiable demands of the hungry ego. Love has taken control.

"The authentic spiritual life helps us to go ever deeper into truth."

Love is the transforming fire that drives this whole spiritual awakening and powers the universe. It is the "intolerable shirt of flame" [1] that relentlessly burns off all illusion or restriction. It calls us to move beyond sympathy, where we can understand what another feels and feel it as if it were our own. It is beyond empathy, where we can identify with the other person's situation and really feel it as they might feel it themselves. It pours through compassion, which calls us to combine feeling with action, the heartfelt desire to care, to be of service, to alleviate suffering. Compassion arising out of this unconditional love spurs us to action, for it is "not simply a sense of sympathy or caring for the person suffering, or a sharp clarity of recognition of their needs and pain, it is also a sustained and practical determination to do whatever is possible and necessary to help alleviate their suffering" [16].

Spiritual awakening opens the door to more love and compassion into the world through the relief of suffering – of individuals, groups and communities and indeed the whole of creation, including ourselves. It is compassion free of attachment, a way of being in the world that does not exhaust us with the burden of caring for others, but which liberates us to care from a place of resting at Home in the Source of infinite love. We do not burn out from this kind of caring, it is not from our own emotional ego batteries that it is drawn; rather it is from that infinite source, a source so vast that it is willing to scatter it seemingly wastefully.

This compassion does not drain us, but comes from the open heart, drawing after much emotional and spiritual work, upon its deepest resource unfettered by all kinds of emotional hang ups or ego attachments. It is not charged with the debilitating desire to fix everything - but rests in humility and deep awareness that we can change very little yet humbly play a part within our capacity. Sometimes we go the extra mile, but more often we simply travel the miles we can through non-attached compassion that does not leave us depleted.

To do so means that our own hearts must be open to the Source and healed of all that gets in the way, otherwise whatever love we hope to express is redacted. The best way we can serve with compassion in the world is to awaken ourselves to our true nature. Of love; from which this compassion then flows like an unstoppable, inexhaustible river. In the fairy story 'The Snow Queen', Hans is unable to love until the splinter of ice is removed from his heart. Icy, heartless people are uncommon, but not rare and perhaps the inevitable products of unresolved wounds in their hearts or the waste land that does not value or foster compassion.

Love, the greatest of all human emotions as St Paul so perfectly expressed [Cor.13:1-13] is not something universally accepted or understood in the waste land. Yet this Love, this *agape*, is not associated with affection, lust or attachment to things or persons. It is a compassionate concern and action for another's and the world's wellbeing, indeed for all of humanity. It is uncluttered by value judgments and rooted in respect and equity. This love has no conditions, not one which says, "I'll love you if you love me" where the undertow is really about meeting the ego's co-dependent needs for gratitude, power, worthiness or acceptance. To the egoic self, remember, love is like a pie where, "if you get a slice, I get less". Love is no pie; it is boundless.

As we have explored in this book, all our Soul Care approaches are grounded in the surrender of the ego will, of the alchemical transmutation of our way of seeing and being so that the soul, the very wellspring of love in the world is set free; liberated into its true nature, to do and to be love. How could it not be so? For the soul is a hologram of the Beloved, of Sacred Unity whose nature is love. Therefore all that emanates from the soul cannot be but love and loving.

The ego, the little or false self, cannot comprehend this love, although it may in time surrender to it. It sees and knows in a way that is alien; its values are an inverse of the soul. And yet it has a power and energy, unwilling yet waiting to be mastered by something other than itself. Its psychology has been mapped in Maslow's[187] classic concept of the hierarchy of needs – that familiar pyramid shape - with the basic needs at the bottom (food, shelter, safety) that have to be met before we can address other needs rising above them, in sequence, to the pinnacle of self-actualisation. The latter is that place where "A man can be what a man must be" as Maslow put it.

In egotistical terms this relates to fulfilling all our hopes, dreams and aspirations and making fullest use of all our attributes. An ego perspective as we have seen is some-what limiting and is the opposite of the spiritual search. Indeed, spiritual seekers tend to subvert the hierarchy theory as we have seen, often forgoing many aspects of need – wealth, security, comfort, approval – in the pursuit of higher goals of going

"The authentic spiritual life helps us to go ever deeper into truth."

Home. These 'goals' as we have seen are diametrically opposite to ego desires, for in spiritual terms we do not self-actualise, we self-immolate to find the Self. In that sense a person does indeed become what a person must be, but not in the terms in which I suspect Maslow intended that statement. The psychological pyramid with its peak is very different from the spiritual ladder of descent into the depths of being. The peak as the maximised ego is a world away from the depths of the boundless soul.

When we look at the great spiritual teachers down the centuries, they offer us shining examples of how to live our lives, to be a living presence of that compassionate consciousness of non-duality. This can sometimes seem like an impossible goal, to be self-actualised beings like a Jesus, Buddha, Prophet or Lao Tzu. And it is, for the goal is not so much to strive to be them, but to be fully ourselves. In discovering our true selves then we find that we are like them. All the Soul Care work we pass through reveals truths like this to us. The work of opening fosters the inpouring of the Divine so that we come to realise that we do not master Truth, it masters us. We come to live in this truth of the mystical, non-dual consciousness. It is the contemplative mind where there is no splitting between this reality and that reality, but a perfect loving awareness of the essential union of All-that-is.

Faith and interfaith

Some of the discussion in these pages has focussed on the merits or otherwise of participating in a religion, a tradition, as a Soul Community; the participation is a spiritual practice in itself. There is no requirement to join a religion in order to get Home, but, as we have explored, all the evidence suggests that on balance it is better to have the strength (and weakness) of a tradition and an associated Soul Community (or several) to draw upon. How do we choose one? I cannot say for sure. Perhaps we need to be cautious about making it our choice at all. Perhaps we might feel called to one, as in my experience, while embracing the truth of others. Perhaps the dominant one of our childhood is the right one to return to, but from a very different place in ourselves. Or perhaps it is right and true to commit to another, maybe even radically different from our origin. Sometimes there might be signs along the way, the promptings from people, literature or events that reinforce a message - the metaphorical 'angels' speaking to us. Drawing upon the discernment resources of our four Soul Care approaches we can be guided to choose our true path, following not what is our will but *the* Will. Sometimes of course there is a happy coincidence of the two!

Just as the spiritual supermarket has emerged in the last century, so too has a wider range of options for simultaneous participation in a religious faith. Some of the latter still tick to very rigid rules of what it is to be 'in' or 'out' of the group. Other faiths, or at least parts of them, are more accommodating to varied religious identity. In my role as an interfaith minister as well as my backstory of wandering through many different traditions, I have found that I can be just as comfortable and encounter the Beloved in a Buddhist meeting or on a Shamanic journey or prayers in a gurdwara or a scripture reading in a synagogue as I can in my home church. Likewise I can find some meetings of these same faiths alienating where they slip into rigid dogma. Some religious Soul Communities are finding it more difficult than others to adapt to participants who have multifaith, interfaith or multiple religious identities. This is odd really, because if we think about it exactly what is a Jew, Buddhist, Moslem, Christian, Hindu or whatever? Are not all faiths riddled with multiple options of beliefs, subgroups, orders or sects?

Furthermore, in view of our previous discussion on 'I-Amness', it is problematic if we define ourselves by a religious or any other label. It's understandable for reasons of social shorthand when someone asks, "Are you a Christian (or Buddhist, Jew, Taoist etc.)?" that we might say "Yes." But we might do so with some inner caution about attachment to yet another identity. When seekers ask me if I participate in my local church I give an honest answer. If they then ask, "Are you a Christian?" it's more difficult to offer a direct answer so I usually say something like, "I'm a follower of the way of Jesus." This can start off a whole new ball game of spiritual exploration about who 'I am' is and whether we can really be defined by our beliefs, labels and identities. My inclination to dig deeply and find my guru in the Christian tradition has not precluded my practice of Tai Chi, joining Sikh friends in worship or delighting in the Friday evening Shabbat prayers when Jewish friends visit.

It seems that some Soul Communities may be learning to embrace people who include beliefs and practices from 'outside'. In doing so they may be facilitating an 'entry' to that faith and its rich possibilities for those who would otherwise feel excluded. I have certainly experienced this recently in meetings of the Quakers, in a United Reformed Church, a Unitarian gathering and a mosque. Such multifaith or

"The authentic spiritual life helps us to go ever deeper into truth."

interspiritual, as it is becoming known, inclusiveness may not yet be that common, but these examples suggest that if we 'shop around' we may find a Soul Community that can offer both breadth and depth. On the other hand, as I have suggested, we may find that we can hold the contradictions while participating in a religion where such inclusiveness is more problematic. Either way, there is much strength in pursuing the possibility of participating in a tradition. Going it alone is hard work and for most of us may well be impossible if we are to approach the obstacles along the way safely and fruitfully. It is also a blessing to have others with whom we can share the bliss and struggle of the journey too. What we bring to a community also influences what we get out of it.

It is not for me to say that a particular way must be followed. Yet, on balance I am inclined to the view that it is better to go deeper into one tradition rather than many (while still embracing the riches we glean from others) and to do that in a Soul Community associated with it. I recognise that this can be tough work, especially for those who no longer have any roots of story, language or participation in a religioun. Many surveys now suggest that, among young people particularly, there is a disinclination to cluster or to follow religious doctrines that are anathema to their personal knowing and to define themselves as 'nones' – spiritual but not religious. Such seekers find their awakening, transformation and relationship to the Beloved through many different options of Soul Communities, Foods, Works and Friends.

These interfaith, interspiritual or multifaith options are ways in which new forms of religious expression and gathering are emerging alongside the rise or fall of the established ones. This movement is characterised by the elements explored in this book and which are underpinned by my own experience – a 'new monasticism' embracing the desire to go deep, to commit to regular spiritual practice, openness to continuous transformation and to seek the truth in all beliefs. This inner exploration is not self-centred, but commits to bringing this expansion of consciousness into engagement with the world, joining in the healing of that which is broken, a concern for ecology and social and political action. New forms of spiritual awakening are blossoming alongside and out of the old. We have yet to see how this will play itself out and how common approaches can be defined permitting dialogue, respect and flourishing for all.

Whatever form we choose, it can be seen that healthy religion helps bind a com-

munity together, the waves on the ocean are countless but they are not self-gener-
ated and they do not exist alone. A religion offers the rites of passage, which bring
meaning and belonging to our lives – the loss of rites of passage is arguably partly
the cause of the socially atomised waste land. It is difficult, if not impossible I believe, to pursue the Way without the strength and challenge of a tradition in which
to express and find it. A tradition offers the ground and the firm foundations often
tried and tested over thousands of years of exploration in which all the mistakes and
delusions have been mapped, responded to, and ways through found. The common notion that we can be 'spiritual not religious' is suspect and often an excuse to
avoid the difficult terrain of participating in a religious tradition/community, built on
some delusion that spiritual exploration should be all about sweetness and light and
exclusively nice people and experiences or that it can be undertaken in solitude. It is
true that the way religion is portrayed and distorted (by followers and those on the
outside alike) hardly helps encourage seekers and those in exile to return. However,
overcoming our hostility to religion and the religious, like overcoming the thought
that we can "go it alone", is itself a subject for rigorous discipline in spiritual work
full of potential for surrender, humility and healing.

There is another aspect to consider when we shift from one religious tradition to
another as we have explored. It happens especially among people from indus-
trialised countries who fall in love with some idealised image of the religions of
aboriginal peoples. The wise know how to honour these traditions. Others pillage
their cultures for the bits that are alluring, project all kinds of notions of perfection
onto them, abuse the originators by our exploitation of their beliefs and fail to 'get'
what they are really all about because we do not have the cultural backdrop and
language. This tendency to project idealised spirituality onto others and avoid our
own cultural traditions reveals much about ourselves and is a product of spiritual
uncertainty in the waste land.

There is wisdom in religious traditions, which we are ill advised to reject out of hand.
And the rejection is understandable in a world where so much of religion and those
who follow it seems mean, savage, excluding and cruel (invariably the opposite of
what the founder of that faith taught). Yet most people of faith are struggling to
be the best human beings they can be, seeking to be inclusive, loving, kind and
generous to themselves and each other as well as dealing with their own spiritual

"The authentic spiritual life helps us to go ever deeper into truth."

conflicts. Simply because such people tend to be unostentatious, quietly getting on with life and using their faith to inform a Way that is full of humility, love and justice we tend not to hear from or about them. Perhaps they are the majority, for whom faith and the holy book are open to interpretation, a food for the soul to be chewed over, reflected upon and used to transform the person, not to lapse into fearful dogmatism that is inflicted on the rest of the world.

For every hard-liner there are people, far more people, whose approach to religion is open and loving, like the Divine. I recall being harangued by someone using a passage from the gospels where Jesus says he is the Way [John 14:6]. In the hands of literalism there is not far to go with that, and at a stroke that phrase has been used to persecute and slaughter non-Christians and indeed many Christians down the ages. Modern scholars and teachers with richer interpretations offer greater hope [14,98] as they peel back the layers of meaning and show breathtaking vistas (for example the deeper meaning of the use of "I am" in Aramaic) of possibility that include rather than exclude, enhance rather than diminish. It seems unwise to limit the Divine and reduce or elevate facts and holy books to the level of the incontestable, for we then make the thing itself a God, a kind of idolatry and blasphemy.

I have learned too that embracing the truth in other faiths does not dilute a commitment to the one we follow ourselves. Quite the reverse, it can strengthen it. Only those whose own faith is built on fragile foundations of which they may not be fully conscious tend to see other faiths as a threat. With true faith, as we explored in Part 8, we are able to escape duality and travel across boundaries to find the common ground, honouring and respecting those of other faiths while digging ever deeper into the well of our own. Diversity of perspective is strength not weakness to faith.

Quoting scripture fluently and with apparent authority can seem difficult to stand against, but it is, as Bonhoeffer remarked [170], a darkness masking as light, hiding shadows of fear and power-seeking. When *mythos* gets buried by *logos*, when interpretation of scripture gets lost in literalism, then all faiths fail both seekers and the Beloved. I recall the challenge of the Dalai Lama at a meeting in Manchester nearly 35 years ago. Most at that meeting were like me exploring Buddhism, but he was not interested (much to everyone's surprise) in gathering converts. Rather he threw out the challenge "Why are you interested in Buddhism? You in the west have all the spiritual answers you need in your Christian roots. There's no need for you to be a Buddhist, what you need is right under your own noses". Needless to say this caused some consternation, but his words have remained with me ever since, and eventually helped me make some difficult choices.

There are many like myself who have been in exile from Christianity for all kinds of reasons, not least the difficulty in reconciling what we know in our hearts to be true with what some religionists throw at us. The post-modern deconstruction and separation of religion has worsened the disconnection. The once-understood routines and rituals of a religion can become lost to us. The language ceases to be familiar and becomes alienating. There tends to be no understanding, unlike in my upbringing, because the language is lost - words like prayer to penance, sacred to sin, repentance to redemption, heaven to hell - none of it means anything anymore or, if it does mean anything, it is usually superficially understood and deeply dismissed.

When working with groups and individuals I often draw on my own religious and spiritual roots in the Christian tradition to illustrate the teaching, while also embracing the truths in other faiths that have fed me. I notice that so often these days Bible stories mean nothing or at best there is only a vague remembrance picked up from our culture or because elements of the Bible stories linger 'in the blood' from childhood. With the lost language has gone the story. I always find Christmas a difficult time in some ways because I can feel like I am either drowning in saccharin from the reductionist, cutesy story and imagery of 'away in a manger' or wearied by the jingle-bells, money-making machine that gets under way it seems ever earlier each year. Indeed Christmas shops on-line and in many towns are open all year these days. In the festival of consumption, a very powerful story has been lost.

On the way home from a class I walked up the long pavement to the railway station in the dark of late afternoon. The footpath was crowded with commuters heading home. I stopped a couple of times to chat and put change in the cups of street people curled up on the floor in doorways. I felt a kind of deep indignation at one point as a couple of well-dressed members of a Christian sect were busy handing out leaflets on either side of the pavement. The pamphleteers seemed unaware of the incongruity of handing out stuff telling people they were on a highway to hell if they didn't believe in Jesus, while fellow humans, homeless and dejected and

"The authentic spiritual life helps us to go ever deeper into truth."

already in their own kind of hell were but inches from their feet. I wondered what kind of Christian story was being transmitted here when right under their noses (literally) was all the Christian action they needed to show people what the faith is. As I walked on my friend spotted this - "Is it any wonder people don't like Christians... did you see that?"

Our discussion continued on the train. "How can you still go to church with all that stuff?" he asked, "I know you don't believe the half of it." He was right on target in some senses. Like anyone participating in a religious tradition I rub up against doctrines and beliefs that I cannot follow. I encounter people whose understanding of the same faith is barely recognisable to me. But of course that's not the point. If we only participate in something where we agree with everything and everyone, then we're probably either in denial or drugged. The authentic spiritual life leads into those gritty places of conflict, challenge and discomfort in the search for truth. It draws us into community where idealised notions are dispelled. It compels us to see where we can hold difference and diversity and yet still participate. It prompts us into discernment of the right Way to follow.

The loss of language and story or the distortion of them, the hypocrisy gap between the talk and the walking of it – these can seem like impenetrable barriers to the precious truths in religious traditions. These truths and the spiritual practices that go with them have stood the test of time despite all that we have done to corrupt them. One of the skills of the spiritual life is learning to navigate these corruptions and get to the wealth that still lies within. Everyone at some level is seeking their way Home, but in the current spiritual supermarket we are either alienated, confused by the religious clutter, spoilt for choice or avoiding the difficult and the deep. Too often religions get hooked on doctrines and rituals to hold the line and provide a degree of spiritual security. In so doing they alienate those for whom these things mean nothing and for whom the need for the contemplative, the mystical, the direct relationship with the Beloved, the expression of authentic action for justice and peace is not satisfied.

I have swum the length and breadth of the New Age river and ended up on a shore, at least for the present, that I had not anticipated. I offer my own stories in this book only as examples, not with any weight of recommendation of which faith you may or may not follow. Indeed it is with some wariness that I have shared them here, the same wariness of sharing with groups or those in spiritual direction. Stories can be used to intoxicate the other with how wonderful we are or share the truth of ourselves and our vulnerabilities and errors. They can encourage transference where the spiritual director gets placed on a pedestal and becomes an idolised father/mother figure or they can help to ensure that the director remains thoroughly ordinary and on the ground. Through the latter others realise that those in teaching roles or any other seekers for that matter are not special, that we use the loo like everybody else! Thus the seeker might be inspired by that ordinariness, that they too can overcome the challenges along the way. Transformation is not the sole province of the special and the gifted, however we may interpret these, but the birthright of all.

So my stories are presented here as one man's experience along the Way in the hope that they aid discernment, not least in the decision to get involved with any spiritual practice or religion. If we have a sense of a 'calling' is it a true one, is it really 'in the blood'? Or is it clouded and influenced by all sorts of unconscious motives like a need to belong, avoid choice confusion or to enter something tough because we feel we must suffer and spirituality is supposed to be like that. These are the very questions we have explored in each Part. They are the substance of discernment along the way with our four Soul Care themes.

Being and belonging

I suspect that ultimately it is not impossible to get into serious spiritual work and Soul Care without at least some degree of involvement in and study of a religious tradition. To pursue our search without it can leave us devoid of roots and support and is a matter for serious reflection and self-examination of motives. Going it alone may indeed work for some people, although I have yet to come across any teacher or tradition that does not require, at least at some point, the discipline of exploring a tradition with other people. Whether that is always an established religion or not is another matter and certainly getting involved with one can be guaranteed to press every one of our buttons! It is packed with the raw material of spiritual awakening and one of the test beds of authentic spirituality. So we think we have become loving? Then try it in the real world of ordinary people. So we think we are so spiritually mature? Then try it in a religion full of difference and difficulty.

"The authentic spiritual life helps us to go ever deeper into truth."

I was asked recently to participate in the Archbishop of Canterbury's 'Conversations' on human sexuality. In an effort to hold people of very diverse views together, carefully facilitated groups were set up across England to explore the issues – the Anglican Church's response to lesbian, gay and transgender people, gay marriage, sexual relations outside of marriage and remarriage of divorced people. All of these are the kind of topics guaranteed to generate fierce debate and risk creating schism in many different religions. Personally I'd long ago given up debating such matters. I had come to the conclusion that the issues were too polarised and that the Anglican Church (I'm an active member of my local parish) would at some stage just have to split. Indeed, I think I'd got to the view that once an established position starts to be argued about then the argument is already lost and change is inevitable, so why bother?

I was curious when I was invited to the 'Conversations' meeting and felt a strong pull to attend, despite the 'what's the point' feeling. I realised, once the discussions got under way, that my complacency was also denial. What the church says and does still matters, not least in how its thinking contributes to the cultural milieu, how it can create 'otherness' of people that somewhere down the line leads to the wife beater and the gay basher. That this is not just a personal or religious issue of sexuality, but one of justice – something in which the Christ I know as Friend was deeply concerned at every level of his ministry.

So I arrived with little hope, assuming there would be scraps between opposites before long. Thanks to excellent facilitators, there wasn't much of that, but the tension was there beneath the surface. When our beliefs are deeply attached to our identity, differing views can feel like an attack and produce fear and anger. Following a polarised discussion on the authority of scripture, I despaired. The discussion wasn't particularly nasty – we had 'house rules' to work with – but I felt that there was no way such opposing views could stay under one roof. It also became clear that there was a group who were not there – I heard much talk of sections within the church who would not join the 'Conversation' fearing that it's very existence was suggestive of change and trying to 'convert' people.

It's my experience that once people get into absolutes of 'scriptural authority' (itself a nebulous concept open to much interpretation) then it seems disconnection from each other is inevitable. It's just not a worldview I can embrace, though I think I can understand it. What interests me at this point, and it is something that was raised but never pursued in depth in the 'Conversation', was not what people believe but why we believe it.

One of the great gifts to modern spiritual direction is psychology. It can help us to see more clearly the drivers that lie behind beliefs lying often deep in the unconscious. For example, I held a conversation with one person on the 'scriptural authority' perspective and felt very strongly her fear that unless she accepted certain biblical phrases at face value, then God would punish her. Another person refused to countenance any other interpretation of scripture but his own, or any shift in the church's position because "If we give way to that, what else will we have to give way to?" While we can understand such fear-based perspectives (although the persons I explored this with did not see any fear, for example, around authority, punishment or sexuality and the 'Conversation' wasn't a therapy group in which to discuss them safely) I find such views deeply alienating and difficult to sit with after a while, even hurtful, as they can make it easy to forget that it is real people that we are dealing with here.

There is a possible downside to the gifts of psychology. Much of psychological theory emphasises our pathological response to ordinary reality – neuroses, psychoses, complexes, addictions, obsessions and assorted other manifestations of the shadow of the unconscious. We can, if we are not careful, slip into a very negative view of what it is to be human. Psychological models also tend to see us as the sum of the baggage of our mind, as separate from the All-that-is and the multitude of various forces that interconnect us with the world beyond our skin and within it. Each morning as a member of the Iona Community I am re-minded in our prayers of the willingness to reach out and connect with the world in which I live and of the "good that is planted more deeply than all that is wrong". Yes, we humans manifest all manner of unhealthy and harmful behaviours and "ways of seeing" [35], but we also manifest immense creativity, ingenuity and compassion.

Fear of death is not the only human driver, any more than the suffering we seek to escape brought on by shame, guilt, worthlessness, unloveableness and all the other demons that haunt us. Despite all this, we humans are far more than these shad-

"The authentic spiritual life helps us to go ever deeper into truth."

ows. For every demon unleashed on the world, we find a thousand more angels of kindness, justice and compassion. The deeply pessimistic view of humanity that so much psychology throws up is not borne out in the reality of the greater goodness that most people seek to bring into their lives, the lives of others and the life of the planet.

There are horrors in existence, but immense beauty too. Beyond the shadows in ourselves lies a love far greater and more powerful. Our spiritual deepening brings us to that realisation. In this we are not alone, the love in each of us is part of the vast ocean of love that undergirds the cosmos. God is too small a word to name the One, yet it must be apparent to anyone that there is a life force, a driving force behind the mystery and our experience of ordinary reality that tells us there is something 'more', something 'beyond', and that it is entirely loving in its nature.

We can say that we have gone 'wrong', that humanity is in error, that the world is full of horrors and we are going to hell on a handcart. Yet from the soul's perspective, everything has its own kind of beauty. To say otherwise is the judgment of ego consciousness and judgment is in the landscape of dualism, it separates. It's all one, it is the infinite variety of consciousness magnificently at play with itself fulfilling all possible manifestations of creation, it is a work of art, a cosmically unfolding work of art. Each of us bears witness to it. Each of us participates in it. We may respond to it with joy and sorrow, but we are not the centre of it – that is an ego-centric response. This vast work of art is not governed by our judgments. Ordinary life, reality, is beautiful, in all its tragedy and wonder (mere surface judgments in the end). We are part of this boundless creative act and it is perfect. Somewhere in the depths of this ocean there is a profound knowing that all is well, that we do not have to be afraid, that we are all doing (it is all doing) exactly what we are (it is) supposed to be doing. Thus we have two choices to participate with or without awareness.

If we accept that we are doomed to live in an overwhelmingly tragic world even God becomes just another object of transference, another fantasy to help us cope with reality and 'save' us from death and suffering. We can also engage in transference towards other objects of 'salvation' – for example the belief that our technology, gene therapy, nanotechnology or any endeavour can be the one that 'saves' us. It could be that this book and my beliefs that underpin it are just another transference, a way of keeping me occupied and hopeful in the face of my inevitable death and the deep unconscious fear of it. Maybe this book and my spiritual life is just another formula for denying the horror of reality while the Beloved is my fantasy knight who I hope will ride to my rescue. The authentic spiritual life helps us to spot such fantasies, projections and transferences and go ever deeper into truth. There we find, what? – that it's all One, that its all Good.

Enlightenment will not change our neuroses, that's what the ego hopes for. There is no bypassing the emotional work. Enlightenment fosters transformation, which is about a different plane of consciousness. Living from that place of true life we then transcend, neutralise, the ego's heroic death defying attachments. We don't just create another transference towards God, we discover that 'ye are gods' [Psalm 82:6, John 10:34]. We no longer look to some authority God to fix it for us, rather we become the ones liberated to participate fully in the co-creation of reality and let go of the our egoic attachment to do the fixing.

Fear (of death, powerlessness, meaninglessness, worthlessness) is the worm at the heart of the psyche. Awakening does not free us from fear, rather what it does is set us free of its grip. We learn to respond to it differently, not in a Pollyanna-ish way of looking to life after death in some harp and cloud filled heaven rather the reality of true life in this moment now. Coming Home sets us free of our neuroses, which are no more than the ego's response to the anxiety of living and all the energy it puts into shoring up the defences or the lies it perpetuates in the face of reality. The ego's responses can seem almost heroic as it plunges itself into the need to succeed, get control or into a multitude of short-term satisfactions. It is a kind of faux heroism, an understandable reflex action as it seeks to cope with all the terrors of being alive and dying.

Yes the world can seem irredeemably tragic and humanity a lost cause, but the whole point of the work in Coming Home is to set us free from that nihilistic trap. Anyone who has taken the first step on the Way has begun the process of getting free into a new vision of the real reality and how to participate in it.

Because of the work I do, I see a difference between the roles and identities that we occupy and the Essence of who we are. There is no such thing as a divorced or gay

"The authentic spiritual life helps us to go ever deeper into truth."

or transgender person, but a human being, a soul who happens to be experiencing these in life. Until we 'get' this, that space between 'Who I am' and 'Who I think I am' (a subject I will revisit in a moment) then biblical authority and/or interpretation just become brickbats to be hurled at each other, provoking our deepest fears in the unconscious. It seems to me that unless these unconscious motives can be safely brought to the fore in such meetings, then the possibility of connection and 'staying under one roof' may be limited. So far as I can see, and from my experience as a spiritual director, religious organisations in general and the church in particular do not have a good track record in being aware of and working with this difficult terrain.

On the last day of the 'Conversations' meeting I experienced a glimmer of hope, that a split may avoidable. I'd deliberately sought out people at the conference whose views I discerned were different from my own. I wanted to listen deeply and see if I could hold opposites. In a conversation with one person whose fear and anger that someone else was trying to 'persuade' him was palpable, we made an effort to really 'see' each other, not just our beliefs, but the full person that holds them – the hurt, fear and anger that comes when deeply held beliefs are challenged. We talked about what we felt, not just about what we think and believe, about each other's lives and stories. Thus we began to see beyond the surface notions of self. We saw that trying to persuade each other (and we both reserved the right to do that!) without *first* seeing each other fully results in feelings of attack and defence.

With our intention to try and connect at a deeper level than simply our beliefs, the anger and fear evaporated. Forgiveness and love replaced them. This, to me, is when Christ is made visible. It was prayer in action - making an effort to really connect fully with a person beyond superficial judgements. To love our neighbour, as Jesus required, before we try out our ideas on each other, might just enable us to live together in the same tent. Thus 'grace and disagreement' (a key theme of the conversations), agreeing to disagree became possible. I came away with hope from that.

I share the above example of the 'Conversations' as the kind of conflict we can expect across a whole range of issues in any religious groupings. They are the grist to the mill of working through relationships in Soul Communities and how we can square our individual response to them – do we participate, walk away, try to change things, work patiently as a path of service, get angry and try and control people? All those buttons, personal and collective, are available to test out our spiritual maturity. In a world of social, economic, political and environmental flux any spiritual grouping is going to be stretched by the tension between its laws and conventions and the changing needs and aspirations of its participants. Our Soul Works, Foods, Communities and Friends provide the support we need to do this to lean always towards Truth.

Participating in a tradition as part of the Work is therefore not without its tribulations. Yet I contrast that with the walk to my local church across idyllic open country. I enter a gathering where all sorts meet, though like most churches in English rural communities there is a dearth of the young and those from ethnic minorities. I have learned that beneath superficial appearances all life is here. In microcosm are all the different views on Christ that wash around the Christian church [188] right now. In the bible class, you can have ten people sitting around and there will be ten different perspectives on a single sentence. This is part of its challenge, and also its joy. Love does not require that we all agree, the boundless Beloved moves in ways that we cannot always perceive – remember, "You never know!"

Being and belonging are basic human drives, so it is natural that most of us seek to cluster with others, looking for that strength of tradition and community and perhaps at first unconsciously seeking that idyllic community of perfect people. As I explored in Part 6, one of the reasons for a Soul Community is to help us shed the illusion that such a body of people exists. Participating in a tradition may provide the depths we seek and the milieu in which to practise what we preach. Like all families there is diversity of view and behaviour, good days, bad days, peace and conflict. The point is that we embrace those diversities and still eat together at the end of the day, still love each other while sometimes being disappointed. Just as mighty spiritual beings like Jesus seemed to be perfectly balanced human beings, so it behoves us to seek that balance in community, holding opposites together we hold the One. Thus in my case I have returned to where I started, perhaps to know it for the first time. I do not say it is forever, but it is for now, after that, "You never know!"

The Beloved I know does not punish, so I asked in relation to church, why me and why here? We all may ask these questions when feeling summoned into something

"The authentic spiritual life helps us to go ever deeper into truth."

that hitherto we would have avoided. I am reminded of the notion in some ideol-ogies that ordinary reality is a school or classroom where we learn the lessons for heaven or the next life. I've always thought that rather reductionist. It makes us mere pupils rather than participants, victims of authority rather than volunteers in the 'Dreaming'. The poet [1] reminds us that we "are not here to learn", rather this is a plane of consciousness in which we have the potential to awake, within the humility that we are all doing exactly what we are supposed to be doing.

Perhaps we are not so much in a classroom as a milieu for a participation in the co-creation of reality. Although at one level we can argue that modern civilisation mitigates against this awakening with its dense attention upon the ego's agenda, at another we might see that it is all One, a kind of divine contract between the Be-loved and the soul for the total immersion in this plane of reality to fulfil the co-cre-ative potential. When we ask the 'why?' questions such theologies may or may not be helpful, but perhaps our job is to throw them into the pot for discernment.

Meanwhile, in discerning whether my prompting back into the church life of my local community was authentic or not I prayed upon it and sought wise council. The Anglican Church, bound to the establishment, riven with strongly held opposing views, in tension between *mythos* and *logos* – a softer landing could surely be cho-sen? This church full of charge and counter charge, with its historical exclusion of so many from left-handed or black people to women and gay people. This church full of big hearted and hard hearted views. Why this church? – Because I am called there, because the love of the Divine is here as much as anywhere, because I heard what my friend said about turning to my guru all those years ago, because of the enormous depth that a tried and tested tradition has to offer. Because like all organ-isations in the post-modern era it is being shaken and stirred into new forms which are yet to be made clear. Because here is a place like anywhere else, full of practical, ethical, spiritual and moral differences and concerns, struggles with diversity, and wonderful fellowship – in short the raw material of any spiritual community. Light and shadow exist in all.

When we feel drawn to a particular community it is important to examine the mo-tives and intentions, to seek prayerfully to know if it is the right community where the Will calls, to discern if it is true. Personally that process has led me to feel at rest in the truth that where I am right now is true to myself, and to the Beloved, the Great Friend. At the same time we need to be aware that if the Will someday calls elsewhere then it must be followed, after due discernment, but followed nonetheless. Right now I find myself in a state of puzzlement, wonder, laughter that it should be this place for me: I did not think I would be here, in this church, my Soul Community in all its bittersweet love, in all its gifts, in all its potential for giving. It could have been anywhere I guess, some other faith or the bottom of a bottle, but it wasn't to be. It is here and now and I trust in it until called otherwise. Thus the words of my wise woman prophet at the beginning of this chapter ring so true.

All we can do is follow what is true, and what is true is often something the we-who-we-think-we-are may not like at first. In my example it has been a turning back to something lost in childhood and distorted by adult experience and not allowing those distortions to keep me away from something precious. The surface layer in many respects may be unappealing, but beneath it lies a rich wisdom tradition that, if we are willing to go there, is a deep well of spirit. Here past all the superficial and distracting is the Christ consciousness guru to whom Ram Dass with blinding precision reintroduced me, this man, this being, this brother, master, teacher, friend in whom God broke into the world and called, "This Way". It has been a deep breathless dive into the known and the unknown, into a tradition with all its spiritual riches and the poverty of its brokenness. Others get called to other Ways, I cannot say better or worse, and the Way once found must be taken and pursued with seriousness if we are to reap the blessings of all that it has to offer. There are no bypasses, no shortcuts, not if our hearts really long for a deep relationship with the One.

Testing the fruit
My spiritual life has been filled with immense highs and lows and who knows, maybe all those theorists and scientists I quoted in Part 2 might be right – that 'God' and the 'God experience' are just delusions or comforters? All my experiences of good and evil, of Beloved and spirit might be mere fabrications of a mind or ego seeking fun, distraction, stories, meaning and significance in the world. Yet that has been tested, not least because I do not get the rewards that the ego would demand - more money, power, fame, pleasure, avoidance of pain. The Way has not shown itself to score highly on 'God' being just a comforter, quite the reverse.

"The authentic spiritual life helps us to go ever deeper into truth."

And there has been testing through discernment by the processes described in this book, which provide a framework for checking out the true from the false; tested by knowing their fruits. We can trust the process, but tie our camels! Thus in the pursuit of God and knowing that we will be called Home, still we have in place the four Soul Care approaches described in this book, just in case, to keep us on our way.

A curious and heart-warming fruit may also be noticed that is not often mentioned in the literature. This changed way of seeing affects every aspect of our lives, past and present. A scene we have looked at many times before suddenly seems more beautiful, more sacred. We linger where once we passed on. A song heard long ago, an ordinary song, is now replete with new meaning. I recall listening with my mum to Doris Day when I was a child and we sang along to "Once I had a secret love". Decades later I heard it not as a song about two people falling in love, but about the discovery of the divine love in the heart. "And that secret love's no secret any more." Coming Home the ordinary often becomes extraordinary. The familiar seen and heard, seen and heard anew.

The soul has descended into matter and longs for Home, but this does not mean that matter is bad, rather the soul on being liberated returning Home free of ego clutter, revels and serves in matter. Union of soul in the Divine after the long purgation of the ego is not disconnection from the world into the Beloved, but connection to the Beloved in the world. There is in some traditions a tendency to deem matter, physical reality, an irrelevance or illusion and something to be escaped.

This is not spirituality but escapism, a symptom of the struggle to get free of ordinary physical reality, the world of matter, because it is perceived as full of suffering. But matter matters, it is part of All-that-is not separate from it. It lives and moves and has its being in the Divine and the Divine lives and moves and has being in the world of matter. In most creation stories, such as the book of Genesis, God creates the physical realm and does not condemn it, but sees it as "good". The alienation from matter is what feeds, for example, nihilism or sexual repression as we explored in Part 8. The Way Home allows us to embrace reality in its fullness, to participate in the world of matter and all planes of consciousness, heaven and earth, beyond these dualistic concepts.

I have encountered being in stuck and painful places with those I love and all that spiritual work has stood me in good stead I know, allowing me to respond to that pain with more patience, love and understanding than hitherto even when that old, little-self part of me would be screaming to have its own way. The Work has allowed me to function more fully and creatively in the world and to experience the joy and the pain of the world more than ever before. Yes the spiritual path can lead us to know the bliss of the world and the love of the Beloved more deeply than had we remained closeted in the safe parameters of the ego, but we come to feel the suffering of the world and All-that-is more deeply too. How could we not do so if we are not to be fully in this moment, in the world and to love it and serve it (not the self) more fully and authentically?

Arid, despairing and painful times are not just about loss, but may include gain, part of the process as much as the pleasant and blissful ones, for in these we come to understand that the stuckness is a precursor to new breakthroughs, new insights, new and more expansive love. Transformation towards wholeness where light and shadow in us have become integrated, the process of individuation is the alchemical process. Turning lead into gold was a metaphor among the ancients for this shift and chemical processes often generate heat, violent reactions and unexpected events. At school in the chemistry class we would put all kinds of things in the crucibles over the Bunsen burner when the master wasn't looking, just to see what would happen. A dangerous prank in retrospect, although what most often happened was the creation of a black, turgid mud. Times of transformation can be like that; *melanosis* in alchemy where what has been produced seems unchanging, black and useless, anything but gold. The experiment seems to have failed, our hopes are dashed, we feel angry or numb or feel like giving up.

Such coldness and aridity towards our soul efforts can be a sign that we need them even more, that the ego is still grasping for power and seeking to hold the soul in its thrall. The value of the 'enemy' - something inside us that makes us feel hopeless or stuck or a person or event coming from outside that makes us feel within unseen or misunderstood or nor accepted – this enemy is a friend too. He/she/it teaches us that we still have work to do, that we need help, that we have deeper to go into humility. It becomes clear then why Hafiz says "pour on more oil" [136] or Rumi prays to "break my heart again" [194] not because they are spiritual sadomasochists, but because

"The authentic spiritual life helps us to go ever deeper into truth."

they know that drawing closer to the Beloved, to Love, is over the twin bridges of suffering and joy; both cross the chasm of time and space on the way Home.

Ah, but the faith, the knowing, the groundedness of experience – all tested in the fires of Soul Friends, Soul Foods, Soul Communities, Soul Works – pull us onwards. The calling like so much true spiritual experience can feel just like that, a pull, a drawing out and towards something often against the will as opposed to a pushing where it is often our will calling the shots. Pushing is an attempt to hurry and "he who is in a hurry delays the things of God" [189]. What we come to know in the calling of the Divine stands truer and outwith anything the rationalist debate can describe or change. After a while it may be that notions of spiritual work fall away, as we come to realise that we have been in charge of very little, if anything; it has been the spirit of the Beloved at work in us. The Way is quite simple you see – a dissolution of ego power, surrendering it (without punishing or blaming) into service, and losing self in Self and the realisation that we did not follow the Way, but it was the Way that was within us working to bring us Home all along.

Words like annihilation and surrender associated with the work on the ego can seem brutal and frightening, at least at first. After a while, it's my experience that once we start to get where this surrender might take us, what a gift is in this annihilation, then we start to long for them, for this *fana*. Although such a longing runs counter to the individualist drive, we begin to sense that somehow that handing ourselves over may not be a loss. There is an exquisite paradox here. Once we experience union we see that "true union differentiates" [72]. In union we discover the truth of our individuality. In the Beloved is the great mystery, we are at One yet individual *at the same time*.

Love and laughter
It's not all fierce grace. There is also bliss, joy, wonder and laughter along the Way, in fact I have laughed more in this search than I thought possible. Soul Care is serious work, but it is playful and happy work too. Indeed the search without laughter is less than human and ought to be subject to some rigorous spiritual testing to see if it is indeed a true path, where the blockages are and what needs to change. For an ability to laugh, in love and joy, is a spiritual attribute too, part of the fullness of our humanity.

Anthony De Mello [190] writes, "The master was in expansive mood. So his disciples sought to learn from him the stages he had passed through in his search for the divine. "God first led me by the hand," he said, "into the Land of Action, and there dwelt for several years. Then he returned and led me to the Land of Sorrows, and there I lived until my heart was purged of every inordinate attachment. That is when I found myself in the Land of Love whose burning flames consumed whatever was left in me of myself. This brought me to the Land of Silence where the mysteries of life and death were bared before my wondering eyes." "Was that the final stage of your quest?" they asked. "No," the master said. "One day God said, 'Today I shall take you to the innermost sanctuary of the temple, to the heart of God himself.' And I was led to the Land of Laughter." The spiritual search is packed with conundrums, confusions and challenges; it is also replete with heart, humour and hilarity.

So often the great spiritual beings of history are portrayed as rather sombre people. Exploring the gospels anew I began to realise that Jesus told jokes, that a study of the Buddha illuminated a man who enjoyed a good belly laugh, that the Prophet must have giggled away too. Divinely-filled beings from all traditions laugh as well, because they are fully human and it is human to laugh with the sheer fun and absurdity, the comic-tragedy of life.

One of my early teachers set me a task of contemplation and began by saying, "Imagine Jesus laughing". It seemed so ridiculous when I began the exercise, for I had projected onto Jesus all my own misconceptions and hang ups and all those images I'd seen or heard since childhood of a rather sweet man but always a very serious one. I sulked and wondered and struggled my way through the meditation, only to burst into hysterical laughter myself at the end! It is useful to remember that laughter is part of spiritual awakening too, in fact any Soul Community or Soul Friend that does not laugh is probably best avoided. For a true community, a true Soul Friend, a true tradition, embraces all aspects of what it is to be human. We reach the "I am" by integrating fully our own "I am" – which is the same, at Home.

After words and forms
We can get stuck on words, not least our names and genders for the Divine. In coming Home we find they are pointers along the Way but they are not the way, the One is beyond typecasting, beyond any labels or descriptions we care to offer, beyond the-

"The authentic spiritual life helps us to go ever deeper into truth."

ology. Even our desire to understand the Beloved is something we learn to put down on the Way. Our images of God, like the images we have of ourselves, have to die if we are to get anywhere near to knowing the Source of All and ourselves beyond image. The old dies into life. I have at home a beautiful feminised statue of the walking Buddha. He has broad hips, full breast and soft elegant frame – conveying that aspect of our Buddha nature, our Essence, our souls, that is integrative of both genders. Many of the founders of the great faiths, most of whom have been men, were profoundly feminine as well as masculine in their teachings and their behaviour – open hearted, compassionate, collaborative, inclusive servants. Integration, holding opposites in harmony, being with mystery, uncertainty and paradox lightly are hallmarks of a maturing spirituality.

All four Soul Care approaches in this book are our contribution to the Work along the Way when we approach them consciously. They are not the Way itself, any more than a map is the real ground it describes. The Work prepares us; purifies our consciousness so that we are readied to receive more and more of the Divine. Fighting or pushing or working with the ego are all traps that keep us attached to it. The purification from the ego's grip heightens our receptivity to the Presence, to learn from it, to receive the inpouring of 'Divine Energy', 'Love', the 'Holy Spirit' or 'Grace' that draws us ever closer to Home. Grace, not our own will, makes us free. Our work is to refine, purify and prepare ourselves to receive this Will through the renunciation of the power of the egoic personality, of self-will into Self-Will.

The heart, the seat of the Divine in us, is set free to be heart-felt and heart-full in the world, governing our identity as the servant of the Divine that it is. The heart's desire is the homing beacon within, flashing out to guide us and remind us who we truly are and why we are here. Soul Care work opens us to that longing, sensitises us so the inpouring of divine grace, strengthens and liberates it. Jesus said, "My yoke is easy and my burden is light" [Matt.11:30] and this is hopeful advice in our spiritual work, as we come to find it less laborious, less effort-full and soften into the Will of the Beloved which takes us and leads us onward. The hope in this is not some wishful thinking in the face of suffering, an ersatz optimism to comfort us. This hope is rooted deeply in the soul that does not require external validation; it is a sure knowing that the Beloved is real, that all things are working towards the whole no matter what our limited five senses may tell us.

We may notice increasingly as we learn to let go into the Divine, that there is more joy and less suffering in our spiritual practice, that it tends to simplify into forms of "prayer and fasting" that do not require striving and painful sacrifice. The yoke no longer weighs us down or pulls us back, the burden is light, not just less heavy but light itself, the true light of the Divine shining more and more in our lives. Light is weightless; it is no burden at all. We can relax more into our life and practice along the Way, for we come to know at some deep level that we are taken care of, drawing us Home with inevitable and unconquerable love.

The Beloved is faceless and formless, all the faces I see are just impressions, constructs of my mind that wants to make sense of 'God' (my heart knows and does not bother with sense, but with the sensation of the One by which it knows). Yet in my ordinary humanity it is hard to connect with the faceless and the formless, the eternal, the unknowable. It locks itself onto a shape or form. Some would argue that the Divine in compassion self-presented in physical form to be seen in the god-filled being of Jesus. Other faiths too have their images, sometimes in human form. Whether these gods we seek are true or false gods is why we need the process of discernment mentioned in this book. Actually, one of the beauties of being in time and space is that we can have it both ways! We can experience the Beloved through our spiritual work as immanent and transcendent, personal and transpersonal.

In the Brothers Karamazov [191] Therapont through his zealous effort is delivered from the world, but he does not break through to the next level of integrating the world. Instead his efforts lead him to be authoritarian and self-righteous and to call "God's curse" down on the world of matter, of ordinary reality. The *Staretz* Zossima, he too has done the spiritual work, but properly nurtured and in contrast to Therapont he becomes full of compassion and in his surrender to the Divine seeks to call down blessing on the world. Leading the spiritual life teaches us that the limits of ordinary human life can be surpassed, that we can go beyond the boundaries set by our egos, our cultures and even beyond death. In our spiritual work we come to know the realm of the infinite and eternal and it is love, only love that breaks these rules. Inescapable love. Love sets us on fire, is fire. It is the primordial stuff of the cosmos, out of which the creation burst forth. That fire burns still, the whole universe is on fire [72] with that creative force and it burns in us too.

"The authentic spiritual life helps us to go ever deeper into truth."

The density of ordinary reality, of ego consciousness, has a gravity all of its own. Soul Work sets us free, gradually (if we are careful) of this pull in giving up to a new centre of gravity so that astronaut-like we can soar to new levels of reality, become aware of All-that-is and not just the bit that first held us in its thrall. To use another metaphor [189] we "learn to be amphibious"; able to dwell in different aspects of reality that are part of one reality, one Sacred Unity; it is merely a question of aware-ness and perception. In leaving our first home we come to cherish and have com-passion for it all the more, to be willing to take care of it and participate in it, but from a completely different place of loving awareness in ourselves. Therapont was incapable of doing this. Paradoxically, by thus being more connected to the earth (in love) we become more sacred not less. Being led, by the Christ consciousness or whatever name by which we call it, that which was 'in the beginning', we are led more deeply into the creation not away from it. When we know the creation, we know a little out of whom and what it was created.

Jesus, like all the great spiritual teachers, showed us the meaning of true freedom to be fully ourselves no matter what the circumstances, that to be fully ourselves we dissolve the false self into the true Self. He breaks free of the gravitational pull of ego consciousness. Being fully ourselves is to escape the gravitational pull, yes, even of identity - I am gay, I am black, I am a woman, I am a man, I am a Christian, I am a Taoist, I am straight, I am a diabetic, I am ... I am... Liberation movements of identity (essential in their way – to surrender an identity we have to have an identi-ty to surrender in the first place) are but staging posts along the way. In acquiring an identity, sometimes seemingly at great cost, the true spiritual seeker comes to know that there is yet further to go, perhaps even scarier, of surrendering even that perhaps hard won label. In emptying himself of the self (the trial in the desert for example) Jesus opens to his true divine nature and thus, being possessed fully of himself, he was able to give himself away completely, to live in the eternal now in, but not captured by, time and space. The ultimate freedom comes after death and resurrection; until then the laws of physics bind Jesus in his body, he can only meet so many people, do so many things. Afterwards is the freedom of the enlightened being, available to all.

I Am

A little while ago I got stuck in my body.

As the round of hospitals and tests and queues filled up the day, I could feel the grumpiness growing, the judgmentalism at others around me and the steadily magnifying self-pity for my own suffering. Weary, I watched some out-of-control kid of maybe 4 or 5 years in the waiting room; inwardly wishing his mother would get her attention out of her mobile 'phone and her can of Coke and get a grip. The wild screams, lack of words and the misshapen head of the child should have told me something. Then his mother called him over and took his soiled T-shirt off to reveal surgical scars the full length and breadth of his body. A drainage bag, catheters and intravenous lines were hidden under clothing. I was overcome by sorrow for the child and remorse at my own chagrin. My bubble of spiritual smugness had been well and truly pricked. I had been given a humbling reminder that despite decades of spiritual work I can so easily slip into fear and forgetting.

I laughed inwardly at my foolishness; blessed the gift of this child who taught me more in seconds about myself and the nature of angels than he could possibly imagine. I watched in wonder at his in-the-moment-ness. Not for him the worry about test results, the frustration at the waiting, the fears of pain and illness. No, his big challenge was how to do something amusing with that pile of old magazines. I tore off a cover, made him a paper aeroplane and realised I was enjoying myself. By the time I was called in to the treatment room I no longer felt trapped. There was a mess of paper on the floor and four other grown-ups were busy with attempts at origami and a child having a wild time demolishing their efforts.

"I don't have a body, I am a body." [192] wrote author Christopher Hitchens before dying of oesophageal cancer in 2011 at the age of 61. I think he was wrong.

I empathise with the challenges he faced as he approached death. Around the time I hit 60, I began to feel that I was under attack from one illness after another, some serious. My thyroid gland was irradiated into extinction. My oesophagus followed the family tradition of developing the pre-cancerous Barratt's syndrome (my brother died of oesophageal cancer) requiring regular gastroscopy and biopsy. My heart

"The authentic spiritual life helps us to go ever deeper into truth."

made a unilateral decision to sometimes skip off to its own rhythm independent of the needs of my body. My colon saw fit to cultivate its own little garden of alien cells. And my prostate decided it was going to buck the trend of the economy at the time and go for growth instead, but not benignly.

Life threatening disease is a good catalyst for taking a rain check on your understanding of self and mortality. Many of my tests and treatments have involved body parts where the sun does not normally shine. Invasion of intimacy produced some deep reflections upon what it is to 'be' a man and to be 'me'. Through many tests and treatments I found my understanding of the boundaries of dignity, intimacy and masculinity all challenged. Behaviours and body parts I associate with manliness and privacy have been exposed and made public. When someone is pushing a finger up your bum or a long instrument up your colon or penis while strangers all around you look on, then notions of dignity and privacy are taken to the edge. Everyday life is packed with spiritual practices, opportunities for humility to help strip us ever closer to the soul's bones.

I found myself sometimes surrendering into almost infantile feelings of vulnerability when uncovered or subject to the power of others. The vulnerability was not just a physical one as tender body parts are exposed and man/woman handled, but deeply ingrained in my psyche about what it was to feel safe, to be in control, to be human. Such experiences flush out many ego attachments to power and identity.

One of my responses to cancer some years ago was to do what I suggest my clients do, to set up a 'healing circle' of conventional and complementary approaches to my health care. One of my team sat me down and said "Well, Stephen, now that you are a cancer patient, let's talk about next steps." I could see her mentally referring me to a counsellor ("in denial!") when I replied, "I don't have cancer. My body has, I don't." I did not wish illness and the fears that come with it to drive me back into the egoic closet, to be possessed by yet another identity after many years of getting free of the ones I already had.

Ego identities are rooted in needs for power, status and roles to keep at bay the fear of being without these. Liberation from identity is also liberation from fear. That is not to say we do not *experience* fear and many other thoughts and feelings at the prospect of the termination of life, or at least the egoic perception of it. *Timor mortis*, the fear of death, is a perfectly natural human response, ingrained in our psyche and physiology. Rather, what the spiritual practice can do is help us not be captured by them. If we defenestrate our perception that "I am this" or "I am that" we are no longer trapped by what 'this' or 'that' thinks or feels or does. Phenomena, like cancer, carry on happening and are very real, but we can approach them differently. With this kind of awareness we respond with greater equanimity to experiences rather than feeling trapped in ping-pong, turbulent reactions. Thus I felt the Hitchens' perception, while understandable, to be profoundly limiting. I live through my body, I have a body, but I am not my body.

We can even deny our fears of death through death cults, by counter-phobic behaviour or by bringing death to others as if to show we have control over it (e.g. of the actions of the death cult of Islamic State in the near east as I write). We transfer our inclination to fetishism to death itself. Fetishism is a form of control when we transfer all our 'stuff' to a narrow point in the environment, making the single thing (an idol, a person, a group, an ideology) the source of salvation for all our shadow. Yet this transference is a kind of cowardice, a turning a way from the courage to live an examined life and participate fully in a world full of paradox, of love and fear, and engage instead with simplistic cubby holes of consciousness and behaviour that do not demand too much of us – too much thinking, too much reflection, too much change…The only way out of this dilemma is to renounce these false gods and embrace our higher power; the last thing the body-and-fear-trapped person wants to do. The way out of our neuroses is to become part of the larger whole and recognise that we *are* part of the larger whole.

If "I am not my body" this does not suggest that we should reject the body, rather to not identify with it. Otherwise we can fall into neglecting the wellbeing of our bodies or see it as something that is 'sinful', requiring suppression or punishment. This leads, in some traditions, to an inclination to hurt the body or put it through extreme asceticism to prove how 'spiritual' we are or how we are no longer controlled by the desires of the flesh and have attained enlightenment. A healthy spirituality recognises the wonder of our bodies as our medium for being in the world. The opening of the heart that accompanies spiritual maturity enables us to extend compassion and service to the world, but also to ourselves. It is not a case of dualism, body *or*

"The authentic spiritual life helps us to go ever deeper into truth."

soul, but of integration, body *and* soul. If 'charity (compassion) begins at home' then there is no better place to start than having care and respect for the body, which includes attention to exercise, sleep, nutrition and so forth and the avoidance of substances and behaviours that do it harm.

In discovering our I-Amness we acknowledge the great gift of our bodies. Yet we also let go of the tendency to get stuck in them as the only thing that we believe we are. We go further than the patterns set, for example, by an inclination to professional labels like 'cancer patient' or by various programmes responding to the needs of addiction, such as AA. After the courage to say "I am an alcoholic" is the embracing of the possibility of 'graduating', of healing beyond it. With humility and strength we may say, "I am a..." without any need to fill the space. We come to rest quite simply in "I Am."

Once during a retreat Rachael, who worked as a radiographer, began exploring her "I Am". She was very attached to all her identities – job, mother, daughter, dancer and so forth. Like all of us, the names are legion, but as she gradually peeled away at each of hers she hit - "If not this, then who am I?" – and became more and more afraid. As she sat with this and explored it deeply, with support, she saw how fear came with all the attachments to her identities. She also saw how the fear, especially the fear of being nothing, was an instrument to claw her back; at one point she had to run out of the room.

She held these strong, dark feelings and thoughts on her return and burst through them into the light at the other side when she realised that not being hooked to "I am a mother" was not terrifying but liberating. It did not mean that she was *nothing* as she feared, but it did mean that she was *no-thing*; thereby free to dance creatively with many aspects of personhood without being chained to any one of them. The "condition of complete simplicity" [1] is what sets us free. There are other startling (for some people) realisations from this too. For if everyone else realises that simply "I Am" with no qualifications added and what is more if the Beloved says this too ("I am that I am" [Ex.3:14] suggesting a condition of both being and becoming) then we are all "I Am"! Beneath and beyond the surface story of ordinary perceptions of reality, deep in the core of our being, we are all one in our I-Amness, the very ground of being.

We find this essential oneness expressed in all traditions together with the possibility of relationship in the Beloved that is simultaneously both deeply personal and unreachably transcendent. To the Hindus, for example, it is Atman and Brahman – Godhead as self and transcendent respectively. We see the same image in the Christian cross – the vertical plane representing the immanent personal Divine, the horizontal plane, the transcendent. Throughout scriptures of all traditions we find these motifs repeated in one form or another; a deep paradox that we are at once of God and human. Ruysbroeck [91] tells us that, "The image of God is found essentially and personally in all mankind. Each possesses it whole, entire and undivided, and all together not more than alone. In this way we are all one, intimately united in our eternal image, which is the image of God and the source in us of all life."

If we approach each other only from the egoic plane we find differentiation and potential for both creativity and conflict. When we approach each other from the plane of contemplative unity the response is very different. Ruysbroeck as a typical mystic speaks much the same language as Quantum physicists a thousand years later. We are at our core one and the same. Costly love (Soul Work) forces us to rethink our notions of separateness and individuality and surrender often long cherished views. Until we do that we cannot 'get' to the essential truth that we are all the same. Mother Julian [193] found this in her 'shewings'; that each of us, everything indeed, is "not just made by God but made of God".

The reaction of Rachael on the retreat to the exploration of her I-Amness follows a familiar pattern. Jung wrote [99] of what happens when the tectonic plates of our consciousness begin to shift: "The fear of meaninglessness is the interregnum from ego to soul orientation". As we move from one plane of consciousness (the one that says "I-am-who-I-think-I-am", which is but a mask for the ego's fear that it is really nothing) into that of "I Am" the ride can be terrifying. Joseph Campbell [60] sees this as the true heroic journey because of the courage it takes: "The agony of breaking through personal limitations is the agony of spiritual growth. Art, literature, myth and cult, philosophy, and ascetic disciplines are instruments to help the individual past his limiting horizons into spheres of ever-expanding realization. As he crosses threshold after threshold, conquering dragon after dragon, the stature of the divinity that he summons to his highest wish increases, until it subsumes the cosmos. Finally the mind breaks the bounding sphere of the cosmos to a realization

"The authentic spiritual life helps us to go ever deeper into truth."

transcending all experiences of form – all symbolisations, all divinities: a realisation of the roar of acknowledgement of our "I-Am" is the flip side of our deepest fear the "I-am-notness". As we pass through the latter we find the joy and liberation of the former. The deepest fear of our mortality, which we have sought to bury with countless false-heroic acts of engagement with ordinary reality from the pursuit of success or power to our myriad addictions, is subsumed in the fearless truth of our immortality of I-amness, our Essence, our soul.

Joy and liberation offer opportunities to dance lightly, dispassionately, non-attached-ly (all words and consequences we have explored in these pages) with many possible roles and identities without clinging. The "I Am" is also the "I Can" of our natures, the place of boundless possibility when freed from attachments and limited perceptions of self. Not being hooked to a role or identity can set us free. This freedom Zossima grasped, but Therapont could not. The latter, stuck with ego, could continue only to stay in its defence-attack mode with those he met and the rest of the world. The former's transformed awareness was not so stuck, his awareness was not neutral but full of compassion in seeing the struggles and joys in the world, from which place he chose to engage with it by responding with an open heart rather than egoic ping-pong reactiveness.

The saying 'charity begins at home' is often interpreted rather meanly. From the point of view of those who awaken it is a truth. Charity (compassion) really does begin at home. When like Zossima we discover it in the depths of our nature, at Home in ourselves and its inexhaustible Source, it ripples out almost wastefully from there to serve.

Sometimes when under pressure we say we want to 'get our life back', but perhaps a healthier response is not to try and get something 'back' in the sense of restoring an old story or attachments, but to see this as an opportunity to let go and discover what Life really is? As we 're-programme' our thought processes (through meditation, cultivating loving awareness, and other approaches to Soul Care) we actually change the brain structure as we examined before. Those old fearful punishing and negative thought patterns embedded in their bunches of brain cells get used less and less. New heart-centred 'superhighways' of compassion in our neurones are reinforced simply because we are using them more instead. Cultivating a change in consciousness produces changes in the brain, reinforcing and sustaining the transformation. It's more than positive thinking; it's a complete change in the way we see ourselves and the world and our way of being – a spiritual transformation.

"Be ye perfect as your father in heaven is perfect" [Matt.5:48] was drummed into us at Sunday School. This seemed a tall order, too tall for a small child. "How could I possible be as perfect as God?" And was told quite simply I couldn't be, but could try. Well, that was me put in my place then and it probably fed a hopelessness and inadequacy that contributed to my giving up religious interest in my teens. Decades later I understood how a moralistic '*logos*' interpretation of that command was too limiting. The word 'perfect' in Aramaic, *g'mar* (the main language of Jesus' teaching among the common people) is best interpreted as meaning 'whole' or 'harmony' or 'one'.

To be perfect in a moralistic sense suggests some form of idealised person who never has a lustful, angry, shaming or any other kind of disconnecting thought or behaviour; in other words never 'sins'. The mystical approach, *mythos*, to 'perfection' rejects this view and instead summons us to ever-greater acceptance of ourselves with all the judgements of our various foibles and limitations. In accepting this multi-patterned identity that each of us carries we find two things happening. First of all the draining energy of judgement that comes with judgement (of ourselves) dissipates. We simply come to rest in acceptance of its presence and secondly, paradoxically, once the fight and rejection goes out of this approach that messy ego being that we carry around with us loses its power. Thirdly, the more we 'see' this identity we carry around with us, the more we see that it is 'not who I am', we begin to put some distance between it and our true Self. This distance gives liminal space in which we can cultivate a new awareness, fresh options for choice. Our I-Amness thus liberated is able to be in the world in loving awareness while at the same time integrating and accepting all the multifarious roles and identities with which we must dance.

Home is not elsewhere
Coming Home is not a retreat from the world; it calls us to action in compassion and love not to withdraw. It is to leave behind the withered and work with the growing. It is to be in the world more fully, how could we not be? For this is Home, there is

"The authentic spiritual life helps us to go ever deeper into truth."

no duality, no 'other', it is all part of the One, just here and now. If we cannot be at Home here there is no other place. Thus we can come to know that 'here and now' in all its magnificent, tragic, boundless, loving possibility. We do not make the darkness of the waste land light by remaining indoors with our torches; we have to take them out into the shadow, to participate fully in the world in whatever way we are called so to do.

The Sufi mystic and poet Jalalu'ddin Rumi [194], currently one of the world's most popular poets, wrote of his religion, "Ours is not a caravan of despair." Famously, through love of his mentor Shams of Tabriz he fell ecstatically into love with the Divine – producing some of the finest love poems to his Beloved on the way. His "hopefulness for God" permeates his work. There is no despair for he sees the Beloved as embracing and welcoming all comers. A Sufi chant and sacred dance based on his words calls out, "Come, come, whoever you are, even though you've broken your vows a thousand times, come, come again." The unconditionally loving One that Rumi directly encountered constantly calls everyone of us Home, no matter who we are, no matter how often we might stray from our best intentions or our best selves. Rumi's God and mine and that of millions of others is the same Beloved and is 'perfect', holy – in the true sense of the word, which is deeply related linguistically (from the Teutonic *haelan*) to our concepts of hale, whole, healthy, hearty, holism; holy, embracing All-that-is in Sacred Unity.

Our task, those who are seeking Home, is to mirror and embody that holy Home here on earth, to create communities of heaven where the sacred principles are mirrored in each moment, here and now, as above so below; a world of love beyond irrelevant distinctions like age, race, sexuality, social class or personal history. A culture of dismemberment, dissection, disconnection, atomising – the waste land – also fragments those who live in it, unless we wake up. Without this awakening we are stuck in the belief that we are separated from each other, the cosmos, ourselves and the Beloved. Spiritual work flows the opposite way. The spiritual life re-members, re-connects, makes whole and holy.

The way home draws us into Rumi's "wild love affair with life". Our spiritual work is not about weird and wonderful experiences or fixity in religion, but getting past these and seeing the world differently, truthfully, full of endless change, refinement, transformation; seeing, being anew in, becoming more sensitised to the Beloved. It is the *via purgativa*, the way of cleansing ourselves of our ideas of self in order to know the Self; a way of seeing that like all love affairs is full of turbulence and calm, bliss and pain. Most of all it is replete with unfathomable, boundless, endlessly in-breaking love in the One in whom that wild love affair is both complete and never ending, still and still moving. Into ourselves, into life, into the One we know and love. Home.

"The authentic spiritual life helps us to go ever deeper into truth."

If we are lucky or patient,
in sacred, silent solitude,
we may catch a glimpse of God
meditating in the timeless moment
between the flashes of the lighthouse,
or the split sunbeam in the waves.
The holy is not bound by altar
or portal carved just so.
It is here, now. Under the pine roof
Where the mouse peeps through
the knot hole, under the glare of
strip lights illuminating the temenos
of the ecstatic ordinary.
If we will only look.
If we only look.
The mountains have their own deep
thoughts, we cannot share them.
Like the Buddha under the Bo tree,
they have gone, gone beyond,
gone beyond the beyond of our reach.
But we can sit and pray
and in our waiting the veil may lift
for just a moment, just a moment.
And if we watch closely, we might just
see something. Don't try to pin it down.
It will move like quicksilver from any grasp,
Lost down the drain of the unconscious.
But sit and pray for just a moment
and watch another universe come into being.
Boom!

Part 11

"Home is the place where, when you have to go there, they have to take you in." [195]

Letter 2

Dear Unknown Friend,

The master poet [1] wrote how we return to where we started and know the place of the first time. About two years ago, having decided to withdraw from the conference/journal circuit after 40 years at it and working in 70 different countries and with thousands of publications…..the last workshop I did was with a group of nurses and I was surprised to find the venue to be no more than a couple of miles from the site of the hospital, now long demolished, where I trained 45 years before. Later I went to teach in a building called Red Bank House in Manchester. The street where I grew up is called Red Bank Road. And I'm sitting in the early hours in a Manchester hotel looking to the hills where that street is. I'm on the third floor of a building that was once an office block in 1968. A modern thing close to what was then a run down railway station, now part of a regeneration project. Unremarkable to others, but to me the station where I would arrive each day for work, a working class lad made good by the standards of the day, who had escaped the factory (I had a white collar and a tie and an umbrella and a brief case!) walking to his office on the third floor of an Inland Revenue building called Highland House.

I can see that station from my hotel window, as I write, which is now the same building as that office block once was. So here I am in the later years *entre la vie et le mort* (why is life a feminine gendered word and death a masculine one *en Francais*?) looking back, literally, at some of the structure of my life and wondering have I really been anywhere, have I really done anything? Do I know any better that place from which I started? Now my life's a film of a teenager with aspirations in an office block who sat a few floors below this old man in the future and if he imagined one thing it was that he would never return to that grey 60's monster, now painted purple, full of beds that guarantee a good night's sleep or your money back. If I could have my

"To become ensouled is to become fully ourselves."

lived-life back, because it fell short of the guarantees or at least the assumptions of ambitions fulfilled and happiness complete, would I do it again? I'll give this hotel a Tripadvisor rating. How many stars will I give my life lived this Way? Time enough for that I must trust. Meanwhile, if spirituality is about dying to self, then that reflection through the window of my office-hotel made me realise that in any life there's an awful lot of self about!

For millions more people in the decade since I wrote the first edition of this book, life has become entertainment – the unlimited possibilities of social media, vast numbers of confessional books and films and TV programmes, 'reality' TV (which by the very nature of its confection is anything but real) and makeover programmes. Life itself has become an even more intense and vast ego distraction from anything that demands depth or a long attention span, just what the ego wants in fact and which the soul experiences as a kind of hell. Millions long for a Way that is 'more'. Some find it. Many don't.

After all, there's plenty of distractions more tempting than the sobriety and self-mastery for the sacrifice (make holy) we make in order to soar to the Beloved, fasting from all those things which get in the way, healing all wounds, getting through all obstructions. Nevertheless something seems to impel our lower nature away from the gravitational pull by which it is seduced. It becomes attracted to the needs of the higher, we pay attention, deep attention, to ourselves in order to see all the blocks and get free of this little, false self. Sometimes the extrication is a smooth birthing, sometimes a brutal extraction without anaesthetic.

Across the planet vast numbers of people are enslaved to systems of governance and ways of seeing that keep them trapped in material and psychological poverty, injustice and deprivation. Down the ages revolutions and ideologies of all sorts have claimed to set the masses free from this bondage, yet their, our, condition remains essentially unchanged. If such movements have their limitations perhaps the authentic way of spirit provides an option. Perhaps through mass personal transformation we may yet see ways of organising our lives commensurate with values and actions rooted in love.

The spiritual cat is out of the religious bag. Ideas and practices once confined to the elites of priests, healers or shamans can now be explored in a world of mass communication and accessible information. Training programmes in faith or ministry of all sorts have been proletarianised, made available to all, for the price of a weekend course or a university module or the flick of a finger on a computer keyboard. While this unrestricted availability runs the risk of deep truths being exploited or subject to shallow understanding or practise, it brings with it the benefit of the vast transmission of awakening and wisdom to enormous numbers of people in ways unheard of in all of history. Perhaps mass transformation is possible simply because the means to do so are now so universally available and increasingly so.

On the other hand this may be merely another delusion. Perhaps the world, or at least one plane of consciousness of it, is doing exactly what its supposed to be doing, that we are confusing the perfection of the beyond with the condition of ordinary reality. Maybe the two really are actually quite different and forever shall be with one being a ground of fermentation to awakening to the other. Perhaps earthly perfection is a delusion albeit a beautiful one, or more accurately its seeming imperfection is its perfection. Ordinary reality is just one of the planes of consciousness in which we exist, one of the ways of seeing; the transformation, the alchemy, is an endless Coming Home in which there is no ending. We are participants in this infinite process of becoming, in awakening and through that acting within our sphere with compassion and action for the transformation of others. Thus there is no end point, no time in which we can say we are 'there', 'home', rather we are *always* Coming Home.

To live and work in ordinary reality demands courage, the courage to be [29], a kind of cosmic heroism to hold onto hope in the face of suffering, to believe and know in the face of horror and despair, to be willing to see all the suffering and human folly and yet still engage with the world and not give up on our relationship in the Beloved. Yes, fear of death and our own inner demons of shame, worthlessness or meaninglessness can seem insurmountable at times. Yes, madness, denial and neuroses can seem like rational options in the face of a crazy world. Yes, to sink into the welcoming arms of the hungry ghosts could be an understandable response to the terror of existence. Yet masses of people do not succumb to these traps and embracing life and infinity find courageous ways to be that set ourselves and others free, to do good, to live from love and not fear.

"To become ensouled is to become fully ourselves."

Years ago, I sat in bed reading by candlelight. In the middle of the night a butterfly (not a moth), a day creature, began to flutter about my head. I was reading about Jung and synchronicity and transformation as I'd just emerged from a life-changing encounter with the Beloved. The butterfly flopped into the candle wax before me, died instantly in the hot wax forever entombed. I still have that candle and the memory of ripples of multiple thoughts and feelings and interpretations of that moment.

In the midst of tragedy long ago a young man said to me, "Love is what's going on." My mind railed against such crazy irrationality. On the surface, the only response is no. Dive deep and look up with the eye of the mystic, the contemplative non-duality and he'd set a truth juddering though my consciousness that would not be stilled until satisfied. I had to learn to swim all over again.

Later in the abbey church on Iona, I was hearing about death in the deep silence in the early hours, the kind of time when prayers of entreaty are emptied out and all we can do is sit and listen. I saw death as a gift of love, as everything as a gift of love if we can only see it. It is as if the soul, upon incarnation, has this written into the small print of the contract. Small print that says 'return guaranteed', a promise that the iron cage of the personality must, by death, be broken and the soul set free of the tight straightjacket of the embodied life. And although we, I, fear death [the I-that-I-think-I-am fears death] somewhere a promise is full-filled. Love, yes even as death sets us, sets me, free; it is a gift, a gift of Love. Oh to be willing to fall in Love that much. Oh to be willing to die into life and live it fully now.

I had a moment, only a couple of months back from the time of writing this edition, when my heart stopped for a second time. On this occasion it was not a managed event as the one in Cairns Hospital. It was during a 'safe' procedure that I became aware that my heart wasn't beating. It lasted only a few breaths, maybe 20 seconds. In that time I noticed I wasn't afraid. I noticed too the increased level of activity of carers around me. I did not have a near-death experience, no out-of-bodyness or tunnel ending in white light or the presence of long-dead loved ones. What I did see was everything around me with a rare intensity. The people, the machines, the computers, the walls of the treatment room, the needles in my arm, the tubes and IV equipment, oh, all of it was in some wondrous way of the same substance. It was all alive, vibrating, shimmering and I was part of it and it was part of me. And it was not neutral or indifferent. I had an intense feeling that I was *in* love, that the whole damn thing was love, that I was not I but some other I watching I…and the I that was watching just new deeply, certainly, that it was all good. Then the electric shock waves pulsed through my body along with a flush of drugs. I suddenly felt the heaviness of my flesh against the operating table, the pain and nausea, a flash of fear, the dull density of ordinary vision and a doctor's reassuring voice and the hand of nurse holding mine.

The kindness was palpable, but unnecessary. I knew I was OK. I knew it was all OK.

Please think back, dear Unknown Friend, to the very beginning of this book when we explored the possible options for causes for such mystical (possibly) experiences. Was it the drugs, a dream, psychosis, a past life memory, a sudden rush of endorphins, a Pollyanna-ish inclination of my psyche to avoid fear, or…or…or…? Sometimes truth punches through all possible explanations, rational or otherwise, to render them re-dundant. Sometimes we are just open to know something as true because of the ripeness of the moment and ourselves. It's as if an angel drops a postcard through our psychic letterbox with a simple note to remind us, re-mind us, that in its essence, in its height and depth beyond ordinary perceptions of one plane of reality, it is all held and it is all good.

Good and God are words that come from the same Teutonic roots. God is not dead in these times as Nietzsche [196] claimed, nor is there no God as the atheists demand, nor is God the God of certainty (male) as some religionists claim. That which does not 'live' in the same sense that the false self lives cannot die. The Divine, the Truth of the Beloved has simply been hidden away in the unconscious when we can no longer accept the reality in the conscious realm. Somewhere there, amidst a kind of perennial waiting, angels with a thousand different faces queue up to call us out and Home.

I cannot say *this* is the Way, or *that* is the Way. In a sense the great Way is not difficult for those who have no preferences, for it is the Way that prefers us! As Hafiz reminded us, we are all invited, that narrows down the choice to going willingly or resisting. Yet with so many doors open to us we are called to become clear, to make choices, to do the work, to celebrate every step of the Way. I hope the words in this book have helped a little in the choosing. And in making that choice, it is clear that the perennial guidance for following the Way is to ensure that you have in place the Soul Friends, Works, Commu-

"To become ensouled is to become fully ourselves."

nities and Foods that will nurture you, keep you and bring you all the struggle and peace you will need in returning Home.

I trust these words have helped make clear the value of discernment in making your choices, when to stick with something and when to let it go depending on how healthy it is for your Way, when to go deeper into surrender so that the Way Home takes you rather than you seek to command it. There is no requirement to hang onto a Soul Friend or Soul Community just for the sake of it and especially if they are harmful, but it is necessary to be very clear about your intentions and consciousness if the time comes to say goodbye to something or someone. The Way is not travelled entirely alone or entirely in company.

The Way may seem far off with many miles to go. Yet, if we cannot find the One here and now, where do we seek? There is nowhere else we can be. Recall, dear Unknown Friend, that 'soul to soul' talk with Ram Dass (Part 5 page 180). Few are destined for the hermitage. Most of us need companions along the way where soul talk can happen. Soul talk to re-mind us that the quest is not in vain, that the Beloved is calling us Home in the mouths of good friends, the signs in the world around us and beyond. With soul talk we can walk through the swampy lowlands of the waste land with an open heart and hope and not be overcome.

To become ensouled is to become fully ourselves. When our deepest Self, which is the One Self, is set free, it has nowhere it needs to go, nothing it needs to say or do. It is simply free to be what it is, utterly present in the moment, sunbathing in, indeed becoming, the radiant light of Love of the Presence of the Friend. In this Presence we know beyond doubt, in faith, that we are loved in the Beloved not because we are superhuman but because of our essential humanity.

The four Soul Care routes we have explored are not the Way in themselves, but they help us along the Way and open us so that it is the Way that takes us ever more, stripping us even of the idea that it is we who are doing all the work of following, seeking, effort-ing. They open us to that inner prompting, to the power that transforms within dissolving all obstructions. It is what some would describe as the bursting forth within of the light of the Christ, the Wisdom, the guru consciousness, the in-breaking of the grace, the power of the Divine which ultimately is the power that is magnetically, forcefully, relentlessly bringing us Home.

The seed of that consciousness is in each of us. Our Soul Care work tills the soil so this seed may blossom; justifies and purifies the ground so that the Divine potential in each of us may come to its fullness. The pattern of the universe is printed on our hearts. Soul Care and the distillation of our egos opens us to the radiant beauty of that pattern, sensitises us to the Divine will so that it can draw out of us the essence of who we are and let it flourish, be revealed and harvested in all its glory.

Soul Care, dear Unknown Friend, is like being a constant gardener. We treasure the beautiful flowers and vegetables, but have to keep the weeds down. The weeding and cultivating never stop, but there are periods of rest, times of enjoying the fruits of our labour. Such is the journey of spiritual maturation, for the true pilgrim, like the gardener, there is never an endpoint, no place or time when we can say we are 'there', just as we mature as human beings from infant to elder, so the maturity of our relationship in the Beloved is one of *always* Coming Home. That maturity is marked by the humility and wisdom to know that we are always learning, that we are forever students, students of love.

My life like yours has been full of times of sorrow and joy, love and fear. There have been times when I have behaved well and risen to being the best I could be, times when I have behaved badly and wounded others and myself. But as we tend the garden of our lives, we learn to forgive, accept, integrate and heal so the heart of the garden itself heals, flourishes and is made whole. In this life, dear Unknown Friend, there is no ordinary life and spiritual life, although it can seem so at times. It is all one; it is a consecrated life when we realise and live this truth. As we continue our work, the beauty of the whole, the perfect place of every part is revealed to us. If we apply ourselves to heartfelt Soul work and play, then that treasure deep within that has longed to be fully and radiantly in the world is revealed. It is free and at Home.

Tend your garden, dear Unknown Friend, tend it well, there is nothing else!

Yours,
In
Love,
A Friend

"To become ensouled is to become fully ourselves."

Part 12

"Your word goes out to call us Home
To the city where angels sing Your praise."[197]

<u>Coming Home</u>

You said, "Home".
I drank the booze of hospitality in a stranger's house.
You said, "Awake".
I slept on the hard mattress of my loneliness.
You said, "Pray".
I bowed low in the temple of despair.
You said, "Dream".
I wove nightmares from threads of steel.
You said, "Light".
I snuffed out candles on the altar of my desires.
You said, "Love".
I hunted bodies under dark lamps.
You said "Come".
I, deaf Icarus, took flight.
You said, "Be Still".
I raced in the grand prix of my thoughts.
You said "Know Me".
I watched Eastenders instead.
You said, "Hold".
I let go Your hand.
You said, "Wait".
I got on the first bus that came along.
You said, "Trust".
I betrayed my soul in a palace of mirrors.

When You caressed me for attention,
I slapped You down.
When You tickled my chin,

I punched You away.
When You plunged a fist into my heart,
I took the hand of fear and ran away.
When You shook me – hard, and hooked –
the pain unmanned me.
I sat up and listened.

Sometimes.

Then slunk away down the long corridor of shadows.
You
Reeled me in.

My mother always said, "It will all end in tears".
Had I known she had the gift of prophecy
I would have bought her bibles
or the black chocolate she loved.
Goddesses deserve worship
when their compassionate eyes stroke
your soul with the melting honey of love.

You said, "Now, come closer".
I drew myself upon Your knee
to await Your orders.
I asked, "When?"
You said, "Now!"
And I?
Fell asleep again.

In the forgetfulness of the Porsche,
the rock concert
or simply an overdrawn bank statement,
I had been offered the womb of Your love.
I self aborted.
Again

But always the hunger.
A bowel-less pain.
The hollow pitiless tomb.

Relentless.

You have sent me living angels down the years.
I pruned their wings and stuffed my duvet with their feathers.
Angels, the kind who fasten your seat belt when you fall drunk in
the back of a taxi.

When You sent the message
this time in an unlooked for brown envelope.
I could only smile.
It seemed simpler
To surrender.
Falling into book and prayer.

Years ago I asked, "What do You want of me?"
You said, "Be My Voice".
Struck dumb by impossible visions,
I ordered another pint.

The Lord Shiva slaughtered the slimy frog of my unworthiness.
"Death is mine not yours to give!", said he.
And I remember,
I looked him straight in the eye
for the first time.

Spinning in the velocity of my own redemption
there was nothing left to do but fall
dizzy
at Your feet.

From apogee to perigee,
in the flick of the serpent's tongue.

In surrender is peace.
In trust is service.

I ask, "What have I learned here?"
You say, "Trust".
I ask, "What do You want of me?"
You say, "Wait".
I ask, "Why offer Your hand?"
You say, "Hold".
I ask, "Where do I begin?"
You say, "Know me".
I ask, "How?"
You say, "Be still".
I ask, "Am I worthy enough?"
You say, "Come".
I ask, "Why?"
You say, "Love".
I ask, "What lies in this dark?"
You say, "Light".
I ask, "How shall I find You?"
You say, "Dream".
I ask, "How shall I stay with You?"
You say, "Pray".
I ask, "What have I become?"
You say, "Awake".
I ask, "What is this place?"
You say, "Home".

References

All Bible references are from the New Revised Standard Version. 1999. OUP. Oxford

[1] Eliot T S 1944 The Four Quartets. Harcourt Brace Jovanovich. London

[2] Davies B In Wright S 1989 Nursing the older patient. Harper. London

[3] Heelas P,Woodhead l, with Seel B, Szerszynski B,Tusting K 2005 The spirituality revolution – why religion is giving way to spirituality. Blackwell. Oxford

[4] Weil S 2000 Waiting for God. Perennial. London

[5] Forster E 1982 Howards End. Penguin classics. London

[6] Prayer for Conversations.2.www.salfordiocese.org.uk/listening2004

[7] Nietzsche F in Frankl V 1959 Man's search for meaning. Rider. London

[8] Tomberg V 2006 Lazarus come forth. Lindisfarne. Great Barrington

[9] Achterberg J 1990 Woman as healer. Ryder. London

[10] Baring A 2013 Dreams of the Cosmos. Archive. Dorset

[11] Palmer P 1993 To know as we are known. Harper & Row, San Francisco

[12] Davie C 1995 Religion in Britain since 1945. Blackwell. Oxford

[13] Finney J 1996 Recovering the past. DLT. London

[14] Douglas-Klotz N 1999 The hidden gospel. Quest. Wheaton

[15] Lee P 1969 Is that all there is? Columbia Records

[16] Sogyal Rinpoche 1992 The Tibetan book of living and dying. Ryder. London

[17] Doyle B 1983 Meditations with Julian of Norwich. Bear. Santa Fe

[18] Underhill E 1942 Practical mysticism. Ariel. Columbus

[19] Bourgeault C 2008 The wisdom Jesus. Shambhala. Boston

[20] Lancaster B 2006 The essence of Kabbalah. Arcturus. London

[21] Einstein A (trans. Harris A) 1984 The world as I see it. Citadel. New York

[22] Climacus J (trans. Luibheid C & Russell N) 1982 The ladder of divine ascent. Paulist. Mahwah

[23] Wilber K 1995 Sex, ecology and spirituality. Shambhala. Boston

[24] Underhill E 1960 The mount of purification. Longmans Green. London

[25] Hilton W (trans. Anon) 2004 The ladder of perfection. Kessinger. Whitefish

[26] Koenig H, McCullogh M, Larson B 2002 Handbook of religion and health. OUP. New York

[27] Pargament K, Koenig H, Tarakeshwar N, Hahn J 2001 Religious struggle as a predictor of mortality among medically ill elderly patients. Arch.Int.Med 161:1881-85

[28] Krause J. 2006 Church-based social support and mortality. Journals of Gerontology series B. 61.S140-146

[29] Tillich P 2000 The courage to be. YUP. Yale

[30] Yang C, Boen C, Gerken K, Li T, Schorpp K, Harris K 2016 Social relationships and physiological determinant longevity across the human life span PNAS 2016 ; doi:10.1073/pnas.1511085112

[31] Griffin J 2010 The Lonely Society? The Mental Health Foundation. London.

[32] Holt-Lunstad J, Smith T, Layton J 2010 Social relationships and mortality risk: a meta-analytic review. PLOS Medicine Journal. 7(7): e1000316

[33] Pert C 1999 Molecules of emotion. Scribner. New York

[34] Wright S 2005 Reflections on spirituality and health. Wiley. Chichester

[35] Macquarrie J 1972 Paths in spirituality. SCM. Trowbridge

[36] Grof S & Grof C (eds.) 1989 Spiritual emergency: when personal transformation becomes a crisis. Putnam. New York

[37] Dennet D 2006 Breaking the spell. Penguin. London

[38] Dawkins R 2006 The God delusion. Bantam. London

[39] Hitchens C 2007 God is not great. Atlantic. London

[40] Sagan C 1997 The demon-haunted world. Headline. London

[41] Hobbes T (ed. Griffith T) Leviathan. Wordsworth. London

[42] Newberg A, D'Aquili E, Rause V 2001 Why God won't go away. Ballantine. New York

[43] Hamer D 2004 The God gene. Doubleday. New York

[44] Schultes R & Hoffman A 1992 Plants of the gods. HAP. Rochester

[45] Edwards L 2013 Awakening Kundalini: the path to radical transformation. Sounds True. London

[46] Cornwell J 1991 Powers of darkness, powers of light. Viking. London

[47] Maslow A 1976 Religions, values and peak-experiences. Penguin. Harmondsworth

[48] Jung C 1961 Modern man in search of soul. Routledge & Kegan Paul. London

[49] Underhill E 1993 (first pub.1910) Mysticism. Oneworld. Oxford

[50] Maxwell M &Tschudin V 1990 Seeing the invisible. Arkana. London

[51] Dossey L 2014 One mind. Hay House. London

[52] Wright S 2011 Contemplation SSP. Cumbria

[53] Wright S & Sayre-Adams J 2007 Sacred Space: right relationship and spirituality in health care. SSP. Cumbria

[54] Wright S 2009 Burnout. SSP. Cumbria

[55] Heinlein R 1961 Stranger in a strange land. Putnam. London

[56] Merton T 1949 Seeds of contemplation. Hollis & Carter. London

[57] Ram Dass 1978 Be here now. Hanuman Foundation. New York

[58] McGrath A 2004 The twilight of atheism. Rider. London

[59] Sartre J in Armstrong K 2001 The battle for God. HarperCollins. London

[60] Campbell J 2008 The hero with a thousand faces. New World Library. Novato

[61] Hutton W 2016 Having too many things can be bad for you. Observer. 31.1.16

[62] Sedalek T 2011 The economics of good and evil. OUP. Oxford

[63] Eliot T 1972 The waste land and other poems. Faber & Faber. London

[64] Gallup Organisation in Hatfield D 1999 New research links emotional intelligence with profitability. The Inner Edge. 1(5) 5-9

[65] Lerner M 2000 Spirit Matters. Hampton Roads. Charlottesville

[66] Wilkinson R & Pickett K 2010 The spirit level. Penguin. London

[67] Sartre J 1965 Nausea. Penguin. New York NY

[68] Yeats W 'The second coming' in Harmon W (ed.) 1998 The Classic Hundred Poems. Columbia University Press. New York

[69] Childre D & Martin H 2011 The Heartmath solution. Piatkus. London

[70] Buber M 1937 I and Thou. Clark. Edinburgh

[71] Schweitzer A 1983 Reverence for life. HarperCollins. London

[72] de Chardin T 1959 The phenomenon of man. Collins. London

[73] Speck P 2003 Working with dying people in Obholzer A and Roberts V (eds.) The unconscious at work. Brunner-Routledge. London

[74] Almaas A 2000 The diamond heart. Shambhala. London

[75] Pennick N 1996 Celtic sacred landscapes. Thames & Hudson. London

[76] Ray P 1996 The integral culture survey. Inst. Noetic Sciences. Sausalito

[77] Thomas R 1999 The I society. The Guardian Archive 17.9

[78] Halevi Y (trans. Levin G) 2002 Poems from the divan. Anvil. London

[79] Cantacuzino M 2013 The forgiveness project. JKP. London

[80] Cavafy C 1995 (trans. Keeley E & Sherrard P) The essential Cavafy. Ecco. Hopewell

[81] Linders E & Lancaster L 2012 Sacred illness: exploring transpersonal aspects in physical affliction and the role of the body in spiritual development. Mental Health, Religion and Culture: 0I:10.1080/13674676.2012.728578

[82] Friedberg J, Suchday S & Shelov D 2007 The impact of forgiveness on cardiovascular reactivity and recovery. International Journal of Psychophysiology.17466400

[83] Wallace H, Exline J & Baumeister R 2008 Interpersonal consequences of forgiveness: does forgiveness deter or encourage repeat offenses? Journal of Experimental Social Psychology 44: 453-460

[84] Worthington E 2005 Handbook of forgiveness. Routledge. New York

[85] Wright S 2012 Yours faithfully. SSP. Cumbria

[86] Storr A 1997 Feet of clay. HarperCollins. London

[87] Proulx A 2005 Close range: Brokeback Mountain and other stories. Harper. New York

[88] Easwaran E 1988 (trans.) The Upanishads. Arkana. London

[89] Guenther M 2002 Holy listening. DLT. London

[90] Tweedie I 1907 Daughter of fire. Golden Sufi Centre. Inverness Calif.

[91] Ruysbroeck J van (trans. Sherwood Taylor F) 1944 The seven steps of the ladder of spiritual love. Dacre. Westminster

[92] Riso D & Hudson R1999 The wisdom of the Enneagram. Bantam. New York

[93] Caplan M 2002 Do you need a guru? Thorsons. London

[94] Leech K 2001 Soul friend – spiritual direction in the modern world. DLT. London

[95] Lao Tzu (trans. Legge J) 1994 Tao te ching. Little Brown. London

[96] Schumacher E 1977 A guide for the perplexed. Abacus. London

[97] Watts A1977 The essential Alan Watts. Celestial Arts. Berkeley

[98] Borg M 1995 Meeting Jesus again for the first time. HarperCollins. New York

[99] Jung C [ed. Shamdasani S] The red book. 2009 Norton. London

[100] Newell JP 1997 Listening for the heartbeat of God. SPCK. London

[101] Krishnamurti J 1982 Krishnamurti's journal. Harper. San Francisco

[102] Wernham S 2003 Personal correspondence

[103] Liebert E 2000 Changing life patterns. Chalice. St. Louis

[104] Whiteaker S 2004 The good retreat guide. Rider. London

[105] Sahajananda J 2003 You are the light. O Books. Alresford

[106] Aronson H 2004 Buddhist practice on western ground: reconciling eastern ideals and psychology. Shambhala. Boston .

[107] Jones A 1982 Exploring spiritual direction: an essay of Christian friendship. Harper & Row. San Francisco

[108] Ball P 2003 Introducing spiritual direction. SPCK. London

[109] Nickalls J (ed.) 1997 The journal of George Fox. RSF. Philadelphia

[110] Childre D & Rozman D 2014 Transforming anger: the Heartmath solution for letting go of rage, frustration and irritation. Piatkus. London

[111] Dewar F 1991 Called or collared. SPCK. London

[112] Levine S 1982 Who dies? Doubleday. New York

[113] Steven K 2000 Iona. St. Andrew Press. Edinburgh

[114] Bradley I 2000 Colonies of heaven. DLT. London

[115] Merton T 1955 No man is an island. Harcourt Brace. New York

[116] Ross H M 1998 Jesus untouched by the church. Ebor. York

[117] Moore T 2009 Writing in the sand. Hay House. London

[118] Barth K in Underhill E 2000 The spiritual life. Oneworld. Boston

[119] Dossey L 2011 Healing words. Harperone. San Francisco

[120] Muktananda Swami 1978 Play of consciousness. SYDA. New York

[121] Ram Dass and Gorman P 1992 How can I help? Knopf. New York

[122] Tennyson A Ulysses in Gardner H (ed.) 1989 The new Oxford book of English verse. OUP. Oxford

[123] Bohm D 1980 Wholeness and the implicate order. Routledge & Kegan Paul. London

[124] Sheldrake R 2012 The science delusion. Cornet. London

[125] Zukav G 1990 The seat of the soul. Simon & Shuster. New York

[126] Shakespeare W 1982 edition. Anthony and Cleopatra. Complete works. Vol. 2. Nelson Doubleday. London

[127] Huxley A 1994 The doors of perception and heaven and hell. Flamingo. London

[128] Palmer G, Sherrard P & Ware L (trans.) 1983 The Philokalia. Faber & Faber. London

[129] Merton T 2005 Contemplative prayer. DLT. London

[130] Lane B 1998 The solace of fierce landscapes. OUP. Oxford.

[131] Dionysius (trans. Rolt C) 1957 Dionysius the Areopagite: on the divine names and mystical theology. SPCK. London

[132] Griffin E (ed.) 2005 Bernard of Clairvaux selected works. Harpercollins. San Francisco.

[133] McTaggart L 2001 The field. Harpercollins. London

[134] Harner M 1990 The way of the Shaman. Harper & Row. San Francisco

[135] Mascaro J (trans.) 1962 The Bhagavad Gita. Penguin. Harmondsworth

[136] Ladinsky D 2002 I heard God laughing – renderings of Hafiz. Sufism Reoriented. Walnut Creek

[137] Smith H in Borg M 1995 Meeting Jesus again for the first time. Harpercollins. San Francisco

[138] Martin L & Robinson J 2005 TV to push the boundaries of sex. The Observer 28.08.05 p4

[139] Bourgeault C 2014 Love is stronger than death. Monkfish. New York

[140] Leloup J (trans. Rowe J) The gospel of Philip. Inner traditions. Rochester

[141] Jamison C 2006 Finding sanctuary. Weidenfield & Nicholson. London

[142] Tyler P 2007 Divine unknowing: lessons from the Christian mystical tradition for healthcare today. Spirituality and health international. 8 [2] 64-73

[143] McCabe H 2002 God still matters. Continuum. London

[144] Baker R & Henry G 1999 Merton and Sufism: the untold story. Fons Vitae. Louisville

[145] Mitchell S 1991 The gospel according to Jesus. HarperCollins. London

[146] Cassian J (ed. Ramsey E) 1997 The conferences. Newman. New York

[147] Estevez E (dir.) 2010 The Way. Filmax Elixir Films. USA

[148] Schuoun F 1963 Understanding Islam. Allen & Unwin. London

[149] Paintner C 2012 Lectio divina. SPCK. London

[150] Torkington D 1977 The hermit. Alba, New York

[151] Riso D & Hudson 1999 The wisdom of the Enneagram. Bantam. New York

[152] Artress L 2006 Walking a sacred path. Riverhead. New York

[153] Westbury V with Pavlinac C 2003 Labyrinths: ancient paths of wisdom and peace. Da Capo. Cambridge.Mass

[154] Anon 1991 Meditations on the tarot. Element. Shaftesbury

[155] Campbell J & Moyers B 1989 The power of myth. Bantam. London

[156] Segal R 1998 The myth and ritual theory. Wiley. Chichester

[157] Watts A 1991 Myth, ritual and Christianity. Beacon. London

[158] Castaneda C 1990 The teachings of Don Juan. Arkana/Penguin. London

[159] Virgil (trans. West D) 2003 The Aeneid. Penguin. Harmondsworth.

[160] Avila T of (trans. Peers E) 200 The interior castle. Dover. New York.

[161] Loyola I of (trans. Puhl L) 2000 The spiritual exercises of St. Ignatius. Vintage. New York

[162] Meister Eckhart (trans. Davies O) 1994 Meister Eckhart selected writings. Penguin. Harmondsworth

[163] Hanh T N 1987 Being peace. Parallax. Berkeley

[164] Needleman J 1993 Lost Christianity. Element. Shaftesbury

[165] Williams E 1967 Beyond belief. Pan. London

[166] Gandhi M 2011 An autobiography. Penguin. Harmondsworth

[167] Hillman J in Zweig C & Abrams J 1991 Meeting the shadow. Tarcher. New York

[168] Fry C 1951 A sleep of prisoners. OUP. Oxford

[169] Frankl V 2004 Man's search for meaning. Rider. London

[170] Bonhoeffer D (ed. de Gruchy J) 1987 Selected writings. Collins. London

[171] Hillesum E 1966 An interrupted life. Owl. New York

[172] Dossey B 2009 Florence Nightingale: mystic, visionary, healer. Davis. Philadelphia

[173] Angelou M 1995 Wouldn't give nothing for my journey now. Virago. London

[174] Ram Dass 2000 Still here. Hodder & Stoughton. London

[175] Mother Theresa in Kornfield J 1993 A path with heart. Bantam. New York

[176] Teasdale W 2001 The mystic heart. New World. Novato

[177] Sahajananda J 2003 You are the light: rediscovering the eastern Jesus. O Books. Alresford

[178] Pannenberg W (trans. Maxwell J) 1977 Faith and reality. Knox. London

[179] Torkington D 1995 The mystic. Hodder & Stoughton. London

[180] Wright S 2011 Beloved. SSP. Cumbria

[181] Campbell J in McLuhan T 1996 Cathedrals of the spirit. Thorsons. London

[182] Anon (trans. Wolters C) 1978. The cloud of unknowing. Penguin. Harmondsworth

[183] von Bingen H (ed. Bowie F) 1995 An anthology. SPCK. London

[184] Swimme B 1984 The universe as a green dragon. Bear. Santa Fe

[185] Vardey L (ed.) 1999 God in all worlds. Pantheon. New York

[186] Laing R in Vardey L (ed.) 1999 God in all worlds. Pantheon. New York

[187] Maslow A 1954 Motivation and personality. Penguin Compass. New York

[188] Barret D 2001 The new believers. Cassel. London

[189] Underhill E 2000 The spiritual life. Oneworld. Boston

[190] de Mello A 1996 Walking on water. Columba. Dublin

[191] Dostoevsky F 1880 (trans. McDuff D 1993) The brothers Karamazov. Penguin. Harmondsworth

[192] Hitchens C 2013 Mortality. Atlantic. New York

[193] John-Julian Father (ed.) 2009 The complete Julian of Norwich. Paraclete. Brewster

[194] Rumi (trans. Barks C) 1997 The illuminated Rumi. Broadway. New York

[195] Frost R 1915 The death of the hired man in North Boston. Holt. New York

[196] Nietzsche F (trans. Common T) 2016 Thus spake Zarathustra. Createspace. London

[197] The Archbishops Council 2000. Common worship. Church House. London

Bibliography,

Other sources of inspiration and recommended reading not otherwise cited in the text. For deeper enquiry into the contemplative way and suggested further reading on that topic see also the companion volume *Contemplation*.

Alexander V (trans.) 2016 The Aramaic New Testament. Alexander. Charleston

Anon. (trans. French R) 1973 The way of the pilgrim. Harper. San Francisco

Armstrong K 1993 A history of God. Ballantine. New York.

Armstrong K 2011 Twelve steps to a compassionate life. Bodley head. London

Attar F ud-din (trans. Darbandi A & Davis D)1984 - the conference of the birds. Penguin. Harmondsworth

Bamford C (trans.) 2000 The voice of the eagle. Lindisfarne. Great Barrington

Becker E 1973 The denial of death. Simon & Schuster. New York

Becker E 1975 Escape from evil. Free press. New York

Benson H 1996 Timeless healing. Schuster. London

Borg M 1997 The God we never knew. HarperCollins. San Francisco

Borg M 1989 The heart of Christianity. Harper. San Francisco

Bradley I 2003 The Celtic way. DLT. London

Bragg M 2011 The book of books. Sceptre. London

Brown N 1959 Life against death: the psychoanalytic meaning of history. Viking. New York

Bruce S 2002 God is dead – secularization in the west. Blackwell. Oxford

Caddy E 1992 God spoke to me. Findhorn press. Findhorn

Cooper A 1995 An encyclopaedia of traditional symbols. Thames and Hudson, London

Dalai Lama 1996 The good heart. Wisdom. Somerville

Dhammapada (trans. Mascaro J) 1973 Penguin. Harmondsworth

Douglas-Klotz N 1990 Prayers of the cosmos. HarperCollins. San Francisco

Douglas-Klotz N 2003 The Genesis meditations – a shared practice for Christians, Jews and Muslims. Quest. Wheaton

Douglas-Klotz N 2005 The Sufi book of life. Penguin. London

Douglas-Klotz N 2006 Blessings of the cosmos. Sounds True. Boulder

Eagleton T 2010 On evil. YUP. London

Ehrenreich B 2014 Living with a wild God. Granta. London

Eliade M 1966 Shamanism. Bollingen. Princeton

Flanagan B & Lanzetta B 2013 Embracing solitude: women and new monasticism. Cascade. Eugene

Fox M 1983 Original blessing. Bear. Santa Fe

Freud S (trans. Brill A) 2010 Collected works. PPS. www.PacPS.com

Galloway K 2010 Living by the rule: the rule of the Iona Community. Wild Goose. Glasgow

Gibran K 1994 The Prophet. Mandarin. London

Gregory of Nyssa (trans. Roth C) 1993 On the soul and the resurrection. St Vladimir's Seminary. New York

Griffiths B 1992 A new vision of reality. Harpercollins. New York

Guru Granth Sahib (trans. Singh P) 2002. OUP. London

Halevi Z 1991 Psychology of Kabbalah. Gateway. Bath

Harvey A 1991 Hidden journey. Bloomsbury. London

Hitchens C 2007 The portable atheist. Da Capo. London

Holden M 2002 Boundless love. Rider. London

Holden R 1996 Happiness now. Coronet. London

Holloway R 2003 On forgiveness. Canongate. Edinburgh

Holloway R 2013 Leaving Alexandria. Canongate. Edinburgh

Housden R 1995 Retreat. HarperCollins. London

Huxley A 1945 The perennial philosophy. Harper and Row. San Francisco

Ibn Al-Arabi (trans. Austin J) 1980 The bezels of wisdom. Paulist. Mahwah

James W 1985 Varieties of religious experience. Penguin. Harmondsworth

Jewish Publication Society 1992 The Torah JPS. Jerusalem

Johnson K & Ord D 2012 The coming interspiritual age. Namaste. Vancouver

Jones J 1996 In the middle of this road we call our life. HarperCollins. London

Julian of Norwich (trans. Skinner J) 1997 Revelation of love. Image. New York

Jung C (trans. Winston C & W) 1995 Memories, dreams, reflections. Fontana. London

Keating T 1994 Intimacy with God. Crossroad. New York

Keating T 2002 Invitation to love: the way of Christian contemplation. Continuum. New York

A Kempis T (trans. Croft A) 2004 The imitation of Christ. Hendrickson. Peabody

Kershaw I 2000 Hitler 1989-1936 Hubris. Norton. London

Kershaw I 2001 Hitler 1936-1945 Nemesis. Norton. London

Kornfield J 1993 A path with heart. Bantam. New York

Kornfield J 2000 After the ecstasy, the laundry. Rider. London

Kubler-Ross E 1975 On death and dying. Spectrum Berkeley

Lanzetta B 2007 Emerging heart: global spirituality and the sacred. Fortress. Minneapolis

Lanzetta B 2015 Path of the heart. Blue Sapphire. San Diego

Lawrence, Brother (trans Klein P) 2004 The practice of the presence of God. Hendrickson. New York

LeShan L 1974 How to meditate. Harpercollins. London

Levine S & Levine O 1995 Embracing the Beloved. Doubleday. New York

Lewis C 1952 Mere Christianity. Harper. San Francisco

Longaker C 1998 Facing death and finding hope. Arrow. London

Lynch G 2002 After religion – generation X and the search for meaning. DLT. London

Maimonides (trans Rabin C) 1952 The guide for the perplexed. Hackett. Cambridge

Main J 1988 The inner Christ. DLT. London

Malinski V (ed) 1990 Rogers' science of unitary human beings. NLN. New York

Matt D 1983 Zohar. Paulist. Mahwah

McEntee R & Bucko A 2015 The new monasticism. Orbis. New York

Mishra P 2004 An end to suffering. Picador. London

Muller W 1999 Sabbath: restoring the sacred rhythm of rest. Bantam. New York

Newell JP1999 The book of creation. Canterbury. Norwich

Newell JP 2000 Echo of the soul. Canterbury. Norwich

Newell JP 2008 Christ of the Celts. Wild Goose. Glasgow

Newell JP 2014 The rebirthing of God. Skylight paths. Woodstock

Newman L 1963 The Hasidic anthology: tales and teachings of the Hasidim. Schoken. New York

Nouwen H 1994 The wounded healer. DLT. London

Nouwen H 1997 The inner voice of love. DLT. London

Nouwen H 2006 Bread for the journey: a daybook of wisdom and faith. HarperOne. New York

O'Malley B 2005 Lord of creation. Canterbury. Norwich

O'Murchu D 2003 Evolutionary faith. Orbis. New York

Pagels E 2006 The Gnostic gospels. Phoenix. London

Palmer M 2001 The Jesus sutras. Piatkus. London

Pannikar R 2013 The rythmn of being. Orbis. New York

Parsons S 2000 Ungodly fear. Lion. Oxford

Prabhu J 2015 Raimon Pannikar: selected writings. Orbis. New York

Qur'an (trans. Dawood N) 1991 Penguin. Harmondsworth

Ram Dass 2011 Be love now. Rider. London

Ram Dass 2013 Polishing the mirror. Sounds true. Boulder

Rank O 1961 Psychology of the soul. Perpetua. New York

Religious Society of Friends 1998 Quaker faith and practice. RSF. London

Roberts J 1974 The nature of personal reality. Amber-Allen. San Rafael

Robinson J (ed.) 1996 The Nag Hammadi library in English. Brill. New York

Rodegast P, Santon J 1987 Emmanuel's book. (also books 2 and 3, 1989 and 1994) Bantam. New York

Rohr R 2009 The naked now. Crossroad. New York

Rohr R 2011 Falling upward. Jossey Bass. San Francisco

Scott W (trans.) 1997 Hermetica. Solo. London

Shah I 1973 The way of the Sufi. Penguin. Harmondsworth

Shanks N 2009 God's energy: the vision and spirituality of the Iona Community. Wild Goose. Glasgow

Shorter B 1996 Susceptible to the sacred. Routledge. London

Shucman H and Thetford W 1972 A course in miracles. CMS. Omaha

Smith H 1991 The world's religions. Harper. San Francisco

Smith P 2011 Integral Christianity: the spirit's call to evolve. Paragon. St.Paul

Spong J 1998 Why Christianity must change or die. Harper. San Francisco

Spong J 2007 Jesus for the non-religious. Harper. San Francisco

St John of the Cross (trans. Zimmerman B) 1973 The dark night of the soul. Clarke. Cambridge

St Theresa of Avila (trans. van de Weyer R) 1995 The interior castle. HarperCollins. London

Sri Aurobindo 1970 The life divine. Sri Aurobindo Ashram. Pondicherry

Tao Te Ching (trans. Le Guin U) 1997 Shambala. Boston

Vaughan F 1995 Shadows of the sacred. Quest.Wheaton

von Goethe J (trans. Stopp E) 1998 Maxims and reflections. Penguin. London

Walsch N 2008 Conversations with God trilogy. Putnam. New York

Zweig C & Abrams J 1991 Meeting the shadow. Tarcher. New York

–

COMING HOME - Notes for the Journey

Index

Always Coming Home

I cannot say there is a point when "It is finished".
Someone has already said that for me.
That gives me hope,
Like this relentless ferry crossing the Sound,
Back and forth.
There is no point when she can say, "There, I'm home".
She is always, like me, coming home.
No point of the journey is fixed, stationary or ever exactly the same.
The land and the waves make sure of that.
If she is fixed at all it is in movement.
Home is not at the end or the beginning,
Or in the limited space in between.
Home is where she always is, fixed or moving, crossing and still.
Unbounded by time and space,
It is in the coming home -
A condition of heart and mind,
An ever-watchful wonder,
A loving awareness of
The unfettered nowness where there is no finish
For there was never a start.
Always, Coming Home.
Drowning, in eternity,
In
Love.

About the author   Stephen G. Wright

Stephen works as a spiritual director and teacher for the Sacred Space Foundation (www.sacredspace.org.uk), guiding group retreats and individual seekers. Before this he had a long and distinguished nursing career in practice and academia gathering an extensive list of publications, an MBE, a Fellowship of the Royal College of Nursing and lots of other letters before and after his name along the way. His life and path of service took a significant about turn with a series of profound and transformative spiritual experiences that led him into giving more time, among other things, to the integration of spirituality into health care – for which he was later made an Honorary Fellow of the University of Cumbria. He has written three books exploring the nature of healing relationships - *Therapeutic Touch* and *Sacred Space – right relationship and spirituality in health care* (both with Jean Sayre-Adams) and *Reflections on spirituality and health*. He continues to work in the UK's NHS in "Heartfullness" educational programmes for healthcare professionals (see youtu.be/YUMBKXjgEN0). Coming Home is rooted in a personal, and continuing, account of spiritual awakening and his work as a spiritual director. For the latter he has received significant training in the presence of several renowned teachers and at the Interfaith Seminary (now OneSpirit) in the UK. His other recent published works include a CD of chants and circle dances (*Song and dance for the Way Home*), poetry (B*eloved* and *Yours, Faithfully*), *Burnout* and *Contemplation*. He lives with his partner in the English Lake District, deepening service and spiritual practice, participating in his local church community and the Iona Community, taking care of his organic garden and enjoying grandfatherhood.

Printed in Great Britain
by Amazon

79332642R00249